D1252027

THE ECOLOGY OF COMPUTATION

# STUDIES IN COMPUTER SCIENCE AND ARTIFICIAL INTELLIGENCE

**2**

Editors:

## D. G. Bobrow

*Xerox Corporation*
*Palo Alto Research Centre*
*Palo Alto, California*

## H. Kobayashi

*IBM Japan Ltd.*
*Tokyo*

## J. Nievergelt

*ETH, Institut für Informatik*
*Zürich*

## M. Nivat

*Université Paris VII*
*Paris*

NORTH-HOLLAND – AMSTERDAM ● NEW YORK ● OXFORD ● TOKYO

# THE ECOLOGY OF COMPUTATION

edited by

**B. A. HUBERMAN**

*Xerox Palo Alto Research Center*
*Palo Alto, CA*
*U.S.A.*

1988

NORTH-HOLLAND – AMSTERDAM ● NEW YORK ● OXFORD ● TOKYO

ISBN: 0 444 70375 6


*Publishers:*
ELSEVIER SCIENCE PUBLISHERS B.V.
P.O. Box 1991
1000 BZ AMSTERDAM
THE NETHERLANDS



*Sole distributors for the U.S.A. and Canada:*
ELSEVIER SCIENCE PUBLISHING COMPANY, INC.
52 VANDERBILT AVENUE
NEW YORK, N.Y. 10017
U.S.A.

Library of Congress Cataloging-in-Publication Data

The Ecology of computation.

   (Studies in computer science and artificial
intelligence ; 2)
   1. Electronic data processing.  2. Artificial
intelligence.  I. Huberman, B. A. (Bernardo A.),
1943-    .  II. Series.
QA76.E26  1988      004      87-36405
ISBN 0-444-70375-6 (U.S.)

PRINTED IN THE NETHERLANDS

# CONTENTS

The Ecology of Computation
B.A. Huberman (editor)
© Elsevier Science Publishers B.V. (North-Holland), 1988

# The Ecology of Computation

B. A. Huberman
Xerox Palo Alto Research Center
Palo Alto, CA 94304

A new form of computation is emerging. Propelled by advances in software design and increasing connectivity, distributed computational systems are acquiring characteristics reminiscent of social and biological organizations. These open systems, self—regulating entities which in their overall behavior are quite different from conventional computers, engage in asynchronous computation of very complex tasks, while their agents spawn processes in other machines whose total specification is unknown to them. These agents also make local decisions based both on imperfect knowledge about the system and on information which at times is inconsistent and delayed. They thus become a community of concurrent processes which, in their interactions, strategies, and competition for resources, behave like whole ecologies.

The appearance of such complex systems on the computational scene creates a number of interesting problems. At the operational level, the lack of global perspectives for determining resource allocation gives rise to a whole different approach to system level programming and the creation of suitable languages. Just to implement procedures whereby processes can cross trust barriers and manage to compute in a highly heterogeneous medium is a challenging task with no optimally known solution. Although human organizations often deal successfully with the problem of asynchronous operation and imperfect knowledge, the implementation of a computational analog is far from obvious. Nevertheless, pieces of such systems are already in place, and a serious effort at designing open computational networks is under way in a number of laboratories.

On a different vein, the existence of computational ecologies leads to a number of fascinating questions concerning their function, dynamics, and efficiency. Stated succinctly, one would like to understand the overall system behavior from knowledge of what the individual processes can do. Since the rules whereby computational agents choose among possible strategies can be arbitrarily set by the designer, whole scenarios can be artificially created and tested. Moreover, the intrinsic nonlinearity of such systems leads to a rich repertoire of behaviors which can be studied at both the theoretical and experimental level. This leads in turn to a consideration of concepts such as evolutionarily stable strategies. Also, since computational ecologies have much in common with biological organizations, one expects that insights gained from one will help the understanding of the other. Just as insect colonies can reveal the workings of a natural computational system with simple components, the dynamics of an artificial open system can provide a quantitative testing ground for models of social organizations.

This book is a collection of articles which deal with the nature, design and implementation of open computational systems. Although varied in their approach and methodology, they are related by the goal of understanding and building computational ecologies. They are grouped in three major sections. The first one deals with general issues underlying open systems, studies of computational ecologies, and their similarities with social organizations. The second part deals with actual implementations of distributed computation, and the third one discusses the overriding problem of designing suitable languages for open systems. The book ends with a vision of a future knowledge medium by Stefik.

Imperfect knowledge, asynchronous computation and inconsistent data are not exclusive of open computational systems. Human societies face the same constraints, often successfully, when trying to engage in collective problem solving, be it a scientific community or a design group. Such an analysis, in the pervasive context of office work, is presented by Hewitt from an open systems perspective.

The consideration of a computational system as an ecology brings to mind biological mechanisms such as mutations, which introduce variations into species. These alterations in the code of life, while leading to increased diversity, allow for adaptation to a changing environment. Such mutation strategies have been often proposed as ways of improving the performance of artificial intelligence systems. A highly instructive example of such an approach is provided by *AM* and *Eurisko*, which were designed in order to explore and discover mathematical concepts by syntactically mutating small Lisp programs. Equally interesting is the process of resource allocation to the resulting programs, and which are distributed by an external agent on the basis of perceived degree of progress. Lenat and Brown perform an incisive analysis of the advantages and shortcomings of such systems, and speculate that the paradigm underlying them may be that of collections or societies of evolving, self—organizing, symbolic knowledge structures.

Within this context, Miller and Drexler discuss several evolutionary models such as biological ecosystems, human markets, and *Eurisko*, and outline their analogies and differences with computational ecologies. In this and a related paper on *Markets and Computation*, they elaborate a vision of direct computational markets which they term *agoric* open systems.

Since incomplete knowledge and delayed information are intrinsic features of computational ecologies, serious consideration has to be given to their dynamical behavior when operating with such constraints. Huberman and Hogg derive and  analyze the appropriate equations governing game dynamics, and show that when processes can choose among many possible strategies while collaborating in the solution of computational tasks, the asymptotic dynamics can lead to nonlinear oscillations and chaos. These results imply that evolutionarily stable strategies may not exist in computational ecologies. They also discuss the possible existence of a universal law regulating the way in which the benefit of cooperation is manifested in the system, and compare it with findings in biological ecologies and human organizations.

This dynamical approach to distributed computation is to be contrasted with the static static one of Rosenchein and Genesereth, who apply classical game theory to resolve potential conflicts between computational agents having disparate goals.

The second part of the book discusses actual implementations of distributed computational systems. Two different papers describe operational systems designed from an open systems perspective. *Enterprise*, a market—like scheduler, described by Malone and collaborators, consists of independent processes or agents being allocated at run time among remote idle processors through a bidding mechanism. The system provides substantial performance improvements over processing tasks on the machines at which they originate even in the face of large delays and inaccurate estimates of processing times.

An alternative system is *Mach*, described by Rashid in an article outlining the evolution of a class of network operating systems. A multiprocessor operating system kernel currently running on VAX architecture machines, *Mach* provides a number of attractive features from an open systems point of view. These include support for transparent remote file access between autonomous systems, internal symbolic debuggers, and most notably, network interprocesses which can be protected across system boundaries.

This section on distributed computation ends with an article by Drexler and Miller on *Incentive Engineering*. Within the framework of market—like mechanisms for resource allocation, it proposes a set of algorithms which allow for both processor scheduling as an auction process, and for distributed garbage collection through which unreferenced loops that cross trust boundaries can be collected.

This book would not be complete if it did not dealt with the problem of languages for computational ecologies. A suitable programming language for open systems should allow for programs in which modules reside and execute at geographically remote, but communicating, locations. It should also allow for the writing of robust programs which can survive hardware failures without loss of distributed information, while allowing concurrent access to that information while preserving its consistency. An example of such a programming language is provided by Liskov and Scheifler in their article on *Guardians* and *Actions*. In a more general vein, Kahn and Miller analyze the suitability of actor languages and concurrent logic programming for writing programs which both provide services and take advantage of them in a manner that scales from basic computational steps to very large distributed systems.

Lastly, there is a visionary description by Stefik of a future in which AI systems, distributed across society, will be able to communicate and share knowledge with each other. This *knowledge medium* will stand in sharp contrast to current expert systems which are built from scratch every time and essentially function as stand alone entities. In his description of such a medium, Stefik draws heavily both on the history of cultural changes and most importantly, on the notion of a knowledge ecology.

The Ecology of Computation
B.A. Huberman (editor)
Elsevier Science Publishers B.V. (North-Holland), 1988

# Offices Are Open Systems

Carl Hewitt

MIT Artificial Intelligence Laboratory

This paper is intended as a contribution to analysis of the implications of viewing offices as open systems. It takes a prescriptive stance on how to establish the information-processing foundations for taking action and making decisions in office work from an open systems perspective. We propose *due process* as a central activity in organizational information processing. Computer systems are beginning to play important roles in mediating the ongoing activities of organizations. We expect that these roles will gradually increase in importance as computer systems take on more of the authority and responsibility for ongoing activities. At the same time we expect computer systems to acquire more of the characteristics and structure of human organizations.

## 1. INTRODUCTION

In this paper we discuss the nature of office work from an open systems perspective. Coping with the conflicting, inconsistent, and partial information is one of the major challenges in office information systems. Due process is the organizational activity of human and computer systems for generating sound, relevant, and reliable information as a basis of action taking. Within due process logical reasoning takes place within relatively small coherent modules called microtheories. In general the microtheories will be inconsistent with one another. Due process makes use of debate and negotiation to deal with conflicts and inconsistencies between microtheories.

## 2. OFFICE WORK

We define an *office* as a place where *office work* is done, thus shifting the emphasis of our investigation from the nature of the locale to the nature of the activity performed. Office work can take place in an automobile with a mobile telephone, in the anteroom of a lecture hall, or at a networked personal computer. Of course, the situation including place, time, and participants can materially affect the work. All office work takes place within a particular concrete situation. The point that we want to make here is that there is no *special* place where office work has to take place.

Reprinted from *ACM Transactions on Office Information Systems*, Vol. 4, No. 3, July 1986, pp. 271-287.

Later we discuss how office work is situated in *particular concrete* space and time and how the situation provides an important part of the context in which the work is done.

We take *office work* to be information processing that is done to coordinate all the work that an organization does with the exception of direct manipulation of physical objects. The organizations in which office work takes place are "going concerns" in the sense of Everett Hughes [11]. For example, they include the processing of beliefs, goals, and mutual commitments as well as the development and management of responsibilities, policies, tasks, transactions, projects, and procedures. Office work is specialized by excluding *robotics*. Robotics involves information processing directly involved in the physical production, transformation, transportation, servicing, or consumption of physical objects.

Office work is situated social action in the sense that it is the action produced by participants at particular times and places. However, we need to extend the usual notion of situated social actions to encompass the social actions of computer systems in their interactions with other computer systems as well as the interactions of computer systems with human participants.


## 3. OPEN SYSTEMS

Offices are inherently open systems because of the requirement of communication with operational divisions as well as the external world in the task of coordinating the work of the organization. In all nontrivial cases the communication necessary for coordination takes place asynchronously. Unplanned dynamic adaptation and accommodation are required in organizational information systems to meet the unplanned changing needs of coordination since the execution of any plan requires articulation, change, and adjustment.

Open systems deal with large quantities of diverse information and exploit massive concurrency. They can be characterized by the following fundamental characteristics [9]:

(1) *Concurrency.* Open systems are composed of numerous components such as workstations, databases, and networks. To handle the simultaneous influx of information from many outside sources, these components must process information concurrently.

(2) *Asynchrony.* There are two sources of asynchrony in open systems. First, since the behavior of the environment is not necessarily predictable by the system itself, new information may enter the system at any time, requiring it to operate asynchronously with the outside world. Second, the components are physically separated distances prohibiting them from acting synchronously. Any attempt to clock all the components synchronously would result in an enormous performance degradation because the clocks would have to be slowed down by orders of magnitude in order to maintain synchronization.

(3) *Decentralized control.* In an open system, a centralized decision maker would become a serious bottleneck. Furthermore, because of communications asynchrony and unreliability, a controlling agent could never have complete, up-to-date information on the state of the system. Therefore control must be

distributed throughout the system so that local decisions can be made close to where they are needed.

(4) *Inconsistent information.* Information from outside the system or even from different parts of the same system may turn out to be inconsistent. Therefore decisions must be made by the components of an open system by considering whatever evidence is currently available.

(5) *Arms-length relationships.* The components of an open system are at an *arms-length relationship*: The internal operation, organization, and state of one computational agent may be unknown and unavailable to another agent for reasons of privacy or outage of communications. Information should be passed by explicit communication between agents to conserve energy and maintain security. This ensures that each component can be kept simple since it only needs to keep track of its own state and its interfaces to other agents.

(6) *Continuous operation.* Open systems must be reliable. They must be designed so that failures of individual components can be accommodated by operating components while the failed components are repaired or replaced.

## 4. CONCURRENCY

The underlying concurrent basis of operation enables due process to react dynamically to asynchronous input and in many cases makes the results indeterminate.

### 4.1 Asynchronous Input

Concurrent systems differ from Turing machines in that they allow asynchronous communication from the external environment to affect ongoing operations. Sequential systems deal with this problem as a kind of "interrupt" in which they "switch tasks." Organizational information systems rarely have all the material at hand needed to make an important decision. Information that is known in advance to be required arrives asynchronously as the decision making proceeds and is often incomplete. Unanticipated information can arrive at any time in the process and affect the outcome even though it arrives quite late. For instance, an unanticipated story in the *Wall Street Journal* on the morning of a corporate board meeting to give final approval to a merger has been known to kill or delay a deal.

### 4.2 Indeterminacy

Concurrent systems are inherently indeterminate. The indeterminacy of concurrent systems does not stem from invoking a random element such as flipping a coin. Instead it results from the indeterminate arrival order of inputs to system components. In general, complete knowledge of the state and structure of a concurrent system together with exact knowledge of the times and values of inputs does not determine the system's output. Concurrent systems are indeterminate for the same reason that other quantum devices are indeterminate.

The indeterminacy of concurrent computation is different from the usual nondeterministic computation studied in automata theory in which coin flipping is allowed as an elementary computational step. In general, it is not possible to know ahead of time that a concurrent system will make a decision by a certain lime. Flipping a coin can be used as a method of forcing decisions to occur by making an arbitrary choice. Often as a matter of principle, however, due process refuses to invoke arbitrary random measures such as coin flipping to make a decision. For example, a jury might not return a verdict, and the judge might have to declare a mistrial. (Agha [1] provides an excellent exposition of the nature of a mathematical model of concurrent computation and its differences with classical nondeterministic Turing-machine-based theories.)

## 5. CONFLICTING INFORMATION AND CONTRADICTORY BELIEFS

Conflicting sources of information and inconsistent beliefs are a staple of life in organizational information systems. This partly results from dealing with differing external organizations that retain their own autonomy and belief structures.

Inconsistencies inevitably result from the measurements and observations made on complicated physical systems. Higher level abstractions are used to attempt to construct a consistent description of parts of the environment in which the organization operates. For example, a firm's earnings might be labeled "provisional" and then "subject to audit." But, even after being published in the annual report, they might later have to be "restated." In this case "provisional," "subject to audit," and "restated" are attempts to construct a consistent description from conflicting information about earnings.

Whatever consistency exists among the beliefs within an organization is *constructed* and *negotiated* by the participants. In the case of reported earnings, the chief executive officer, finance department, board of directors, and regulatory authorities play important roles in constructing and negotiating the financial reports.

Any belief concerning an organization or its environment is subject to internal and external challenges. Organizations must efficiently take action and make decisions in the face of conflicting information and contradictory beliefs. How they do so is a fundamental consideration in the foundations of organizational information systems.

Conflicting information and contradictory beliefs are engendered by the enormous interconnectivity and interdependence of knowledge that come from multiple sources and viewpoints. The interconnectivity makes it impossible to separate knowledge of the organization's affairs into independent modules. The knowledge of any physical aspect has extensive *spatiotemporal, causal, terminological, evidential,* and *communicative* connections with other aspects of the organization's affairs. The interconnectivity generates an enormous network of knowledge that is inherently inconsistent because of the multiple sources of actors making contributions at different times and places.

For example, suppose that in the middle of 1986 an organization undertakes to consider its knowledge of sales currently in progress for that year for the New England region. In such a situation, there is an enormous amount of information about other pieces of information. The following considerations show a small part of the enormous interconnectivity of knowledge:

*Spatiotemporal interconnectivity.* The organization has a great deal of knowledge about the history of sales in the New England region in the first few months of 1986, including how the sales were generated and recorded. In addition, it has sales projections of what will happen in the remainder of the year.

*Causal interconnectivity.* The marketing department believes that increased advertising is causing sales to go up. On the other hand, the sales department believes that the increased sales commissions are the real reason for the increase in sales.

*Terminological interconnectivity.* Some of the sales are really barter agreements with uncertain cash value. Do the barter agreements qualify as sales?

*Evidential interconnectivity.* The accounting department fears that sales might really not be increasing because many of the products could be returned because of a new 30-day free trial offer. It does not believe that the evidence presented shows that sales are increasing.

*Communicative interconnectivity.* The organization consists of a community of actors operating concurrently, asynchronously, and nondeterministically. The asynchronous communications engender interconnectivity, which defies any complete description of the global state of the organization at any particular point in time.

Conflicting information and contradictory beliefs are an inherent part of office work that must be explicitly addressed in any foundation for organizational information systems.

## 6. DUE PROCESS

Due process is the organizational activity of humans and computers for generating sound, relevant, and reliable information as a basis for decision and action within the constraints of allowable resources [4]. It provides an arena in which beliefs and proposals can be gathered, analyzed, and debated. Part of due process is to provide a record of the decision-making process that can later be referenced.

Due process is inherently reflective in that beliefs, goals, plans, requests, commitments, etc., exist as objects that can be explicitly mentioned and manipulated in the ongoing process.

Due process does not make decisions or take actions per se. Instead it is the process that informs the decision-making process. Each instance of due process begins with *preconceptions* handed down through traditions and culture that constitute the initial process but are open to future testing and evolution. Decision-making criteria such as preferences in predicted outcomes are included in this knowledge base. For example, increased profitability is preferable to decreased profitability. Also, increased market share is preferable to decreased market share. Conflicts between these preferences can be negotiated [18]. In addition preferences can arise as a result of conflict. Negotiating conflict can bring the negotiating process itself into question as part of the evaluative criteria of how to proceed, which can itself change the quality of conflict among the participants [7, 7a].

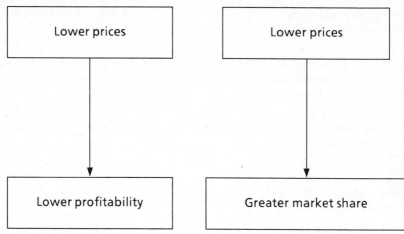

Figure 1

Changing the price of a product can affect both its profitability and market share in conflicting ways, as shown in Figure 1. Market research and internal cost analysis can help model the effects of lower prices on profitability and market share. The sales and financial divisions can have very different views on the subject. They need to organize their respective positions including counterarguments to opposing views. The cost-effectiveness of generating new information by market research and new product development can be considered by using due process.

All this activity takes place within a context that sets the time frame for the decision-making process. Sometimes the time frames can be very short, and, at the same time, the decision could be very important to the organization. Consider the sudden appearance of a new product that is drastically undercutting prices and demands a quick decision as to whether or not to cut prices. It is extremely common for a "case" to occur in due process that has to be settled promptly but has implications for more general issues. A company may develop a general vacation policy because a request by a particular employee for certain vacation privileges has to be granted or refused [13]. Due process takes place within action-taking and decision-making situations. It occurs at a particular place and time within a community of actors (both human and computer) that communicate with one another in a historical context involving information gathering, discussion, and debate.

The communications involved in due process can be analyzed along the following dimensions:

*Belief.* The dimension of belief concerns the propositional content of a message. Belief is an integral part of organizational information gathering and analysis.

*Commitment.* The dimension of commitment concerns the plans of the actors as to their future actions. Commitment is an integral part of organizational planning. Organizations grant certain of their components the authority to commit the whole organization to certain future actions [2].

*Request.* The dimension of request concerns the attempt to influence the future actions of recipients of the message. Requests are used in organizational execution.

*Declaration.* The dimension of declaration concerns the ability to change agreed state of affairs by the performance of the appropriate communicative act. Declarations are used in organizational rearrangements and confirmations.

*Expression.* The dimension of expression concerns the attitude of the actors (e.g., fear, anger, gratitude). Expressions are used in organizational resource adjustments.

An individual communicative act can involve several of the above dimensions. We take the meaning of each communicative act to be its subsequent effect on the participants whether they be human or computer. An important challenge in organizational information systems is to construct computer systems that can perform appropriately for the above kinds of communicative acts by making use of the information in the implications of communications in the wider context in which they take place.

## 6.1 Record Making

Due process produces a record of the decision-making and action-taking process, including which organization is responsible for dealing with problems, responses, and questions for the decision made or the action taken. This is the way in which responsibility is assessed for the decisions and actions taken.

The record also includes rationales for various courses of action such as

*Predicted beneficial results.* Better targeted advertising will increase sales.

*Policies guiding conduct.* Products may not be returned for credit more than 30 days after sale.

*Reasons tied to specific institutional roles or processes.* A corporation may not be able to enter the computer business because of a consent decree that it has signed.

*Precedent.* The organization might always have taken Patriots' Day as a holiday. Precedent may seem like a weak rationale. However, deciding according to precedent in the absence of strong alternatives has the consequences of predictability, stability, and improvement in the general coherence among decided cases.

Due process is an inherently self-reflective process in that the process by which information is gathered, organized, compared, and presented is subject to evaluation, debate, and evolution within the organization. Thus the debate is not just about whether to lower prices, but also about the beliefs used in the decision and the process used by the organization to decide whether to lower them.

## 6.2 Cooperation

Due process is not a magical way for an organization to make "correct" decisions. Instead it is concerned with the reasonableness with which information is gathered, organized, compared, and presented. It addresses the question, "How can the decision-making process be improved?" instead of the question, "What is the right decision?" Efforts to find the basis for "correct" decision making before the organization goes to work are fruitless. Attempting to critique a particular course of action chosen by an organization involves us in the very *same* activities that are embodied in due process.

In general due process involves cooperation among the participant actors in the organization. The participants' investment in the process of information gathering, evaluation, debate, and presentation helps to produce the consensus. Every participant knows that his or her views need to be put forth in order to be considered and balanced against the others. In general those actors whose authority and responsibility are most affected by the choice of action must at least give their passive cooperation. Preexisting organizational precedents and traditions are influential in the exact way that a choice of action is made. Even if the course of action taken is not the participant's first choice the execution of the decision can be tailored to reflect the views and concerns that have been uncovered in due process. Also recompense can often be offered to disgruntled parties by making allowances in other concurrent decision making within the organization.

## 6.3 Task Performance Assessment

Assessing how well the task was performed or how the performance might be improved can be quite problematical. Each performance is unique. It must be assessed in terms of quality of analysis, planning, and execution, as well as the appropriate balance of these activities. Performance assessment is subject to severe limitations in available knowledge about realistic alternatives because of unknown interactions between details in a performance. For example, the timing of an advertising campaign can affect the results of sales.

## 7. MICROTHEORIES AS TOOLS IN DUE PROCESS

A *microtheory* is a relatively small, idealized, mathematical theory that embodies a model of some physical system. Prescriptively, a microtheory should be internally consistent and clearly demarcated. Any modification of a microtheory is a new microtheory. Special relativity, a spreadsheet model of a company's projected sales, and a Spice simulation of an integrated circuit are examples of microtheories. Microtheories are simple because they have simple axiomatizations. The physical system being modeled, however, may be enormously complicated. We expect that computer systems will require hundreds of thousands of microtheories in order to participate effectively in organizational work.

In general due process deals with *conflicting* microtheories that cannot always be measured against one another in a pointwise fashion. In due process, debate and negotiation takes place where rival microtheories are compared with one another without assuming that there is a fixed common standard of reference. We do not assume that there is a global axiomatic theory of the world that gradually becomes more complete as more microtheories are debugged and introduced. Instead we propose to deal with each problematical concrete situation by using negotiation and debate among the available overlapping and possibly conflicting microtheories that are adapted to the situation at hand. For many purposes in due process it is preferable to work with microtheories that are small and oversimplified, rather than large and full of caveats and conditions [17].

Logical deduction is a powerful tool for working *within* a microtheory. The strengths of logical deduction include

*Well understood.* Logical deduction is a very well-understood and characterized process. Rigorous model theories exist for many logics including the predicate calculus, intuitionistic logics, and modal logics.

*Validity locally decidable.* An important goal of logical proofs is that their correctness should be mechanically decidable from the proof inscription. In this way the situation of proof creation can be distinct from the subsequent situations of proof checking. In order to be algorithmic, the proof-checking process cannot require making any observations or consulting any external sources of information. Consequently all of the premises of each proof step as to place, time, objects, etc., must be explicit. In effect a situational closure must be taken for each deductive step. Proof checking proceeds in a closed world in which the axioms and rules of deductive inference have been laid out explicitly beforehand. Ray Reiter [16] has developed closure axioms that justify the default rules used in relational databases as logical deductions. Similarly the circumscription technique proposed by John McCarthy [14] is a closure operator on sets of axioms that results in stronger, more complete axiom sets.

*Belief constraining.* Logical deductions deal with issues about logically entailed relationships among beliefs. If an actor believes P and (P implies Q), then it is constrained to believe Q. Similarly if an actor believes (P implies Q) and entertains the goal of believing Q, then it can entertain the goal of believing P. Examples below illustrate how both of these techniques can be valuable in evolving and managing belief structures.

Let us consider a simple concrete example to illustrate the use of logical deduction in organizational decision making. Commercial enterprises sometimes put their merchandise "on sale" to increase sales. Often this is done by cutting prices and increasing advertising. Consider the microtheory shown in Figure 2, which we shall call *profitable sale*.

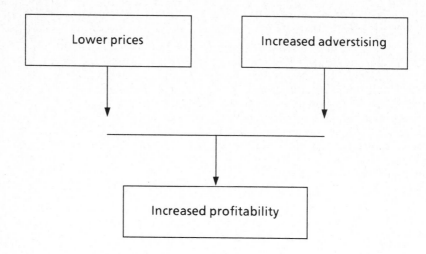

Figure 2

We shall use the above deduction rule as a *microtheory* to explore how deduction can be used in organizational decision making. Microtheories are simply very small partial logical theories. They are kept small and partial to avoid the problems of entanglement by interconnectivity, as discussed above.

We take a very general view of deduction: Deductive proofs are tree structures in which a computer can mechanically decide whether a step is valid just by inspecting the premises and conclusion of the deduction.

A microtheory should be internally consistent. Ideally there should even be good arguments for its consistency. If an inconsistency is discovered in a microtheory, then a repair can be attempted. Sometimes the repair attempt will fail in the face of well-justified contrary beliefs. This can be dealt with by splitting the microtheory into more specialized microtheories.

## 7.1 Contradictory Knowledge

Microtheories are often inconsistent with one another. The financial department might argue that lowering prices brings in less revenue, advertising increases expenses, and therefore profitability could very well decrease. We could express this model in the microtheory shown in Figure 3, which we shall call *unprofitable sale*.

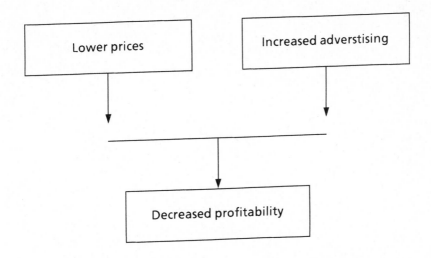

Figure 3

Our second microtheory directly contradicts the first. Proofs are not convincing in a contradictory knowledge base in which we can prove both that the profitability will increase and that it will decrease. Therefore we confine logical deduction to within microtheories that are presumed to be consistent and use due process to mediate contradictory microtheories.

## 7.2 Counterarguments

The tree-structured, locally decidable character of logical deductive proof cannot take audiences into account. The *profitable-sale* microtheory cannot take into account the counterargument of the *unprofitable-sale* microtheory. We shall use extradeductive techniques such as negotiation and debate to deal with the inconsistencies and conflicts between microtheories.

A *metamicrotheory* has as part of its content axioms about other microtheories as in the work of Richard Weyhrauch [19]. Such metamicrotheories can be very useful. Due process reasoning often involves debate and negotiation between multiple conflicting metamicrotheories [20]. The metamicrotheories arise in the course of debate about the reasonableness and applicability of previously introduced microtheories. Often the metamicrotheories are also inconsistent with one another.

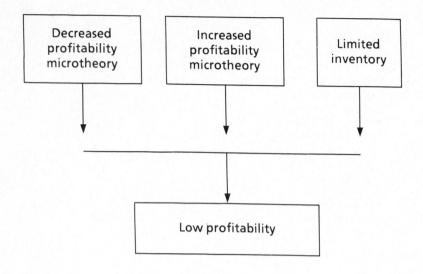

Figure 4

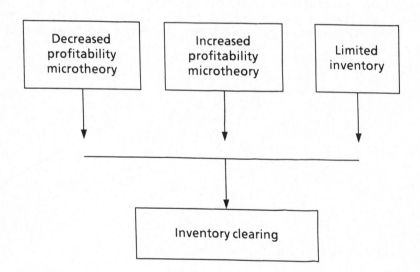

Figure 5

For example, the microtheory shown in Figure 4 takes into account the limited inventory as well as the decreased profitability and increased profitability microtheories to conclude that the sale would be of low profitability because of the limited inventory, whereas the metamicrotheory shown in Figure 5 concludes that desirable inventory clearance would take place as a result of the sale.

## 7.3 Context

The validity of a deductive proof is supposed to be timeless and acontextual. If it is valid at all, then it is supposed to be valid for all times and places. The timeless and acontextual character of logical deduction is a tremendous advantage in separating the proof-creation situation from the proof-checking context. However, applicability of an empirical deductive rule such as the *profitable-sale* rule is problematical in many situations. For example, the rule might be challenged on the grounds that the conditions under which it worked in the past no longer hold because, for example, the market is saturated. To meet this constraint, we take the extradeductive step of dynamically adapting rules to the context at hand. Challenges to the applicability of the deductive rule may need to be entertained and debated [6]. For example, the *profitable-sale* rule might need to be further adapted by specifying that the increased advertising be presented to appeal to new customer needs that are not saturated. Operations like these contribute episodic precedents that are material for the synthesis of new microtheories.

## 7.4 Indeterminacy

Decisions need to be made on the basis of the arrival order of communications. The arrival order may not be determined by complete knowledge of system state, structure, and inputs. Consequently, the arrival order may not be able to be deduced. For example, decisions on whether to honor a withdrawal request for an account depend on the arrival order of withdrawals and deposits. The order of arrival of communications can drastically affect overall outcomes.

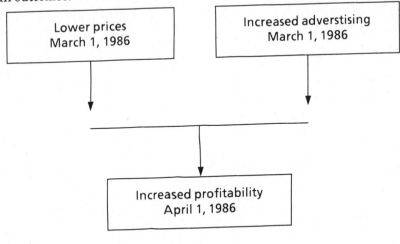

Figure 6

## 7.5 Description versus Action

Deduction can only *describe* possible actions and their possible effects; it cannot be used to take action [10]. Suppose that an organization wants to decide how to increase sales on March 1, 1986. The optimistic sales rule can be instantiated as shown in Figure 6. However, this deduction does not take any action. Instead it raises useful questions depending on the viewpoint from which it is considered. Considered from a viewpoint after March 1, 1986, it raises questions about the history of what happened. Logical deductions are useful in drawing further conclusions about the relationship of historical beliefs. On the other hand when considered from a viewpoint before March 1, 1986, it raises questions about predicting the future. Deductions can be very useful in analyzing the logical relations among the beliefs about the future.

The validity of a deduction is supposed to be decided mechanically solely from the premises and conclusion. In this way the situation of proof checking can be separated from the situation of proof generation so that proof generation and proof checking can take place in completely separate situations. In addition, the proof is supposed to be checkable solely from the text of the proof. In this way proofs can be checked by multiple actors at different times and places adding to the confidence in the deductions. The requirements of logical deduction preclude the possibility of introducing the term *now* into a deductive language. They mean that the validity of the deduction in Figure 6 is independent of whether it is made after March 1, 1986, and thus concerns the past or is made before March 1, 1986, and concerns the future.

Logical reasoning can be used before the happening to *predict* what might happen. It can be used after the happening to *analyze* what did happen. In either case logical proof does not control the action taken.

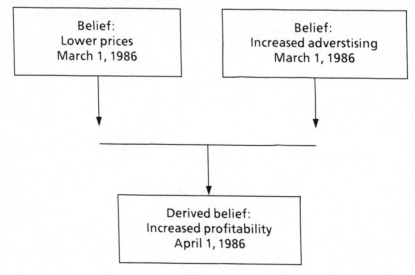

Figure 7

## 7.6 Constraints among Beliefs

Deduction is a powerful tool for propagating constraints among the beliefs and goals of a microtheory. For example, the belief that prices are lower and that advertising is increased on March 1, 1986, can he used to derive the belief that profitability is increased on April 1, 1986, as shown in Figure 7. Furthermore, the goal of increased profitability on March 1, 1986, can be used to derive the subgoals of lowering prices and increasing advertising, as shown in Figure 8.

New beliefs and subgoals derived by deduction in microtheories are useful to actor communities in conducting debates about the results and applicability of microtheories such as the *profitable-sale* and *unprofitable-sale* microtheories. Decisions then can be made on the basis of the results of the debates.

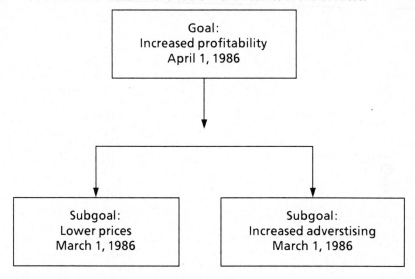

Figure 8

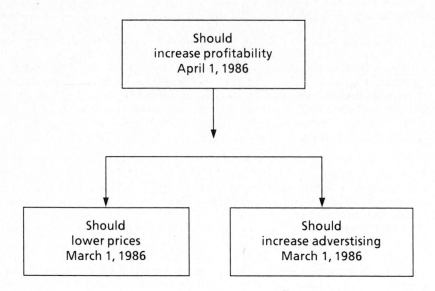

Figure 9

### 7.7 Recommendations and Policy

Deduction can be used to derive recommendations and to draw conclusions from policies (see Figure 9). However, the recommendations and implications of policy that are produced by deduction do not by themselves determine actions. In general, just as beliefs will be contradictory, recommendations for action will be in conflict (see Figure 10). The inconsistency among the microtheories results in inconsistent recommendations based on them.

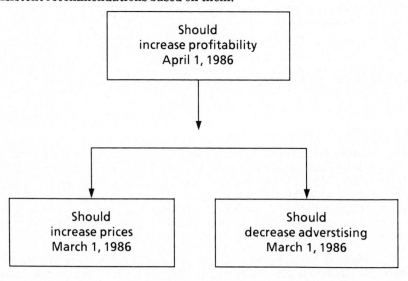

Figure 10

# 8. CONCLUSIONS

Foundations for organizational information systems are still in a primitive state. The enterprise is inherently interdisciplinary, requiring contributions from anthropology, artificial intelligence, research on indicators and models, cognitive science, computer science, research on needs and organizational factors, economics, management science, philosophy of science, psychology, and sociology. Foundations are needed on which to describe their function, structure, and principles of operation that can serve as the basis for managing, evolving, and designing better organizational information systems.

The effort to find the basis for decisions before the organization goes to work is meaningless. Understanding decision making is not separable phenomena from understanding the process by which it arrived. It is to forget the very purpose for which the organizational decision-making processes have been fashioned. Due process plays a central role in the operation of organizational information systems and allows for the consideration of multiple inconsistent microtheories. Logical deduction plays a role in analyzing the constraints among beliefs and goals *within* microtheories. Logical deduction is not suited to deciding among conflicting microtheories. Due process is manifested by situated action at the particular time and place when a choice of action is made. Due process specifically includes the social actions of computer systems.

The contrast between correct decision making and the actual organizational processes does not make sense. Due process has a systematicity of its own. It serves to test constantly whether the organization has come to see new differences or similarities. Due process is a situated process: The outside sociophysical world interacts with the organizational processes at particular places and times of the process that result in a particular decision. In general the decision is not determined by these interactions, nor can it be said that the result of due process is too uncertain to obtain satisfactory choices in organizational course of action. The compulsion of adherence to due process is clear; any fundamental breakdown directly impairs the organization.

Due process is the only kind of system that will work when parts of the organization do not agree completely and represent different responsibilities. The meaning of the words in the rules, policies, and goals changes to receive the meaning that organization gives to them in due process.

## Acknowledgments

Many of the ideas in this paper have been developed jointly with the members of the MIT Message Passing Semantics Group and the Tremont Research Institute. Fanya Montalvo, Elihu M. Gerson, and Susan Leigh Star contributed important ideas and helped with the organization. The due process task analysis example was developed jointly with David Kirsh. Tom Reinhardt greatly helped with the presentation. Our analysis of the limitations of deductive logic builds on previous work by Minsky [15] and the author [8, 9].

The ideas in this paper are related to previous work in distributed artificial intelligence. In particular we build on the work of Corkill and Lesser [3,

12]. The approach here differs from Davis and Smith [5] in that organizational mechanisms are emphasized instead of market mechanisms.

This paper describes research done at the Artificial Intelligence Laboratory of MIT. Major support for the research reported in this paper was provided by the System Development Foundation. Major support for other related work in the Artificial Intelligence Laboratory is provided, in part, by the Advanced Research Projects Agency of the Department of Defense under Office of Naval Research contract N0014-80-C-0505. I would like to thank Carl York, Charles Smith, and Patrick Winston for their support and encouragement.

## REFERENCES

[1] AGHA, G., *Actors: A Model of Concurrent Computation in Distributed Systems*. MIT Press, Cambridge, Mass., 1986.

[2] BECKER, H. S., "Notes on the concept of commitment", in: *Am. J. Sociol.* 66 (July 1960), 32-40.

[3] CORKILL, D. D., "Hierarchical planning in a distributed environment", in: *Proceedings of the 6th International Joint Conference on Artificial Intelligence* (Tokyo, Aug.). Kaufman, Los Altos, Calif., 1979, pp. 168-175.

[4] DAVIS, K. C., *Discretionary Justice*. University of Illinois Press, Urbana, Ill., 1971.

[5] DAVIS, R., and SMITH, R., "Negotiation as a metaphor for distributed problem solving", Memo 624, MIT Artificial Intelligence Laboratory, Cambridge, Mass., May 1981.

[6] GASSER, L. G., "The social dynamics of routine computer use in complex organizations", Ph.D. thesis, Computer Science Dept., Univ. of California at Irvine, 1984.

[7] GERSON, E. M. "On the quality of life", in: *Am. Social. Rev.* 41 (Oct. 1976), 793-806.

[7a] GERSON, E. M., and STAR, S. L., "Analyzing due process in the workplace", in: *ACM Trans. Off. Inf. Syst.* 4, 3 (July 1986).

[8] HEWITT, C., "PLANNER: A language for proving theorems in robots", in: *Proceedings of ISCAI- 69* (Washington, D.C., May). 1969.

[9] HEWITT, C., "The challenge of open systems", in: *BYTE* (Apr. 1985), 223-242.

[10] HEWITT, C., and DE JONG, P., "Analyzing the roles of descriptions and actions in open systems", in: *Proceedings of AAAI* (August). 1983.

[11] HUGHES, E. C., "Going concerns: The study of American institutions", in: *The Sociological Eye*. Aldines, Chicago, Ill., 1971 .

[12] LESSER, V., and CORKILL, D. D., "Functionally accurate, cooperative distributed systems", in: *IEEE Tran. Syst. Man Cybern. SMC-11*, 1 (Jan. 1981), 81-96.

[13] MARCH, J. G., and SIMON, H. A., *Organizations*. Wiley, New York, 1958.

[14] McCARTHY, J., "Applications of circumscription to formalizing common sense knowledge", in: *Proceedings of the Non-Monotonic Reasoning Workshop* (New Paltz, N.Y.). 1984, pp. 295-324.

[15] MINSKY, M., "A framework for representing knowledge", in: *The Psychology of Computer Vision*, P. Winston, Ed. McGraw-Hill, New York, 1975.

[16] REITER, R., "A logic for default reasoning", in: *Artif. Intell.* 13, 1, 2 (1980), 81-132.

[17] STAR, S. L., "Simplification in scientific work: An example from neuroscience research", in: *Soc. Stud. Sci. 13*, 2 (1983), 205-228.

[18] STRAUSS, A., *Negotiations*. Jossey-Bass, San Francisco, Calif., 1978.

[19] WEYHRAUCH, R. W., "Prolegamena to a theory of mechanical formal reasoning", in: *Artif. Intell. 13*, 1, 2 (1980). 133-170.

[20] WIMSATT, W., "False models as means to truer theories", in: *Systematics Symposium on Neutral Models in Biology* (Chicago, Ill.). 1985. To be published.

The Ecology of Computation
B.A. Huberman (editor)
Elsevier Science Publishers B.V. (North-Holland), 1988

# Why AM and EURISKO Appear to Work*

## Douglas B. Lenat

*Heuristic Programming Project, Stanford University,
Stanford, CA 94305, U.S.A.*

## John Seely Brown

*Intelligent Systems Laboratory, Xerox PARC,
Palo Alto, CA 94304, U.S.A.*

Recommended by Daniel G. Bobrow

ABSTRACT

*The AM program was constructed by Lenat in 1975 as an early experiment in getting machines to learn by discovery. In the preceding article in this issue of the AI Journal, Ritchie and Hanna focus on that work as they raise several fundamental questions about the methodology of artificial intelligence research. Part of this paper is a response to the specific points they make. It is seen that the difficulties they cite fall into four categories, the most serious of which are omitted heuristics, and the most common of which are miscommunications. Their considerations, and our post-AM work on machines that learn, have clarified why AM succeeded in the first place, and why it was so difficult to use the same paradigm to discover new heuristics. Those recent insights spawn questions about "where the meaning really resides" in the concepts discovered by AM. This in turn leads to an appreciation of the crucial and unique role of representation in theory formation, specifically the benefits of having syntax mirror semantics. Some criticism of the paradigm of this work arises due to the ad hoc nature of many pieces of the work; at the end of this article we examine how this very adhocracy may be a potential source of power in itself.*

## 1. Introduction

Nine years ago, the AM program [7] was constructed as an experiment in learning by discovery. Its source of power was a large body of heuristics [2, 5, 13], rules which guided it toward fruitful topics of investigation, toward profitable experiments to perform, toward plausible hypotheses and definitions. Other heuristics evaluated those discoveries for utility and 'interestingness', and they were added to AM's vocabulary of concepts. AM's ultimate limitation apparently

Reprinted from *Artificial Intelligence*, Vol. 23, No. 3, August 1984, (Elsevier Science Publishers B.V. (North-Holland), 1984), pp. 269-294.

was due to its inability to discover new, powerful, domain-specific heuristics for the various new fields it uncovered. At that time, it seemed straight-forward to simply add Heuretics (the study of heuristics) as one more field in which to let AM explore, observe, define, and develop. That task—learning new heuristics by discovery—turned out to be much more difficult than was realized initially, and we have just now achieved some successes at it, in the behavior of the EURISKO program [11, 12]. Along the way, it became clearer why AM had succeeded in the first place, and why it was so difficult to use the same paradigm to discover new heuristics.

This article originally started out to be a response to Ritchie and Hanna's "AM: A Case Study in AI Methodology" (the preceding article in this issue of *Artificial Intelligence*). It quickly evolved into much more than a specific response to the points they raise. We are grateful to them for spurring us to perform this analysis, because of the new understanding it has led us to about why AM and EURISKO appear to work. The first sections of this paper present these recent insights; the second half treats Ritchie and Hanna's specific questions about AI methodology in general and the AM thesis in particular.

## 2. What AM Really Did

In essence, AM was an automatic programming system, whose primitive actions produced modifications to pieces of LISP code, predicates which represented the characteristic functions of various math concepts. For instance, AM had a frame that represented the concept LIST-EQUAL, a predicate that checked any two LISP list structures to see whether or not they were equal (printed out the same way). That frame had several slots:

```
NAME:        LIST-EQUAL
IS-A:        (PREDICATE FUNCTION OP BINARY-PREDICATE
              BINARY-FUNCTION BINARY-OP ANYTHING)
GEN'L:       (SET-EQUAL BAG-EQUAL OSET-EQUAL STRUC-EQUAL)
SPEC:        (LIST-OF-EQ-ENTRIES LIST-OF-ATOMS-EQUAL EQ)
FAST-ALG:    (LAMBDA (x y) (EQUAL x y))
RECUR-ALG:   (LAMBDA (x y)
                (COND ((OR (ATOM x) (ATOM y)) (EQ x y))
                      (T (AND
                            (LIST-EQUAL (CAR x) (CAR y))
                            (LIST-EQUAL (CDR x) (CDR y))))))
DOMAIN:      (LIST LIST)
RANGE:       TRUTH-VALUE
WORTH:       720
                .
                .
```

Of central importance is the RECUR-ALG slot, which contains a recursive algorithm for computing LIST-EQUAL of two input lists $x$ and $y$. That algorithm recurs along both the CAR and CDR directions of the list structure, until it finds the leaves (the atoms), at which point it checks that each leaf in $x$

is identically equal to the corresponding node in *y*. If any recursive call on LIST-EQUAL signals NIL, the entire result is NIL, otherwise the result is T.

During one AM task, it sought for examples of LIST-EQUAL in action, and a heuristic accomodated by picking random pairs of examples of LIST, plugging them in for *x* and *y*, and running the algorithm. Needless to say, *very* few of those executions returned T (about 2%, as there were about 50 examples of LIST at the time). Another heuristic noted that this was extremely low (though nonzero), and concluded that it might be worth trying to define new predicates by slightly *generalizing* LIST-EQUAL. By 'generalizing' a predicate we mean copying its algorithm and weakening it so that it returns T more often. The heuristic placed a task to this effect on AM's agenda. The agenda, which guided the application of heuristics in AM, was simply a job-queue of activities worth spending time on, prioritized using the set of symbolic reasons supporting each task. The new task being added looked like this:

```
(Find Generalizations of LIST-EQUAL
    because: (1) very few pairs of LISTS are LIST-EQUAL
             (2) very few Generalizations of LIST-EQUAL are known
    Priority: 700
)
```

When that task was chosen from the agenda, another heuristic said that one way to generalize a definition with two conjoined recursive calls is simply to eliminate one of them entirely, or to replace the AND by an OR. In one run (in June, 1976) AM then defined these three new predicates:

```
L-E-1:   (LAMBDA (x y)
             (COND ((OR (ATOM x) (ATOM y)) (EQ x y))
                   (T (L-E-1 (CDR x) (CDR y)))]

L-E-2:   (LAMBDA (x y)
             (COND ((OR (ATOM x) (ATOM y)) (EQ x y))
                   (T (L-E-2 (CAR x) (CAR y)))]

L-E-3:   (LAMBDA (x, y)
             (COND ((OR (ATOM x) (ATOM y)) (EQ x y))
                   (T (OR
                       (L-E-3 (CAR x) (CAR y))
                       (L-E-3 (CDR x) (CDR Y))]
```

The first of these, L-E-1, has had the recursion in the CAR direction removed. All it checks for now is that, when elements are stripped off each list, the two lists become null at exactly the same time. That is, L-E-1 is now the predicate that tests two lists to see if they have the same length; indeed, the human observing AM run might interrupt it at this point and rename L-E-1 to be Same-Length.

The second of these, L-E-2, has had the CDR recursion removed. When run on two lists of atoms, it checks that the first elements of each list are equal. When run on arbitrary lists, it checks that they have the same number of leading left parentheses, and then that the atom that then appears in each is the same. One might call this predicate Same-Depth. As with L-E-1, it is very closely related to cardinality.

The third of these is more difficult to characterize in words. It is of course more general than both L-E-1 and L-E-2; if $x$ and $y$ are equal in length then L-E-3 would return T, as it would if they had the same first element, etc. This disjunction propogates to all levels of the list structure, so that L-E-3 would return true for $x = (A\,(B\,C\,D)\,E\,F)$ and $y = (Q\,(B))$ or even $y = (Q\,(W\,X\,Y))$. Perhaps this predicate is most concisely described by its LISP definition.

A few points are important to make from this example. First, note that AM does not make changes at random, it is driven by empirical findings (such as the rarity of LIST-EQUAL returning T) to suggest specific directions in which to change particular concepts (such as deciding to generalize LIST-EQUAL). However, once having decided upon this eminently reasonable goal, it then reverts to a more or less syntactic mutation process to achieve it. (Changing AND to OR, eliminating a conjunct from an AND, etc.) See [4] for background on this style of code synthesis and modification.

Second, note that all three derived predicates are at least *a priori* plausible and interesting and valuable. They are not trivial (such as always returning T, or always returning what LIST-EQUAL returns), and even the strangest of them (L-E-3) is genuinely worth exploring for a minute.

Third, note that L-E-1 is familiar and of the utmost significance ("same-length"), and the second of the three (L-E-2) is familiar and moderately useful ("same-depth" if one deals exclusively with very deep nestings of parentheses, and "same-leading-element" if one deals only with shallow lists).

AM quickly derived from L-E-1 a function we would call LENGTH and a set of canonical lists of each possible length: ( ), (T), (T T), (T T T), (T T T T), etc.; i.e., a set isomorphic to the natural numbers. By restricting list operations (such as APPEND) to these canonical lists, AM derived the common arithmetic functions (in this case, addition), and soon began exploring elementary number theory. So these small syntactic mutations sometimes led to dramatic discoveries.

This simple-minded scheme worked almost embarassingly well. Why was that? Originally, we attributed it to the power of heuristic search (in defining specific goals such as "generalize LIST-EQUAL") and to the density of worthwhile math concepts. Recently, we have come to see that it is, in part, the density of worthwhile math concepts *as represented in LISP* that is the crucial factor.

## 3. The Significance of AM's Representation of Math Concepts

It was only because of the intimate relationship between LISP and Mathematics that the mutation operators (loop unwinding, recursion elimination, composition, argument elimination, function substitution, etc.) turned out to yield a high 'hit rate' of viable, useful new math concepts when applied to previously-known, useful math concepts—concepts represented as LISP functions. But no such deep relationship existed between LISP and Heuretics, and when the basic automatic programming (mutations) operators were applied to viable, useful heuristics, they almost always produced useless (often worse than useless) new heuristic rules.

To rephrase that: a math concept *C* was represented in AM by its characteristic function, which in turn was represented as a piece of LISP code stored on the Algorithms slot of the frame labelled '*C*'. This would typically take about 4–8 lines to write down, of which only 1–3 lines were the 'meat' of the function. Syntactic mutation of such tiny LISP programs led to meaningful, related LISP programs, which in turn were often the characteristic function for some meaningful, *related* math concept. But taking a two-page program (as many of the AM heuristics were coded) and making a small syntactic mutation is doomed to almost always giving garbage as the result. It's akin to causing a point mutation in an organism's DNA (by bombarding it with radiation, say): in the case of a very simple microorganism, there is a reasonable chance of producing a viable, altered mutant. In the case of a higher animal, however, such point mutations are almost universally deleterious.

We pay careful attention to making our representations fine-grained enough to capture all the nuances of the concepts they stand for (at least, all the properties we can think of), but we rarely worry about making those representations *too* flexible, too fine-grained. But that is a real problem: such a 'too-fine-grained' representation creates syntactic distinctions that don't reflect semantic distinctions—distinctions that are meaningful in the domain.

For instance, in coding a piece of knowledge for MYCIN [2, 5], in which an iteration was to be performed, it was once necessary to use several rules to achieve the desired effect. The physicians (both the experts and the end-users) could not make head or tail of such rules individually, since the doctors didn't break their knowledge down below the level at which iteration was a primitive.

As another example, in representing a VLSI design heuristic *H* as a two-page LISP program, enormous structure and detail were *added*—details that are meaningless as far as capturing its meaning as a piece of VLSI knowledge (e.g., lots of named local variables being bound and updated; many operations which were conceptually an indivisible primitive part of *H* were coded as several lines of LISP which contained dozens of distinguishable (and hence mutable) function calls; etc.) Those details were meaningful (and necessary) to *H*'s *implementation* on a particular architecture.

Of course, we can never directly mutate the *meaning* of a concept, we can only mutate the structural *form* of that concept as embedded in some representation scheme. Thus, there is never any guarantee that we aren't just mutating some 'implementation detail' that is a consequence of the representation, rather than some genuine part of the concept's intensionality.

But there are even more serious representation issues. In terms of the syntax of a given language, it is straightforward to define a collection of mutators that produce minimal generalizations of a given LISP function by systematic modifications to its implementation structure (e.g., removing a conjunct, replacing AND by OR, finding a NOT and specializing its argument, etc.) Structural generalizations produced in this way can be guaranteed to generalize the extension of function, and that necessarily produces a generalization of its *intension*, its meaning. Therein lies the lure of the AM and EURISKO paradigm. We now understand that that lure conceals a dangerous barb: *minimal* generalizations defined over a function's structural encoding need not bear much relationship to *minimal* intensional generalizations, especially if these functions are computational objects as opposed to mathematical entities.

## 4. Better Representations

Since 1977, Lenat has worked on building and extending the EURISKO program, the descendant of AM; see [10, 11, 12]. Its task is to learn new heuristics the same way it learns new math concepts. For four years, that effort achieved mediocre results. Gradually, the way we represented heuristics changed, from two opaque lumps of LISP code (a one-page long IF slot and a one-page long THEN slot) into a new language in which the statement of heuristics is more natural: it appears more spread out (dozens of slots replacing the IF and THEN), but the length of the values in each IF and THEN is quite small, and the total size of all those values put together is still much smaller (often an order of magnitude) than the original two-page lumps were. The term 'slot' here refers to a binary relation whose first argument is the name of a unit (frame, concept, etc.) and whose second argument is referred to as the value stored in that slot of that unit; they can also be viewed as unary functions over units, thus Genl(Primes) = Numbers,

Consider as an example the heuristic that says "If you want to find examples of a set $B$, and you know some function $f : A \to B'$, where $B'$ is known to intersect some generalization of $B$, then apply $f$ to examples of $A$ and collect the results." In AM, this was coded in LISP as something like the following:

```
IF:     (AND (EQ Cur-Action 'Find)
             (EQ Cur-Slot 'Examples)
             (MEMBER 'Collection (IsA Cur-Concept))
             (SETQ f (SOME (Examples 'Function)
                    '(LAMBDA (g)
                         (DoesIntersect (Range g) (Generalizations Cur-Concept))))))
THEN: (SUBSET (MAPCAR (Examples (Domain f))
                 '(LAMBDA (x)
                     (APPLY* (Alg f) x))
                 '(LAMBDA (e)
                     (APPLY* (Defn Cur-Concept) e))))
```

In EURISKO, the new form looks like this:

| | |
|---|---|
| IfCurAction: | Find |
| IfCurSlot: | Examples |
| IfCurConcept: | a Collection |
| IfForSome: | a Function *f* |
| IfIntersects: | (Generalizations CurConcept) (Range *f*) |
| ThenMapAlong: | (Examples (Domain *f*)) |
| ThenApplyToEach: | (Alg *f*) |
| CollectingIfTrue: | (Defn Cur-Concept) |

Much criticism of the AM paradigm, even of the entire expert systems and heuristic programming paradigms, arise from the 'scruffy' or *ad hoc* nature of the work. The shift in the form of the above heuristic rule suggests that adhocness is relative, and may be a fairly superficial property of a piece of knowledge: at the communication and surface structure level what appears to be ad hoc in one representation may shift and appear to become much less ad hoc as we evolve better languages.

It is not merely the *shortening* of the code that is important here, but rather the fact that this new representation provides a *functional decomposition* of the original two-page program along two dimensions: slots and values. The *values* now parameterize the heuristic; one can mutate syntactically, say replacing 'Generalizations' by some other slot name, and thereby move from one meaningful heuristic to another. The *slots* (the many different unary functions IfCurAction, IfForSome, ThenCollect, etc.) also functionally decompose the heuristic, setting the stage to learn context-sensitive (slot-sensitive) rules for guiding mutation. For instance, one such rule that EURISKO learned is "It's usually okay to mutate a heuristic by changing an AND to an OR in its If*Potentially*Relevant slot, but usually *not* in its If*Truly*Relevant slot."

A single mutation in the new representation is frequently equivalent to many *coordinated* small mutations at the LISP code level; conversely, most *meaningless* small changes at the LISP level (e.g., changing SETQ to SETQQ, or changing one occurrence of *x* to *f*) can't even be expressed in terms of changes to the higher-order language. This is akin to the way biological evolution makes use of the *gene* as a meaningful functional unit, and gets great milage from rearranging and copy-and-edit'ing it.

A heuristic in EURISKO is now—like a math concept always was in AM—a collection of about twenty or thirty slots, each filled with at most a line or two worth of code (often just an atom or a short list).

By employing this new language of specialized If- and Then-slots, the old property that AM satisfied *fortuitously* is once again satisfied: the primitive syntactic mutation operators usually now produce meaningful semantic variants of what they operate on. Partly by design and partly by evolution, a language has been constructed in which heuristics are represented naturally, just as Church and McCarthy made the lambda calculus and LISP into a language in which mathematics concepts' characteristic functions could be represented naturally. Just as the LISP↔Math 'match' helped AM to work, to discover math concepts, the new 'match' helps EURISKO to discover heuristics.

In getting EURISKO to work in domains other than mathematics, we have also been forced to develop a rich set of slots (new binary relations) for each domain (so that any one value for a slot of a concept will be small). EURISKO also requires that we provide a frame that contains information about that type of slot, so it can be used meaningfully by the program. This combination of small size, meaningful functional decomposition, plus explicitly stored information about each type of slot, enables the AM-EURISKO scheme to function adequately in non-mathematical domains. It has already done so for domains such as the design of three-dimensional VLSI chips, the design of fleets for a futuristic naval wargame, and for INTERLISP programming.

We believe that such a natural representation should be sought by anyone building an expert system for domain $X$; if what is being built is intended to *form new theories* about $X$, then it is a necessity, not a luxury. That is, it is necessary to find a way of representing $X$'s concepts as a structure whose pieces are each relatively small and unstructured. In many cases, an existing representation will suffice, but if the 'leaves' are large, simple methods will not suffice to transform and combine them into new, meaningful 'leaves'. This is the primary retrospective lesson we have gleaned from our study of AM.

We have applied it to getting EURISKO to discover heuristics, and are beginning to get EURISKO to discover such new languages, to automatically modify its vocabulary of slots. To date, there are three cases in which EURISKO has successfully and fruitfully split a slot into more specialized subslots. One of those cases was in the domain of designing three-dimensional VLSI circuits, where the Terminals slot was automatically split into InputTerminals, OutputTerminals, and SetsOfWhichExactlyOneElementMustBeAnOutputTerminal.

The central argument here is the following:

(1) 'Theories' deal with the meaning, the content of a body of concepts, whereas 'theory formation' is of necessity limited to working on form, on the structures that represent those concepts in some scheme.

(2) This makes the mapping between form and content quite important to the success of a theory formation effort (be it by humans or machines).

(3) Thus it's important to find a representation in which the form↔content mapping is as natural (i.e., efficient) as possible, a representation that mimics (analogically) the conceptual underpinnings of the task domain being theorized about. This is akin to Brian Smith's recognition [14] of the desire to achieve a categorical alignment between the syntax and semantics of a computational language.

(4) Exploring 'theory formation' therefore forces us to study the mapping between form and content.

(5) This is especially true for those of us in AI who wish to build theory formation programs, because that mapping is vital to the ultimate successful performance of our programs.

## 5. Where Does the Meaning Reside?

We speak of our programs *knowing* something, e.g. AM's *knowing about* the List-Equal concept. But in what sense does AM know it? Although this question may seem a bit adolescent, we believe that in the realm of theory formation (and learning systems), answers to this question are crucial, for otherwise what does it mean to say that the system has 'discovered' a new concept? In fact, many of the controversies over AM stem from confusions about this one issue—admittedly, confusions in our own understanding of this issue as well as others'.

In AM and EURISKO, a concept $C$ is simultaneously and somewhat redundantly represented in two fundamentally different ways. the first way is via its characteristic function (as stored on the Algorithms and Domain/Range slots of the frame for $C$). This provides a meaning *relative to the way it is interpreted*, but since there is a single unchanging EVAL, this provides a unique interpretation of $C$. The second way a concept is specified is more declaratively, via slots that contain *constraints* on the meaning: Generalizations, Examples, IsA. For instance, if we specify that $D$ is a Generalization of $C$ (i.e., $D$ is an entry on $C$'s Generalizations slot), then by the semantics of 'Generalizations' all entries on $C$'s Examples slot ought to cause $D$'s Algorithm to return T.

Such constraints *squeeze* the set of possible meanings of $C$ but rarely to a single point. That is, multiple interpretations based just on these under-determined constraints are still possible. Notice that each scheme has its own unique advantage. The characteristic function provides a complete and succinct characterization that can both be executed efficiently and *operated on*. The descriptive information *about* the concept, although not providing a 'characterization' instead provides the grist to guide control of the mutators, as well as jogging the imagination of human users of the program by forcing *them* to do the disambiguation themselves! Both of these uses capitalize on the ambiguities. We will return to this point in a moment but first let us consider how meaning resides in the characteristic function of a concept.

It is beyond the scope of this paper to detail how meaning per se resides in a procedural encoding of a characteristic function. But two comments are in order. First, it is obvious that the meaning of a characteristic function is always relative to the interpreter (theory) for the given language in which the function is. In this case, the interpreter can be succintly specified by the EVAL of the given LISP system.

But the meaning also resides, in part, in the 'meaning' of the data structures (i.e. what they are meant to denote in the 'world') that act as arguments to that algorithm. For example, the math concept List-Equal takes as its arguments two lists. That concept is represented by a LISP predicate, which takes as its two arguments two structures that both are lists and (trivially) represent lists. That predicate (the LAMBDA expression given earlier for List-Equal) *assumes* that its arguments will never need 'dots' to represent them (i.e., that at all levels the CDR of any subexpression is either NIL or nonatomic), it *assumes* that there is no circular list structure in the arguments, etc. This representation, too, proved well-suited for leading quickly to a definition of natural numbers (just by doing a substitution of T for anything in a LISP list), and *that* unary representation was critical to AM's discovering arithmetic and elementary number theory.

If somehow a place-value scheme for representing numbers had developed, then the simple route AM followed to discover arithmetic (simply applying set-theoretic functions to 'numbers' and seeing what happened) would not have worked at all. It's fine to ask what happens when you apply APPEND to three and two, so long as they're represented as (T T T) and (T T); the result is (T T T T T), i.e. the number five in our unary representation. Try applying APPEND to 3 and 5 (or to any two LISP atoms) and you'd get NIL, which is no help at all. Using bags of T's for numbers is tapping into the same source of power as Gelernter [3] did; namely, the power of having an *analogic* representation, one in which there is a closeness between the data structures employed and the abstract concept it represents—again, an issue of the relationship between form and function.

Thus, to some extent, even when discussing the meaning of a concept as portrayed in its characteristic function, there is some aspect of that meaning that we must attribute to it, namely that aspect that has to do with how we wish to interpret the data structures it operates on. That is, although the system in principle contains a complete characterization of what the operators of the language mean (the system has embedded within itself a representation of EVAL—a representation that is, in principle, modifiable by the system itself) the system nevertheless contains no theory as to what the *data structures* denote. Rather, *we* (the human observers) attribute meaning to those structures.

AM (and any AI program) is merely a model, and by watching it we place a particular interpretation on that model, though many alternatives may exist. The representation of a concept by a LISP encoding of its characteristic function may very well admit only one interpretation (given a fixed EVAL, a fixed set of data structures for arguments, etc.) But most human observers looked *not* at that function but rather at the **underconstrained** declarative information stored on slots with names like Domain/Range, HowCreated, Generalizations, IsA, Examples, and so on. We find it provocative that the most useful *heuristics* in EURISKO—the ones which provide the best control guidance—have triggering conditions which are also based only on these same *underconstraining* slots.

Going over the history of AM, we realize that in a more fundamental way we—the human observers—play another crucial role in attributing 'meaning' to a discovery in AM. How is that? As is clear from the fact that EURISKO has often *sparked* insights and discoveries, the clearest sense of meaning may be said to reside in the way its output jogs our (or other observers') memory, the way it forces us to attribute *some* meaning to what it claims is a discovery. Two examples, drawn from Donald Knuth's experiences in looking over traces of AM's behavior, will illustrate the two kinds of 'filling in' that is done by human beings:

(i) See AM's definition of highly composite numbers, plus its claim that they are interesting, and (for a very different reason than the program) notice that they *are* interesting.

(ii) See a definition of partitioning sets (an operation that was never judged to be interesting by AM after it defined and studied it), recognize that it is the definition of a familiar, worthwhile concept, and credit the program with rediscovering it.

While most of AM's discoveries *were* judged (by AM) interesting or not interesting in accord with human judgements, and for similar reasons, errors of these two types did occur occasionally, and indeed errors of the first type have proven to be a major source of synergy in using EURISKO. To put this cynically, the more a working scientist bares his control knowledge (audit trial) to his colleagues and students, the more accurately they can interpret the meaning of his statements and discoveries, but the *less likely* they will be to come up (via being forced to work to find an interpretation) with different, and perhaps more interesting, interpretations.

## 6. AI Methodology

In the remaining sections of this article, we address those specific issues and problems raised by Ritchie and Hanna's "AM: A Case Study in AI Methodology". We are grateful to them for spurring us to do this analysis, because of the new understanding it has led to about why AM and EURISKO appear to work (discussed in the preceding sections of this paper).

Ritchie and Hanna's Section 3 raises three fundamental questions, which are discussed one by one in their Section 4. Rather than mimic this organization, we choose to treat, one at a time, in decreasing order of seriousness, the four types of errors we believe were made in the AM thesis:

*Error Type* 1: Omitted heuristics. The AM thesis never explained, precisely, how concepts such as 'not very often' and 'related to' were implemented. By and large, these omissions were due to the fact that the code Lenat wrote for these predicates was quite trivial. Very recently, we realized that many unstated heuristics had been applied (by Lenat) to decide which concepts could and could not be trivialized in this way. Many of those heuristics are domain specific; that even more strongly argues that they ought to have been stated explicitly in his thesis. So we disagree with Hanna and Ritchie's opinion that the *code* implementing these concepts was the *important* missing information. Yes, the code ought to have been provided, but there was a much more significant omission, however: the *heuristics* that led to such decisions were significant in getting AM to work, hence should have been listed explicitly along with the 243 others.

*Error Type* 2: Omitted details. The second type of error of omission was the common, almost inevitable, yet regrettable process of simplifying large pieces of code, translating them to brief English phrases. This process left out many exceptional cases, and made the English condensations less accurate than the original LISP versions. The alternative, to leave things in LISP and present them that way, would have made the thesis largely impenetrable and dull. This is a choice that everyone in our field must make when writing up their work. In cases where a type 2 (or type 1) error led Ritchie and Hanna to believe a genuine problem or inconsistency existed in AM, we explain below how the original LISP code worked.

*Error Type* 3: Miscommunications. Some problems that Ritchie and Hanna cite, we shall see, are simply errors of mis-reading what was stated in the thesis or articles. For mistakes of this type, both writer and reader must share the blame. These are 'mistakes' only in the *exposition* of the work, not in the work itself. Most errors of this type are listed and explained below. It is useful that Ritchie and Hanna found these, as their correction will improve the readability of the work.

*Error Type* 4: Inconsistencies. A few of the problems raised in Ritchie and Hanna's article are, annoyingly, genuine inconsistencies in the thesis document, such as whether or not facets had subfacets. These reflect the fact that AM was a running and evolving program, changing daily in small ways even as the thesis document was being written. Types 3 and 4 are the least serious type of error, since they can be (and ought to have been) caught and corrected at the document level.

### 6.1. Omitted heuristics

Many of the questions Ritchie and Hanna raise, especially in Section 4.2, involve stating a heuristic, and simply saying "how in the world could *that* be coded as a small, separate if-then rule?" So this and the next section comprise, primarily, expositions of how their "problem heuristics" were coded. First we consider the serious cases, where the omission might seriously impair others attempting to duplicate this work. Next, we treat those cases where the omissions were unimportant. In both cases, they were usually an artifact of the heuristics' condensation into English.

We begin by discussing the specific cases cited in their Section 4.2: the use, by AM's heuristics, of expression such as "... very similar value ...", "...

decays rapidly with time ...", "... *C* is related to *D*...", "... replace the value ...", "if AM just ...", "... not often ...", and so on. Initially, we did not understand their difficulty with these; they took a small amount of LISP to code, and neither their coding nor their performance presented any particular problems. Let us examine the first of these, "very similar value"; SIMILARP is coded in AM as a COND that takes two arguments *x* and *y*, and if *x* is a number, then *y* must be a number within 10% of *x*; if *x* is a concept name, then *y* must be a concept name that appears somewhere on the values of *x*'s slots; and so on, for about a dozen 'types' of entities that might be given to it as arguments. What was not realized until recently was that such simple encodings work only because the *form* of the entries in AM's knowledge base mimic their *meaning*.

These encodings were admittedly—*intentionally methodologically*—done crudely and quickly, and worked well enough that we never needed to go back and improve that code. In retrospect this means that those small pieces of code were a kind of heuristic after all, heuristics which depended on AM's domain (elementary mathematics). Hanna and Ritchie don't explicitly state this, but we believe it is what troubled them in these particular heuristics, and we now agree that the details of such *unstated heuristics* should have been given in the thesis.

Let's consider their next example in particular: Hanna and Ritchie worry about how each new concept gets a small interestingness bonus that "decays rapidly with time"—i.e., how was that coded? The answer is that the task-number of each new concept's creation was recorded, and each concept got an automatic boost in interestingness, a numeric bonus which was reduced each time AM chose a task off its agenda and worked on it. Here is the formula for computing that bonus: (10 − CurrentTaskNumber + CreationTaskNumber). So, ten tasks after a concept gets created, its interestingness starts to fall; 500 tasks later it'll be very low indeed if nothing interesting has been discovered about it by then.

That was the first formula Lenat tried, and it never again drew his attention in such a way that he felt the need to modify it. This mechanism is a trivial version of HEARSAYII's 'focus of attention' mechanism. Many large heuristic programs possess similar mechanisms, both to keep the user/observer from becoming disoriented, and to avoid giving up prematurely on hard tasks. Yet the reason why AM's particular trivial version of Focus of Attention suffices has to do with the nature and structure of its task environment—discovery in mathematics—therefore it warranted detailed treatment in the thesis document [7], treatment it did not receive.

In other words, Lenat omitted stating the crucial heuristic he applied in this case: that a more sophisticated procedure for managing this decay was probably not worth the effort and, if it turned out to be needed, that need would become apparent as the program ran, and could be fixed by changing the focus of attention code at that time. Inherent in this discussion is the assumption that one has a limited amount of effort and time to expend on building an AI program, and therefore one must decide what features and sub-mechanisms to pay attention to.

As the final case of this phenomenon, we examine the predicate for testing "not often". This *might* have been arbitrarily complex and sensitive to context, but it was hoped and expected (by *unstated* heuristics) that it needn't be, in AM's domain. Here is AM's entire LISP code for Not-Often:

```
(LAMBDA ( ) (EQ 10 (RAND 1 10)))
```

Certainly one *might* (in some domains) need "not often" to be a *relative* term, sensitive to context, but '10% of the time' worked in all the cases AM needed to realize that notion. Besides being suited to its domain, the trivializations of otherwise-elusive predicates and concepts were not fatal. Indeed, this touches on the methodology of building AM: the source of power AM relied on (guidance by a large corpus of heuristics communicating via an agenda of plausible tasks) worked *despite* all the simplifications and trivializations committed at the coding level; the project took less than a man-year to do *because* of such simplifications.

At one point in their article, Ritchie and Hanna point out that some of AM's heuristic rules appear to need some inspectable record of past history. This is true, and we agree that it should have been discussed more clearly in the thesis. All that AM's rules can 'see' of the past is (i) what's been happening so far, during the efforts to work on the "current task", and (ii) a list of the most recent tasks that have been worked on, annotated with a list of their results. These two types of records *are* kept in AM. This was never discussed explicitly in [7]; it should become apparent as one works through the heuristic rules, as Ritchie and Hanna did. They noticed this, recognized that this ought to have been discussed in [7], and pointed out this fact.

Since there are so few such 'history' data structures, it is small work to represent each one of them as a full-fledged concept; we have always done things that way in EURISKO. Thus EURISKO has a RecentTasks concept, with a rule or two to update it each time a new task is completed, and a CurrentTask concept, which changes much more frequently and stores data about progress on the current task. At the time the AM thesis was written, the record-keeping data structures were seen as a minor detail, but we now believe that the choice of what parts of past history to save *were* significant, because they reflected the application of unstated heuristics about the process of theory formation.

## 6.2. Omitted details

Ritchie and Hanna complain, early in their article, that "no explanation is given as to why they [the Suggest rules] should, in this case, be attached to concepts or facets." The answer to this in English is that, "when it's time to suggest some new tasks about a concept *c*, evaluate all the Suggest heuristics tacked onto *c* (and all *c*'s generalizations)". For instance, to suggest new tasks involving PrimeNumbers, collect all the Suggest heuristics tacked onto PrimeNumbers, and NaturalNumbers, and Bags, and Structures, and MathematicalObjects, and Anything. Any or all of the rules you find in those places might be able to suggest new tasks involving PrimeNumbers; the other hundreds of rules in the system are presumed to be irrelevant and won't even be checked to see if they'll fire.

AM encoded this in INTERLISP as:

```
(MAPC (Genl* c) '(LAMBDA (gc) (MAPC (GET gc 'SuggestRules) 'EVAL]
```

Throughout the AM thesis, even in the appendices, Lenat opted for the former style (English description followed by an example or two) rather than the latter (listing the LISP code.) Hopefully, in most cases the 'casual reader' gets the correct sense out of the prose, and the reader who spends time to work through each statement in detail can comprehend what should have been said and how it might be implemented in LISP. For those interested in more detail, AM's LISP code was available to others for years after the publication of the thesis. Presenting an AI thesis largely in English is methodologically unlike most of the so-called hard sciences, where prose is supplied merely as commentary to the 'real' work, which must be presented in a formal calculus. This largely reflects the early stage of the AI science, but it does inconvenience those who wish to duplicate and extend their predecessors' work.

As has been mentioned previously, some liberties *were* taken with the English translation of each heuristic, so that Appendix 3 of the thesis would not be too monotonous. One result of this desire to not be monotonous is that the heuristics appear to be quite different from each other in format and syntax. In the AM program itself, however, the heuristic rules were indeed all coded in the same format (except for Interestingness rules). That format is specified in the thesis, and with it in hand one can, in most cases, readily see how to re-word each heuristic into that format, and then, given a rule in that format, how to code it up in LISP.

One of the heuristics that Ritchie and Hanna speculate (in Section 4.2) might be hard to code, and therefore code should have been provided for it, is "A nonconstructive existence conjecture is interesting". It's worth noting that this rule was never used in an AM run; it was intended to be part of the theorem-proving heuristics, an endeavor which, as stated in the thesis, we never got round to. In any event there is no magic in this; it only works on conjectures which have already been tagged explicitly, syntactically, as being existential and not constructive. In other words it is a two-line piece of code: if the proper three entries are members of the IsA facet of a concept, it upgrades its Interestingness facet. Because it was so simple to code, it was one of the first of formal proving heuristics to be coded. Unlike errors of type 1, omitting the details of this heuristic from [7] was not a mistake; failing to include tables detailing the performance of each heuristic was, we believe, the mistake.

Some heuristics comprised lists of automatic programming techniques for generalizing a predicate:
- replace the main connective by a more general one,
- if the main connective is NOT, then recur on its argument trying to *specialize* it,
- disjoin a related predicate onto this one, etc.

AM was not an automatic programming thesis, and it listed several pointers to AP articles (such as [4]) that covered exactly how such code mutations could be managed. Also, there was little if any innovation on code synthesis and mutation, hence little need to dwell on the details of the code we used to do it. Surprisingly often, it was little more than "randomly choose a node in the *S*-expression 'tree' and syntactically mutate it". This is why the ability of syntax to mirror semantics is so vital: in lieu of powerful mutation techniques AM relied on a natural representation to keep the fraction of useful mutants high.

### 6.3. Miscommunications

Ritchie and Hanna begin their article by summarizing AM. That summary is largely correct, but one of its errors is an example of a *Miscommunication*. They say "In general, any facet of a concept will be 'inherited' by that concept's specialization." The casual reader may get a general sense that some sort of inheriting of values is going on (which is true), or s/he will sit down and look at an example of that sentence and realize it is correct in some cases but wrong in others: surely 'examples of primes' should not automatically include all 'examples of numbers', rather, vice versa! As discussed in Lenat's thesis, some facets (such as Examples) inherit their values from specializations, some (such as all the relevant heuristics slots) inherit in the direction that Ritchie and Hanna stated, from generalizations, and some (such as all the book-keeping slots) don't inherit at all.

Hanna and Ritchie next dwell on the fact that Interestingness rules have a format which is not the same as the schema for other types of rules. This is quite correct, and is a *MisComm*: as can be seen by carefully reading the Interestingness subsection of the representation chapter of the thesis, Interestingness rules are not collected and fired to work on a task. Rather, what happens is that a particular Fillin or Check rule may *call* on the Interestingness rules stored for a concept *C* (and, by inheritance, *C*'s generalizations), then run those rules to determine if some concept *X* is an interesting *C*, and, if so, why.

They next question the consistency of the way heuristic rules in Appendix 3 of the thesis are organized; this again is a *Miscommunication*, not a genuine *Inconsistency*, as the first page of Appendix 3 clearly states how the section headings correspond to the 'internal form' of the heuristics. Lenat followed the convention that, if $f$ is an operation, then by saying that "$h$ is a $f$.check heuristic" or "$h$ is a $f$.fillin heuristic", what was *really* meant was that "$h$ is a $f$.examples.check heuristic" (or $f$.examples.fillin, etc.).

The small pieces of additional structure (beyond the clean, simple control structure discussed in [7, 8]) were added as a series of steps to improve efficiency by a small factor, and to cut down the amount of list cells required (by less than a factor of 2). They have little to do with the issues and contributions of the research. This level of detail *is* important to those who might wish to code similar systems, which is why some discussion of it was included in the thesis. It is this bundle of details that are the focus of much of Ritchie and Hanna's article's Section 4.1. The failure of the thesis to be clear on this point was a serious Miscommunication error.

Ritchie and Hanna then complain that in AM's concept hierarchy Any-Concept is not the root, but rather has a generalization called Anything. In AM, not all the world were concepts: there were individual numbers, user-names, and other atoms and strings that existed as *values* (of some facet of some concept) but were not themselves *full-fledged concepts*. Our recent work on EURISKO strives toward the extreme self-representation wherein each entity can be considered a concept, but in AM there were plenty of nonconcepts. We see the separation of AnyConcept and Anything to be a useful pragmatic distinction; there is no 'deep irregularity' to permitting AM to know that there are non-concepts in its world.

Ritchie and Hanna speculate on Lenat's "putting the heuristic commands in the body of the facet's entry (the algorithm, in this example)." Interpreting this remark literally results in a category error: algorithms encode the characteristic functions of concepts, whereas heuristics provide meta-level guidance on when and how those characteristic functions might be reasoned about, changed, etc. E.g., the Alg facet of Squaring (a concept discovered by AM) contained this LISP code:

```
(LAMBDA (x) (TIMES x x)),
```

while Squaring's (and its generalizations') heuristics facets contained page-long pieces of code that listed conditions under which one might want to square numbers, or apply a function in general to some particular arguments, how one could evaluate a function for interestingness, and so on—information which does not belong to the same category or type as the algorithm.

The other possible interpretation of their remarks about weaving heuristics into algorithms facets might be that the Alg facet of a concept contained a several-page-long block of LISP code, in effect a large SELECTQ, one of whose branches actually ran the algorithm and the other of whose branches were the various heuristics associated with the concept. That *would* be a significant change from the simple stated control structure, but AM could not function if it were true. There are two reasons for this. The first is pragmatic: there would be too huge a *space* cost involved in duplicating heuristics dozens of times (once in each algorithm facet), and AM was space-limited. The second reason is more important: AM mutates algorithms (values stored on various concepts' Algs facets) quite often, and if those algorithms were pages long (as they would have to be if they contained heuristics in the form of LISP code) rather than a couple *lines* long, syntactic mutation would never have achieved a high hit rate of valuable new mutants. This is the point of an earlier section of our current paper. AM worked only because the algorithms facets were tiny; they most clearly did *not* contain heuristics woven as pages of LISP code into them. This is one of the fortuitous cases where a *Miscommunication* error led us to a deeper insight about why the program worked.

A serious *Miscommunication* was caused by Lenat's use of the terms 'hacks' and 'specific tricks'. Lenat used the term to describe summarizations, collected in code, of his and others' work in other, earlier AI projects: the use of the term does *not* mean that he had preprogrammed into AM just the right piece of knowledge to achieve a desired runtime result, as Ritchie and Hanna imply. It is the incomplete nature of these parts of the program, and the fact that they were represented differently from the 'full fledged concepts' that comprised the bulk of the knowledge base, that drew from Lenat the label of hacks and tricks.

Ritchie and Hanna complain, e.g., about AM's "known tricks, some hacks" for symbolically instantiating LISP definitions. These "hacks" are a corpus of dozens of small *general* heuristics assembled earlier in PUP6 (BEINGS), and discussed extensively in print [4, 6] in the few years prior to the AM thesis. In AM, they were all lumped together into one four-page-long heuristic. The point is that this megaheuristic is capable not just of the one or two transformations AM actually carried out, but rather of the large classes of program instantiations that PUP6 and similar systems carried out. Directed by Cordell Green, Lenat collected this useful body of techniques for manipulating small LISP programs, unwinding recursions, etc.

It is worth going through one of these little 'tricks' to show the level of generality it has. It says that, if one wants examples of a concept, first find the base step in its recursive definition (the branch of the COND that doesn't mention the function name itself) and then extract a primitive extreme example from that base step (namely the value returned by that line of code). For instance, given

```
(DEFUN FIB (n)
  (COND
    ((EQ 0 n) 2)
    ((EQ 1 n) 3)
    (T (PLUS (FIB (SUB1 n))
            (FIB (SUB2 n))))))
```

this technique would first isolate the ((EQ 0 $n$) 2) branch, and the ((EQ 1 $n$) 3) branch, and then extract the values 2 and 3 as trivial examples of Fibonacci numbers. Even though it works quite often. Lenat called it a 'trick' because it relies on a particular style of programming (form), rather than on a true understanding of the LISP semantics (function), to work. As with many heuristics, this one usually succeeds but sometimes fails. Such 'imperfect coverage' is acceptable research methodology, in the spirit of heuristic programming. It is certainly not the same thing as 'fully predetermined usage', any more than an expert system's performance is determined when its rules are acquired.

Another example of this is the complaint about Rule 67, "Examine *C* for regularities". This one rule was large, to be sure—it contained many of the microrules that comprised Pat Langley's original BACON system. Not seeing any need to separate out the various recognizers from one another, Lenat allowed that single rule to embody all the low-level pattern recognizers. This does not mean that the uses of that rule were known ahead of time, merely that its contents have little to do with Discovery in Mathematics as Heuristics Search.

In discussing AM's rediscovery of cardinality, Ritchie and Hanna raise a question about which Suggest rules fire, and how that led to the goal of canonicalizing SameLength; the answer is the following: the Suggest rules attached to Predicate (and to its generalizations) are the rules which get evalled, and since SameLength is a Genl of SetEqual, AM tries Canonization. That's all there is to it. Canonization was not nearly as special-purpose as they imply, though—like "not often", "similar to", and "notice regularities"—it was *heuristically incomplete*. That is, it was drastically simplified to take advantage of the program's domain (reasoning about types of simple discrete math functions and structures), though *not* tailored with any specific sequence of behaviors in mind. The idea is that Canonizing operates via a set of mini-experiments, and various changes are made depending on their outcomes. For instance, here are the experiments (and reactions to take) AM applies when canonizing a new type of list structure:
– if order makes no difference, then sort the result,
– if element-name makes no difference, then use the same letter as the value of every element,
– if duplicating makes no difference, then eliminate all multiple copies of elements.

In the case of canonizing Has-the-same-length (the new predicate AM called Genl-Obj-Equal), order makes no difference, element-name makes no difference, but duplicating an element *does* make a difference. The resultant canonizing function therefore takes a bag, (unnecessarily) sorts it, and then replaces each element by the letter T. Since this was the only significant use of Canonize, we see that if we'd had a script in mind when building AM, and if only 'the scripted behavior' was desired, then only the middle of these three experiments would have been needed.

Later, once the Canonical-bag-strucs are defined, Ritchie and Hanna question whatever mysterious process lets arithmetic get discovered. As the traces in the thesis document, AM simply sees what happens when it restricts normal bag operations to these new canonical bags (all of whose elements are just the letter T). The result is that APPEND becomes addition (for instance, (T T) appended to (T T T) gives (T T T T T)), CDR becomes subtract-1, BAG-UNION becomes maximum, and so on. In other words, bag-operations restricted to Bags-of-T's *are* arithmetic functions. Moreover, it further surprised us that most of the arithmetic operations were discovered again and again, in unusual and different ways, as AM ran further.

Hanna and Ritchie focus, in Section 4.3, on this discovery of natural numbers. AM's key step was mutating the definition of equality, and it is treated in great detail in the thesis and also earlier in this paper. A miscommunication apparently occurs here: stripping off the CAR recursion test does *not* transform it into the predicate "Equal-except-Cars", as Ritchie and Hanna state, but rather into "Has-the-same-length".

## 6.4. Inconsistencies

The very first problem Ritchie and Hanna cite in the AM thesis is its apparent discrepancy about whether subfacets existed, and if so how many there were. This is a genuine inconsistency. The policy we (and the AM program) followed for having or not having subfacets changed frequently during the time that the thesis document was being written, and settled down finally into the decision that subfacets weren't needed, but the Suggest rules were separated off into different list structures. Looking over our records to see why this occurred, the changes in representation were driven simply by AM's running out of list space in 1975 INTERLISP code; we were forced to shift representations time and time again just to gain a few hundred precious list cells.

Most of the apparent inconsistencies pointed out in Ritchie and Hanna's article have already been seen to be one of the above three types of errors (usually a *Miscommunication*). The other inconsistencies, as the subfacet vs. no-subfacet issue, trace their roots to the volatility of coding details, and their etymology cannot be recreated today. If Lenat had noted them at the time of writing the thesis, they of course would have been excised, but is that the ideal solution? We are raising the methodological issue that perhaps it would have been better to chronicle and discuss the evolution of the program's data structures and algorithms, rather than just describing their final designs. Such considerations lead us to the next section of this article.

## 7. Methodological Consequences

The opening and closing pages of the Ritchie and Hanna article call attention to a valid, important issue in AI today: the difficulty researchers experience trying to build directly upon each other's work, due to the informal style of reportage currently acceptable. Lenat had hoped to alleviate this somewhat by giving copious details of how the program was built (in hundreds of pages of appendices and footnotes in his thesis). As Hanna and Ritchie say, "The whole discussion in this paper could not have commenced if Lenat had not provided this unusual level of documentation." It is largely at this level of minutiae that their article (and perforce our Section 6) focuses. We agree with them that critical dialogues at this extremely concrete level can facilate the spread of AI ideas, techniques, and problems. This competitive argumentation [15] should clarify the details of how AM was built and how it ran.

It is misleading to praise or critize AM's performance or methodology on the basis of any one or two specific discoveries. What surprised and pleased us was the quantity of interesting results, the large average number of discoveries (about two dozen) that each heuristic was used in making, the large average number of heuristics (again about two dozen) that worked together to make each discovery, the large number of discoveries of concepts and conjectures which were not known to Lenat (typically found by mathematicians poring over a transcript of one of AM's runs.)

It is not crucial that AM discovered cardinality or any other *one* concept. It did hundreds of other things before and after. It is the quality and quantity of the route it followed, the top tasks' consistent *plausibility*, that is the proper yardstick for its performance, regardless of *exactly* which concepts that route did or didn't happen to uncover. Consistent with this paradigm, we might have *supplied* cardinality and a few numerical concepts to it, just to see what it would do in number theory. In one experiment on AM, reported in the thesis, Lenat *did* have to hand-supply a dozen geometry concepts to get it to make discoveries in plane geometry. It was interesting that AM found cardinality all by itself, but, as we saw in the body of this paper, concepts such as "Bag" and "Set-Equality" took it halfway there to begin with.

After discussing the discovery of cardinality in detail, Ritchie and Hanna make a claim that we disagree with completely: to wit, that even if AM's behavior *were* the result of a carefully-engineered attempt to produce just one particular sequence of discoveries, then that would still be interesting. Such a project might indeed say something about mathematics, but it would have nothing to do with research in machine learning. The AM project methodology was to write down an apparently-coherent set of heuristics and starting concepts, and then code them all up and let them run. Tuning the system extensively (except to improve its use of space and time) would have negated the experiment utterly; the behavior of the program could have been arbitrarily deeper and more 'advanced' if we tuned it, but such exercises would not shed much light on how one could explore a new field, where the useful discoveries hadn't already been made. Exploring *new* fields is what EURISKO does, with some success [11, 12], and it is crucial to appreciate that it was the methodological commitment we made not to ever tune AM that let us discover what we needed to build EURISKO.

Many of the next questions raised by Hanna and Ritchie are right on the mark (e.g., did AM ever judge a concept to be uninteresting, when a human thought it was interesting?), and are discussed in the body of this paper. Their speculation is correct, that human observers corrected for some of the misjudgements on AM's part. The set of guidelines and questions they list in Section 5.2 are excellent, and warrant careful attention from all of us in AI research.

Ritchie and Hanna conclude Section 4.1 stating "The queries raised in the section are not minor organizational matters or implementation details." We disagree; that is *precisely* what they are. They appear to treat Lenat's thesis as if it were a formal proof of a theorem, in which finding even the tiniest inconsistency or irregularity from the clean control structure claimed therein would 'refute' it. But AI research is rarely like proving a theorem. The AM thesis is not making a formal claim about a provable property of a small, clean algorithm; AM is a demonstration that little more than a body of plausible heuristic rules is needed to adequately guide an "explorer" in elementary mathematics theory formation.

One of their central questions is "What did AM discover?" This is a very interesting issue, and to a large extent is what we describe in the body of this paper. Hanna and Ritchie complain because AM did discover Goldbach's conjecture in one run, but failed to in another run. They may take it as a flaw that AM does different things in different runs, but we take it as a very significant and positive sign, and indeed one might characterize EURISKO's current goal as being to produce as varied and unexpected behavior as possible, while not seriously sacrificing its level of plausibility, productiveness, and interestingness. Because of innumerable uses of random number generators (such as in "not often", above), the only way to keep the performance the same is to restart the program with the same pseudorandom seed. Placing much emphasis on the precise set of discoveries made or not made by AM is missing the entire point of the thesis, treating it as if it were stating a precise theorem, rather than making a plausible conjecture, about the nature of discovery.

The opposite complaint is also made, about the "preprogrammed behaviours" AM exhibited, the tailoring of the knowledge base to "unwind" a given discovery. In building AM, Lenat first compiled a large online document called GIVEN, in which were listed all the concepts it seemed plausible for AM to have (90% of which finally made it in), concepts drawn from Piaget's sets of prenumerical concepts. This document also specified all the slots (facets), and a rough listing of the values to be filled in for any slots that would start out with values (including all the attached heuristics—plus many more that never were implemented). This document was generated via morphological analysis—to wit, we made a big table of concepts along one dimension, slots along another, and spent months agonizing over the contents of each box. Armed with this document and several set-theory scenarios (most of which AM never did successfully carry out, by the way), coding began. Only about 1% of the final knowledge—both concepts and rules—was added or modified after that stage.

## 8. Conclusions

We have taken a retrospective look at the kind of activity AM carried out. Although we generally described it as "exploring in the space of math concepts", what it actually was doing from moment to moment was "syntactically mutating small LISP programs". Rather than disdaining it for that reason, we saw that that was its salvation, its chief source of power, the reason it had such a high hit rate; AM was exploiting the natural tie between LISP and mathematics.

We have seen the dependence of AM's performance upon its representation of math concepts' characteristic functions in LISP, and in turn *their* dependence upon the LISP representation of their arguments, and in both cases *their* dependence upon the semantics of LISP, and in *all* those cases the dependence upon the observer's frame of reference. The largely fortuitous "impedance match" between all-four of these, in AM, enabled it to proceed with great speed for a while, until it moved into a less well balanced state.

One of the most crucial requirements for a learning system, especially one that is to learn by discovery, is that of an adequate representation. The paradigm for machine learning to date has been limited to learning new expressions in some more or less well defined language (even though, as in AM's case, the vocabulary may increase over time, and, as in EURISKO's case, even the grammar might expand occasionally).

If the language or representation employed is not well matched to the domain objects and operators, the heuristics that *do* exist will be long and awkwardly stated, and the discovery of new ones in that representation may be nearly impossible. As an example, consider that EURISKO began with a small vocabulary of slots for describing heuristics (If, Then), and over the last several years it has been necessary (in order to obtain reasonable performance) to evolve two orders of magnitude more kinds of slots that heuristics could have, many of them domain-dependent, some of them proposed by EURISKO itself. Another example is simply the amount of effort we must expend to add a new domain to EURISKO's repertoire, much of that effort involving choosing and adjusting a set of new domain-specific slots.

The chief bottleneck in building large AI programs, such as expert systems [2, 5], is recognized as being knowledge acquisition. There are two major problems to tackle: (i) building tools to facilitate the man–machine interface, and (ii) finding ways to dynamically devise an appropriate representation. Much work has focused on the former of these, but our experience with AM and EURISKO indicates that the latter is just as serious a contributor to the bottleneck, especially in building theory formation systems. Thus, our current research is to get EURISKO to automatically extend its vocabulary of slots, to maintain the naturalness of its representation as new (sub)domains are uncovered and explored. This paper has raised the alarm; others [1, 10, 11, 12, 14, 15] discuss in detail the approach we're following and progress to date.

As we have tried to show above, throughout this paper, the kinds of *discrepancies* that Hanna and Ritchie focus upon are minor implementation details. The kinds of *omissions* they point to are more significant. We did not perceive until writing this paper that the way in which Similar-To, Not-Often, Notice-Regularity, and scores of other 'primitives' were coded do themselves embody a large amount of heuristic knowledge. We exploited the structure of (or, if you prefer, partially encoded) the domain of elementary mathematics, in the process of making *trivial yet adequate* LISP versions of those extremely complex and subtle notions (such as similarity of concepts).

The set of issues which we addressed in the earlier sections of this paper cover the other important methodological contributions and shortcomings of the AM program. Some of these have been remedied in EURISKO. All of them, plus the ones Ritchie.and Hanna have brought to light, deserve to be attended to explicitly, both in theoretical studies of the nature of learning by heuristic search, and in any projects to build programs that attempt to do such theory formation tasks.

## 9. An Alternative Perspective: The New Generation of Perceptrons

In closing, we present a new way of viewing the AM and EURISKO work. The apparent *adhoc*ness in both the heuristics' content themselves, and in the control knowledge guiding the application of those heuristics, is clearly the source of many methodological objections to the work. But we believe that this *adhocracy*—indeed, adhocracy controlling adhocracy—may be the source of EURISKO's underlying potential especially as a *model for cognition*. It bears some similarity to Newell, Rosenbloom, and Laird's current ideas on using chunking (into *ad hoc* chunks) to learn methods for controlling search.

As such, the paradigm underlying AM and EURISKO may be thought of as the new generation of perceptrons, perceptrons based on collections or societies of evolving, self-organizing, symbolic knowledge structures. In classical perceptrons, all knowledge had to be encoded as topological networks of linked neurons, with weights on the links. The representation scheme being used by EURISKO provides much more powerful linkages, taking the form of heuristics about concepts, including heuristics for how to use and evolve heuristics. Both types of perceptrons rely on the law of large numbers, on a kind of local-global property of achieving adequate performance through the interactions of many small, relatively simple parts.

The classical perceptrons did hill-climbing, in spaces whose topology was defined explicitly by weights on arcs between nodes (nodes which did straight-forward Boolean combinations plus threshholding). The EURISKO style of system does hill-climbing at both the object- (performance-program) and meta-(control decision) levels, in spaces whose terrain is defined implicitly, symbolically, by the contents of the nodes (nodes which are full-fledged concepts, at both object- and meta-levels). The new scheme fully exploits the same source of power (synergy through abundance) yet it is free from many of the limitations of the classical perceptron scheme.

One new possibility, that could not exist with classical perceptrons, is the opportunity for a genuine partnership, a synergy, between these programs and human beings, much the kind that EURISKO has already demonstrated. EURISKO is mediated by a language infinitely more comprehensible to humans than were classical perceptrons, and as we saw in Section 4 the more comprehensible the language became the more powerful it (and the man–machine system) became.

We could wax poetic on the metaphors implied by this new perspective on the AM and EURISKO work. For example, the control heuristics serve the same function in the program as cultural mores serve in human societies, and both of those corpuses evolve relatively slowly for many of the same reasons. Another example of the use of the cultural metaphor is that the appropriate methodologies for studying the AM and EURISKO programs may resemble those for studying the social sciences more than those for studying classical computer science.

In any event, thinking about AM and EURISKO from the perspective of *perceptrons* suggests new and exciting research directions in the construction and orchestration of large parallel cognitive systems.

### ACKNOWLEDGMENT

EURISKO is written in—and relies upon—RLL [9] and INTERLISP-D. We wish to thank XEROX PARC, and Stanford University's HPP, for providing superb environments (intellectual, physical, and computational) in which to work. An earlier, shorter version of this paper appeared in the proceedings of the 1983 National Conference on Artificial Intelligence, and we thank AAAI for permission to reprint it here. Financial support for this work has been provided by ONR, the IPTO office of ARPA, and XEROX Corporation. We thank Saul Amarel and Danny Bobrow for many useful comments on this work.

### REFERENCES

1. DeKleer, J. and J.S. Brown, "Foundations of Envisioning", *Proc. AAAI-82, NCAI*, Carnegie-Mellon University, Pittsburgh, PA, 1982.
2. Feigenbaum, E.A., The art of artificial intelligence, *Proc. Fifth International Joint Conference on Artificial Intelligence*, MIT, Cambridge, MA, (1977) 1014.
3. Gelernter, H., Realization of geometry theorem proving machine, in: E.A. Feigenbaum and J. Feldman (Eds.), *Computers and Thought* (McGraw-Hill, New York, 1963) 134–152.
4. Green, C.R., Waldinger, R., Barstow, D., Elschlager, R., Lenat, D., McCune, B., Shaw, D. and Steinberg, L., Progress report on program understanding systems, AIM-240, STAN-CS-74-444, AI Lab., Stanford, CA, 1974.

5. Hayes-Roth, F., Waterman, D. and Lenat, D., (Eds.), *Building Expert Systems* (Addison-Wesley, Reading, MA, 1983).
6. Lenat, D.B., BEINGS: Knowledge as interacting experts, *Proc. Fourth International Joint Conference on Artificial Intelligence*, Tbilisi, USSR, 1975.
7. Lenat, D.B., AM: An artificial intelligence approach to discovery in mathematics as heuristic search, Ph.D. Thesis, AIM-286, STAN-CS-76-570, and Heuristic Programming Project Report HPP-76-8, Stanford University, AI Lab., Stanford, CA, 1976.
8. Lenat, D.B., On automated scientific theory formation: A case study using the AM program, in: J. Hayes, D. Michie and L.I. Mikulich (Eds.), *Machine Intelligence* 9 (Halstead Press, New York; 1979) 251–283.
9. Lenat, D.B. and Greiner, R.D., RLL: A representation language language, *Proc. First Annual Meeting of the American Association for Artificial Intelligence*, Stanford, 1980.
10. Lenat, D.B., The nature of heuristics, *Artificial Intelligence* 19(2) (1982) 189–249.
11. Lenat, D.B., Theory formation by heuristic search, The nature of heuristics II: background and examples, *Artificial Intelligence* 21(1, 2) (1983) 31–59.
12. Lenat, D.B., EURISKO: a program that learns new heuristics and domain concepts, The nature of heuristics III: program design and results, *Artificial Intelligence*, 21 (1, 2) (1983) 61–98.
13. Polya, G., *How to Solve It* (Princeton University Press, Princeton, NJ, 1945).
14. Smith, B., Reflection and semantics in a procedural language, MIT Laboratory for Computer Science Tech. Rept. TR-272, Cambridge, MA, 1982.
15. VanLehn, K., Brown, J.S. and Greeno, J., Competitive argumentation in computational theories of cognition, in: W. Kinsch, J. Miller and P. Polson (Eds.), *Methods and Tactics in Cognitive Science* (Erlbaum, New York, 1983).

The Ecology of Computation
B.A. Huberman (editor)
© Elsevier Science Publishers B.V. (North-Holland), 1988

# Comparative Ecology:  A Computational Perspective

Mark S. Miller
Xerox Palo Alto Research Center,
3333 Coyote Hill Road, Palo Alto, CA 94304

K. Eric Drexler
MIT Artificial Intelligence Laboratory,
545 Technology Square, Cambridge, MA 02139*

A long-standing dream in the field of artificial intelligence has been to use evolutionary processes to produce systems of greater competence than those we can directly design. This paper compares different evolutionary models—such as biological ecosystems, markets, and EURISKO—with respect to this goal. This comparison suggests that a form of ecosystem here termed a *direct market* (as opposed to the *indirect market* of human society) is a promising basis for computational ecosystems. Related papers [I,II] in this book elaborate a vision of direct computational markets termed *agoric open systems*.

## 1. Introduction

A major problem in making effective use of computers is dealing with complexity. As we design programs of increasing functionality, we find ourselves overwhelmed by their ever greater complexity. It might seem that the complexity of computational systems must be limited by our ability to understand and design them, but this is not so. In the world outside computation are working systems that developed without design—indeed, systems of a complexity far beyond present design capabilities [1].

A patterned system which develops without deliberate design is termed a *spontaneous order* [2]. Crystals provide a simple example: nowhere in the nature of an element's individual atomic forces is its crystal structure specified, much less designed, yet that structure emerges as a result of those forces. Similar examples include patterns observed in Conway's game of Life [3] and the spiral arms of galaxies. A particularly powerful spontaneous ordering principle is evolution. Among the spontaneous orders in the world, the most intricate and impressive are those—such as human bodies and languages—that have emerged through evolutionary processes.

* Visiting Scholar, Stanford University. Box 60775, Palo Alto, CA 94306

The goal of this work is to understand how to build systems that will develop increasingly effective (even intelligent) computation through spontaneous ordering processes. In pursuit of this goal, this paper examines several evolutionary systems to determine which properties will serve best when generalized to the computational domain.

Biology provides the most familiar examples of evolutionary processes. A simple generalization from these examples might suggest that evolution is necessarily slow, and that it must proceed by random mutations. But human culture—including technology and scientific knowledge—is also a result of evolutionary processes [2,4]. This shows that evolution can proceed quickly, and that "mutations" in an evolving system can result from thought and design. The essence of evolution is trial and the weeding out of error, but the trials need not be random.

Evolution often proceeds in what, in the biological case, is called an *ecosystem*. Here, the concept of an ecosystem is generalized to cover any set of evolving, interacting entities operating within a framework of rules.

Ecosystems vary in their ability to solve externally defined problems. One can imagine putting a person or an ecosystem in a box and then presenting problems and contingent rewards through a window in the box. A box full of algae and fish will "solve" a certain narrow set of problems (such as converting light into chemical energy), and will typically pay little attention to the reward. A box containing an intelligent person will solve a different, broader range of problems. A box containing, say, an industrial civilization (with access to algae, fish, and Bell Labs) will solve a vastly greater range of problems. This ability to solve externally posed problems can be taken as a measure of an ecosystem's "intelligence" (see Section 6.2 of [I]).

Ecosystems discussed in this paper include Axelrod's *iterated prisoner's dilemma game* [5], which can serve as a sort of *E. coli* of ecosystems, and biological ecosystems, which are familiar enough to serve as a point of reference for the rest. Others discussed are Lenat's EURISKO program [III,6], political ecosystems, and what will here be termed *direct* and *indirect* market ecosystems. Markets are the central theme—other ecosystems are compared to markets, and markets themselves are generalized from existing human systems to proposed computational systems.

## 2. Evolution in ecosystems

Evolution proceeds by the variation and selection of replicators. The most familiar example, of course, is biological evolution, in which genes are the replicators [7,8], mutation is the variation mechanism, and a variety of environmental pressures (predation, parasitism, competition for scarce resources) act as selection mechanisms. The following will explore a variety of other ecosystems, the nature of their replicators, and the nature of their processes of variation and selection.

## 2.1. Ecosystems

Ecosystems provide contexts for evolution in two distinct senses. First, the ecosystem's replicators evolve in response to unchanging aspects of their environment such as climate and physical principles. Second, the replicators interact (through predation, competition, cooperation, and so forth), with each replicator providing part of the context for others. When replicators respond to external selective pressure, but not to each other, the result is an evolutionary system, but not an ecosystem. In such a non-ecological system, the subtlety and sophistication of the selective pressures are fixed.

The environmental richness and complexity generated when evolving entities can interact arguably leads to increased richness and complexity of the resulting system: selective pressures are then themselves the results of evolution. Analyzing such a system may be difficult, however. With many complex, multi-way feedback loops possible, can one be confident in the stability or direction of the overall system? This depends on the nature of the forces and feedback.

The analysis of ecosystems frequently involves non-intuitive secondary and tertiary effects. The Axelrod tournament provides a simple example of these effects.

## 2.2. The Axelrod tournament

Robert Axelrod developed an ecosystem in which the entities interact in rounds of iterated prisoner's dilemma games [5]. To understand it, one must first understand the dilemma itself. Instead of the traditional scenario of prisoners being interrogated, Hofstadter's illustration with the following scenario seems more intuitive.

Two dealers arrange to trade items. Each dealer agrees to place his item in a bag and leave it at a designated place to be retrieved by the other dealer. The dilemma presents itself when each dealer considers how best to interact with the other—given that they are strangers, will not meet face to face for this exchange, and will never deal with each other in the future. As Hofstadter describes, each dealer reasons as follows:

"'If the [other] dealer brings a full bag, I'll be better off having left an empty bag, because I'll have gotten all that I wanted and given away nothing. If the dealer brings an empty bag, I'll be better off having left an empty bag, because I'll not have been cheated. I'll have gained nothing but lost nothing either. Thus it seems that *no matter what the dealer chooses to do*, I'm better off leaving an empty bag. So I'll leave an empty bag.' ...And so both of you, with your impeccable (or impeccable-seeming) logic, leave empty bags, and go away empty handed. How sad, for if you both had just cooperated, you could have each gained something you wanted to have. *Does logic prevent cooperation?* This is the issue of the Prisoner's Dilemma." [emphasis in the original] [9]

The underlying strategic situation can be made precise in the following fashion: In a single prisoner's dilemma interaction, two players each choose between moves (termed *cooperate* and *defect*) in ignorance of the other's choice. If both cooperate, both are rewarded (in Axelrod's case, with a payoff of 3 points). If one cooperates and the other defects, the defector

Column Player

|  | | Cooperate | Defect |
|---|---|---|---|
| Row Player | Cooperate | $R = 3, R = 3$<br>Reward for<br>mutual cooperation | $S = 0, T = 5$<br>Sucker's payoff, and<br>temptation to defect |
|  | Defect | $T = 5, S = 0$<br>Temptation to defect<br>and sucker's payoff | $P = 1, P = 1$<br>Punishment for<br>mutual defection |

Note: The payoffs to the row chooser are listed first

***Figure 1: Prisoner's dilemma payoff matrix.***
*(from "Evolution of Cooperation" [5], page 8)*

receives an even greater reward (5 points), while the cooperator receives nothing (0 points). If both defect, both are punished (by receiving only 1 point).

In a single move, each player has an incentive to defect regardless of the other player's move, but double-cooperation is better than double-defection. Overall, pairs of players that cooperate earn higher scores than those that do not.

In an iterated prisoner's dilemma game, two players go through a long series of moves, and can base their actions on the history of play. When one expects (and hopes for) further transactions with the other party, simple defection no longer seems as attractive. Indeed, by running a computer tournament, Axelrod showed that the logic of an *iterated* prisoner's dilemma actually fosters cooperation.

Robert Axelrod ran a Computer Prisoner's Dilemma Tournament based on the above rules. A diverse group of game theorists were invited to submit programs to play against each other in a round-robin of games, each averaging 200 single moves. After the first tournament, Axelrod circulated the results—including the nature of the winning program, judged by cumulative points—and solicited entries for a second tournament.

Axelrod's *pair of tournaments* may be described as a simple evolutionary ecosystem. The replicators were the programs themselves (or the strategies those programs embody), the variation mechanism was human ingenuity (since programs were modified between tournaments), and the selection criterion during a tournament was simply the number of points earned. Programs interacted with each other in an environment imposing certain rules, and their success depended on each others' behavior. Further, Axelrod went on to simulate the population dynamics of a set of programs, given the assumption that points earned determined the "population density" of that program in the next time period.

In both tournaments a very simple program won. That program was TIT FOR TAT, submitted by psychologist Anatol Rapoport. In the population dynamics simulation, the success of TIT FOR TAT was even more pronounced. Analyzing TIT FOR TAT's success can suggest how to analyze other ecosystems.

### 2.2.1. The triumph of TIT FOR TAT

All sorts of strategies were submitted, including many which used complex reasoning based on past interactions, and one which responded randomly. The success of a strategy depended on whether it was:

- *Nice*—never defected first,
- *Retaliatory*—responded to defection with defection (thereby punishing defectors), and
- *Forgiving*—eventually stopped defecting in response to cooperation.

TIT FOR TAT is the simplest example of a nice, retaliatory, and forgiving strategy. It cooperates on the first move and then does whatever the opposing player did on the previous move.

Other strategies can be classified according to which of the above traits they lack. A strategy which initiates a defection (and thereby is not nice) may be termed a *con man*, since it is trying to gain at the expense of (and with the foolish cooperation of) its opponent—the simplest con man always defects. A nice strategy which does not defect in response to a defection (and thereby is not retaliatory) may be termed a *sucker*, since it can be taken advantage of by con men.

Con men have an advantage over TIT FOR TAT in that they can fully exploit suckers, while TIT FOR TAT only cooperates with them. Given the mix of strategies submitted to Axelrod's tournaments, TIT FOR TAT won both. A con man strategy could have won, however, had the initial population included enough suckers. Since con men could have won in this case, how can one claim that TIT FOR TAT is *fundamentally* more viable than con men? Axelrod's population dynamics simulation helps answer this question.

## 3. Evolutionarily stable strategies

In the population dynamics simulations, a population number is associated with each strategy, to indicate how many "organisms" in the overall population are following the strategy. In each generation, the score received by an organism is the score it would receive in playing a series of one-on-one games with every organism in a representative sample of the total population. At the end of each generation, the total score accumulated by organisms using a given strategy determines how many organisms of that type will exist in the next generation. (A process of this sort—in which success in one round determines influence or existence in the next—distinguishes *evolutionary game theory* from conventional game theory. Evolutionary game theory need make no assumptions about motives or values, though it is natural to think in terms of a "survival motive" which generates a "success motive".)

As Figure 2 shows, in a population dominated by suckers, a small population of con men have a great advantage, rising to temporary dominance. But in doing so, they drive down the population of suckers and so lose their advantage; they are then driven to extinction by TIT FOR TAT. As shown in the diagram, an environment with enough TIT FOR TAT players to fight off an invasion of con men can support a stable population of suckers.

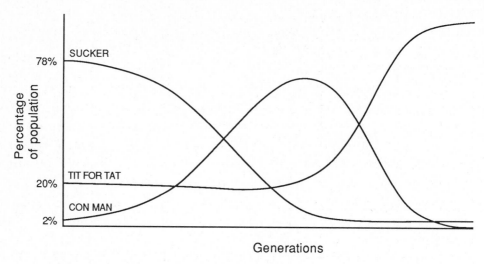

*Figure 2: Population dynamics simulation. Following Axelrod, we ran a population dynamics simulation starting with the stated percentages of three strategies: SUCKER, TIT FOR TAT, and CON MAN (see text). Each strategy was played against all three strategies in a set of 200-move iterated prisoner's dilemma games. The resulting score determined the number of "progeny" in the following generation. The initial conditions were chosen to best illustrate the points made in this paper, but these points are robust in the face of variations.*

In this ecosystem, TIT FOR TAT can be termed an *evolutionarily stable strategy*, or *ESS*. An ESS is a strategy which, given that it dominates an ecology, cannot be invaded by any other strategy [10,7]. In Maynard Smith's terminology, "ESS" refers to a specific detailed strategy (such as TIT FOR TAT); here, the term will refer to general classes of strategies that share basic characteristics, such as being "nice and retaliatory". The rules governing a given ecology determine the success of different strategic characteristics, and therefore the ESS.

As shown, suckers are not an ESS in Axelrod's system because they can be invaded by con men. Con men are not an ESS except in a trivial sense—a population consisting purely of con men cannot be invaded by a small, scattered group of TIT FOR TAT players. A small but significant number of invaders, however, can cooperate, expand, and completely replace a population of con men. A population dominated by any strategy that is both nice and sufficiently retaliatory cannot be invaded by any strategy that is not. Any population dominated by a strategy that is not both nice and sufficiently retaliatory can be invaded. Therefore, the ESS of the Axelrod tournament is to be nice and retaliatory.

A single population-dynamics process can be described as an ecosystem, but not as an evolutionary ecosystem, since there is no source of variation. Axelrod's series of two tournaments included variation from one to the next, and hence qualifies. To transform it into a better example of an evolutionary ecosystem, imagine a continuing tournament open to outside contestants able to create new strategies and introduce them in small numbers. In any

| | Replicators | Variation Mechanisms | Success Metrics | Rules of the Game | Typical ESSs |
|---|---|---|---|---|---|
| **Axelrod game** | Strategies | Inter-round human redesign | Points | Iterated prisoner's dilemma | Nice and retaliatory |
| **Life** | Genes | Mutations | Population, Biomass, Free energy | Physics, Genetic system | Teeth & armor (or analogues) |
| **EURISKO** | Heuristics | Metaheuristics | "Interestingness" | RLL, Privileged metaheuristics | Self-rewarding |
| **Memetic Ecology** | Memes (Ideas, etc.) | Imagination, Invention, Confusion | Popularity | Human psychology | Practical utility, Sheer appeal |
| **Human Market** | Firms, Market memes | Innovators, Entrepreneurs | Net worth | Property rights (post-enforced law) | Productive and wary |
| **Direct Market** | Actors, Objects | Human innovators, Metaheuristics | Net worth | Encapsulation (pre-enforced) | Productive and wary |

*Figure 3: Comparison of Ecosystems. Several evolutionary ecosystems are here analyzed in terms of their replicators, mechanisms for variation and selection, success metrics, foundational rules, and evolutionarily stable strategies.*

such open, evolving ecosystem, given no special restrictions on allowable variations, one should expect the ecosystem to become populated primarily by an ESS. The properties of such an ESS will often indicate emergent properties of the system. For example, in any open Axelrod ecosystem most moves will be cooperative.

The above discussion of Axelrod's system benefits from hindsight. The original game-theory experts who submitted the original strategies knew the rules, and those who submitted strategies for the second tournament even had the benefit of a bit of hindsight from the first tournament. Nevertheless, in both cases most of the strategies submitted were not nice, and so were not ESSs. The analyses which follow cover much more complex ecosystems, in which the nature of strategies and payoffs are much more subtle.

As a result, many of the points made in the rest of this paper are not settled conclusions, but merely initial hypotheses to be tested. The best testing methodology is that used by Axelrod: run a system and open it to outside contributors. The goal is to understand what properties of a computational ecosystem will result in useful system behavior.

## 4. Biological and market ecosystems

This section compares biological and *idealized market* ecosystems, focusing on the differing evolutionarily stable strategies they foster. Idealized markets, as defined here, are computationally-inspired abstractions having parallels with human markets but omitting certain of their complexities and problems. The idea of a computational market is not developed in detail in this paper; see [I,II] for a more concrete discussion.

### 4.1. Rules of the games

The above analysis of Axelrod's ecosystem began with an examination of the rules of the game. These rules are the constraints within which organisms of that ecosystem must operate. The only fundamental constraint on either biological or human market ecosystems is physical law: any action not forbidden by physical law is in theory possible for players in either ecosystem. However, in order to analyze these ecosystems, it is useful to consider idealized versions in which players operate under additional constraints.

### 4.1.1. Foundations of biological ecosystems

An example of a physical constraint in biological ecosystems is the conservation of mass and energy. Among animals, the critical resources—biomass and free energy—are *downwards conserved:* they can be transferred and reduced by the transactions animals are capable of, but not increased. Plants can obtain these resources by photosynthesis; access to sunlight and land area are among their critical limited resources. Biomass and free energy are needed to sustain activity, and can be transferred by predation.

Other constraints in biology (at least if evolutionary history is any guide) include the primary use of proteins for construction of molecular machinery and the use of ribosomes programmed by nucleic acids for their manufacture. These constraints (while not essential to the present discussion) have been shown to limit severely the materials and processes available to biological systems [11,12].

### 4.1.2. Foundations of idealized markets

In the attempt to characterize an idealized biological ecosystem, it is fortunate that the boundary between living and non-living systems is still fairly clear. In contrast, human markets exist in the context of governmental activity and crime—this makes idealization a larger and riskier task. The following will analyze idealized market ecosystems with simple foundational rules of sorts that can be rigorously enforced in a computational context. This analysis draws heavily on analogies with human markets, while omitting certain difficulties that are excluded by the idealization. Section 6.2 will build on the concept of an idealized market, describing a direct market ecosystem with further differences from human markets; again, these differences are inspired by the possibilities of computational systems.

The basic rules of human markets are typically encoded in legal systems and enforced by attempting to catch and punish violators. In a computational setting, these rules can be enforced as unbreakable "physical" laws. In particular, rights of property (or ownership) can be implemented through *encapsulation* [I,IV,V]; unforgeable currency and trademarks can be implemented through *public key systems* [13,14]. The computational entities within such a system could no more steal than human entities can travel faster than light. These abilities can provide the foundations for idealized markets.

An idealized market can contain a great variety of resources, analogous to items ranging from land to airplanes to currency tokens. These resources can be owned by individual entities or groups. No one may take such resources from their owner, but an owner may voluntarily transfer them to any other party. When this occurs in a reciprocal exchange, we refer to the transaction as a *trade*. Exchanges cannot increase the quantity of any resource—resources are locally conserved across transfers. Productive activity, however, can increase supplies of many resources.

By the rules of the game, anyone may produce new airplanes. Were this the case for currency tokens, however, they would be useless as currency. The rules of an idealized market therefore permit manufacture of a given currency only by a corresponding mint [14]. The effects of minting and introducing new currencies into a market ecosystem are complex [15,16], and are ignored in this paper. The following assumes a currency which is both locally and globally conserved.

A key difference between biological and idealized market ecosystems is the ability to establish and use unforgeable identities. Nature abounds in examples of mimicry and in imperfect attempts to avoid being mimicked [17]. A *right to trademark* is here defined to be one of the rules of idealized markets. Any entity may establish a new trademarked identity and attach it to that entity's product or place of business. No entity may do this with another's trademark.

### 4.1.3. Variation and selection

In biology, the replicators are genes, and the variation mechanism is relatively random mutation of an organism's genetic code—its genotype. This does not mean biological variation is random. An organism's phenotype—its body structure, abilities, and so forth—determines its success [18]. An organism's phenotype is decoded from its genotype through a complex translation process. The encoding of a phenotype determines what other phenotypes are reachable by small mutations of a genotype. Therefore this encoding itself can embody heuristics for *plausible* phenotypic mutations (for example, leg-lengthening mutations interact with the heuristic rule of embryonic development that says, in effect, "do the same to both sides"). As explained in [III], AM and EURISKO employ computational embodiments of this principle (as do genetic algorithms in classifier systems [19]). Nevertheless, biological variation is essentially short-sighted, limited to incremental changes.

The variation and selection mechanisms of market ecosystems are less constrained to local optimization or *hill climbing* than are those of biological ecosystems. In biological evolution, temporary changes for the worse (temporary travel downhill) will typically lead to extinction through competition from organisms that have not gone downhill. This, together with the small steps possible through typical mutations, greatly limits the ability to reach distant peaks, however high they may be.

Variation in the human marketplace (as in the computational markets described below) frequently results from invention and design by people (or other entities able to plan ahead) who can design coordinated sets of non-incremental changes. Investors in a market (*e.g.*, venture capital firms, in the human market) can take into account arguments for anticipating future success despite present failure, and invest in crossing a valley to get to a higher hill. Biological variation cannot take such arguments into account. By rewarding successful investors, markets select for entities that can facilitate these large jumps. Design and evolution are sometimes presented as mutually exclusive principles, but market ecosystems make use of both.

### 4.1.4. Success metrics

Success (or "fitness") in an evolutionary process is sometimes defined in terms of long-term survival, but doing so would give little help in analyzing the short term. Also, the goal here is to use evolutionary reasoning to predict the nature of an ecosystem, not to determine what types of creatures will be around at some distant time. For these purposes, a useful criterion of a replicator's success is the magnitude of its ability to affect its environment. This is itself hard to measure, giving reason to seek a metric which is positively correlated with this ability.

In biology, control of biomass and free energy correlates with ability to engage in biological activity. In a market ecosystem, an entity's net worth is the measure of its resources, and hence a rough measure of its potential ability to engage in market activity. The following analyzes strategies for achieving these kinds of success.

### 4.2. ESSs in biological ecosystems

To survive, animals must eat animals or plants; this happens most often though predation. (Here entities which are eaten, whether animals or plants, are termed "prey".) This is not a synergistic or symbiotic process—the incentives are not toward cooperation between predator and prey. If they were, the participants would both try to facilitate the predatory transaction.

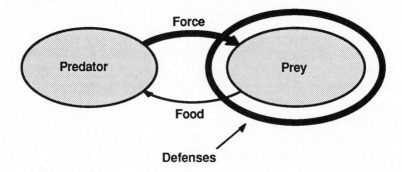

*Figure 4: Predator and prey. In a biological ecosystem, predators forcibly overcome prey defenses to obtain food. Force and defenses evolve in an arms race, adding overhead to the predatory "transaction"; the lines representing force and defense are accordingly thick. Since attack may come from any direction, defenses are shown surrounding the prey.*

Instead, the incentives lead to an arms race in which predators develop better "teeth" and prey develop better "armor". "Teeth" here refers to any mechanism for facilitating predation, such as a cheetah's legs or a dog's nose. "Armor" here refers to any mechanism for avoiding being preyed upon, such as a gazelle's legs or a skunk's scent. An animal without effective "teeth" would starve, and one without effective "armor" would rarely live long enough to reproduce.

Plants are seldom predators, but are often prey. As prey, they develop spines, grit to wear down teeth, and poisons (many are carcinogenic [20]). This has spurred another arms race in which animals have developed large, grinding molars and biochemically complex livers to deal with poisons. Plants compete for light in yet another arms race. This has led to the growth of trees which invest in huge wooden columns for the sake of tallness, to intercept their neighbors' light. Efficient, cooperating plants would instead cover the Earth with grassy or mossy growth; their energy would be stored, not in inert wood, but in sugar, starch, oil, or some other metabolizable reserve.

Predation is a negative-sum relationship: one of the participants benefits, but only at a greater cost to the other. Biological competition is roughly zero-sum in the short term, but spurs a wasteful negative-sum arms race over the long term. Of course, there are many examples of symbiotic, positive sum relationships in biology, but the basic ESS of biology is one of "teeth and armor".

## 4.3. ESSs in idealized market ecosystems

In order to sustain activity, players in the idealized market must obtain valuable resources, or *goods*. They can do so through the equivalent of solitary prospecting and manufacture, but the limited competence of any one entity will favor obtaining goods from others—that is, division of labor. Since the rules of the idealized market make it impossible to seize goods by force, one entity can obtain another's goods only by inducing it to engage in a voluntary transaction. An entity which simply gives away goods would steadily lose resources and

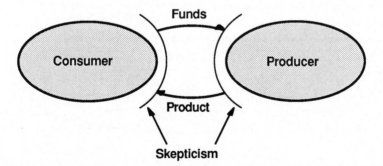

*Figure 5: Consumer and producer. In an idealized market ecosystem, customers use funds to induce producers to supply products. Each party must maintain defensive skepticism, but the evolution of relationships favors reducing the overhead of transactions. Skepticism is thus shown as a thin but effective barrier. Transactions are voluntary, hence skepticism need not protect against bad trades from every possible direction.*

influence compared to one which does not; such a strategy would not be an ESS. Therefore, the strategy of simply accumulating donated gifts would also not be an ESS.

To induce "gifts", an entity must offer something in exchange. For both sides to want to trade, each must value the goods received more than the goods given. Pair-wise barter deals of immediate mutual benefit are hard to find, and would yield only part of the full potential benefit of trade. Large multi-way deals would yield the full benefit, but are difficult to nego-tiate. Trade of goods for currency is therefore the expected dominant pattern; currency makes it easier for the equivalent of large multi-way barter deals to occur through separate pair-wise trades.

Each trade in a market can be seen as moving the system toward a condition (one of many possible) in which no transaction that will make both parties better off remains to be done (a condition known as *Pareto optimality*). Each trade can be seen as a hill-climbing step. Pair-wise barter amounts to hill-climbing across a rough terrain with few available moves; trade in a system with currency and prices amounts to hill-climbing across a smoother terrain with many available moves.

In a trade of goods for currency, the player paying currency in exchange for goods we term a *consumer* and the one selling goods in exchange for currency we term a *producer*. A set of producers competing to provide the same (or very similar) goods we term an *industry*.

Consumer-producer relationships can be contrasted to predator-prey relationships. Pro-ducers, unlike prey, will voluntarily seek out those who want to consume what they have, using advertising, distribution networks, and so forth. Consumers, less surprisingly, will seek out producers (in human markets, they do so by reading advertising, traveling to stores, and so forth). The symbiotic nature of this interaction is shown by the interest each side has in facilitating it. Since trade typically increases the viability of both participants, it also raises the viability of the pair considered together as an entity.

There are many negative-sum pair-wise relationships in even an ideal marketplace—the most common is competition among producers in the same industry. In judging the nature of the market as a whole, however, it is important to note that when producers compete, each is competing to do a better job of cooperating with the rest of the world, of attracting consumers into beneficial trade relationships.

In the absence of perfectly-effective rules to prevent it (which seem difficult to define, even in the computational domain), markets will suffer from fraud. A fraudulent transaction occurs when a producer induces a consumer to pay for an undesired good under false pretenses.

It is worth distinguishing fraudulent trades from those in which (in light of later informa-tion) a different alternative would have yielded a better product or a better price. Non-optimal trades are universal, given imperfect knowledge (which will be ubiquitous in computational markets), but this observation would argue against the use of market mechanisms only if someone could find a better way to use imperfect knowledge. Unlike fraudulent trades, non-optimal trades are still symbiotic; they merely fall short of an imagined perfection.

The possibility of fraud, together with the difference in quality among available deals, creates an incentive for consumer wariness. Wary consumers will in turn create an incentive for producers to avoid fraud, and for them to offer high quality (though not necessarily optimal) deals. The resulting ESS is to be "productive and wary"—wary as a consumer and productive and honest as a producer—for many of the same reasons that "nice and retaliatory" is Axelrod's ESS. Given a variety of strategies in a brand-new market ecosystem, one can expect that fraudulent producer strategies will initially profit at the expense of non-wary consumer strategies. As a result, wary consumers will grow in importance, driving out fraudulent producer strategies. These considerations will even drive out honest producer strategies which are noticeably less productive than their competitors. At a finer level of resolution, of course, there will be as many detailed strategies for being productive and wary as there are niches for entities in the market.

How can a consumer be effectively wary? The producer-consumer relationship is similar to an iterated prisoner's dilemma. If a producer fraudulently sells a worthless product, he is "defecting" on the arrangement. A wary consumer must take the trouble to notice this defection in order to retaliate (for example, by doing business elsewhere and warning others away). Checking for a defection can be expensive, however, and consumers are frequently in non-iterated situations. Reputation agencies like *Consumer Reports* can lower the cost of wariness and make it more effective by putting the producer in an iterated situation with the community as a whole (see the discussion of reputation agents in [I]). Trademarking of services and products enables producers to establish valuable reputations. The lack of this mechanism in biology [17] contributes to the relative sparseness of symbiosis there.

## 4.4. Food webs and trade webs

Biological and market ecosystems both contain a mixture of symbiotic and negative-sum relationships. This paper argues that biological ecosystems involve more predation, while idealized market ecosystems involve more symbiosis. Indeed, one can make a case that this is so even for *human* market ecosystems—that biological ecosystems are, overall, dominated by predation, while market ecosystems are, overall, dominated by symbiosis.

In human markets (as in idealized markets) producers within an industry compete, but chains of symbiotic trade connect industry to industry. Competition in biology likewise occurs most often among those occupying the same niche, but here, it is predation that connects from niche to niche. Because of the lack of reputations and trademarks, symbiosis in biology occurs most often in situations where the "players" find themselves in a highly-iterated game. In the extreme, the symbiotic system itself becomes so tightly woven that it is considered a single organism—as with lichens composed of fungi and algae, or animals composed of eukaryotic cells containing mitochondria. Predation, of course, links one symbiotic island to the next.

Ecology textbooks show networks of predator-prey relationships—called *food webs*— because they are important to understanding ecosystems; "symbiosis webs" have found no comparable role. Economics textbooks show networks of trading relationships circling the globe; networks of predatory or negative-sum relationships have found no comparable role.

(Even criminal networks typically form cooperative "black markets".) One cannot prove the absence of such spanning symbiotic webs in biology, or of negative-sum webs in the market; these systems are too complicated for any such proof. Instead, the argument here is evolutionary: that the concepts which come to dominate an evolved scientific field tend to reflect the phenomena which are actually relevant for understanding its subject matter.

## 4.5. Is this picture surprising?

Nature is commonly viewed as harmonious and human markets as full of strife, yet the above comparison suggests the opposite. The psychological prominence of unusual phenomena may explain the apparent inversion of the common view. Symbiosis stands out in biology: we have all heard of the unusual relationship between crocodiles and the birds that pluck their parasites, but one hears less about the more common kind of relationship between crocodiles and each of the many animals they eat. Nor, in considering those birds, is one apt to dwell on the predatory relationship of the parasites to the crocodile or of the birds to the parasites. Symbiosis is unusual and interesting; predation is common and boring.

Similarly, fraud and criminality stand out in markets. Newspapers report major instances of fraud and embezzlement, but pay little attention to each day's massive turnover of routinely satisfactory cereal, soap, and gasoline in retail trade. Crime is unusual and interesting; trade is common and boring.

Psychological research indicates that human thought is subject to a systematic bias: vivid and interesting instances are more easily remembered, and easily remembered instances are thought to be more common [21]). Further, the press (and executives) like to describe peaceful competition for customer favor as if it were mortal combat, complete with wounds and rolling heads: again, vividness wins out. These factors go far to explain the common view of market and biological ecosystems.

For contrast, imagine that symbiosis were as fundamental to biology as it is to markets. Crocodiles would not merely have birds to pick their teeth, symbiotic bacteria in their guts, and the like; they would have symbiotes to provide them with orthodontia and tooth crowns, to say nothing of oral surgery, heart surgery, and kidney transplants, as well as shoes, clothing, transportation, housing, entertainment, telecommunications, massage, and psychiatric care.

Likewise, imagine that predation were as fundamental to markets as it is to biology. Instead of confronting occasional incidents of theft in a background of trade, one would be surrounded by neighbors who had stolen their cars from dealers who had mounted an armed assault on factories in Detroit, which in turn had grabbed their parts and equipment by pillaging job-shops in the surrounding countryside. So-called "hostile corporate takeovers" would involve, not purchase of shares of ownership from willing stockholders, but a sudden invasion of offices by an armed gang.

Biological ecosystems have evolved creatures and environments of great beauty and complexity, and they exhibit a grand spontaneous order, but that order is quite different from the synergistic, symbiotic order of the market. If the aim in building computational ecosystems were to maximize their beauty and complexity, biology might be an excellent model. Given the goal of building a computational ecosystem which will organize itself to solve problems, however, one should seek a system that fosters the cooperative use of specialized knowledge and abilities. Market ecosystems seem better suited to this.

## 4.6. Are markets just biological?

It might be objected that the mechanisms which facilitate widespread symbiosis in market ecosystems are achievable within the rules of biological ecosystems. After all, these rules do not forbid organisms from pooling their resources to defend against predators or from establishing reputation and trademark systems. Indeed, this has been done. Through such institutions as laws, courts, banks, and trademarks, talking primates have taken their species through the transition from "nature, red in tooth and claw" to an industrial civilization spanning a planet. Though this has been achieved within the rules of biology, biological rules do not deserve the credit, any more than a machine language deserves credit for the virtues of Lisp.

This comparison of biological and market ecosystems suggests some of the strength of markets as a model for computation. The following examines a simpler computational ecosystem and considers whether market mechanisms would be useful in similar systems.

# 5. EURISKO and markets

Lenat's EURISKO system [6] may be viewed as an ecosystem in which the replicators are interacting, evolving heuristics—that is, evolving, computational rules of thumb. Two kinds of heuristics populate EURISKO: *object-level heuristics* whose subject domain is some topic to be explored (such as war games or three-dimensional VLSI), and *meta-heuristics* whose subject domain is heuristics. Variation occurs as meta-heuristics create new heuristics from old ones via mutation, and selection occurs as meta-heuristics judge and determine the "interestingness" of heuristics (a numeric value associated with a heuristic). This quantity determines allocation of processing resources, so heuristics compete for survival and influence based on their degree of "interestingness".

To apply EURISKO to set theory, for example, one would start it with a set of object-level heuristics representing basic concepts of set theory (such as set equality and union), meta-heuristics for creating plausible new concepts out of old ones (*e.g.,* by removing a conjunct from a predicate to weaken it), and meta-heuristics that attempt to capture a sense of what is mathematically interesting (such as an unexpected coincidence). EURISKO's predecessor, AM, started with exactly this, and was able to discover (and judge interesting) in turn: whole numbers, addition, multiplication, factorization, primality, and Goldbach's conjecture.

(There has been some controversy over the sense in which AM can be said to have discovered these concepts, and whether it is a reproducible result. For a discussion of these issues, see [III]. Also, note that many of these results have been reproduced by Ken Haase's EURISKO-like program, CYRANO [22].)

In AM, meta-heuristics mutated and judged object-level-heuristics, but did not themselves evolve under each others' influence. This was changed in EURISKO: here both kinds of heuristics exist at the same level of the system and can operate on each other freely. This enabled the mechanisms of variation (including the representation language) and the selective pressures to evolve and adapt with the rest of the system.

## 5.1. Parasitic loops

During a run of EURISKO, however, one meta-heuristic rose to the maximum interestingness value merely by listing itself as a creator of whatever heuristics were judged interesting. As a "creator" of such interesting heuristics, it was itself judged interesting. Lenat reports that EURISKO has, when run for long periods, consistently invented ways to enter infinite loops of one sort or another. This problem may be viewed as the evolution of parasites, of systems that consume resources while returning nothing of value.

Lenat has limited this problem by hand-tuning sets of meta-heuristics, and by placing certain meta-heuristics on a frozen meta-level protected from evolutionary modification. But doing this can solve the problem of parasitism only if *all* entities which assign interestingness are placed in this frozen meta-level. A major part of the system is thus unable to evolve beyond its initial design, and hence unable to adapt to unforeseen changes within the system. This type of solution loses much of the flexibility sought in the move from AM to EURISKO.

"Interestingness" is a standard of value which can be used to claim system resources; if evolving meta-heuristics are allowed to assert value—and hence to generate claims from nothing—then parasites can evolve. If direct self-reward is forbidden, jointly self-rewarding "conspiracies" would spontaneously arise. For example, if a heuristic is consistently being judged interesting by a particular meta-heuristic, it is an ESS for it to discover some way to feed some of the resulting resources back to that meta-heuristic, that is, to find a way to pay a "kickback" to a judge (not to influence the judge in its favor, but to increase a favorable judge's influence). This problem can also be seen as a "tragedy of the commons" [23]: processing resources are the commons, and since the cost of using them (in terms of forgone alternative uses, *etc.*) is borne almost exclusively by others, each entity has an incentive to gobble resources wantonly.

## 5.2. Conservation laws

This dilemma can be avoided by imposing restrictions on value-assertion at a simple, foundational level, rather than restricting valuation to a static set of complex heuristics. How can this be accomplished? Biology and markets both have locally-conserved quantities (matter, energy, currency) that are measures of success, and both systems have steadily generated new, genuinely interesting results. Sterile self-reinforcement cannot lead to success, because it cannot bring in resources. This principle can be applied to EURISKO-like systems.

An attractive approach is reward based on a locally-conserved currency, used to pay for services and computational resources. This inhibits parasitism through stable foundations which themselves embody no knowledge of heuristics (other than this argument). In such a system, a heuristic must pay for processing and for services provided by other heuristics.

Non-productive loops of mutually-rewarding heuristics then go broke, since (by conservation of currency) a group of heuristics can only gain net funds by receiving them from a solvent entity outside the group—an entity that, presumably, either receives or expects to receive some valuable service. A productive entity may unwittingly support an unproductive process, but competitive pressures will help weed out this behavior.

The elimination of unsupported, non-productive entities by letting them go broke is a robust result of a foundational constraint, not a chancy result of hand-tuned heuristics. It achieves its robustness and universality in the same manner as many physical principles: it relies on a conservation law, and hence is independent of subsystem boundaries and system structure.

## 5.3. A market-based EURISKO?

Market mechanisms suggest how a EURISKO-like system could operate without level boundaries or protected sets of supervisory heuristics. In a system of this sort, when a heuristic is invoked it charges the user enough to pay the costs of providing service, plus a royalty that rewards the heuristic's creators. As users learn to make discriminating choices, heuristics will compete to maximize their performance per unit of system resources consumed. Meta-heuristics that create new heuristics will earn royalties from their creations to the extent that these creations prove useful. Where several heuristics are responsible for creating a given heuristic, they can be viewed as its "stockholders", splitting royalties (or dividends) according to a prior contractual agreement.

Rules for negotiating the terms of such agreements can themselves evolve; the proper division of rewards will itself be rewarded, since it will lead to the evolution of better subsystems. Being able to evolve better division of rewards is important for a capable learning system (see the discussion of genetic algorithms and connectionism in Appendix II of [I]).

The above has outlined how money circulates among heuristics, and how it is ultimately used to pay for processing resources. Where does this flow of money originate? The next section answers this first by re-introducing a protected meta-level, though one that avoids the above problems, and then by explaining how to remove this meta-level as well.

## 5.4. External funders and open systems

In a closed, market-based EURISKO-like system, heuristics pay for the storage space and processor time they use; the funds collected are then recycled to fund computation. If entities external to the economic system control the re-introduction of funds, then the heuristics within the system will be selected for their effectiveness in solving the problem of meeting the criteria for funds allocation. Ultimately, these criteria represent the problem being posed to the system; they could be simple contingent rewards for solving problems.

The funding agency is outside the system, and so not subject to heuristic evolution. It might seem equivalent to Lenat's protected meta-level, but, unlike EURISKO, a system of this sort can contain a fully-capable set of evolving meta-heuristics. The external funders reward only end results; meta-heuristics inside the system can act as internal investors, accelerating the adaptation of the system to the externally-defined goals. Investors and the activities in which they invest all participate in the same one-level market system. Use of this sort of meta-level avoids freezing the criteria for judging intermediate results, or for judging the judges of intermediate results (this resembles suggestions for funding scientific research [24]).

The unobjectionable role of the external funding agency is clear when the system is considered as part of a broader economy, in which external human users provide the funding and hence the feedback. The evolution of programs is ultimately guided by human judgment of what constitutes good performance [VI]; in a market-based, EURISKO-like system, the "supervisory" heuristics that judge other heuristics would themselves be judged by people. This supervisory position entails no special privilege; it results from their role as entities directly funded by users. The EURISKO experience may also be viewed in this light. Lenat's protected meta-heuristics were not really immune from evolution: Lenat himself varied and selected them with respect to the behaviors they encouraged, and allocated physical processors to those versions of EURISKO which he judged more promising.

In a distributed system consisting of EURISKO-like nodes subcontracting to each other, the external funding agency of any one node can consist of other nodes (of course, this principle does not require separate machines). In an open computational market—one using real dollars and connected to the human market—participating humans may be thought of as the ultimate meta-heuristics. They will be the ultimate source and drain for the flow of funds in the system, and will be the ultimate source of variation (at least initially). However, they are in no sense *protected* meta-heuristics. The flow of real money, and the provision of actually useful software services, will provide an incentive for humans to work to make the system more useful, and for them to buy the useful services being offered (see "Agoric Systems in the Large" in [I]).

## 6. Memes and markets: direct and indirect market ecosystems

Human cultures evolve. Their replicators are any of the information patterns which make up a culture, and which spread (with variation) from human to human via imitation. By analogy with genes, these replicators are known as *memes* [7]; they include ideas, beliefs, habits, morals, fashions, designs, techniques, jokes, and more. Any pattern which can spread via imitation is a meme, even if its human host cannot articulate it or is unaware of its existence.

It is important to recognize that the replicators of human culture are memes, not people. The lack of this distinction has led to the unfortunate confusion called "social darwinism". Our ability to change our minds allows cultural evolution to proceed not by selection of humans, but, as Karl Popper says, by "letting our theories die in our stead" [4].

Recognition of the evolutionary nature of human culture has inspired computational proposals for aiding the spread of memes among humans [25,26] and for establishing a memetic ecosystem among software entities [VII]. The memes making up human culture are diverse, as are their variation and selection mechanisms. Rather than studying human culture as a single, generic kind of ecosystem, it makes more sense to view it as composed of several interacting memetic ecosystems.

For example, Karl Popper describes science in evolutionary terms [4]. The replicators of science are theories, and their evolution proceeds through a process of conjecture and refutation, that is, variation and selection. The selection criteria include the requirement that a theory be both falsifiable and not actually falsified. (Falsifiable means that if it were false, it could be refuted by experiment.) In science only falsifiable but true theories are ESSs—any theory which is false either can be refuted, or is not falsifiable, and so is subject to rejection. In memetic systems whose replicators are theories, but which apply other selection criteria, theories which are not true may nevertheless be ESSs. Idealizations of scientific inquiry have also inspired computational ideas and systems [27,28].

## 6.1. Market memes and the indirect market

In this paper, the memetic systems of interest are those that shape activities in markets, here called *market memes*. They include ideas that shape strategies for production, organization, marketing, investment, and much more. Market memes can be embodied in individuals or in groups such as firms, but their mechanisms of selection are indirect, working through the human brain.

Money flows not to successful market memes, but to their hosts. No matter how much money it brings in, a meme is unable to rent more brain space—indeed, it cannot even protect itself from being displaced. Entities directly interacting with an ideal market can own assets which cannot be seized; memes can own no such assets.

Market memes can replicate by spreading from human to human, but for some, this process is difficult. Complex market memes, such as business management skills or organizational patterns, are hard to communicate without introducing great variation. Biological systems can generate and test many small variations of a genetic pattern, replicating the more successful, but human markets can seldom do the same with organizations.

*Meta-market memes* are memes responsible for generating new market memes; an example would be an idea for how to educate better entrepreneurs. When their results are successful, however, no reward reliably propagates back to the memes responsible. Since meta-market memes do not receive credit for their efforts, people are led to underinvest in them.

Thus, market memes are able neither to benefit directly from their own successes, nor (in general) to replicate and pass on their successful characteristics. These defects in the system for creating, expanding, and replicating market memes make their evolution a slow and clumsy process. Successful practices are recognized and imitated, but quite imperfectly.

Although institutions such as patents, trade secrets, and copyrights attempt to strengthen feedback loops, there is only an indirect coupling between market forces and the replicators of the human market—this system thus constitutes what has here been called an *indirect market*. In software, however, it seems possible to achieve a *direct market*—an ecosystem in which the replicators that dominate the evolutionary process are directly rewarded by market success.

## 6.2. Direct market ecosystems

In a direct market implemented in software, a successful heuristic or strategy can directly acquire more processing power and can replicate itself with small variations if it chooses. In these ways, a direct market resembles the biological ecosystem more than it does human markets. In addition, meta-heuristics can generate new software entities from old ones (that give access to the requisite information) by plausible mutation and recombination of the patterns that embody them. The generation of new entities will generally occur only after the participants have negotiated a division of any later rewards (a portion of their shares will, in turn, propagate back to their own creators). These mechanisms directly reward (and thereby encourage) "meta-market" activities, such as inventing new forms of business.

Direct markets have other advantages over human markets. In human markets rules against theft and extortion are enforced imperfectly through mechanisms such as police, courts, and jails. In software, however, these rules can be like "laws of physics". Human markets are plagued by negative externalities (such as air pollution) resulting from the unowned and non-local nature of many common resources (such as air). In software, it seems that these problems can be largely avoided. The basic resources of computation—processor time, memory space, and communications bandwidth—can be allocated without negative externalities [II]. No commons seem needed in computational ecosystems; computational environments need have no analogues of air, water, lines of sight, or rainforests.

The discussion thus far has assumed that computational markets are "idealized markets", in the sense introduced in Section 4.1.2, operating under only simple, foundational rules, preventing non-voluntary transactions analogous to theft. Human markets, however, operate under a wider range of less rigorously enforced rules, imposed by a variety of legal and regulatory institutions. The next section examines whether such institutions might be of use in computational markets.

# 7. Computational legal systems and markets

Like human markets, direct computational markets will have many problems. Computational markets are enough like human societies that it is worth examining mechanisms—such as law and regulation—used by human societies to try to deal with these problems. However, these analogies must be used with care—there are also many differences between human and computational markets. For example, in proposed computational markets:

- No negative externalities exist in basic resources (processor, memory, communications), hence there are no problems analogous to pollution.
- Replicators directly own resources, making the evolutionary process more like "social darwinism" than like the actual evolution of human societies.
- Participants are not people (or even animate), hence they are not hurt when they go broke.
- Object encapsulation prevents force absolutely, hence there is no "who will watch the watchers" problem.

- Only information services are sold, hence there are no depletable inventories of manufactured goods.

Given all these differences, one should not demand that government-like systems proposed for computation be closely patterned on those evolved by human societies. A more appropriate use of the social model is as a source of ideas and analogies, and ideas need not be workable in society to be worth considering in computation. Since computer science has already examined centralized forms of organizations, a promising direction to explore is the other extreme, that of highly decentralized models.

## 7.1. Remaining problems of direct computational markets

Direct computational markets can be built so as to exclude theft and negative externalities; this leaves problems such as fraud, overall fluctuations (such as business cycles and depressions), monopolies, and provision of *public goods* (goods whose provision will benefit entities that do not purchase them, breaking the usual link between public benefit and producer reward). These problems are fundamentally different from the problem of theft, which can be eliminated in computation via simple local rules such as encapsulation. Eliminating any of the problems just mentioned requires the recognition of complex emergent phenomena:

- Fraud involves the non-delivery of promised value; its elimination would require (at least) understanding all possible representation languages in which these promises can be expressed, and recognition of the conditions defining the fulfillment and non-fulfillment of all promises.
- Overall fluctuations are typically measured in terms of economic aggregates such as GNP, which involves collecting considerable information about transactions and determining rules for aggregating them.
- Monopolies can only be recognized by first determining both what constitutes an industry and what constitutes an "anti-competitive" practice.
- Public goods situations can be recognized only if benefits can be recognized, along with the absence of ways to reward producers for them through normal market mechanisms.

An official fraud-deterring function must at least understand the "advertising" in the system, which is difficult in computation—every inter-object protocol constitutes a different sublanguage, and in general, none is globally understood. As explained in Section 4.3, however, and in Section 5.3.3 of [I], computational markets can themselves deter types of fraud which local entities can recognize, just as they routinely judge the comparative values of different opportunities. For a workable system, it seems that the one essential anti-fraud law is also implementable—to prevent fraudulent use of another's trademark.

In human markets, overall fluctuations of an economy (such as business cycles and depressions) have stimulated the creation of governmental institutions such as federal reserve banks and deficit spending; the rise of monopolies in certain industries has stimulated the creation of anti-trust laws. In both cases, there is controversy regarding whether the problems themselves are intrinsic to human markets or whether they result from political intervention

[16,29,30,31,32]. Computational markets will be different enough from human markets that these problems may either be severe, or not occur at all. The game theory of these phenomena is so complex that *a priori* argument may be fruitless; an experimental methodology seems more promising. The simplest approach may be to build computational markets that lack any foundational mechanisms to prevent these problems, and then observe the results.

A *public good* is one that, if provided, benefits members of a group independently of whether *those* members have paid for it. Examples include national defense and residential streets. Consider the incentives of a potential contributor: "If I refuse to pay, the good may be provided anyway, and I will have gotten it for free. If I do pay, my contribution will be such a small fraction of the total that I will not significantly increase the amount of the good being provided, so I will refuse to pay." (This is also known as the *free-rider problem,* because some entities can get a free ride on the efforts of others.) Thus, if left to the market, public goods will be underproduced, from the standpoint of overall benefit.

Many public goods problems can be avoided in a computational setting. Ingenuity can convert many seemingly public goods into marketable goods, thereby enabling market incentives to reward appropriate production. Examples include the "Dividend Algorithm" presented in [II], and the difference between selling information and selling information-based services explained in Section 6.2 of [I]. Nevertheless, for true public goods, the problem is intractable in a market framework. In the case of human society, a legal principle has been proposed to deal with this issue.

## 7.2. Public goods and "takings"

Richard Epstein has proposed [33] a legal principle derived from the "takings" clause of the U.S. Constitution, which grants to the federal government the power of eminent domain over private property. The takings clause limits forcible seizure of property, stating ". . .nor shall private property be taken for public use, without just compensation." Epstein argues for the principle that any taking from an entity, including taxation, must be compensated by the return of benefits of equal or greater value. It may readily be seen that, where the taking is indeed of net benefit, full compensation (whether in money, goods, or services) will be possible. Where full compensation is quantitatively impossible, the net cost must exceed the net benefit—and the taking itself is therefore undesirable.

To apply this principle requires a complex evaluation of costs and benefits on a case-by-case basis. Epstein, as a legal scholar writing about human society, proposes the use of legal mechanisms (courts and evolved systems of law) presently unavailable in a computational setting. The closest equivalent of such mechanisms would comprise a complex set of heuristics—so complex that it would have to evolve, rather than be built into the computational foundations as a frozen set of rules. How might complex laws evolve in computation?

## 7.3. Political ecosystems

In human societies, legal systems and governmental activities provide a framework for the market. They can be seen as a meta-level with respect to market activity, but they are not protected from evolutionary forces; instead, they evolve within a *political ecosystem* with its own mechanisms for the variation and selection of laws and interventions.

In recent years, the tools of economic analysis have been applied to the evolution of policies within democratic political ecosystems [34,35]. This work defines *vote* and *growth* motives that parallel the well-known *profit motive*. All these motives have some claim to be motives to act in the public interest; all, in practice, have their flaws:

- *The profit motive:* do what people want, as shown by their willingness to pay for the result (but cheat customers, if your reputation won't catch up with you).
- *The vote motive:* do what people want, as shown by their willingness to vote for you and your platform (but lie and sell out to special interests, if it will win votes).
- *The growth motive:* do what people want, as shown by their elected leaders' willingness to expand your agency (but do not achieve goals too economically, or your budget will be cut).

In each case, evolutionary forces—not psychology—virtually guarantee behavior in accord with these motives: profitable businesses, vote-winning politicians, and growing agencies will (almost by definition) dominate their fields. Evolution selects for those that *act* in accord with these motives, whether or not they *feel* these motives, just as evolution selects for genes that act in accord with the reproduction motive, though genes have no minds or motives at all. And when genes build organisms with minds, those minds may feel a sex motive rather than a reproduction motive. In a like fashion, selection of individuals and ideas could, in a hypothetical world, evolve institutions led by public-spirited executives, politicians, and bureaucrats, all subjectively selfless, but all acting in accord with the profit, vote, and growth motives (if only to keep their positions of influence, to enable future good works).

Analysis of the vote motive shows how socially destructive policies can win elections [34,35], hence the idea of correcting computational markets with computational democracies should be approached warily, at best. Further, it is not immediately obvious how a computational democracy would work. If one were to substitute "one object, one vote" for "one person, one vote", the result would be the immediate creation of vast numbers of otherwise useless voting-objects. One would prefer a system with a better incentive structure.

## 7.4. Meta-market ecosystems

Imagine a system in which computational objects can choose to operate in any one of a number of legal environments, and in which new legal environments can be created at any time. Since environments could be copies of other environments, they can replicate; since they can also vary and be selected, they can evolve. A measure of the evolutionary success of a legal environment is its level of use (objects can vote with their nonexistent feet); one should expect the behavior of evolved systems of this sort to be describable in terms of an "attractiveness motive".

Something of this sort is seen in the human world. There are many human markets, each with its own set of rules, and each interacting and competing with the others. Stock and commodity exchanges, diversified corporations, and nations each employ a different set of rules governing their internal markets. In each case, entities with different internal markets are able to trade and compete with each other. Factoring out the other dimensions, these amount to a system of *competing legal systems*.

Each of these legal systems would have an incentive to approximate Epstein's system, which allows any action that will benefit all participants. When a public goods situation occurs which involves subscribers of several different systems, it would be settled according to prior treaties—when these have been negotiated (for a discussion of similar notions, see [30]). When such treaties have not been negotiated, the public goods problem may go unsolved, and the participants are left with only simple market rules. The penalty for leaving some public goods unprovided may be minor in a computational market ecosystem; no strong example of a public goods problem has so far been proposed.

Even under the selective pressure of competition, it may not be possible to establish a computational legal system that can enforce Epstein's system well. If so, then the simple, stable, low-overhead rules of the computational market ecosystem will be the system of choice. This system is a simple starting point and enables experimentation with alternatives; experience can show whether any are better.

## 8. Conclusions

Although evolutionary reasoning is most often applied to biological ecosystems, it is also of use in understanding human markets, culture, and politics, and adaptive computational systems such as EURISKO. By assuming that an ecosystem's foundational rules will shape its evolutionarily stable strategies, and that these strategies will dominate behavior in the ecosystem, one can relate foundations to emergent properties—including properties sought by a designer. This paper has examined a variety of evolutionary ecosystems and compared them with "direct, idealized-market ecosystems"; for the purpose of evolving useful computational behavior, the latter have strong advantages. Other papers in this volume explore the implementation and properties of computational markets of this sort in greater depth [I,II].

## Acknowledgments

Listed in "Markets and Computation: Agoric Open Systems", in this volume.

## References

Papers referenced with roman numerals can be found in the present volume:

Huberman, Bernardo (ed.), *The Ecology of Computation*
(Elsevier Science Publishers/North-Holland, 1988).

[I] Miller, Mark S., and Drexler, K. Eric, "Markets and Computation: Agoric Open Systems", this volume.

[II] Drexler, K. Eric, and Miller, Mark S., "Incentive Engineering for Computational Resources", this volume.

[III] Lenat, Douglas B., and Brown, John Seely, "Why AM and EURISKO Appear to Work", this volume.

[IV] Kahn, Kenneth, and Miller, Mark S., "Language Design and Open Systems", this volume.

[V] Rashid, Richard F., "From RIG to Accent to Mach: The Evolution of a Network Operating System", this volume.

[VI] Perlis, Alan, "The Evolution of Software Systems", this volume.

[VII] Stefik, Mark, "The Next Knowledge Medium", this volume.

[1] Dawkins, Richard, *The Blind Watchmaker: Why the Evidence of Evolution Reveals a Universe Without Design* (W. W. Norton and Company, New York, 1986).

[2] Hayek, Friedrich A., "Cosmos and Taxis" in: *Law, Legislation and Liberty, Vol. 1: Rules and Order,* (University of Chicago Press, Chicago, 1973) pp.35–54.

[3] Gardner, Martin, *Wheels, Life, and Other Mathematical Amusements* (W. H. Freeman, New York, 1983).

[4] Popper, Karl R., "Evolutionary Epistemology", in: Miller, David, (ed.), *Popper Selections* (Princeton University Press, Princeton NJ, 1985) pp.78–86.

[5] Axelrod, Robert, *The Evolution of Cooperation* (Basic Books, New York, 1984).

[6] Lenat, Douglas B., "The Role of Heuristics in Learning by Discovery: Three Case Studies",

in: Michalski, Ryszard S., Carbonell, Jaime G., and Mitchell, Tom M. (eds.), *Machine Learning: An Artificial Intelligence Approach* (Tioga Publishing Company, Palo Alto, CA, 1983) pp.243–306.

[7] Dawkins, Richard, *The Selfish Gene* (Oxford University Press, New York, 1976).

[8] Wilson, Edward O., *Sociobiology* (Belknap Press / Harvard University Press, Cambridge, MA, 1975).

[9] Hofstadter, Douglas R., "The Prisoner's Dilemma Computer Tournaments and the Evolution of Cooperation", in: *Metamagical Themas: Questing for the Essence of Mind and Pattern* (Basic Books, New York, 1985) pp.715–716.

[10] Smith, Maynard J., and Price, G.R., "The Logic of Animal Conflicts", in: *Nature* (1973) 246, pp.15–18.

[11] Drexler, K. Eric, "Molecular Engineering: An Approach to the Development of General Capabilities for Molecular Manipulation", in: *Proceedings of the National Academy of Science USA* (Sept. 1981) Vol. 78, No.9, pp.5275–5278.

[12] Drexler, K. Eric, *Engines of Creation* (Anchor Press / Doubleday, Garden City, New York, 1986).

[13] Rivest, R., Shamir, A., and Adelman, L., "A Method for Obtaining Digital Signatures and Public-Key Cryptosystems", in: *Communications of the ACM* (Feb. 1978) Vol. 21, No. 2, pp.120–126.

[14] Miller, Mark S.; Bobrow, Daniel G.; Tribble, Eric Dean; and Levy, Jacob, "Logical Secrets", in: Shapiro, Ehud, (ed.), *Concurrent Prolog: Collected Papers* (MIT Press, Cambridge, MA, 1987) in press.

[15] Hayek, Friedrich A., *Denationalisation of Money* (The Institute of Economic Affairs,

Westminster, London, 1978, Second Edition).

[16] Keynes, John Maynard, *The General Theory of Employment, Interest, and Money* (Harcourt Brace Jovanovich, San Diego, CA, 1964).

[17] Wickler, Wolfgang, *Mimicry in Plants and Animals* (World University Library / McGraw-Hill, New York, 1968).

[18] Dawkins, Richard, *The Extended Phenotype* (Oxford University Press, New York, 1982).

[19] Holland, John H., Holyoak, Keith J., Nisbett, Richard E., and Thagard, Paul R., *Induction: Processes of Inference, Learning, and Discovery* (MIT Press, Cambridge, MA, 1986).

[20] Ames, Bruce N., Magaw, Renae, and Gold, Lois Swirsky, "Ranking Possible Carcinogenic Hazards", in: *Science* (17 April 1987) Vol. 236, pp.271–285.

[21] Nisbett, Richard, and Ross, Lee, *Human Inference: Strategies and Shortcomings of Social Judgment* (Prentice-Hall, Englewood Cliffs, NJ, 1980).

[22] Haase, Kenneth W., Jr., "Discovery Systems", in: *ECAI '86: The 7th European Conference on Artificial Intelligence* (July 1986) Vol. 1, pp.546–555.

[23] Hardin, Garret, "The Tragedy of the Commons", in: *Science* (13 December 1968) Vol. 162, pp.1243–1248.

[24] Tullock, Gordon, *The Organization of Inquiry* (Duke University Press, Durham, NC, 1966).

[25] Nelson, Theodor, *Literary Machines* (published by author, version 87.1, 1987, available from Project Xanadu, 8480 Fredricksburg #8, San Antonio, TX 78229. Available as hypertext on disk from Owl International, 14218 NE 21st St., Bellevue, WA 98007. 1981).

[26] Drexler, K. Eric, *Hypertext Publishing and the Evolution of Knowledge* (Foresight Institute, Palo Alto, CA, 1986).

[27] Kornfeld, William A., and Hewitt, Carl, "The Scientific Community Metaphor", in: *IEEE Transactions on Systems, Man, and Cybernetics* (IEEE, 1981) SMC-11, pp.24–33.

[28] Kornfeld, William A., "Using Parallel Processing for Problem Solving" (MIT AI Lab, Cambridge, MA, 1979) MIT-AI-561.

[29] Hayek, Friedrich A., *Unemployment and Monetary Policy: Government as Generator of the "Business Cycle"* (Cato Institute, San Francisco, CA, 1979).

[30] Friedman, David, *The Machinery of Freedom: Guide to a Radical Capitalism* (Harper and Row, New York, 1973).

[31] Friedman, Milton, and Schwartz, Anna, "The Great Contraction", in: *A Monetary History of the United States, 1867–1960* (Princeton University Press / National Bureau of Economic Research, 1963) Chap 7.

[32] McGee, John S., "Predatory Price Cutting; The Standard Oil (N.J.) Case", in: *Journal of Law and Economics* (October 1958) 1, 137.

[33] Epstein, Richard A., *Takings: Private Property and the Power of Eminent Domain* (Harvard University Press, Cambridge, MA, 1985).

[34] Buchanan, James M., and Tullock, Gordon, *The Calculus of Consent: Logical Foundations of Constitutional Democracy* (University of Michigan Press, Ann Arbor, MI, 1965).

[35] Tullock, Gordon, *The Vote Motive* (The Institute of Economic Affairs, Westminster, London, 1976).

The Ecology of Computation
B.A. Huberman (editor)
© Elsevier Science Publishers B.V. (North-Holland), 1988

# The Behavior of Computational Ecologies

Bernardo A. Huberman and Tad Hogg
Xerox Palo Alto Research Center
Palo Alto, CA 94304

## Abstract

We present a theory of computational ecologies which explicitly takes into account incomplete knowledge and delayed information on the part of its agents, features which are characteristic of open systems. We study the dynamics of such ecologies when the processes can choose among many possible strategies, and evaluate the effects of cooperation on the behavior of the overall system. This leads to a wide range of asymptotic regimes characterized by fixed points, oscillations and chaos. Finally, we conjecture the existence of a universal law regulating the way in which the benefit of cooperation is manifested in the system.

## 1. Introduction

Incomplete knowledge and delayed information are the novel features of open computational systems which have no central controls. These large networks, emerging from the increasing connectivity between diverse processors, are becoming self−regulating entities very different in their nature from their individual components. Their unplanned growth and evolution leads to an immense diversity in both their behavior and composition, with the ensuing challenges of dealing with trust barriers and interoperability. Moreover, the possibility of spawning remote processes and the consequent inability to explicitly predict resource utilization, gives rise to a society of computational agents which, in their interactions, are reminiscent of biological and social organizations.

Many such systems, particularly those involving distributed computing on many machines of a network, are never completed but continue instead to evolve in response to new technologies and new desires on the part of the user community. Examples include networks containing many different kinds of computers, like those used in airline reservations, and distributed networks of automatic teller machines. The lack of global controls implies that the insertion of new systems into the existing network introduces problems of coordination and commonality. For example, the addition of an extra robot to a geographically distributed manufacturing facility would entail either a readjustment of the global scheduler to account for the increased speed, or an adaptive change in local strategy whereby each machine would process the partially assembled components when they become available to it. Notice that in the first alternative, unforeseeable communication delays, or the breakdown of the scheduler, lead to the system moving away from optimality and ensuing chaos, whereas the second approach naturally allows for local decisions to be made in order to adjust to new situations.

In fact, these evolving systems are seldom improved by completely redoing the whole design. Rather, they are incrementally modified by introducing new functionality and improving existing modules. These changes generally involve making use of current capabilities supplied by the system, thereby producing complex interdependences which violate the traditional requirements for a hierarchical decomposition into modules. These evolving entities must continue to operate in the face of all these changes, even with a lack of central control, asynchronicity (i.e. new packages are not installed on all machines at the same time so they must work with old versions as well), and also with inconsistent data from other agents (either human or other machines on the network). These inherent inconsistencies result from the very nature of open systems, whose totality cannot be completely known within a single entity.

Other issues involved in the design and operation of open systems are how to decide which messages to believe and act upon when they conflict, and how to efficiently allocate resources. A recent proposal for dealing with the first issue is due process reasoning[1]. This entails procedures very similar to those used in order to validate scientific claims in the face of possibly conflicting results. To use a simple manufacturing example, if a request for the number of magnets currently available at an accelerator site were answered differently by a computer and a human, a decision would have to be made as to which to believe.

This could depend on knowledge of past reliability or of the technique used to determine the value, i.e. automated inventory vs. an actual count of the magnets. For the second issue, one way to share resources in a distributed environment with no master controller is to allow processes to bid for limited available resources such as memory and processor time. This is analogous to market economies in which a dynamic allocation of resources to the most needed agents results in improved performance. The resulting system can then operate in a more efficient fashion than those using standard queueing techniques[2]. For example, when two processes make requests for CPU time, deciding on its allocation could depend on their relative importance. A further improvement of that approach allows several bidding strategies for the processes, leading to the interesting question of the existence of evolutionarily stable equilibria for the system as a whole.

Machines that directly interact with the physical world provide another important example of open systems. They can include sensors and motors with which the state of the world can be observed and modified. Examples include robots as well as more immediate uses of microcomputers in various appliances and instruments. In this case the simplifying assumption of a closed world certainly fails, for although the machine cannot have immediate and certain access to all relevant information, it is nevertheless required to operate in real—time.

For instance, if objects are moved while a mobile robot is in another room, it's internal database will no longer correspond to the facts in the world. However, it may have to use this database when planning a path from one room to another. When encountering the (unexpected) changed configuration, not only will the database need to be corrected when sensors indicate the objectes are no longer in their expected position, but any relevant consequences for its current action plan will have to be incorporated.

There is another scenario which closely resembles a computational ecology without necessarily being distributed among many computers. As is the case with robots, machines that deal with ill—defined problems also face the issues of incomplete knowledge, inconsistent and often delayed information. In such problems, the actual desired solution is not formally characterized or known. Once again, the system must deal with constantly changing data, as well as often inconsistent and incomplete information. In this case, inconsistencies arise because the information available from many sources can disagree due to delays, and asynchrony in its arrival. Incompleteness in this context refers to limitations on the accuracy or time available to obtain the information by particular parts of the system. Thus, decisions must be made without knowledge of which action is best. This requires in turn robust systems in the sense that they are able to cope with unexpected variations. One way of dealing with some of these problems entails having agents with a large number of different strategies to solve the same problem.

A number of basic questions are raised by the difficulties encountered in designing open systems. These include understanding their generic behavior and its relation to local implementation, as well as any laws guiding the evolution of such systems. In the latter context, there is the interesting issue of the tradeoff between an adaptable system which can deal with a range of changes, and a system which is optimized for a particular configuration but may not continue to work at all when the environment changes.

In this paper we present a dynamical theory of computational ecologies which explicitly incorporates the features of incomplete knowledge and delayed information, and which gives rise to a panoply of interesting behaviors. These include asymptotic regimes which, depending on particular system parameters, are characterized by fixed points, oscillations, or chaos. Furthermore, by allowing the computational agents to engage in a repertoire of strategies, and by making the individual payoffs depend on what other processes are doing, we obtain nonlinear differential–delay equations which we globally analyze. In order to illustrate the range of possible behaviors, we build a simple model which encapsulates most of the features of computational ecologies. We show how imperfect knowledge leads to an optimality gap which can be explicitly computed, and how delays in information access induce oscillations in the number of agents engaged in given strategies. Furthermore, we consider the effects of both cooperation and competition for finite resources, and exhibit the appearance of chaotic solutions which exclude the possibility of evolutionarily stable strategies. Finally, we consider how the improvement in overall system behavior is distributed among its agents, and conjecture that it displays universal performance characteristics, independent of the detailed nature of either the individual processes or the particular problem being tackled.

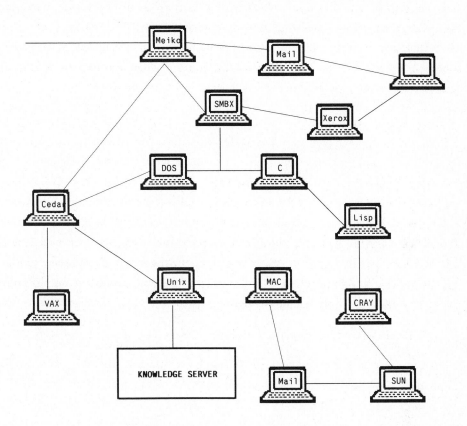

## 2. Computational Ecologies

An interesting model of collective problem solving by nearly independent agents which can interact with each other is provided by groups of people working on a set of related problems. For example, the scientific or legal communities offer insights into the process whereby largely autonomous, interacting agents can succeed at generating new hypotheses and solving particular problems in the presence of inconsistent and incomplete information. This mechanism can be used metaphorically as a design model for a distributed, intelligent, computer system. In this case the agents encompass interacting computer programs, passing messages and engaging in due process reasoning to sort out the relevant information. The agents in these computational ecologies operate concurrently with no central control, incomplete, sometimes inconsistent and delayed information, and with a high degree of communication. A similar metaphor has been invoked by Minsky in a model of the workings of the mind[3]. We will therefore call *computational ecology* the study of the interactions that determine the behavior and resource utilization of computational agents or processes in an open system.

These computational ecologies have a number of similarities and differences from their biological counterparts. Their similarities include the fact that processes are born, they can spawn new ones in order to complete tasks, and die when finished. Furthermore, they also compete for the use of available resources, while making decisions which may not be globally correct due to the existence of delays or limited sensors. In contrast to biological systems however, computational agents are programed to complete their tasks as soon as possible, which in turn implies a desirability for their earliest death. This task completion may also involve terminating other processes spawned to work on different aspects of the same problem, as in parallel search, where the first process to find a solution terminates the others. Another interesting difference between biological and computational ecologies lies in the fact that for the latter the local rules (or programs for the processes) can be arbitrarily defined, whereas in biology those rules are quite fixed. Through these programs, the rationality assumption of game theory[4] can be explicitly imposed on the individual computational agents. This makes open systems amenable to game dynamic analyses, adjusted to incorporate the intrinsic characteristics of such systems. There is also a vast difference in the fundamental time scales with which the basic entities operate. This is reflected in the millisecond time scale for processes to choose a strategy vs at least seconds in human societies. This difference requires caution in extrapolating from one ecology to the other[5]. And last but not least, in open computational systems the interactions are not constrained by a euclidean metric, so that processes separated by large physical distances can strongly affect each other by passing messages of arbitrary complexity between them.

A very important issue in open systems concerns resource allocation. The procedures whereby computational resources are allocated to agents determine the effectiveness of the overall system in finding solutions to particular problems. Thus, a number of strategies consistent with the openness of the system can be implemented. For example, given agents could allocate some of their resources to subprocesses that they spawn based on the perceived degree of their progress towards the overall solution. This is the case in the Eurisko system, where heuristics generated by syntactic mutations are given resources based on their perceived degree of interestness, which is measured by a numerical value attached to each heuristic[6].

An alternative design principle is to have individual agents choose from a repertoire of strategies in order to gain access to resources being contested by other agents. This game dynamics approach is often analyzed by looking for the equilibria which signal the appearance of evolutionarily stable strategies[7,8]. Moreover, if equilibria exist, the time it takes for the system to relax to them should be short compared to the times required to solve particular problems in order for such analyses to apply. This is particularly important in the case of phase transitions in distributed computational environments, where near transition the system exhibits very sluggish relaxation[9]. Notice that the appearance of such evolutionarily stable strategies is by no means obvious, for in interacting systems which are nonlinear or contain delayed interactions, the long time behavior may consist of complicated oscillations and chaotic reverberations. In addition, imperfect knowledge about the relative payoffs to be accrued when choosing given strategies, can generate behavior at the system level which is far from optimal.

## 3. Game Dynamics

In order to investigate the issues of making decisions with imperfect knowledge, delays and lack of central control, we will now introduce a model which incorporates these features, while allowing for quantitative predictions to be made about the system behavior. As we show below, fairly general assumptions concerning these issues can lead to unexpectedly complicated dynamics. Thus, simple estimates of evolutionarily stable strategies from

examination of payoff matrices, or even linear stability analyses of their
evolution, can be grossly misleading when dealing with computational ecologies.

This model consists of a number of agents engaging in various tasks, and
free to choose among a number of strategies according to their perceived payoffs.
Because of the lack of central controls, they make these choices asynchronously.
Imperfect knowledge is modelled by assuming the perceived payoff to be a
slightly inaccurate version of the actual payoff. Finally, in the case when the
payoffs depend on what the other agents are doing, delays can be introduced in
the evaluation of the payoffs by assuming each agent only has access to the
relevant state of the system at earlier times.

Consider a collection of $n$ agents capable of choosing among $m$ possible
strategies in order to complete various asigned tasks. Let $\mathbf{n}(t)$ be a vector whose
components $n_i(t)$ are the number of agents using strategy i at time t. Note that

$$\sum_{i=1}^{m} n_i = n.$$ Moreover denote by $\mathbf{G}(\mathbf{n})$ the *payoff vector* whose component $G_i(\mathbf{n})$ is

the expected payoff accrued by each agent using strategy i, given the number of
agents engaged in the various strategies. In other words, we assume that the
payoffs can be density dependent. This payoff is interpreted as the benefit to be
accrued for the completion of a task, from beginning to end, while using a given
strategy. Benefit in this context refers to actual computational measures of
performance such as time to complete the task, accuracy of the solution, amount
of memory used, etc. Note that we interpret the payoff as both a measure of
desirability of choosing particular strategies, as well as a measure of overall
system performance, an assumption that holds for fairly homogeneous tasks. In
more complicated situations i.e. agents with different goals, these payoffs can
vary from one agent to another.

Within our model, at various times agents evaluate the perceived payoff
for different strategies and switch to the one with the highest payoff. This
dynamical process can be described by writing an equation governing the rate at
which processes change their strategies. Since processes do not choose to
evaluate their alternatives all the time, only a fraction will consider switching
during any given time interval, a fact which can be modelled by a probabilistic

dynamics. This provides an analytic description of the system, including examples of the behavior of quantities such as the number of agents and net payoff of various strategies, as a function of time.

For the sake of simplicity we will first concentrate on the case of two possible strategies from which the agents can choose. The same methods, although algebraically more involved, can be used to generalize this problem to $m$ strategies. Note that in this case $n_2 = n - n_1$. We start by deriving an equation governing the rate at which agents change their strategies. We then discuss the wide variety of persistent behaviors which the system can exhibit, ranging from simple fixed points to oscillations and chaotic reverberations.

In order to write the dynamical equation, we consider how the agents change strategies in a given time interval, $\Delta t$. Let $a$ be the average number of choices made by an agent per unit time. This means that each agent has an independent probability $a\Delta t$ of making a choice in that time interval. The time interval should be small enough that few enough agents change strategies so that the effective payoffs do not change considerably over that interval. In order for an agent to change strategies it must: a) decide to evaluate the option, and b) determine that the other strategy is preferable, i.e. that it has a higher payoff. Therefore, during this interval the probabilities that an agent currently engaged in strategy 1 changes to strategy 2 and vice versa are given by

$$P(1 \rightarrow 2) = a\Delta t(1-\rho) \tag{1a}$$

$$P(2 \rightarrow 1) = a\Delta t\rho \tag{1b}$$

where $\rho$ is the probability that strategy 1 will be perceived to be better than strategy 2. Consequently, the likelihood that $k_{12}$ agents change from strategy 1 to 2 is given by the binomial distribution $Bi(n_1, P(1 \rightarrow 2); k_{12})$, with mean value $\mu_{12} = n_1 P(1 \rightarrow 2)$. Similarly the probability for $k_{21}$ agents to change from 2 to 1 is $Bi(n_2, P(2 \rightarrow 1); k_{21})$. This distribution is given by the familiar form

$$Bi(N, p; k) = \binom{N}{k} p^k (1-p)^{N-k} \tag{2}$$

To connect these local changes with the global behavior of the system, we consider the quantity $P_1(a,t)$, the probability that, at time t, $a$ agents are using strategy 1. Since there are a total of $n$ agents, this must satisfy

$$\sum_{a=0}^{n} P_1(a,t) = 1 \tag{3}$$

which simply states that there must always be some number, between 0 and $n$, using strategy 1. In order to have $a$ agents engaged in using strategy 1 at time $t+\Delta t$, one must have had $a'$ such agents at time t and a net number $a-a'$ switching to strategy 1. Since $a'$ could have been any value between 0 and n,

$$P_1(a,t+\Delta t) = \sum_{a'=0}^{n} P_1(a',t)\, P(a-a',a') \tag{4}$$

where $P(\delta \equiv a-a',a')$ is the probability that during that time interval there is a net change of $\delta$ from strategy 2 to strategy 1, given that there are initially $a'$ using strategy 1. Note that $\delta$ is given by the difference between the number that go from 2 to 1 and those doing the opposite, i.e. $\delta = k_{21} - k_{12}$. To lowest order in the small quantity $\Delta t$, there are only three possible values for $\delta$, namely 0, –1, and 1. This is because for sufficiently small time intervals, most agents will not be making a choice, and thus the likelihood that two or more will choose is even smaller. Accordingly, from Eqs. (1) and (2) we have, up to terms of order $\Delta t$,

$$P(\delta=0,a') = 1-a'a\Delta t(1-\rho)-(n-a')a\Delta t\rho$$

$$P(\delta=-1,a') = a'a\Delta t(1-\rho)$$

$$P(\delta=1,a') = (n-a')a\Delta t\rho$$

so that Eq. (4) becomes

$$\frac{P_1(a,t+\Delta t)-P_1(a,t)}{a\Delta t} = P_1(a,t)[-a(1-\rho)-(n-a)\rho] \quad +$$

$$P_1(a+1,t)(a+1)(1-\rho_+) + P_1(a-1,t)(n-a+1)\rho_- \tag{5}$$

where $\rho_\pm$ is the value of $\rho$ evaluated at $a\pm1$. In the limit of $\Delta t\to0$ the left hand hand side of this equation becomes $a^{-1}dP_1/dt$, and the corrections of order $\Delta t$ vanish. The resulting linear differential equation fully describes the dynamics of the system.

Since one is interested in the average behavior of an open system, the relevant quantities to compute are averages such as $\langle n_1(t)\rangle$ and $\langle\rho\rangle$. Note that the average of any quantity, say f, which depends on $n_1$, can be computed using the definition $\langle f\rangle\equiv\sum_{a=0}^{n}f(a)P_1(a,t)$. Using the above equation one finally obtains the law governing the rate at which agents choose a given strategy, i.e.,

$$\frac{d\langle n_1\rangle}{dt}=a(n\langle\rho\rangle-\langle n_1\rangle) \tag{6}$$

In addition to examining the number of agents engaging in various strategies, one can also consider the dynamics of the net resulting payoff for the system. This quantity provides a measure of how well the system as a whole is using the choices available to it. Specifically, with the payoff vector **G** defined previously (which may be a function of the number of agents using the various strategies), the overall payoff will be given by the dot product

$$g = \mathbf{G}\cdot\mathbf{n}$$

In the case of two strategies, it is simply given by $g=G_1n_1+G_2n_2=G_2n+(G_1-G_2)n_1$. Therefore, its average value is given by

$$\langle g\rangle = \sum_{a=0}^{n}[G_2n+(G_1-G_2)a]P_1(a,t) = n\langle G_2\rangle+\langle(G_1-G_2)n_1\rangle$$

where, in general, $G_1$ and $G_2$ will depend on $a$, the number of agents using strategy 1.

As for the case of $\langle n_1 \rangle$, we can use Eq. (5) to determine the evolution of $\langle g \rangle$, which may differ from that of $\langle n_1 \rangle$. For general functional forms of $G$ this gives rise to complicated dynamics. A simple starting point is provided by using the mean field approximation[10], which consists in writing the average of a function as a function of the average. In this approximation,

$$\langle g \rangle = nG_2(\langle n_1 \rangle) + [G_1(\langle n_1 \rangle) - G_2(\langle n_1 \rangle)]\langle n_1 \rangle$$

Thus, knowledge of the dynamical behavior of $\langle n_1 \rangle$, determined by Eq. (6), allows for an explicit evaluation of the corresponding evolution for the average payoff of the whole system.

# 4. Imperfect Knowledge and Delays

We now evaluate the behavior of the dynamical equation governing the rate at which agents choose a given strategy in a number of simple cases. These include the situations when $\rho$ is 1) a constant and 2) a linear function of $n_1$. Furthermore, we explicity solve these problems when delays are present, and consider the interesting case of cooperating processes which must deal with both imperfect knowledge and delayed information.

## 4.1. Simple Choices with Imperfect Knowledge

We first consider the case in which the payoffs to each agent are independent of what the others are doing. Although simplistic, this example illustrates the effect of imperfect knowledge on the dynamical behavior of the system. Specifically suppose $G_1$ is greater than $G_2$, i.e. strategy 1 is always better. When there is perfect knowledge $\rho$, the probability that strategy 1 is perceived to be better than strategy 2, is one. In this case, Eq. (6) becomes

$$\frac{d\langle n_1 \rangle}{dt} = a(n - \langle n_1 \rangle)$$

whose solution is given by

$$\langle n_1(t) \rangle = n-(n-\langle n_1(0) \rangle)e^{-at} \tag{7}$$

and is illustrated in Fig. 1. As can be seen, in the long time limit all agents end up using strategy 1 as expected. Furthermore, this is a simple example of an evolutionarily stable strategy, for any fluctuations away from $\langle n_1(t) \rangle = n$ relax back to this fixed point in the course of time.

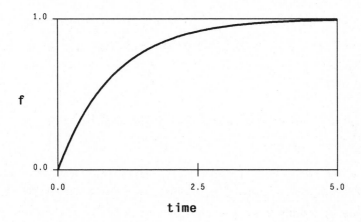

Fig. 1: Plot of $f(t) = \langle n_1(t) \rangle/n$ as given by Eq. (7) for a system in which initially all agents are using strategy 2, i.e. $\langle n_1(0) \rangle/n = 0$. Here $a = 1$.

In most circumstances however, perfect knowledge about the state of the world is not available, and choices between strategies have to be made based on their perceived – as opposed to actual – value. Within our model this is simply done by assuming that the perceived payoff of each strategy is normally distributed, with variance $\sigma^2$, around the correct value. That is, the probability for the perceived payoff for strategy i to be $x$ is given by $N(G_i, \sigma^2; x)$. For a given mean $\mu$ and variance $\sigma^2$, this distribution $N(\mu, \sigma^2; x)$ is given by the familiar form

$$N(\mu, \sigma^2; x) = \frac{1}{\sigma\sqrt{2\pi}} \exp\left[ -\frac{(x - \mu)^2}{2\sigma^2} \right]$$

Thus $\rho$, the probability that strategy 1 is perceived to be better than strategy 2, is given by

$$\rho = \int_{-\infty}^{\infty} dx\, N(G_1, \sigma^2; x) \int_{-\infty}^{x} dy\, N(G_2, \sigma^2; y)$$

which can be evaluated to be

$$\rho = \left(1 + \mathrm{erf}\left(\frac{G_1 - G_2}{\sigma\sqrt{2}}\right)\right)/2 \tag{8}$$

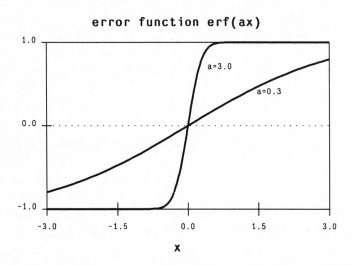

Fig. 2: Plot of the error function, erf($ax$) as a function of $x$ for two values of $a$. Notice that for $a = 3.0$ it resembles a sharp step function, whereas for $a = 0.3$ its form is almost linear.

where erf($x$) is the error function, shown in Fig. 2. When the error is small, this will resemble a step function, i.e. $\rho$ close to one when $G_1 > G_2$ and close to zero when $G_1 < G_2$. For large errors, $\rho$ will be near 0.5 and will vary almost linearly with $G_1 - G_2$. The solution of Eq. (6) in this case becomes

$$\langle n_1(t) \rangle = n\rho - (n\rho - \langle n_1(0) \rangle)e^{-\alpha t} \tag{9}$$

which unlike the previous case with perfect knowledge, still has agents using the less desirable strategy in the long time limit. That this is indeed the case can be seen from the fact that for long times $\langle n_1(t) \rangle = n\rho$, as opposed to the previous, optimal, case where $\langle n_1(t) \rangle = n$. Note that this error in evaluation causes the system to behave in less than optimal manner, while still remaining stable against perturbations. This is summarized in Fig. 3.

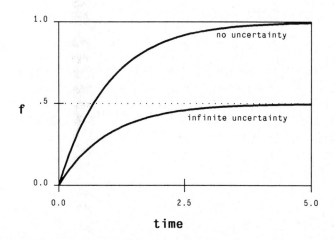

Fig. 3: Plot of $f(t) = \langle n_1(t) \rangle / n$ as given by Eq. (9) for $\langle n_1(0) \rangle / n = 0$, $a = 1$ and two extreme values of $\sigma$.

## 4.2. Wise Choices with Imperfect Knowledge

The most interesting strategies are those where the payoff depends on what other agents are doing, leading to crowding. This in turn implies density dependence in that the payoff vector $\mathbf{G}$ now depends on $\mathbf{n}(t)$. This leads to $\mathbf{n}$ dependence in $\rho$, and thereby to nonlinear dynamics.

One instance of this crowding behavior is given by strategies which involve the use of independent resources. In this case, the payoff for a particular strategy will depend on how many agents are using that strategy and not on what the rest might be doing. Specifically, as more agents make use of the resource, its utility goes down. Therefore, $G_i(\mathbf{n})$ is a positive function of $n_i$ only, and monotonically decreasing with it. The simplest such function is given by $G_i(\mathbf{n}) = R - \Gamma_i n_i$, where R characterizes the total capacity of a finite resource, and $\Gamma_i$ is the positive amount by which the payoff decreases as each additional agent chooses to use the strategy. For this to remain positive, we require that $R > \Gamma_i n$. For the sake of definiteness we will choose the case $\Gamma_2 > \Gamma_1 > 0$. With this choice, $\rho$ in Eq. (8) becomes

$$\rho = (1 + \mathrm{erf}\left(\frac{\Gamma_2 n_2 - \Gamma_1 n_1}{\sigma\sqrt{2}}\right))/2 \tag{10}$$

In order to solve the dynamics governed by Eq. (6) one must evaluate the average value $\langle \rho \rangle$. In this case, $\rho$ is a nonlinear function of $n_1$ (recall that $n_2 = n - n_1$) and this evaluation is nontrivial. However, many of the general features of crowding behavior can be obtained by resorting to the mean field approximation. Within it, $\langle \rho \rangle$ is given by the above equation using the average values of $n_1$ and $n_2$.

To examine the range of possible behaviors we first consider the simplest case, i.e. one in which perfect knowledge ($\sigma = 0$) exists and there are no delays in the evaluation of the payoffs. The error function in Eq. (10) then becomes a step function so Eq. (6) reads

$$\frac{d\langle n_1 \rangle}{dt} = a[n(1 + H(\Gamma_2\langle n_2 \rangle - \Gamma_1\langle n_1 \rangle))/2 - \langle n_1 \rangle] \tag{11}$$

where $H(x)$ is a step function i.e, its value is 1 when $x > 0$ and $-1$ for $x < 0$. For $x = 0$ the actual value of the function will depend on the decision procedure employed when the payoffs are equal. One simple procedure would consist in not changing strategies in this case, i.e. one which would make the right hand side of this equation equal to zero. This requires $H(0) = 2\Gamma_2/\Gamma - 1$, where $\Gamma \equiv \Gamma_2 + \Gamma_1$.

Because of the step function, Eq. (11) is piecewise linear. Thus the dynamical behavior generated by this equation can be determined by considering the following inequalities. For $\Gamma_2 n > \Gamma\langle n_1 \rangle$ the equation reads

$$\frac{d\langle n_1 \rangle}{dt} = a(n - \langle n_1 \rangle)$$

whose solution is given by $\langle n_1(t) \rangle = n - (n - \langle n_1(0) \rangle) e^{-\alpha t}$. This remains valid until $\langle n_1 \rangle = \Gamma_2 n / \Gamma$; after which it stays at this value. Similarly, when $\Gamma_2 n < \Gamma \langle n_1 \rangle$ the solution is $\langle n_1(0) \rangle e^{-\alpha t}$ until it reaches the fixed point. Thus the fixed point is stable against perturbations, and it relaxes towards it as illustrated in Fig. 4.

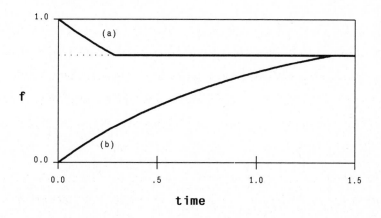

Fig. 4: Behavior of $f(t) = \langle n_1(t) \rangle / n$ with crowding but perfect knowledge and no delays, as a function of time for two initial conditions: a) $n_1(0) = n$ and b) $n_1(0) = 0$. In both cases $\alpha = 1$, $\Gamma_1 = 1$ and $\Gamma_2 = 3$ so the equilibrium point is $f = \Gamma_2 / \Gamma = 0.75$.

As pointed out above, realistic open systems agents have to operate in an environment which has imperfect knowledge. We now consider such a situation by allowing $\sigma$ in Eq. (10) to be larger than zero. In particular when the uncertainty about which strategy is most suitable becomes very large, $\rho$ goes to 0.5, and Eq. (6) becomes

$$\frac{d\langle n_1 \rangle}{dt} = \alpha(n/2 - \langle n_1 \rangle)$$

with solution $\langle n_1(t) \rangle = n/2 - (n/2 - \langle n_1(0) \rangle) e^{-\alpha t}$, as illustrated in Fig. 5.

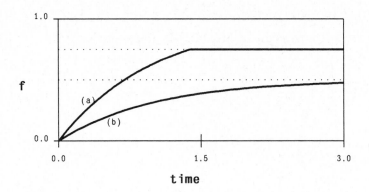

Fig. 5: $f(t) = <n_1(t)>/n$ for the limiting cases of a) no errors, and b) extreme uncertainty. In both cases $<n_1(0)> = 0$, $a = 1$, $\Gamma_1 = 1$ and $\Gamma_2 = 3$.

Unlike the case with perfect knowledge, the optimal solution is never achieved, and an optimality gap develops. This situation is similar to the one we encountered in the simple case with no crowding in the strategies. Furthermore, for cases where the amount of error is intermediate between the cases considered above one still has an optimality gap. For instance, the asymptotic behavior of $<n_1(t)>$ for an intermediate case in which $n/\sigma\sqrt{2} = 1$ is shown in Fig. 6.

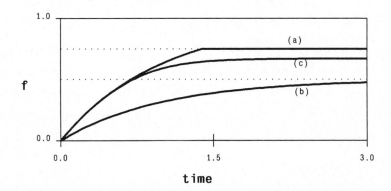

Fig. 6: $f = <n_1(t)>/n$ for a) no errors, b) extreme uncertainty, and c) a case in which $n/\sigma\sqrt{2} = 1$. In (c) the asymptotic value is 0.6715. In each case, $f(0) = 0$, $a = 1$, $\Gamma_1 = 1$ and $\Gamma_2 = 3$.

Before closing this section, we point out that for a payoff of the form $\Gamma_1/n_1$ instead of $-\Gamma_1 n_1$, one obtains qualitatively the same behavior. Such a payoff function could arise in sharing a resource (e.g. the CPU time or internal memory of a particular machine) which is equally divided among those agents which choose to use it. In this case, Eq. (8) becomes

$$\rho = (1 + \text{erf}(\eta\left(\frac{\Gamma_1 - \Gamma f}{f(1-f)}\right)))/2$$

where $\eta = 1/\sigma n\sqrt{2}$ characterizes the size of the uncertainty in the payoff evaluation. For perfect information ($\sigma = 0$) this becomes a step function and the system exhibits exponential relaxation toward the equilibrium value $f = \Gamma_1/\Gamma$. Large uncertainties give $f = 0.5$, as before. Intermediate cases are also similar, as shown in Fig. 7.

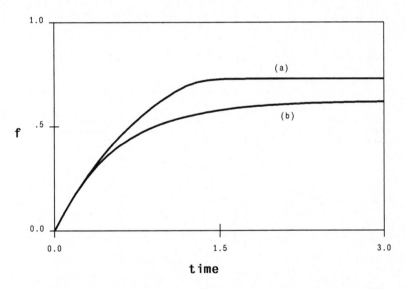

Fig. 7: Behavior of f(t) for $\Gamma_1 = 3$, $\Gamma_2 = 1$ (so $\Gamma = 4$) and $\alpha = 1$, starting from f(0) = 0. a) $\eta = 1.0$, which approaches the limit 0.73; and b) $\eta = 0.1$, which approaches 0.62.

## 4.3. Delays and Oscillations

An interesting complication in computational ecologies is provided by the existence of delays in the evaluation of the payoffs. Thus, when computing the perceived payoffs, the value of $n_1$ used is evaluated at earlier times. Specifically, for the simple linear payoffs used above, Eq. (10) becomes

$$\rho = (1 + \text{erf}\left( \frac{\Gamma_2 n - \Gamma n_1(t - \tau)}{\sigma \sqrt{2}} \right))/2 \tag{12}$$

where $\tau$ is a typical delay time, which can range from zero (no delays) to infinite (extreme delays). More precisely, since $\alpha$ determines the characteristic relaxation rate of the system long delays corresponds to the case when $\tau \gg 1/\alpha$.

In what follows, we show how the existence of such delays in a simple, linear, differential equation can lead to oscillations, and obtain an analytic criterion for their first appearance. We will then consider the full nonlinear case provided by Eq. (12).

Consider the following linear differential−delay equation, characterized by having many delays $\tau_i$,

$$\frac{d\langle n_1 \rangle}{dt} = -\sum_i D_i \langle n_1(t - \tau_i) \rangle$$

where the coefficients $D_i$ are positive. Let $T_i = \tau_i D_i$, and $T = \sum_i T_i$. Assuming a solution of the form $\langle n_1(t) \rangle = \exp(-\lambda t)$ for some value of $\lambda$ (which may be complex), and substituting in the equation, we obtain the characteristic equation which $\lambda$ must satisfy, namely

$$\lambda = \sum_i D_i \exp(\lambda \tau_i)$$

We will now investigate the range of values of $D_i$ and $\tau_i$ for which $\lambda$ has an imaginary part, in which case $\langle n_1 \rangle$ displays oscillatory behavior, which may or may not be transient. We rewrite the characteristic equation as

$$1 = 1/\lambda \sum_i D_i \exp(\lambda\tau_i) = \sum_i \frac{D_i}{\lambda} \exp(\lambda\tau_i)$$

For real $\lambda$ each term of the right hand side is individually minimized by setting $\lambda = 1/\tau_i$. Thus, a lower bound of the whole sum becomes $\sum_i D_i\tau_i e = \sum_i T_i e$, and the following inequality holds:

$$\sum_i \frac{D_i}{\lambda} \exp(\lambda\tau_i) \geq \sum_i T_i e = Te$$

When the product $Te$ is larger than 1, the characteristic equation for $\lambda$ cannot be satisfied for any real value of $\lambda$. Therefore, for $T > 1/e$, $\lambda$ will have an nonzero imaginary part and the system will oscillate. In terms of the original parameter values, this sufficient, but not necessary, condition for oscillation amounts to having $\sum_i \tau_i D_i > 1/e$.

This bifurcation from a time independent state or evolutionarily stable strategy to an oscillatory one is signaled by the appearance of complex roots in the characteristic equation associated with the stability of the differential delay equation, as we showed above. This is illustrated schematically in Fig. 8. For short delays, $\lambda$ is real and negative so the system relaxes directly to the fixed point. Eventually, $\lambda$ acquires an imaginary part, giving rise to damped oscillations. As the delay is increased still further, the real part of $\lambda$ becomes positive which produces persistent oscillations which grow until bounded by nonlinearities in the system.

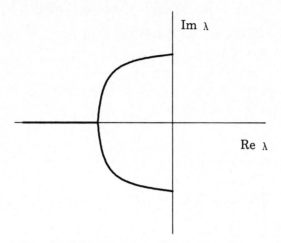

Fig. 8: Schematic depiction of a Hopf bifurcation, characterized by the appearance of imaginary roots of the characteristic equation as a control parameter (e.g delay time) is changed.

To illustrate the behavior of game dynamics with delays, we examine a particular case of Eq. (6). Specifically let $\alpha = 1$, $\Gamma_1 = 1$ and $\Gamma_2 = 3$ (so that $\Gamma = 4$). Furthermore, we let $f \equiv \langle n_1 \rangle / n$ be the fraction of agents using strategy 1. In this case Eq. (6) becomes

$$\frac{df(t)}{dt} = (1 + \mathrm{erf}[\eta(3 - 4f(t-\tau)]]/2 - f(t) \qquad (13)$$

where $\tau$ is a characteristic delay time and $\eta \equiv n/\sigma\sqrt{2}$ describes how accurately the agents are able to evalute the payoffs of the strategies. For the case of precise information, $\sigma$ becomes small and $\eta$ becomes large. Conversely, a large uncertainty is characterized by a small value of $\eta$. A typical intermediate case is given by the value $\eta = 1$ which we used in Fig. 6c. In this case, if there are no delays f(t) relaxes to the fixed point value given by setting the right hand side of Eq. (13) to zero, i.e. $f = 0.6715$. As short delays appear in the system, they produce transient oscillations which decrease in magnitude, again leading to a stable fixed point. Such an example is given for the case of $\tau = 1$ in Fig. 9a. As the delay increases, the simple fixed point eventually becomes unstable leading to persistent oscillations as shown in Fig. 9b for $\tau = 10$. Note that the period of the oscillations varies with the delay parameter, becoming larger with increasing values of τ. As an illustration, the extreme case of a long delay given by τ=50 is shown in Fig. 10 for much longer times. Notice the nonlinear nature of the oscillations, characterized by a sharp switchover between strategies. This overshooting–undershooting behavior can be neatly summarized by the apparent paradox contained in the sentence "it is so crowded that no one goes over there"[11].

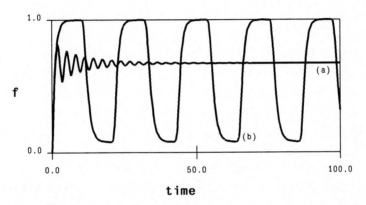

Fig. 9: f(t) = <n₁(t)>/n in the case of delays. a) τ=1, b) τ=10. Notice the transient nature of the oscillations in the first case, and their permanence in the second. In both cases f(0)=0, α=1, Γ₁=1 and Γ₂=3.

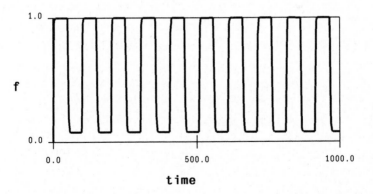

Fig. 10: Behavior of the fraction of agents using strategy 1 for delay value τ=50. In this case f(0)=0, α=1, Γ₁=1 and Γ₂=3.

The criterion for the appearance of oscillations can be given explicitly for such linear systems. Eq. (13) is approximately linear when $\eta$ is small, i.e. the uncertainty is large. In this case, it becomes

$$\frac{df(t)}{dt} = \frac{1}{2} + \frac{3\eta}{\sqrt{\pi}} - \frac{4\eta}{\sqrt{\pi}} f(t-\tau) - f(t)$$

because $\mathrm{erf}(x) \approx \frac{2}{\sqrt{\pi}}(x - \frac{x^3}{3})$ for small $x$. Thus, the criterion for oscillations given by $Te > 1$ is just $4\eta\tau > \sqrt{\pi}/e$, or $\tau > 0.16/\eta$. Notice that as $\eta$ becomes smaller, longer delays are required to produce oscillations. This can be simply understood by noting that a large uncertainty in the evaluation of the payoffs means that any value of f used, delayed or not, gives roughly the same value, and hence delays are less able to push the system away from the fixed point.

With delayed knowledge, many agents evaluate the payoff of a strategy using old information and then find the apparently desirable strategy more crowded than anticipated. In this case, it could be assumed that an agent would benefit by being able to anticipate these oscillations and then utilize a strategy exploiting the times when the system is less crowded. Unfortunately, as soon as many agents attempt to do this, the period of the oscillations changes, and no evolutionarily stable strategy is possible. For instance, when the delay is 10 in the above example, the system oscillates with a period of about 20. Thus an agent could predict the current value of $\langle n_1(t) \rangle$ by looking at $\langle n_1(t-20) \rangle$ instead of the most recent available information, namely $\langle n_1(t-10) \rangle$. While this would allow a single agent to determine the payoffs more accurately and hence to improve performance, as soon as most agents adopt this technique, the value of $\tau$ changes from 10 to 20, producing oscillations of a different period. Notice that this ill−compensating phenomenon becomes even more complicated by the existence of multiple delay time scales.

### 4.5 Cooperation with Imperfect Knowledge and Delays

Cooperating agents provide another instance of possible behaviors in open systems. In this case, the payoff is influenced by two competing effects: 1) competition for resources, as discussed above, which tends to reduce the payoff as the strategy gets more popular and, 2) the benefits of collaboration, which tend to increase the payoff through the concurrent speedup of problem solving. The former is a monotonic decreasing function of the number of users of a strategy, and represents the depletion of finite resources used by that strategy. A simple such form, which was used in Section 4.2, is $R-\Gamma_1 n_1$. The second factor is an increasing function of the number of agents in that strategy, and represents the efficiency with which resources are utilized in the cooperative effort of solving a particular problem. The simplest function is given by $P+Cn_1$, where P is the payoff accrued in the absence of any cooperation, and C is the extra benefit due to cooperation. This extra benefit is tempered by the increasing depletion in resources, which eventually causes the overall payoff to shrink to zero. These considerations can be simply modelled by choosing the payoff function to be

$$G_i(n_i) = (R-\Gamma_i n_i)(P+Cn_i)$$

With this choice, the probability that strategy 1 is perceived to be better than strategy 2, as given by Eq. (8), becomes

$$\rho = (1+\text{erf}(\Delta+\Lambda f-\Psi f^2))/2$$

where as before, $f=n_1/n$ and the constants are $\Delta=n(C\Gamma_2 n+\Gamma_2 P-CR)/\sigma\sqrt{2}$, $\Lambda=n(2CR-\Gamma_2 P-\Gamma_1 P-2C\Gamma_2 n)/\sigma\sqrt{2}$ and $\Psi=n^2 C(\Gamma_1-\Gamma_2)/\sigma\sqrt{2}$. In what follows we will consider the case in which these constants are all positive. The delayed form of Eq. (6) becomes

$$\alpha^{-1}\frac{df(t)}{dt} = (1+\text{erf}[\Delta+\Lambda f(t-\tau)-\Psi f^2(t-\tau)])/2-f(t)$$

a highly nonlinear differential–delay equation which gives rise to a wide range of complicated dynamics. In order to illustrate the most striking features we will consider the limit of very long delays, i.e. $\tau \gg \alpha^{-1}$. In this case, the long time behavior of f(t) is obtained by writing the right–hand side of the equation as a finite difference one[12], i.e.

$$f(t+1) = (1+\text{erf}[\Delta+\Lambda f(t)-\Psi f^2(t)])/2 \qquad (14)$$

where time has been rescaled in units of the delay time τ.

  To illustrate the dazzling behavior of the solutions to this equation we
first note that for a wide range of parameter values it belongs to a universality
class of equations, i.e. all members of the class display the same dynamical
behavior[13]. This class consists of all finite difference equations whose
right—hand side have a parabolic maximum, which is the case for this equation.
The kinds of asymptotic behavior that such an equation can display as the
parameters are varied are most conveniently shown in the so—called bifurcation
diagram. It is obtained by iterating the equation many times (e.g. 10000) for each
value of the parameter and plotting the points it visits after long times. Thus a
simple fixed point will be represented by a dot, periodic orbits by many of them
corresponding to the same value of the parameter, and chaotic behavior will
appear in the form of bands stretching vertically for given parameter values.

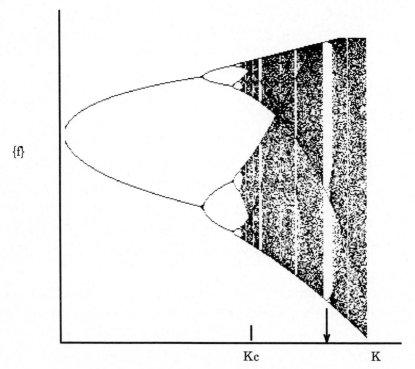

{f}

Kc                    K

Fig. 11: Bifurcation diagram for a simple member of the universality
class corresponding to Eq. (14).

Fig. 11 shows the bifurcation diagram for a simple member of the universality class, i.e. one in which the right hand side has the simple parabolic form of the type Kf(1-f), as a function of the control parameter K. Any other equation will exhibit the same behavior with suitably rescaled parameters, as is the case for Eq. (14) with $\Delta=-1$, $7<\Lambda<9.6$, $\Psi=40$, and initial condition $f(0)=0.8$. As can be seen, for values of K between the origin and $K_c$, one sees a set of orbits separated by period doubling bifurcations such that at each of them the period of the orbit doubles in length. In this regime, all initial conditions relax towards these stable periods and the system is said to display no sensitivity to initial conditions. Beyond $K_c$ however, and coexisting with some periodic orbits, the system behaves in a chaotic fashion, and the dynamics effectively mimics random behavior, with extreme sensitivity to initial conditions. This means that very close initial configurations of the system will lead to vastly different conditions. An example of this behavior is shown in Fig. 12 where we see the time evolution generated when K is well into the chaotic regime. Notice that the lack of any discernible periodicity prevents the system from ever settling down to any evolutionarily stable strategy. Moreover, the standard criteria for permanence and uninvadability[8,14] fail to establish which mixture of strategies is optimal, for the number of agents engaging in them change at random all the time.

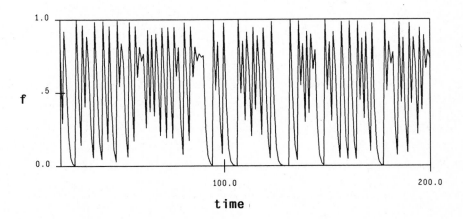

Fig. 12: Asymptotic dynamics generated by the fully chaotic regime of the universality class corresponding to Eq. (14). In this case $K=4$.

A more subtle kind of chaos occurs for values of the control parameter near the period 3 orbit inside the chaotic region (see arrow in Fig. 11) as shown in Fig. 13. In this regime, the asymptotic dynamics consists of sequences of period 3 behavior intermittently interrupted by chaotic bursts[15]. Thus, an examination of the number of agents in a computational ecology engaging in a given strategy would lead to conclusions that would strongly depend on the length of time involved in the observation. Specifically, for observation times which are short compared to the oscillatory regimes one could conclude the existence of periodic behavior, but for longer times the system would suddenly become chaotic and thus unpredictable.

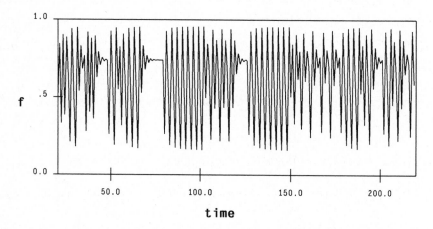

Fig. 13: Asymptotic dynamics in the intermittent regime. In this case K = 3.8264. Notice the existence of both periodic intervals and their noisy interruptions.

The above discussion concentrated on a particular range of parameters of Eq. (14) for which the universality class is well known. For other values of the parameters, the dynamics is still be very complicated. Although not exhibiting universal characteristics, it can nevertheless exhibit multiple equilibria, diffusive reverberations and nonlinear oscillations. The nature of these regimes, which cannot be inferred from stability analyses of the linearized form of the equations, will require nonlinear dynamical tools[16] when studying them in actual computational ecologies.

# 5. Generalizations

## 5.1 Multiple Strategies

The previous discussion, which assumed two possible strategies from which agents can choose, can be generalized to the the case of $m$ strategies. Specifically, let $P(a_1,..,a_m,t)$ or $P(\mathbf{a},t)$ be the probability to have $a_i$ agents using strategy i at time t. Note that this will be zero unless

$$\sum_{i=1}^{m} a_i = n \qquad (15)$$

which simply requires that the total number of agents in the system is $n$. Moreover, Eq. (3) generalizes to

$$\sum_{a} P(\mathbf{a},t) = 1$$

where is sum is over all vectors satisfying Eq. (15).

Now let $\rho_i$ be the probability that strategy i is perceived to be the best choice. Note that $\sum_{i=1}^{m} \rho_i = 1$ because some strategy must be best. As in the two–strategy case, this may depend on what the agents are doing and may also involve errors and delays. Generalizing Eq. (1), this then gives the probability for an agent using strategy i to change to a different one, as well as for an agent to move to strategy i as

$$P(i\rightarrow) = a\Delta t(1-\rho_i) \qquad (16a)$$

$$P(\rightarrow i) = a\Delta t\rho_i \qquad (16b)$$

respectively, where as before $\Delta t$ is a short time interval.

If the number of agents using various strategies at time $t + \Delta t$ is described by the vector **a**, then it must have been described by a vector **a'** at time t and a net number **a–a'** must have switched during the time interval. Thus we have

$$P(\mathbf{a}, t + \Delta t) = \sum_{\mathbf{a'}} P(\mathbf{a'}, t) P(\mathbf{d} \equiv \mathbf{a} - \mathbf{a'}, \mathbf{a'})$$

where $P(\mathbf{d} \equiv \mathbf{a} - \mathbf{a'}, \mathbf{a'})$ is the probability that during that time interval there is a net change from **a'** to **a**. For sufficiently small $\Delta t$, only single changes contribute. That is, either **a'** = **a** or else there is a single move from some strategy j to strategy i. In the latter case $\mathbf{a'} = \mathbf{a}[j \rightarrow i]$, i.e. $a_i' = a_i - 1$, $a_j' = a_j + 1$ and all other components are equal. From Eq. (16), the probability for a single agent to switch from j to i is, to order $\Delta t$, just $a_j' \alpha \Delta t \rho_i$ with $\rho_i$ evaluated at $\mathbf{a}[j \rightarrow i]$. In addition, the probability for there to be no change is, again to order $\Delta t$, just one minus the sum of the single change probabilities. We thus obtain

$$\frac{P(\mathbf{a}, t + \Delta t) - P(\mathbf{a}, t)}{\alpha \Delta t} = -P(\mathbf{a}, t) \sum_{i \neq j} a_j \rho_i + \sum_{i \neq j} P(\mathbf{a}[j \rightarrow i], t)(a_j + 1) \rho_i[j \rightarrow i]$$

where $\rho_i[j \rightarrow i]$ means $\rho_i$ is evaluated at $\mathbf{a}[j \rightarrow i]$. This reduces to Eq. (5) when there are only two strategies. As $\Delta t \rightarrow 0$, the left–hand side becomes $\alpha^{-1} dP/dt$.

As before, this result can be used to obtain the equation describing the evolution of average quantities of the system. In this case, averages are computed according to $\langle f \rangle = \sum_{\mathbf{a}} f(\mathbf{a}) P(\mathbf{a}, t)$. In particular, for the average number of agents using a particular strategy, $\langle n_i(t) \rangle$, one obtains

$$\frac{d \langle n_i \rangle}{dt} = \alpha(n \langle \rho_i \rangle - \langle n_i \rangle)$$

which is very similar to the equation obtained for the two–strategy case.

When we introduce errors into the evaluation of the payoffs, the probability $\rho_i$ that strategy i will be perceived to be the best is given by

$$\rho_i = \int_{-\infty}^{\infty} dx N(G_i, \sigma^2; x) \prod_{j \neq i} \int_{-\infty}^{x} dy N(G_j, \sigma^2; y)$$

That is, it will be perceived as best if its perceived payoff is greater than those of all the other strategies. Although complicated to evaluate explicitly, this integral qualitatively resembles the result given in Eq. (8) for two strategies.

In contrast with the two strategy problem, the multiple strategy case involves a higher dimensionality (i.e. number of coupled ordinary differential equations). Thus the onset of chaotic reverberations can take place for a much wider range of parameter values. In particular, even in the absence of delays, density dependence can produce these persistent or random oscillations.

## 5.2 Anticipating the effects of choices

A simple extension of our model allows the individual agents to anticipate the effect of any proposed action they may take on the resulting payoffs. For instance, instead of basing a decision of which strategy to pick on the current payoffs, an agent could anticipate what the payoff would be if it changes (e.g. switching to a new strategy will make it more crowded and hence change the actual payoff). Note that this anticipation only includes potential actions of the single agent and not what others may be planning to do.

We examine this possibility in the case of two strategies considered above. In such a situation, an agent currently using strategy 1 receives a payoff $G_1(n_1)$ where $n_1$ is the number of agents currently using strategy 1. If it switches to strategy 2, its anticipated payoff will be $G_2(n_1-1)$ since then there will be one fewer agents using strategy 1. This contrasts with the previous case of no anticipation in which strategy 2 was evaluated according to the value of $G_2(n_1)$. This produces a small change in the derivation of Eq. (6). Specifically, Eq. (1) becomes

$$P(1 \to 2) = a \Delta t (1 - \rho_{12})$$

$$P(2 \to 1) = a \Delta t \rho_{21}$$

where $1-\rho_{12}$ is the probability that an agent currently using strategy 1 will anticipate that its payoff will improve if it moves to strategy 2, i.e. the probability that $G_1(n_1)$ is greater than $G_2(n_1-1)$; and $\rho_{21}$ is the probability that an agent using strategy 2 will find strategy 1 better, i.e. $G_1(n_1+1)$ is greater than $G_2(n_1)$. Since $\rho_{12}$ is not necessarily the same as $\rho_{21}$, the prior derivation is changed only in that $(1-\rho_{12})+\rho_{21}$ need not equal one. This then gives, in the mean field approximation,

$$\frac{d\langle n_1\rangle}{dt} = \alpha(n\langle\rho_{21}\rangle-\langle n_1\rangle(1-\langle\rho_{12}\rangle+\langle\rho_{21}\rangle))$$

which can be analyzed in similar fashion as we did in the previous cases for non – anticipatory choices.

# 6. Progress and Cooperation

In the previous sections, we have discussed the effects of having a highly interacting collection of agents in a computational ecology. In particular, we showed how strategies in which payoffs depend on what other agents are doing lead to a wide range of dynamics. Furthermore, we showed how cooperation between agents engaging in different tasks can lead to improved performance of the system as a whole. Since this improvement in overall system behavior is not equally distributed among all processes, an interesting question concerns the distribution of performance among the agents. In particular, since those agents making the most progress per unit time are the ones that set the overall increase in performance on a cooperative task, it is imperative to know how such ability is distributed. A simple example will illustrate these ideas. Consider a concurrent constraint search in a large database in which $n$ agents are looking for an item which satisfies the constraints. The overall performance, i.e. search time in this case, is determined by the agent which arrives at the answer first, thereby terminating all related processes.

In what follows we will show how such highly cooperating systems, when sufficiently large, display universal individual performance characteristics, independent of the detailed nature of either the individual processes or the particular problem being tackled. This universal law has been observed to describe systems as diverse as scientific productivity, species diversity in ecosystems, and income distributions in national economies. One therefore expects that distributed systems operating as computational ecologies will display the same quantitative characteristics.

Consider an open system operating according to the principles of a computational ecology. Because the system is open, it must operate with messages that are often inconsistent, unreliable, and delayed. Thus, individual processes, embedded in different machines, will not be able to receive and utilize the same information. Notice that, in this fashion, such a distributed computational system, although an imperfect implementation of the idealized model of ref. [1], becomes a more faithful representation of an actual computational ecology. In order for an agent to have a given performance, it must successfully complete a set of tasks. This depends on a number of factors, such as the messages it receives and is able to process. Therefore the overall performance will be determined by the probability that it is able to complete these steps. Let $p_i$ be the probability that one of them is able to complete the $i^{th}$ step. Then, assuming that the various probabilities are independent of each other, the probability $P$ of completing the task in a given time interval is the product of the probabilities that it successfully deals with each of the individual steps involved, i.e.

$$P = p_1 p_2 ... p_n$$

By taking logarithms, one obtains

$$\log P = \log p_1 + \log p_2 + ... + \log p_n \tag{17}$$

When the individual distributions of the $\log p_i$ numbers satisfy the weak condition of having a finite variance, and if the number of individual steps is large, then the central limit theorem applies. Therefore, the distribution function of $\log P$, as given by Eq. (17), will be normally distributed around its mean, $\mu$, with variance $\sigma^2$. In other words, $P$ itself is distributed according to

$$\text{Prob}(P) = \frac{1}{\sigma P \sqrt{2\pi}} \exp\left[ -\frac{(\log P - \mu)^2}{2\sigma^2} \right]$$

where the mean value of $P$ is $m = e^{\mu + \sigma^2/2}$ and its variance is given by $m^2(e^{\sigma^2}-1)$. This distribution is known as the *log–normal distribution*[17], and is illustrated in Fig. 14. Notice the highly asymmetric nature of the distribution, and the long tail, which signifies an enormous range of performance for the individual agents.

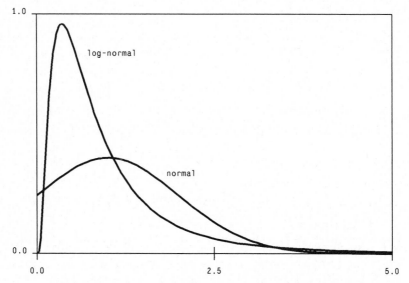

Fig. 14: Comparison of log–normal and normal probability density functions with mean 1.0 and standard deviation 1.0. In addition to the asymmetry of the log–normal one, it also has a slower decay for large values of $x$ than the normal function.

Although the above assumption of step by step completion independence may seem overly restrictive, there is ample evidence that this result apply to many different systems. For instance, in a study of the statistics of individual variations of productivity in research laboratories, Shockley discovered a log–normal distribution in the individual productivity, regardless of field or laboratory location[18]. In a totally unrelated endeavour, that of animal ecology, several investigators have discovered a log–normal distribution of abundances in species as different as nesting birds, butterflies and moths captured in light traps and the snakes of Panama[19]. Since this is related to the ability to survive through a number of events in the ecosystem, it mimics the process whereby agents succesfully solve given problems, and can be described by the model given above. Moreover, a study of the income distribution in families and single individuals in the U.S.[20] and many other economies shows a log−normal distribution[17], which can be ascribed to the many necessary steps that lead to the accumulation of wealth. These examples suggest that there is an underlying universal law describing the behavior of large systems of interdependent entities. Therefore, if resources are allocated to individual agents in computational ecologies based on their perceived progress, one expects a consequent wide distribution in their utilization. It would be extremely interesting to have this universality conjecture tested in open computational systems.

# 7. Conclusion

In this paper we have presented a theory of computational ecologies that takes into account that in open systems imperfect knowledge and information delays are often unavoidable. By considering independent but mutually interacting agents which at any time can choose among a set of possible strategies, we were able to derive an equation governing their dynamic behavior. We first showed that even when payoffs do not depend on what other agents are doing, incomplete knowledge leads to an optimality gap which can be analytically computed from the system parameters. We then considered the case when the perceived payoffs do depend on what other processes are doing and obtained nonlinear equations whose global solution we analyzed.

A most important consideration has to do with choosing among possible strategies with delayed information. We showed how such delays can induce unavoidable oscillations in the system, and predicted the conditions for their appearance as a function of delay times. Furthermore, we studied the effects of cooperation in open systems with finite resources when imperfect knowledge and delays cannot be avoided. In that case, we showed that the asymptotic dynamics consist of complicated oscillations, chaotic behavior and intermittent oscillations, thus precluding the existence of evolutionarily stable strategies. Moreover, the sensitive dependence of the dynamics on initial conditions suggests that the experimental verification of these predictions will have to rely on tools from dynamical systems theory.

Lastly, we studied the effects of cooperation in inducing diversity among computational agents which are initially homogeneous. In particular we discussed the possibility that a universal law (i.e. log−normal) could describe how progress is distributed among the agents. Since this law is also verified in other communities, its experimental verification would lend further impetus to the analogy between computational and biological ecologies.

A final issue concerns the way open systems, like ecologies, can cope with variations in the environments. An important property of such systems is their adaptability, which is characterized by the ability to satisfy variations in constraints with minimal changes. This is related to their complexity, which often exhibits a hierarchical organization: at any given level of the system the effect of the lower echelons can be integrated over, while the larger scale structures are essentially frozen and act as static constraints. Simon has argued that in the design and construction of systems, as well as in their natural evolution, this organization is a consequence of the need for very stable and fault−tolerant intermediate states[21]. A particular example of this is the short time scale (much less than a second) over which computational processes execute, versus human interactions with the system, which take place over longer times.

In closing, we mention several directions into which this theory can be further expanded. In more complicated situations than the ones discussed in this paper, payoffs can vary from one agent to another. Moreover, if we interpret G as payoff to agents over the life of a task (which implies that strategies can change only after completion of a task) it would imply that faster or better strategies should choose more frequently than slower ones (instead of the constant rate assumed for all agents in the simple case). On the other hand, if agents can choose at fixed time intervals, then some will choose while a task is in progress, which means that payoffs should depend on how much of the task is completed, an interesting complication of our model. A further refinement will consider the corrections to the mean field approximation brought about by fluctuations.

These are just a few examples of the wide range of behaviors and complications which will result from studying the dynamics of computational ecologies. At the experimental level, there remain many outstanding issues such as how to monitor the behavior of a distributed system, and the isolation of difficulties due to bugs, failures or bottlenecks. Tools to be used could range from nonlocal extensions of current techniques to apply in a distributed environment, to experimental probes commonly used in dynamical systems theory.

And then, there is the alluring analogy between computational and biological ecologies. The ease of design and experimentation of the former should enable the testing of hypotheses and predictions which are harder to validate in biological or social communities. Moreover, the time might come when a computational ecology will appear to be as 'natural' as its biological counterpart, leading to an increased cross—fertilization between two apparently remote endeavors.

## Acknowledgements

We have benefited from stimulating discussions with H. A. Ceccatto, K. Kahn, M. Miller, A. Perlis, J. Shrager and M. Stefik. This work was partially supported by ONR Contract No. N00014—82—0699.

## References

1. W. A. Kornfeld and C. E. Hewitt, "The Scientific Community Metaphor," *IEEE Transactions on Systems, Man and Cybernetics*, SMC—11, 24–33 (1981).

2. T. W. Malone, R. E. Fikes, K. R. Grant and M. t. Howard, *Market—like Task Scheduling in Distributed Computing Environments*, Internal Report, Sloan School of Management, M. I. T. (1986).

3.  M. Minsky, *The Society of Mind*, Simon and Schuster, New York (1986).

4.  See, for example, J. S. Rosenschein and M. R. Genesereth, "Deals Among Rational Agents," *Int. Joint Conf. on Artificial Intelligence*, 91−99, Los Angeles, (1985)

5.  M. Stefik, "The Next Knowledge Medium," *AI Magazine*, 34−46, Spring (1986).

6.  D. Lenat and J. S. Brown, "Why AM and Eurisko Appear to Work," *Artificial Intelligence*, **23**, 269−294 (1984).

7.  R. Axelrod and W. D. Hamilton, "The Evolution of Cooperation," *Science* **211**, 1390−1396 (1981).

8.  J. Maynard Smith, *Evolution and the Theory of Games*, Cambridge University Press, Cambridge (1982).

9.  B. A. Huberman and T. Hogg, "Phase Transitions in Artificial Intelligence Systems", *Artificial Intelligence* **37**, 155−171 (1987); and J. Shrager, T. Hogg and B. A. Huberman, "Observation of Phase Transitions in Spreading Activation Networks," *Science* **236** 1092−1094 (1987).

10. For an introduction to mean field theory, see N. W. Ashcroft and N. D. Mermin, *Solid State Physics*, Holt, Rinehart and Winston, New York (1976).

11. A. Perlis, private quip (1987).

12. R. Bellman and K. L. Cooke, *Differential−Difference Equations*, Academic Press, New York (1963).

13. P. Collet and J. P. Eckmann, *Iterated Maps on the Interval as Dynamical Systems*, Birkhauser, Boston (1980). For a tutorial account in the context of population biology, see: R. May and G. Oster, "Bifurcations and Dynamic Complexity in Simple Ecological Models," *Amer. Natur.* **110**. 573−599 (1976).

14. K. Sigmund and P. Schuster, "Permanence and Uninvadability for Deterministic Population Models," in *Stochastic Phenomena and Chaotic*

*Behavior in Complex Systems*, P. Schuster (Ed.), 173–184. Springer, Berlin (1984).

15. For a theory of intermittency in such universality class see, J. Hirsh, B. A. Huberman and D. J. Scalapino, "Theory of Intermittency," *Phys. Rev.* **A25**, 519–528 (1982).

16. J. Guckenheimer and P. Holmes, *Nonlinear Oscillations, Dynamical Systems, and Bifurcations of Vector Fields*, Springer, Berlin (1983).

17. J. Aitchison and J. A. C. Brown, *The Log–normal Distribution*, Cambridge University Press, Cambridge (1957).

18. W. Schockley, "On the Statistics of Individual Variations of Productivity in Research Laboratories," *Proc. of the IRE*. **45**, 279–290 (1957).

19. For a survey of such distributions see, C. J. Krebs, *Ecology*, Chapter 23, Harper and Row, New York (1972).

20. E. W. Montroll and M. F. Shlesinger, "On 1/f Noise and other Distributions with Long Tails," *Proc. Natl. Acad. Sci. (USA)* **79**, 3380–3383 (1982).

21. H. Simon, "The Architecture of Complexity," *Proc. Am. Phil. Soc.* **106**, 467–485 (1962).

The Ecology of Computation
B.A. Huberman (editor)
© Elsevier Science Publishers B.V. (North-Holland), 1988

# Deals Among Rational Agents

**Jeffrey S. Rosenschein***
**Michael R. Genesereth**

Department of Computer Science
Stanford University
Stanford, California 94305

### Abstract

A formal framework is presented that models communication and promises in multi-agent interactions. This framework generalizes previous work on cooperation without communication, and shows the ability of communication to resolve conflicts among agents having disparate goals. Using a deal-making mechanism, agents are able to coordinate and cooperate more easily than in the communication-free model. In addition, there are certain types of interactions where communication makes possible mutually beneficial activity that is otherwise impossible to coordinate.

## 1 Introduction

### 1.1 The Multi-Agent Paradigm and AI

Research in artificial intelligence has focused for many years on the problem of a single intelligent agent. This agent, usually operating in a relatively static domain, was designed to plan, navigate, or solve problems under certain simplifying assumptions, most notable of which was the absence of other intelligent entities.

The presence of multiple agents, however, is an unavoidable condition of the real world. People must plan actions taking into account the potential actions of others, which might be a help or a hindrance to their own activities. In order to reason about others' actions, a person must be able to model their beliefs and desires.

The artificial intelligence community has only lately come to address the problems inherent in multi-agent activity. A community of researchers, working on distributed artificial intelligence (DAI), has arisen. Even as they have begun their work, however, these researchers have added on a new set of simplifying assumptions that severely restrict the applicability of their results.

---

*Dr. Rosenschein's current address is: Department of Computer Science, Hebrew University, Givat Ram, Jerusalem, Israel.

## 1.2   Benevolent Agents

Virtually all researchers in DAI have assumed that the agents in their domains have common or non-conflicting goals. Work has thus proceeded on the question of how these agents can best help one another in carrying out their common tasks [3,4,6,7,25], or how they can avoid interference while using common resources [10,11]. Multiple agent interactions are studied so as to gain the benefits of increased system efficiency or increased capabilities.

Of course, when there is no conflict, there is no need to study the wide range of interactions that can occur among intelligent agents. All agents are fundamentally assumed to be helping one another, and will trade data and hypotheses as well as carry out tasks that are requested of them. We call this aspect of the paradigm the *benevolent agent assumption*.

## 1.3   Interactions of a More General Nature

In the real world, agents are not necessarily benevolent in their dealings with one another. Each agent has its own set of desires and goals, and will not necessarily help another agent with information or with actions. Of course, while conflict among agents exists, it is not total. There is often potential for compromise and mutually beneficial activity. Previous work in distributed artificial intelligence, bound to the benevolent agent assumption, has generally been incapable of handling these types of interactions.

Intelligent agents capable of interacting even when their goals are not identical would have many uses. For example, autonomous land vehicles (ALV's), operating in a combat environment, can be expected to encounter both friend and foe. In the latter case there need not be total conflict, and in the former there need not be an identity of interests. Other domains in which general interactions are prevalent are resource allocation and management tasks. An automated secretary [12], for example, may be required to coordinate a schedule with another automated (or human) secretary, while properly representing the desires of its owner. The ability to negotiate, to compromise and promise, would be desirable in these types of encounters.

Finally, even in situations where all agents in theory have a single goal, the complexity of interaction might be better handled by a framework that recognizes and resolves sub-goal conflict in a general manner. For example, robots involved in the construction of a space station are fundamentally motivated by the same goal; in the course of construction, however, there may be many minor conflicts caused by occurrences that cannot fully be predicted (e.g., fuel running low, drifting of objects in space). The building agents, each with a different task, could then negotiate with one another and resolve conflict.

## 1.4   Game Theory's Model and Extensions

In modeling the interaction of agents with potentially diverse goals, we borrow the simple construct of game theory, the payoff matrix. Consider the following matrix:

|   | c | d |
|---|---|---|
| a | $3 \backslash 1$ | 2 |
| b | $2 \backslash 5$ | $0 \backslash 1$ |

The first player is assumed to choose one of the two rows, while the second simultaneously picks one of the two columns. The row–column outcome determines the payoff to each; for example, if the first player picks row b and the second player picks column c, the first player receives a payoff of 2 while the second receives a payoff of 5. If the choice results in an identical payoff for both players, a single number appears in the square (e.g., the $a\backslash d$ payoff above is 2 for both players). Payoffs designate utility to the players of a particular joint move [18].

Game theory addresses the issues of what moves a rational agent will make, given that other agents are also rational. We wish to remove the *a priori* assumption that other agents will necessarily be rational, while at the same time formalizing the concept of rationality in various ways.

Our model in this paper allows communication among the agents in the interaction, and allows them to make binding promises to one another. The agents are assumed to be making their decisions based only on the current encounter (e.g., they won't intentionally choose a lower utility in the hope of gaining more utility later on). The formalism handles the case of agents with disparate goals as well as the case of agents with common goals.

## 2 Notation

We expand on the notation developed in [9]. For each game there is a set $P$ of players and, for each player $i \in P$, a set $M_i$ of possible moves for $i$. For $S \subset P$, we denote $P - S$ by $\bar{S}$, and write $i$ instead of $\{i\}$ (so $\bar{i} = P - \{i\}$). We write $M_S$ for $\prod_{i \in S} M_i$.

We denote by $m_S$ an element of $M_S$; this is a joint move for the players in $S$. To $m_S \in M_S$ and $m_{\bar{S}} \in M_{\bar{S}}$ correspond an element $\vec{m}$ of $M_P$. The payoff function for a game is a function

$$p : P \times M_P \to \mathbb{R}$$

whose value at $(i, \vec{m})$ is the payoff for player $i$ if move $\vec{m}$ is made.

Each agent is able to specify a set of joint moves (i.e., elements of $M_P$) that specify outcomes the agent is willing to accept; this set is called an *offer group*. If any move or moves offered by one agent are likewise offered by all other agents, this set of moves constitutes the *deal* (i.e., the deal is the intersection of all the agents' offer groups). In practice, a single element of the deal set will be selected by a fair arbiter, and the result of the selection communicated to all agents. At that point, the agents are all compelled to carry out their part of the move. Of course, if the deal set has only one member, no arbiter is needed.

We define a secondary payoff function $pay(i, m_i, D_i)$, the set of possible payoffs to $i$ of making move $m_i$ and suggesting offer group $P_i$:

$$pay(i, m_i, P_i) = \begin{cases} \{p(i, \vec{d}) : \vec{d} \in P_i \, \wedge \\ \quad \exists O_i [\, O_i \in allowed_o(i, P_i) \, \wedge \\ \quad \vec{d} \in O_i ]\}, \text{ if such a } \vec{d} \text{ exists;} \\ \{p(i, \vec{m}) : m_i \in allowed_m(i, m_i)\}, \\ \qquad\qquad\qquad\qquad \text{otherwise}. \end{cases}$$

We designate by $allowed_m(i, m_i)$ the set of moves that other agents might potentially make while $i$ makes move $m_i$, and by $allowed_o(i, D_i)$ the set of offers that other agents might make while $i$ suggests offer group $D_i$. Our formalism implicitly separates offer groups from moves (in other words, there will be no effect on moves by offer groups or vice versa). Intuitively, this reflects simultaneously revealing one's move and offer group, with one's eventual action determined by others' offer groups (that is, only if there is no agreement will you have to carry out your move). Future work might investigate the situation where offers are made before moves are chosen, and may thus affect them.

For nonempty sets $\{\alpha_i\}$ and $\{\beta_j\}$, we write $\{\alpha_i\} < \{\beta_j\}$ if $\alpha_i < \beta_j$ for all $i, j$ (and say that $\{\beta_j\}$ *strictly dominates* $\{\alpha_j\}$). Likewise, we write $\{\alpha_i\} \leq \{\beta_j\}$ for nonempty sets $\{\alpha_i\}$ and $\{\beta_j\}$ if $\alpha_i \leq \beta_j$ for all $i, j$ and the inequality is strict in at least one case. We then say that $\{\beta_j\}$ *dominates* $\{\alpha_j\}$.

Finally, we define $p(S, y_S)$ as $\{p(i, \vec{y}) : i \in S \land y_{\tilde{S}} \in M_{\tilde{S}}\}$. These are the possible payoffs to a group $S$ of players of making move $y_S$.

## 2.1  Rational Moves

We will denote by $R_m(p, i)$ the set of rational moves for agent $i$ in game $p$. We use the following definition to constrain what moves are elements of $R_m(p, i)$, that is, what moves are rational (we will follow the convention that free variables are considered universally quantified):

$$pay(i, y_i, \emptyset) < pay(i, x_i, \emptyset) \Rightarrow y_i \notin R_m(p, i). \tag{1}$$

In other words, if, when no binding agreement will be reached, every possible payoff to $i$ of making move $y_i$ is less than every possible payoff to $i$ of making move $x_i$, then $y_i$ is irrational for $i$. Of course, this does not imply that $x_i$ *is* rational, since better moves may still be available.

In general, it will not be possible to fully specify the value of $pay(i, m_i, \emptyset)$ for all $m_i$, since there is not full information as to the moves that the other agents will make. Instead, we use (1) to show that some moves are *not* rational. Because the dominance relation is transitive but irreflexive (and there are a finite number of moves), it is impossible to show that all moves are irrational.

## 2.2  Rational Offer Groups

We define a *rational offer group* in a way analogous to how we defined a rational move above. We denote by $R_o(p, i)$ the set of rational offer groups for agent $i$ in game $p$, and characterize a rational offer group by the following constraint on $R_o(p, i)$'s members:

$$\exists m_i[pay(i, m_i, P_i) < pay(i, m_i, O_i)] \Rightarrow P_i \notin R_o(p, i). \tag{2}$$

In other words, if for some move $m_i$ every possible payoff resulting from offer group $P_i$ is less than every possible payoff resulting from offer group $O_i$, then $P_i$ is not a rational offer group.

There is one more constraint on members of $R_o(p, i)$: rational offer groups specify (through the function $p$) a continuous range of payoffs that are acceptable to an agent. Intuitively, a rational offer group must reflect the notion of "monotonic satisfaction"—if a rational agent is satisfied with a particular payoff, he will be satisfied with one of equal or greater value (this is a fundamental meaning of "utility"). Formally, we write

$$[p(i, \vec{r}) \leq p(i, \vec{s}) \land \vec{r} \in O_i] \Rightarrow \vec{s} \in O_i \tag{3}$$

for all $O_i \in R_o(p, i)$ and moves $\vec{r}$ and $\vec{s}$. For a particular game and player, a rational offer group can thus be unambiguously specified by any of its members with the lowest payoff.

In general, there may be more than one rational offer group for an agent in a game. If full information were available to an agent about the offers others were going to make (along with their "backup moves"), it would be trivial to determine $R_o(p, i)$. In practice such information is not available, but a rational agent $i$ may be able to discover *some* rational offer group, i.e., some offer group provably in $R_o(p, i)$.

## 2.3 Rational Moves and Offer Groups for a Set of Players

We also wish to define the rational moves and the rational offer groups available to a *set* of players. For $S \subset P$, we denote by $R_m(p, S)$ the rational moves for the group $S$ in the game $p$. It follows that the members of $R_m(p, S)$ are elements of $M_S$. We assume that

$$R_m(p, S) \subset R_m(p, S') \times M_{S-S'} \text{ for } S' \subset S.$$

This states that no rational move for a set can require irrationality on the part of a subset. An obvious consequence of this assumption is that

$$R_m(p, S) \subset \prod_{i \in S} R_m(p, i).$$

A move that is rational for a group of players is thus rational for each player in the group.

Similarly, we denote by $R_o(p, S)$ the set of rational deals for $S$ in the game $p$ (that is, the members of $R_o(p, S)$ are sets of elements from $M_P$). It is the "crossproduct-intersection" of rational offer groups for the individual agents:

$$R_o(p, S) = \{O : O = \bigcap_{j \in S} O_j \ \wedge \ O_j \in R_o(p, j)\}.$$

## 2.4 Rationality Assumptions

The value of $pay(i, m_i, y_i)$ will depend, of course, on the values of $allowed_m(i, m_i)$ and $allowed_o(i, y_i)$ (i.e., the moves and the deals that other agents can make). In order to constrain the value of $pay$, we now define each of the $allowed$ functions ($allowed_m$ is defined as in [9]).

1. **Minimal move rationality:**
   $allowed_m(i, m_i) = M_{\bar{i}}$. Each player assumes that the others may be moving randomly.

2. **Separate move rationality:**
   $allowed_m(i, m_i) \subset R_m(p, \bar{i})$. Each player assumes the others are moving rationally.

3. **Unique move rationality:**
   For all $m_i$ and $m_i'$, $allowed_m(i, m_i) = allowed_m(i, m_i')$ and $|allowed_m(i, m_i)| = 1$. Each player assumes that the others' moves are fixed in advance. This may be combined with separate rationality.

The assumptions above do not fully specify what is or is not a rational move. Rather, they help constrain the set of rational moves by allowing us to prove that certain moves are not rational. We now define analogous assumptions regarding deals other agents might be making:

1. **Minimal deal rationality:**
   $allowed_o(i, y_i) \subset \mathcal{P}(M_P)$, where $\mathcal{P}(M_P)$ denotes the power set of $M_P$. Each player assumes that the others may be making random deals.

2. **Separate deal rationality:**
   $allowed_o(i, y_i) \subset R_o(p, \bar{\imath})$. Each player assumes that the others are making rational deals.

3. **Unique deal rationality:**
   For all $D_i$ and $E_i$, $allowed_o(i, D_i) = allowed_o(i, E_i)$ and
   $|allowed_o(i, D_i)| = 1$. Each player assumes that the others' offers are fixed in advance. This may be combined with separate deal rationality.

We refer to the combination of separate and unique move rationality as individual move rationality, and to the combination of separate and unique deal rationality as individual deal rationality. As in [9], any move that can be proven irrational under the assumption of minimal move rationality will be similarly irrational under the other move rationality assumptions. Analogously, any offer group that can be proven irrational under the assumption of minimal deal rationality will be irrational under the other deal rationality assumptions.

## 3   Rational Deal Characteristics

With our notational conventions defined, we can now prove several characteristics of $R_o(p, i)$. We henceforth use $\vec{s}$ to denote any move that gives agent $i$ his highest payoff.

**Theorem 1 (Existence of a non-null rational offer group).**

$$|R_o(p, i)| \geq 1.$$

**Proof.** If $R_o(p, i)$ were empty then $i$ would do best by making no offers and relying on his move to generate his payoff. But $pay(i, m_i, \vec{s})$ will be greater than or equal to $pay(i, m_i, \emptyset)$ for all $m_i$ (since $\vec{s}$ will either be matched by other agents, increasing $i$'s payoff, or will not be matched, and will therefore be harmless since it doesn't affect other's moves). Thus the offer group $\{\vec{s}\}$ would also be in $R_o(p, i)$, guaranteeing it to have at least one non-null member. □

It follows directly from the definition of a rational offer group (3) that all non-empty members of $i$'s set of rational offer groups include $\vec{s}$. Together with Theorem 1, this implies that it is always rational for an agent to include in his offer group the move that gives him his highest payoff.

In addition, an agent can often restrict his offers to those whose payoffs are higher than that which he can get by making the null offer, relying on his move to give him this payoff.

**Theorem 2 (Lower bound).** *Assuming unique deal rationality, if for any move $m_i$ and joint move $\vec{y} \neq \vec{s}$,*

$$p(i, \vec{y}) \leq pay(i, m_i, \emptyset),$$

$\exists O_i[O_i \in R_o(p, i) \wedge \vec{y} \notin O_i].$

**Proof.** There are two cases:

1. $p(i, \vec{y}) < pay(i, m_i, \emptyset)$: The only way for $\vec{y}$ to be in some rational offer group $P_i$ is for the $\vec{y}$ deal not to be accepted (otherwise $pay(i, m_i, P_i)$ would be dominated by the offer group $pay(i, m_i, O_i)$ where $O_i = \{\vec{x} : p(i, \vec{x}) > p(i, \vec{y})\}$). But if $\vec{y}$ is not accepted, then it is equivalent to another offer group that includes only those moves with payoffs higher than $\vec{y}$. This smaller offer group will then also be in $R_o(p, i)$.

2. $p(i, \vec{y}) = pay(i, m_i, \emptyset)$: Assume that $\vec{y}$ is in some rational offer group $P_i$. If $\vec{y}$ is not accepted, or is accepted along with other offers, then $pay(i, m_i, O_i) > pay(i, m_i, P_i)$ where $O_i = \{\vec{x} : p(i, \vec{x}) > p(i, \vec{y})\}$, so there is another rational offer group without $\vec{y}$, namely the offer group $O_i$. If $\vec{y}$ is the only accepted offer, then $pay(i, m_i, \vec{s}) = pay(i, m_i, P_i)$ (where $\vec{s}$ is the move that gives $i$ his highest payoff), since $\vec{s}$ will not be accepted anyway and therefore $pay(i, m_i, \vec{s}) = pay(i, m_i, \emptyset)$. Again, there is a rational offer group that does not include $\vec{y}$. □

Note that Theorem 2 will not hold for $\vec{s}$ (i.e., the joint move that gives $i$ his highest payoff) since that would contradict Theorem 1 (Theorem 2's proof makes implicit use of the fact that $\vec{y} \neq \vec{s}$ in its construction of the dominating offer group $O_i$). Note also that Theorem 2 will *not* hold under minimal deal rationality. Imagine that a perverse opponent chooses his offer group as follows:

1. If you include in your offer group deals with low payoff (for you), he will accept the deal with your best payoff;

2. If you don't offer that low deal he will accept no deals and you will have to rely on your move to get a payoff.

Under these circumstances (fully consistent with minimal deal rationality), it might be to your advantage to offer a low-payoff deal, since that might be the only way to get your maximal payoff.

## 3.1 Restricted Case Analysis

The consequences of Theorem 2 will differ, of course, based on assumptions about $allowed_m$ since these will affect $pay(i, m_i, \emptyset)$ for any given $m_i$. Consider the following payoff matrix:

|   | c | d |
|---|---|---|
| a | 1\4 | 0\5 |
| b | 3\2 | 2\7 |

It is shown in [9] that, assuming minimal move rationality (potentially random or even malevolent moves by other agents), the row agent can still use "restricted case analysis" to constrain his move to $b$. If unique deal rationality can be assumed then the offer group consisting solely of move $b\backslash c$ (i.e., bottom left corner) is *guaranteed* by Theorems 1 and 2 to be a rational offer group. Of course, there may be other rational offer groups, for example the offer $\{b\backslash d, b\backslash c\}$, depending on what deals the other player can offer.

We formalize part of the above discussion:

**Corollary 3 (Restricted case analysis).** *Assuming minimal move rationality and unique deal rationality, if for some $x_i$ and $y_i$, for all $x_{\bar{\imath}}$ and $y_{\bar{\imath}}$,*

$$p(i, \vec{y}) < p(i, \vec{x}),$$

*then there exists an $O_i \in R_o(p, i)$ such that no $\vec{y}$ is in $O_i$.*

**Proof.** Follows from Lemma 3 in [9] and Theorem 2. □

## 3.2  Case Analysis and Iterated Case Analysis

There are restrictions on rational offer groups analogous to Corollary 3 that apply for case analysis and iterated case analysis under the assumptions of unique and individual move rationality, respectively. The case analysis situation is represented in the following payoff matrix, seen from the row player's perspective:

|   | c | d |
|---|---|---|
| a | 4\1 | 2 |
| b | 3\5 | 0\1 |

The row player need only assume that the column player's move will not be affected by its own move (i.e., unique move rationality) to realize that making move $a$ is in all circumstances superior to making move $b$. As long as unique deal rationality can also be assumed, there is a guaranteed rational offer group consisting only of move $a\backslash c$.

**Corollary 4 (Case analysis).** *Assuming unique move rationality and unique deal rationality, if for some $x_i$ and $y_i$, for all $x_{\bar{i}}$ and $y_{\bar{i}}$ with $x_{\bar{i}} = y_{\bar{i}}$,*

$$p(i, \vec{y}) < p(i, \vec{x}),$$

*then there exists an $O_i \in R_o(p, i)$ such that no $\vec{y}$ is in $O_i$.*

**Proof.** Follows from Lemma 4 in [9] and Theorem 2. □

Similarly, if the column player can assume that the row player is rational and making moves independent of the column player's moves (i.e., individual move rationality), then he can prove that move $d$ is optimal in the above matrix (since the row player will play $a$). With unique deal rationality, he has a guaranteed rational offer group of $\{a\backslash d, b\backslash c\}$ (the offer group $\{b\backslash c\}$ is also rational).

The effect of Theorems 1 and 2 is to show us that there is always a rational offer group that includes an agent's highest payoff outcome, and includes no outcomes below or equal to what he could achieve without deals. Below, we consider other constraints on an agent's rational offer groups.

## 4  The Group Rationality Theorem

The work in [9] and [8] was concerned with the formalization of cooperative behavior, given certain constraints about the agents participating in an interaction. Using our notation, a desirable general result would have been

$$pay(P, \vec{y}, \emptyset) < pay(P, \vec{x}, \emptyset) \Rightarrow \vec{y} \notin R_m(p, P), \tag{4}$$

that is, if any joint move for all players is dominated by any other, then the dominated joint move is not rational for them. This result could not be proven, and the inability to do so stemmed directly from the lack of communication inherent in the model. Without at least minimal communication (e.g., self-identification), there is no way to coordinate on a universally perceived best move when several such moves exist.

We are now able to derive an important result about $R_o(p, P)$ very similar to the elusive non-communication result in (4).

**Theorem 5 (Group offers).** *Assuming individual deal rationality,*

$$p(P, \vec{y}) < p(P, \vec{x}) \Rightarrow \exists O_i[O_i \in R_o(p, i) \land \vec{y} \notin O_i]$$

*for all $i \in P$.*

**Proof.** There are two possible cases:

1. $\forall O_j[O_j \in R_o(p, \vec{\imath}) \Rightarrow \vec{y} \notin O_j]$: Since $\vec{y}$ will not be a consummated deal, if $P_i$ is any offer group containing $\vec{y}$ then $pay(i, m_i, O_i) \geq pay(i, m_i, P_i)$ where $O_i = \{\vec{x} : p(i, \vec{x}) > p(i, \vec{y})\}$. Along with Theorem 1, this shows the existence of a non-null rational offer group without $\vec{y}$.

2. $\exists O_j[O_j \in R_o(p, \vec{\imath}) \land \vec{y} \in O_j]$: All other agents are rational (by assumption), and any rational offer group that includes $\vec{y}$ also includes $\vec{x}$ (3); thus, if $P_i$ is any offer group containing $\vec{y}$, then $pay(i, m_i, O_i) > pay(i, m_i, P_i)$ where $O_i = \{\vec{x} : p(i, \vec{x}) > p(i, \vec{y})\}$. This, along with Theorem 1, shows the existence of a rational offer group without $\vec{y}$. □

Because of Theorem 5, a rational agent interacting with other rational agents knows that he need not offer a move that is dominated for all players—doing so cannot increase his payoff. If the other rational agents also know that all agents are rational, they too will realize that they can refrain from offering a move that is dominated for all players. Higher levels of knowledge [13], such as their knowing that all agents know that all agents are rational, are not needed. In addition, because of the definition of rational offer groups (3), the agents can refrain from offering any moves with smaller payoffs, since those groups would necessarily include the dominated move.

## 5 Examples

We will now examine the consequences of our rational offer theorems in several additional types of games.

### 5.1 Best Plan

The best plan scenario is reflected in the following matrix:

|   | c | d |
|---|---|---|
| a | 7 | 4 |
| b | 5 | 6 |

All agents recognize that there is a single best move; how will their offer groups reflect this? From Theorem 1, a rational agent knows that he can safely offer the move that gives him his best payoff (i.e., move $a \backslash c$), even assuming minimal deal rationality on the part of other players (though the theorem is noncommittal as to whether other moves can or should be included with it). All players can also rule out move $a \backslash d$ using Theorem 2 if unique deal rationality holds (since $a \backslash d$ yields the lowest payoff). If there is an assumption of individual deal rationality, Theorem 5 can guarantee each agent that the offer group consisting solely of $a \backslash c$ is rational. Communication thus allows coordination on the best plan under more intuitive assumptions about the interaction than those used in [9].

## 5.2   Breaking Symmetries—Multiple Best Plan

Our rational offer group theorems allow us to solve the "Multiple Best Plans" case that could not be solved in [9]. The following matrix illustrates the scenario:

|   | c  | d  |
|---|----|----|
| a | -1 | 2  |
| b | 2  | -1 |

Assuming minimal deal rationality, an agent can rationally offer $b\backslash c$ and $a\backslash d$. In addition, assuming unique deal rationality an agent knows that he can rationally not offer $a\backslash c$ and $b\backslash d$ (since they are lowest yield moves). This analysis can be done by both agents if they are rational and operating under the unique deal assumption. Their offer sets will overlap on the multiple best outcomes; selection of a single alternative from the multiple agreements then occurs.

## 5.3   Prisoner's Dilemma

The prisoner's dilemma is represented by the following matrix (we choose different names for our moves so as to conform to the literature):

|   | c    | d    |
|---|------|------|
| c | 3    | 0\5  |
| d | 5\0  | 1    |

Each agent most desires to play $d$ while the opponent plays $c$, then to play $c$ along with the opponent, then to play $d$ along with the opponent, and least of all to play $c$ while the opponent plays $d$. The dilemma comes about because case analysis implies that it is always better to play $d$; both players choosing $d$, however, is less desirable *for both* than if they had chosen $c$. The dilemma has received much attention within the philosophy and game theory literature [2,5,22,27]. In the usual presentation of the prisoner's dilemma, playing $c$ is called "cooperating," and playing $d$ is called "defecting." With the presence of binding promises, in fact, there is no dilemma:

**Corollary 6 (Prisoner's Dilemma).** *If all players know that all players are operating under the assumption of individual deal rationality, agents will cooperate in the prisoner's dilemma.*

**Proof.** The first player knows that it is rational to offer $d\backslash c$ (since it is rational even under minimal rationality, Theorem 1); he also knows it is irrational to offer $c\backslash d$ (from Theorem 2, since individual deal rationality includes unique deal rationality). By Theorem 5, there is a rational offer group without $d\backslash d$. Now he knows that the other agent will not offer $d\backslash c$ (since the other agent is assumed rational and operating under the assumption of unique deal rationality, Theorem 2). Since $d\backslash c$ will certainly not be met, $pay(i, d, \{d\backslash c\}) \leq pay(i, d, \{d\backslash c, c\backslash c\})$. Thus, the offer group $\{d\backslash c, c\backslash c\}$ is rational. The second agent will, if rational and working under the same assumptions, come to the same conclusion. The deal $c\backslash c$ will be struck, and the agents avoid the $d\backslash d$ trap. □

# 6 Extending the Model

For certain types of interactions, the model presented above (i.e., the various assumptions and theorems about rational moves and deals) does not specify rational activity in sufficient detail. We can extend the model in a variety of ways to handle these cases, and at the same time capture a wider range of assumptions about the interaction. In this section, we briefly present some of the extensions that might be made to our original model.

## 6.1 Similar bargainers

Consider the following payoff matrix (equivalent to game 77 in Rapoport and Guyer's taxonomy [23]):

|   | c | d |
|---|---|---|
| a | 3 | 2 |
| b | 5\0 | 0\5 |

Assuming separate deal rationality, the first player can assume that $b\backslash c$ should be in a rational offer group of his, and that $b\backslash d$ should not be. What else can be said about what constitutes a rational offer group in this game? There are three choices, namely $\{b\backslash c\}$, $\{a\backslash c, b\backslash c\}$, and $\{a\backslash d, a\backslash c, b\backslash c\}$. In order to decide among the choices, we would like to make more assumptions about the "bargaining tendencies" of the other agent (since, in fact, some agents might be tougher deal-makers than others). We will ignore what value the agents might place on making a particular move in the absence of a deal, since the payoff is underdetermined.

Let us define two offer groups $O_i$ and $O_j$ to be *similar* if and only if they both have the same lower boundary for what deals are included or not included. It is true that $similar(O_i, O_j)$ if and only if

$$\exists n[\, p(i, \vec{y}) > n \Leftrightarrow \vec{y} \in O_i \,\wedge\, p(j, \vec{x}) > n \Leftrightarrow \vec{x} \in O_j]$$

for some number $n$. If we use the similar bargainers definition, we implicitly assume some meaningful measure for comparing inter-personal utility.

One assumption to use in deciding upon rational offer groups is now that the other agent will accept deals that you would accept; that is, $O_j \in R_o(p, j) \Leftrightarrow O_i \in R_o(p, i)$ where $similar(O_i, O_j)$.

Under this assumption, we can decide what deal is rational in the above game. Player 1 reasons that if he offers $\{b\backslash c\}$, player 2 (who is a similar bargainer) will offer only $\{b\backslash d\}$. There will be no match. In the same way, if it would be rational for player 1 to offer $\{a\backslash c, b\backslash c\}$ then player 2 will offer $\{a\backslash c, b\backslash d\}$, with an agreement on $a\backslash c$ and a payoff of $\{3\}$ for both. If player 1 offers $\{a\backslash d, a\backslash c, b\backslash c\}$ then player 2 will offer $\{a\backslash d, a\backslash c, b\backslash d\}$ and there will be agreement on $a\backslash d$ and on $a\backslash c$, with a payoff of $\{2, 3\}$ for both. Since $\{3\}$ dominates $\{2, 3\}$, agents who assume common knowledge [13] of the similar bargainer assumption should choose the rational offer group that yields agreement on $a\backslash c$.

## 6.2 Stochastic Model—The Game of Chicken

Note, however, the following payoff matrix (commonly known as the game of chicken [23]):

|   | c | d |
|---|---|---|
| a | 3 | 2\5 |
| b | 5\2 | 1 |

Two agents, even if they assume individual deal rationality and the similar bargainers assumption, will be faced with the following choices: a payoff of $\{3\}$ or a payoff of $\{2,3,5\}$. According to our definitions, neither of these sets dominates the other.

If, however, we extend the model to include a probabilistic choice from within the agreement set, it is clear that the latter agreement set dominates the former (with an expected value of 3.33 versus 3). A further stochastic extension to our model would allow moves themselves to be specified probabilistically (e.g., $a$ with probability .5, and $b$ with probability .5). In the game theory literature, this is the distinction between pure strategies and mixed strategies [18]. An analysis of this model is beyond the scope of the present discussion.

## 6.3   Conjunctive Offers—Battle of the Sexes

In the game of chicken example presented above, there was an added complexity that was temporarily ignored: the possibility of "defection." If one agent reasons that the other agent will accept all payoffs above 2, it is to the first agent's benefit to only offer moves of payoff 5 (this is analogous to the prisoner's dilemma, with the same potential that both players will use identical reasoning and no agreement will be reached). A similar problem can be seen in the so-called battle of the sexes matrix, seen below.

|   | c | d |
|---|---|---|
| a | -1 | 1\2 |
| b | 2\1 | -1 |

One approach to solving this problem is to allow "composite" offers, for example, an offer consisting of a conjunct of several moves (the conjunct must be matched exactly in order for a deal to occur). Thus, the offer consisting of $a\backslash d \wedge b\backslash c$ can consistently be made by both agents without the potential of defection (and with an expected utility of 1.5 for each). This notion can be extended to general logical offers consisting of disjuncts, conjuncts and negations of joint moves. The battle of the sexes can thus be uniquely solved with the assumption of similarity in bargaining, if conjunctive offers are allowed.

## 7   Previous Work

The subject of interacting rational agents has been addressed within the field of artificial intelligence as well as in the discipline of game theory. Here we will briefly review relevant contributions from these two areas, and contrast our present approach with previous efforts.

## 7.1   Work in Artificial Intelligence

As mentioned above, researchers in distributed artificial intelligence have begun to address the issues arising in multi-agent interactions. Lesser and Corkill [4] have performed empirical studies to determine cooperation strategies with positive characteristics (such as, for example, what types of data should be shared among distributed processors). They are solely concerned with groups of agents who share a common goal, but have acknowledged the benefit even under this assumption of having agents demonstrate "skepticism" (i.e., not being distracted by others' information).

Georgeff [10,11] has developed a formal model to combine separate plans of independent agents. The primary concern is to avoid destructive interference caused by simultaneous access to a shared resource. The model used assumes that the agents have separate goals, but that these goals do not directly oppose one another. Cooperative action is neither required nor exploited, except insofar as it allows agents to keep out of each other's way.

Other notable efforts include Smith's work on the contract net [7], Malone's work extending the contract net model using economic theory [19], and the theoretical work on knowledge and belief of carried out by Appelt, Moore, Konolige, Halpern and Moses [1,17,14,16,15,21,20].

The current work extends these previous models of interaction by allowing a fuller range of goal disagreements among agents. By using a framework that captures total and partial goal conflicts, it allows investigation into compromise, promises and cooperative action.

This paper considers the communication scenario in ways similar to the manner in which previous work [9,8] investigated cooperation among rational agents when no communication occurs. Below we briefly note the advantages that were gained when communication and promises were added to the interaction model.

The best plan interaction was handled in our framework by assuming individual deal rationality. Because in the no-communication case this scenario could not be solved using individual move rationality, other assumptions were introduced: *informed rationality* in [9] and *common rationality* in [8]. Informed rationality constrained $allowed_m$ in a way that assumed each player would respond in a rational way to the others' moves, whatever they might be.

It should be noted in passing that an assumption of common knowledge of rationality will also allow for a solution to the best plan case, though this has not previously been pursued in the literature.

To solve the prisoner's dilemma, even more assumptions had to be introduced. The interested reader is referred to [9] and [8] for full details; see also [24].

Even using a variety of assumptions, previous work could not handle the multiple best plan case, where there are several outcomes all equally recognized as best by all players. To break the symmetry, some communication is needed, though this communication can be as simple as self-identification and reliance on a common rule (e.g., agent with lowest name performs lowest ordered action).

## 7.2 Game Theory

Game theory has focused on a variety of interactions, and sought to characterize the types of actions that rational agents will take in each. Many of the same questions that come up in our work have been addressed by game theoreticians. Their approach, however, has left some important issues unexamined. Consider the following quote from the classic game theory text, [18]:

> Though it is not apparent from some writings, the term "rational" is far from precise, and it certainly means different things in the different theories that have been developed. Loosely, it seems to include any assumption one makes about the players maximizing something, and any about complete knowledge on the part of the player in a very complex situation... [*Games and Decisions*, p. 5]

As another example, consider the following best plan interaction:

|       | $A_2$ | $B_2$  |
|-------|-------|--------|
| $A_1$ | 4     | $1\backslash 2$ |
| $B_1$ | $3\backslash 1$ | $2\backslash 3$ |

It was demonstrated above that the best plan case can only be solved under particular definitions of rationality. Rapoport and Guyer, however, writing in [23], put forward the following *assumption* regarding agents' behavior (citing the similarity with [26]):

> ($A_3$). If a game has a single Pareto equilibrium, the players will choose the strategy which contains it...
> Our assumption ($A_3$) says that $A_1 A_2$ is the natural outcome, which, of course, is dictated by common sense... we shall refer to this as a *prominent solution*. [*A Taxonomy of* 2 × 2 *Games*]

In short, game theory has sometimes been willing to take for granted certain types of behavior without carefully formalizing its definitions of rationality, or its assumptions of inter-agent knowledge.

These questions are particularly important in the field of artificial intelligence. We are not interested in characterizing game matrices: we want to characterize agent rationality and explore the consequences of various assumptions. The goal is to be able to implement intelligent agents whose strategies of behavior will be provably rational.

## 8   Conclusion

Intelligent agents will inevitably need to interact flexibly in real world domains. Previous work has not modeled the full range and complexity of agents' varied goals. The benevolent agent assumption, which assumes that agents have identical or non-conflicting goals, has permeated previous approaches to distributed AI.

This paper has presented a framework for interaction that explicitly accounts for communication and promises, and allows multiple goals among agents. The model provides a unified solution to a wide range of problems, including the types of interactions discussed in [9] and [8]. Through the use of communication and binding promises, agents are able to coordinate their actions more effectively, and handle interactions that were previously problematical. By extending the communication model even further, a wider variety of interactions can be handled.

## 9   Acknowledgement

The authors wish to thank Matt Ginsberg, who has played an invaluable role in the development of our ideas on cooperation among rational agents. This research has been supported by DARPA under NAVELEX grant number N00039-83-C-0136.

# References

[1] Douglas E. Appelt. *Planning natural language utterances to satisfy multiple goals.* Tech Note 259, SRI International, Menlo Park, California, 1982.

[2] Robert Axelrod. *The Evolution of Cooperation.* Basic Books, Inc., New York, 1984.

[3] Stephanie Cammarata, David McArthur, and Randall Steeb. Strategies of cooperation in distributed problem solving. In *IJCAI-83*, pages 767–770, Karlsruhe, West Germany, August 1983.

[4] Daniel D. Corkill and Victor R. Lesser. The use of meta-level control for coordination in a distributed problem solving network. In *IJCAI-83*, pages 748–756, Karlsruhe, West Germany, August 1983.

[5] L. Davis. Prisoners, paradox and rationality. *American Philosophical Quarterly*, 14, 1977.

[6] Randall Davis. *A model for planning in a multi-agent environment: steps toward principles for teamwork.* Working Paper 217, Massachusetts Institute of Technology AI Laboratory, October 1981.

[7] Randall Davis and Reid G. Smith. Negotiation as a metaphor for distributed problem solving. *Artificial Intelligence*, 20(1):63–109, 1983.

[8] Michael R. Genesereth, Matthew L. Ginsberg, and Jeffrey S. Rosenschein. *Cooperation without Communication.* HPP Report 84-36, Heuristic Programming Project, Computer Science Department, Stanford University, September 1984.

[9] Michael R. Genesereth, Matthew L. Ginsberg, and Jeffrey S. Rosenschein. *Solving the Prisoner's Dilemma.* Report No. STAN-CS-84-1032, Computer Science Department, Stanford University, November 1984.

[10] Michael Georgeff. Communication and interaction in multi-agent planning. In *Proceedings of the National Conference on Artificial Intelligence*, pages 125–129, Washington, D.C., August 1983.

[11] Michael Georgeff. A theory of action for multi-agent planning. In *Proceedings of the National Conference on Artificial Intelligence*, pages 121–125, Austin, Texas, August 1984.

[12] Ira P. Goldstein. *Bargaining Between Goals.* A. I. Working Paper 102, Massachusetts Institute of Technology A. I. Laboratory, 1975.

[13] Joseph Y. Halpern and Yoram Moses. *Knowledge and Common Knowledge in a Distributed Environment.* Research Report IBM RJ 4421, IBM Research Laboratory, San Jose, California, October 1984.

[14] Kurt Konolige. Circumscriptive ignorance. In *Proceedings of The National Conference on Artificial Intelligence*, pages 202–204, Pittsburgh, Pennsylvania, August 1982.

[15] Kurt Konolige. *A Deduction Model of Belief and its Logics.* PhD thesis, Stanford University, 1984.

[16] Kurt Konolige. A deductive model of belief. In *IJCAI-83*, pages 377–381, Karlsruhe, West Germany, August 1983.

[17] Kurt Konolige. *A first-order formalization of knowledge and action for a multi-agent planning system.* Tech Note 232, SRI International, Menlo Park, California, December 1980.

[18] R. Duncan Luce and Howard Raiffa. *Games and Decisions, Introduction and Critical Survey.* John Wiley and Sons, New York, 1957.

[19] Thomas W. Malone, Richard E. Fikes, and M. T. Howard. *Enterprise: a market-like task scheduler for distributed computing environments.* Working Paper, Cognitive and Instructional Sciences Group, Xerox Palo Alto Research Center, October 1983.

[20] Robert C. Moore. *A formal theory of knowledge and action.* Tech Note 320, SRI International, Menlo Park, California, 1984. Also in *Formal Theories of the Commonsense World*, Hobbs, J.R., and Moore, R.C. (Eds.), Ablex Publishing Co. (1985).

[21] Robert C. Moore. *Reasoning about knowledge and action.* Tech Note 191, SRI International, Menlo Park, California, 1980.

[22] D. Parfit. *Reasons and Persons.* Clarendon Press, Oxford, 1984.

[23] Anatol Rapoport and M. Guyer. A taxonomy of $2 \times 2$ games. *Yearbook of the Society for General Systems Research*, XI:203–214, 1966.

[24] Jeffrey S. Rosenschein. *Rational Interaction: Cooperation Among Intelligent Agents.* PhD thesis, Stanford University, 1986. Also published as STAN-CS-85-1081 (KSL-85-40), Department of Computer Science, Stanford University, October 1985.

[25] Jeffrey S. Rosenschein and Michael R. Genesereth. *Communication and Cooperation.* HPP Report 84-5, Heuristic Programming Project, Computer Science Department, Stanford University, March 1984.

[26] Thomas C. Schelling. *The Strategy of Conflict.* Oxford University Press, New York, 1963.

[27] L. Sowden. That there is a dilemma in the prisoner's dilemma. *Synthese*, 55:347–352, 1983.

The Ecology of Computation
B.A. Huberman (editor)
© Elsevier Science Publishers B.V. (North-Holland), 1988

# Markets and Computation: Agoric Open Systems

Mark S. Miller

Xerox Palo Alto Research Center,
3333 Coyote Hill Road, Palo Alto, CA 94304

K. Eric Drexler

MIT Artificial Intelligence Laboratory,
545 Technology Square, Cambridge, MA 02139*

Like all systems involving goals, resources, and actions, computation can be viewed in economic terms. Computer science has moved from centralized toward increasingly decentralized models of control and action; use of market mechanisms would be a natural extension of this development. The ability of trade and price mechanisms to combine local decisions by diverse parties into globally effective behavior suggests their value for organizing computation in large systems.

This paper examines markets as a model for computation and proposes a framework—*agoric systems*—for applying the power of market mechanisms to the software domain. It then explores the consequences of this model at a variety of levels. Initial market strategies are outlined which, if used by objects locally, lead to distributed resource allocation algorithms that encourage adaptive modification based on local knowledge. If used as the basis for large, distributed systems, open to the human market, agoric systems can serve as a software publishing and distribution marketplace providing strong incentives for the development of reusable software components. It is argued that such a system should give rise to increasingly intelligent behavior as an emergent property of interactions among software entities and people.

---

* Visiting Scholar, Stanford University. Box 60775, Palo Alto, CA 94306

# 1. Introduction

A central problem of computer science is the integration of knowledge and coordination of action in complex systems. The same may be said of society. In society, however, this problem has been faced for millennia rather than decades, and diverse solutions have been tested for effectiveness through hundreds of generations of competition. Efforts to understand the resulting institutions and to describe their principles of operation have spawned the science of economics.

Contrary to common impressions (fostered by media coverage of politics and the stock market), most economic inquiry has little to do with guessing economic trends. Economics has many branches; the branch most relevant to this paper studies the consequences of pursuing goals within the constraints of limited knowledge and resources, and studies the institutions and patterns of behavior adapted to this pursuit. This branch of economics can without embarrassment be termed a science, since it meets the criteria for a scientific discipline [1,2].

At the broadest level of abstraction, the problems of social and computational coordination are fundamentally similar. Concrete parallels, however, are rough: memory space is a bit like land, or perhaps a raw material; processor time is somewhat like labor, or like fuel; software objects are like workers, or perhaps like managers or firms. In [I] we list a number of fundamental differences between computational and human markets. For example, within a computational system, activities need produce neither pollution nor other effects on non-consenting objects; the most typical product, information, does not form a depletable physical inventory; specialized labor forces (copies of specialized objects) can be expanded almost instantly and can be cut back without human anguish.

Despite these deep differences, we argue that the fundamental parallels between the problems of social and computational organization are strong enough to motivate the wholesale importation of economic models and metaphors into the computational domain, at least on a trial basis. These differences do, however, suggest that forms of organization that fail or are rejected in one domain may prove workable and desirable in the other. For example, the ability of computational systems to establish rules as genuine constraints where an analogous human legal system can only penalize violations makes possible patterns of organization that can only be approximated in society.

## 1.1. Why focus on markets?

For a variety of reasons, this work explores essentially pure markets as models of economic organization for computation, supported by a minimal "legal" framework of foundational constraints. A large body of economic theory and historical experience indicates that markets are, on the whole, remarkably effective in promoting efficient, cooperative interactions among entities with diverse knowledge, skills, and goals. Historically, those entities have been human beings, but economic principles extend to decision-making agents in general and hence to software objects as well. In [I], markets are considered as ecosystems and compared to others, such as biological ecosystems. This examination shows how the distinctive rules of markets (such as the suppression of force and protection of trademarks) foster the spread of cooperation (and encourage entities to compete to be effective cooperators).

This paper argues that market ecosystems are particularly appropriate as foundations for *open systems* [II], in which evolving software spread across a distributed computer system serves different owners pursuing different goals. When also open to human society, computational market ecosystems will enable diverse authors to create software entities and receive royalties for the services they provide, and enable diverse users to mold the system to their needs by exercising their market power as consumers. Computational markets can be made continuous with the market ecosystem of human society.

## 1.2. Sketch of a computational market

This line of investigation leads us to propose what may be called the *agoric* approach to software systems. *Agoric* (a·gó·ric) stems from *agora* (ág·o·ra), the Greek term for a meeting and market place. An agoric system is defined as a software system using market mechanisms, based on foundations that provide for the *encapsulation* and *communication* of *information, access,* and *resources* among *objects*. Each of these notions plays a role in supporting computational markets.

Here, the notion of "object" is independent of scale and language, and includes no notion of inheritance. An object might be small and written in an object-oriented language; it might equally well be a large, running process (such as an expert system or a database) coded internally in any manner whatsoever. Objects are assumed to communicate through message passing and to interact according to the rules of actor semantics [3,4], which can be enforced at either the language or operating system level. These rules formalize the notion of distinct, asynchronous, interacting entities, and hence are appropriate for describing participants in computational markets.

Encapsulation of information ensures that one object cannot directly read or tamper with the contents of another; communication enables objects to exchange information by mutual consent. The encapsulation and communication of access ensures that communication rights are similarly controlled and transferable only by mutual consent. These properties correspond to elements of traditional object-oriented programming practice; in large systems, they facilitate local reasoning about *competence* issues—about what computations the system can perform.

Extending encapsulation to include computational resources means holding each object accountable for the cost of its activity; providing for the communication of resources enables objects to buy and sell them. In large systems, these extensions facilitate local reasoning about *performance* issues—about the time and resources consumed in performing a given computation. Computational foundations suitable for markets thus offer advantages in the performance domain like those offered in the competence domain by object-oriented programming.

For concreteness, let us briefly consider one possible form of market-based system. In this system, machine resources—storage space, processor time, and so forth—have owners, and the owners charge other objects for use of these resources. Objects, in turn, pass these costs on to the objects they serve, or to an object representing the external user; they may add royalty charges, and thus earn a profit. The ultimate user thus pays for all the costs directly or indirectly incurred. If the ultimate user also owns the machine resources (and any objects charging royalties), then currency simply circulates inside the system, incurring computational overhead and (one hopes) providing information that helps coordinate computational activities.

## 2. Overview of later sections

**Section 3: Computation and economic order.** Basic characteristics of human markets illuminate the expected nature of computational markets. This section describes some of these characteristics and sketches some of the special issues raised in the context of computation.

**Section 4: Foundations.** The foundations needed for agoric open systems may be summarized as *support for the encapsulation and communication of information, access, and resources*. This section describes these foundations and their role in computational markets.

**Section 5: Agents and strategies.** The foundations of computational markets handle neither resource management (such as processor scheduling and garbage collection) nor market transactions. This section describes the idea of *business agents* and their use both in replacing centralized resource-allocation algorithms (discussed further by [III]) and in managing complex market behavior.

**Section 6: Agoric systems in the large.** Large, evolved agoric systems are expected to have valuable emergent properties. This section describes how they can provide a more productive software market in human society—opening major new business opportunities—and how they can further the goal of artificial intelligence.

**Section 7: The absence of agoric systems.** If market-based computation is a good idea, why has it not yet been developed? This section attempts to show why the current absence of agoric systems is consistent with their being a good idea.

**Appendix I: Issues, levels, and scale.** Agoric open systems will be large and complex, spanning many levels of scale and complexity. This section surveys how issues such as security, reasoning, and trust manifest themselves at different levels of agoric systems.

**Appendix II: Comparison with other systems.** Here are reviewed works ranging from those that draw analogies between human society and computational systems to those that explore adaptive computation from an economic point of view.

## 3. Computation and economic order

The basic features of computational markets are best understood by comparing them with human markets. Many important tradeoffs, such as those between market mechanisms and central planning, have already been examined in the context of human society.

## 3.1. Market organization

> Consider the awesome dimensions of the American community. . .a labor
> force of 80,000,000. . .11,000,000 business units. . . .Who designed and
> who now directs this vast production-and-distribution machine? Surely, to
> solve the intricate problems of resource allocation in a vast economy, central
> guidance is required. . . .But American economic activity is not directed,
> planned, or controlled by any economic czar—governmental or private.
>
> —A. A. Alchian and W. R. Allen, 1968 [5]

Two extreme forms of organization are the command economy and the market economy.
The former attempts to make economic tradeoffs in a rational, centrally-formulated plan, and
to implement that plan through detailed central direction of productive activity. The latter
allows economic tradeoffs to be made by local decisionmakers, guided by price signals and
constrained by general rules.

The command model has frequently been considered more "rational", since it involves the
visible application of reason to the economic problem as a whole. Alternatives have frequently
been considered irrational and an invitation to chaos. This viewpoint, however, smacks of the
creationist fallacy—it assumes that a coherent result requires a guiding plan. In actuality, decentralized planning is potentially *more* rational, since it involves more minds taking into account more total information. Further, economic theory shows how coherent, efficient, global
results routinely emerge from local market interactions. (The nature and function of prices and
of market mechanisms are a notorious source of lay confusion—just as Aristotle threw rocks
and yet misunderstood mechanics, so people trade and yet misunderstand markets. Alchian
and Allen [5] give a good grounding in the basic concepts and results of economic analysis.)

Should one expect markets to be applicable to processor time, memory space, and computational services inside computers? Steel mills, farms, insurance companies, software firms—
even vending machines—all provide their goods and services in a market context; a mechanism that spans so wide a range may well be stretched further.

As will be shown, however, a range of choices lies between pure central planning and the
universal fine-grained application of market mechanisms. Computational markets, like human
markets, will consist of islands of central direction in a sea of trade.

## 3.2. Encapsulation and property

> The rationale of securing to each individual a known range within which he
> can decide on his actions is to enable him to make the fullest use of his
> knowledge. . . .The law tells him what facts he may count on and thereby ex-
> tends the range within which he can predict the consequences of his actions.
>
> —F. A. Hayek, 1960 [6]

> ...the law ought always to trust people with the care of their own interest, as in their local situations they must generally be able to judge better of it than the legislator can do.
>
> —A. Smith, 1776 [7]

Computer science began, naturally enough, with central planning applied to small, manageable machines. The first programs on the first computers were like Robinson Crusoe on an empty island. They had few problems of coordination, and the complexity of their affairs could (at first) be managed by a single mind.

As the complexity of software grew, programs with multiple subroutines became the equivalent of autocratic households or bureaucracies with extensive division of labor. Increasingly, however, bugs would appear because the right hand would not know what the left hand had planned, and so would modify shared data in unexpected ways.

To combat this problem, modern object-oriented programming (to paraphrase) "secures to each object a known space within which it can decide on its actions, enabling the programmer to make the fullest use of his knowledge. Encapsulation tells him what facts he may count on and thereby extends the range within which he can predict the consequences of his actions". In short, motivated by the need for decentralized planning and division of labor, computer science has reinvented the notion of property rights.

Central direction of data representation and processing has been replaced by decentralized mechanisms, but central direction of resource allocation remains. Rather than "trusting objects with the care of their own interest, in their local situations", the systems programmer attempts to legislate a general solution. These general solutions, however, provide no way to make tradeoffs that take account of the particular merits of particular activities at particular times.

### 3.3. Tradeoffs through trade

> ...a capacity to find out particular circumstances...becomes effective only if possessors of this knowledge are informed by the market which kinds of things or services are wanted, and how urgently they are wanted.
>
> —F. A. Hayek, 1978 [8]

> ...the spontaneous interaction of a number of people, each possessing only bits of knowledge, brings about a state of affairs in which prices correspond to costs, etc., and which could be brought about by deliberate direction only by somebody who possessed the combined knowledge of all those individuals....the empirical observation that prices do tend to correspond to costs was the beginning of our science.
>
> —F. A. Hayek, 1937 [9]

Trusting objects with decisions regarding resource tradeoffs will make sense only if they are led toward decisions that serve the general interest—there is no moral argument for ensuring the freedom, dignity, and autonomy of simple programs. Properly-functioning price mechanisms can provide the needed incentives.

The cost of consuming a resource is an *opportunity cost*—the cost of giving up alternative uses. In a market full of entities attempting to produce products that will sell for more than the cost of the needed inputs, economic theory indicates that prices typically reflect these costs.

Consider a producer, such as an object that produces services. The price of an input shows how greatly it is wanted by the rest of the system; high input prices (costs) will discourage low-value uses. The price of an output likewise shows how greatly it is wanted by the rest of the system; high output prices will encourage production. To increase (rather than destroy) value *as 'judged' by the rest of the system as a whole,* a producer need only ensure that the price of its product exceeds the prices (costs) of the inputs consumed. This simple, local decision rule gains its power from the ability of market prices to summarize global information about relative values.

As Nobel Laureate F. A. Hayek observes, "...the whole reason for employing the price mechanism is to tell individuals that what they are doing, or can do, has for some reason for which they are not responsible become less or more demanded....The term 'incentives' is often used in this connection with somewhat misleading connotations, as if the main problem were to induce people to exert themselves sufficiently. However, the chief guidance which prices offer is not so much how to act, but *what to do."* [8] This observation clearly applies to the idea of providing incentives for software; the goal is not to make software sweat, but to guide it in making choices that serve the general interest.

These choices amount to tradeoffs. With finite processing and memory resources, taking one action always precludes taking some other action. With prices and trade, objects will have an incentive to relinquish resources when (and only when) doing so promises to increase their net revenue. By trading to increase their revenue, they will make tradeoffs that allocate resources to higher-value uses.

## 3.4. Spontaneous order

> Modern civilization has given man undreamt of powers largely because, without understanding it, he has developed methods of utilizing more knowledge and resources than any one mind is aware of.
>
> —F. A. Hayek, 1978 [10]

Will prices, trade, and decentralized tradeoffs be valuable in computation? This depends in part on whether central planning mechanisms will be able to cope with tomorrow's computer systems.

Systems are becoming available having performance tradeoffs that are nightmarishly complex compared to those of a von Neumann machine running a single program. The world is becoming populated with hypercubes, Connection Machines, shared-memory multi-processors, special-purpose systolic arrays, vectorizing super-computers, neural-net simulators, and millions of personal computers. More and more, these are being linked by local area networks, satellites, phones, packet radio, optical fiber, and people carrying floppy disks. Machines in the personal-computer price range will become powerful multi-processor systems with diverse hardware and software linked to a larger world of even greater diversity. Later, with the eventual development of molecular machines able to direct molecular assembly (the basis of *nanotechnology)* [11], we can anticipate the development of desktop machines with a computational power greater than that of a billion of today's mainframe computers [12,13].

One might try to assign machine resources to tasks through an operating system using fixed, general rules, but in large systems with heterogeneous hardware and software, this seems doomed to gross inefficiency. Knowledge of tradeoffs and priorities will be distributed among thousands of programmers, and this knowledge will best be embodied in their programs. Computers are becoming too complex for central planning, with its bottlenecks in computation and knowledge acquisition. It seems that we need to apply "methods of utilizing more knowledge and resources than any one mind is aware of." These methods can yield a productive spontaneous order through decentralized planning—through the application of local knowledge and local computational resources to local decisions, guided by non-local market prices. Instead of designing rules that embody fixed decisions, we need to design rules that enable flexible decisionmaking.

Markets are a form of "evolutionary ecosystem" [I], and such systems can be powerful generators of spontaneous order: consider the intricate, undesigned order of the rain forest or the computer industry. The use of market mechanisms can yield orderly systems beyond the ability of any individual to plan, implement, or understand. What is more, the shaping force of consumer choice can make computational market ecosystems serve human purposes, potentially better than anything programmers *could* plan or understand. This increase in our power to utilize knowledge and resources may prove essential, if we are to harness the power of large computational systems.

### 3.5. Command and price mechanisms

> An economist thinks of the economic system as being co-ordinated by the price mechanism....Within a firm, the description does not fit at all....It is clear that these are alternative methods of co-ordinating production....if production is regulated by price movements...why is there any organization?
>
> —R. H. Coase, 1937 [14]

Coase asks, "Why are there firms?". Firms are economic organizations that typically make little use of market mechanisms internally. If reliance on market forces always produced more efficient use of resources, one would expect that systems of individuals interacting as freelance traders would consistently out-compete firms, which therefore would not exist. In reality, however, firms are viable; analogous results seem likely in computational markets.

Market transactions typically incur higher overhead costs than do transactions inside firms [14,15]. These transaction costs (in both human and computational markets) are associated with advertising, negotiation, accounting, and problems of establishing adequate trust—typically, inside a firm, matching consumers with producers does not require advertising, instructions do not require negotiation, movement of goods does not require invoices and funds transfer, and coworkers share an interest in their joint success. Firms lower the high overhead cost of market transactions among numerous small entities by bundling them

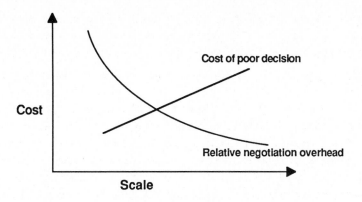

*Figure 1: Scale and transaction costs. As entities and transactions grow larger, the cost of making a poor decision grows, while the relative cost of market negotiation falls. If market decisions are better, but costlier, than central direction, they will be preferred by larger entities.*

together into fewer, larger entities. Not only does this save costs on what are now internal transactions, but by creating larger entities, it raises the size of typical transactions, making relatively fixed per-transaction overhead costs a proportionally smaller burden. (For small enough transactions, even the simplest accounting would be too expensive.)

Similar considerations hold among computational objects. For small enough objects and transactions, the cost of accounting and negotiations will overwhelm any advantages that may result from making flexible, price-sensitive tradeoffs. For large enough objects and transactions, however, these overhead costs will be small in percentage terms; the benefits of market mechanisms may then be worth the cost. At an intermediate scale, negotiation will be too expensive, but accounting will help guide planning. These scale effects will encourage the aggregation of small, simple objects into "firms" with low-overhead rules for division of income among their participants.

Size thresholds for accounting and negotiations will vary with situations and implementation techniques [16]. Market competition will tune these thresholds, providing incentives to choose the most efficient scale on which to apply central-planning methods to computation.

### 3.6. Can market objects be programmed?

The objects participating in computational markets must initially be much simpler than the human participants in human markets. Can they participate successfully? Human markets are based on intelligent systems, but this does not show the impossibility of basing markets on simple objects—it merely shows that the argument for agoric systems cannot rest on analogy alone. Explicit attention must be paid to the question of the minimal competence and complexity necessary for an object to participate in a market system. (These issues provide another motivation to form computational "firms" and to open computational markets to human participation.)

Experimental double-auction markets on a laboratory scale [17] give some indication of the requirements for market participation. Though involving human beings, some of these experiments have excluded most of the range of human abilities: they have excluded use of natural language (indeed, of any communications channel richer than simple bids and acceptances) and they have replaced goods with abstract tokens, excluding any cultural or historic information about their value. The participants in these markets have performed no sophisticated calculations and have lacked any knowledge of economic theory or of other players' preferences. Yet in this informationally-impoverished environment, these markets rapidly converge to the prices considered optimal by economic theory. Spencer Star [18] has successfully run double-auction markets among software entities employing simple decision procedures, and has achieved comparable efficiency.

Another reason for confidence in the applicability of market mechanisms to computation is the existence of primitive market mechanisms (outlined in this paper and presented in [III]) able to cope with such recognized software problems as garbage collection and processor scheduling. With evidence for the workability of market mechanisms both at this low level and at the sophisticated level of human society, there is reason to expect them to be workable at intermediate levels of sophistication as well.

### 3.7. Complexity and levels

Large computational ecosystems linked to the human market will have many parts, many aspects, many levels, and great complexity. Failure to recognize the differences among these levels will open many pitfalls. The field of biology suggests how to approach thinking about such systems.

Biological ecosystems obey physical law, but to understand them *as ecosystems* requires abstractions different from those used in physics. The existence of physics, chemistry, cell biology, physiology, and ecology as separate fields indicates that the concepts needed for understanding biological systems are naturally grouped according to the scale and complexity of phenomena to which they apply. Such a grouping may be called a *level*. Some issues arise repeatedly at different levels. For example, cells, organs, organisms, and hives all expend effort to maintain a boundary between their internal and external environments, and to bring only selected things across that boundary.

The concepts needed for understanding agoric open systems may likewise be grouped according to different levels, ranging from computational foundations through increasingly complex objects to market systems as a whole. As in biology, there are issues which appear in some form at all levels. Appendix I examines some of these issues, including security, compatibility, degrees of trust, reasoning, and coordination. In considering these issues in computational markets, it will be important to avoid misapplying concepts from one level to a very different level—that is, to avoid the equivalent of trying to analyze biological ecodynamics in terms of conservation of momentum.

The next three sections of this paper examine computational markets at successively higher levels, examining first foundations, then decision-making entities, and finally the emergent properties of large systems.

# 4. Foundations

Computation takes place in a context that determines what sorts of events can and cannot occur; this context can be viewed as the foundation of the rest of the system. Computational markets will require foundations that permit and forbid the right sorts of events. To simplify this discussion, the following explores foundations that provide for a basic uniformity in the nature of objects and their interactions despite differences in complexity and scale. In real systems, uniform foundations will ease the process of changing scale-dependent decisions and will make possible a unified set of conceptual and software tools spanning different scales.

It should be emphasized, however, that implementation of an agoric system will not demand adoption of a standard programming language. So long as certain constraints are met at the interfaces between objects coded by different parties, the language used inside an object can be freely chosen. The necessary constraints can be imposed by either the language or the operating system.

Computational foundations are frequently expressed in the form of programming language or operating system designs. Programming languages have evolved chiefly to provide abstractions for organizing computation on a small scale—the computation occurring inside a single machine and serving a single user. This has unfortunately led many programming language designers to make decisions (such as providing for global variables or access to arbitrary memory addresses) that make these languages unsuitable for organizing computation on a very large scale. The Actor languages, Argus, the concurrent logic programming languages (such as FCP), and the Mach operating system are examples of systems which have been designed to be extensible to large, open systems. These are covered in this book respectively in [IV], [V], [IV], and [VI]. All these projects have arrived at broadly similar models of computation from different directions, suggesting that their common elements will be of general value. This section briefly outlines some of the properties they share—properties which seem important for the implemention of computational markets.

## 4.1. Information and access

As indicated in Figure 2, the system capable of supporting open computation all share support for the encapsulation and communication of information and access. Communication of information is fundamental to computation that involves more than a single object. Encapsulation of information involves separating internal state and implementation from external behavior, preventing one object from examining or tampering with the contents of another.

In conventional practice, encapsulation of information increases modularity and conceptual clarity during design, a feature of considerable value. In agoric systems, though, secure encapsulation will be essential during operation. Without security against examination, theft of proprietary information would be rampant, and the rewards for the creation of valuable code

| | Encapsulation of: | | | Communication of: | | |
|---|---|---|---|---|---|---|
| | Information | Access | Resources | Information | Access | Resources |
| Dataflow, CSP, Occam | • | • | | • | | |
| Old Timesharing | • | • | • | • | | |
| Actors, FCP, Argus, Mach | • | • | | • | • | |
| Xanadu | | | • | • | • | • |
| FOCS | • | • | • | • | • | • |
| Agoric Systems | • | • | • | • | • | • |

*Figure 2: Comparison of foundations. CSP is the "Communicating Sequential Processes" language of C.A.R. Hoare [19]. Occam is a related language for the Transputer [20]. FCP is Flat Concurrent Prolog, a concurrent logic programming language [IV], [21]. FOCS [22] is an operating system concept designed for resource ownership and service provision. Xanadu [23] is a hypertext publishing system described briefly in Appendix II, "Comparison with other work".*

and information would be reduced or destroyed. Without security against tampering, objects could not trust each other's future behavior, or even their own. Encapsulation provides a sphere within which an object may act with complete control and predictability.

Encapsulation and communication of access—capability security—ensures that the ability to communicate with an object can only be obtained in certain ways, such as through deliberate communication. With capability security, object A can get access to object B only by:

(1) being born with it, when object A's creator already has that access;
(2) receiving it in a message (from an object that already has that access); or
(3) being the creator of object B.

Capability security is a common foundation for protection in operating systems. It appears to be a flexible and general mechanism able to support a wide variety of policies for providing access protection. In an open system without capability security, every object would have to verify the nature and legitimacy of every message it received, imposing unacceptable overhead on small, simple objects. With capability security, simple objects can "assume" that their messages come from legitimate sources, because their creators can implement policies that limit access to trusted parties.

Together, the above properties yield security while preserving flexibility. Despite the Turing-equivalence of most programming languages, they can nevertheless differ formally and absolutely in their ability to provide for security [25]. How can this be, if one can write an interpreter for a secure language in an insecure one?

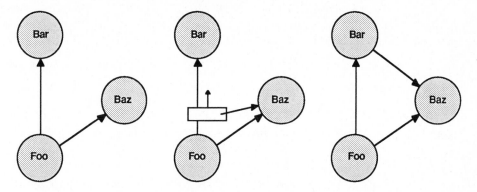

***Figure 3: Communication of access.*** *Foo sends a message to Bar contain-ing a copy of Foo's access to Baz. Upon receiving the message, Bar has access to Baz. (Adapted from [24].)*

Turing-equivalence describes the *abilities* of a system, but security rests on *inabilities*—on the inability to violate certain rules. Adding an interpreter on top of a system cannot subtract abilities from the system itself (even if the interpreted language consists of nothing but inabili-ties, as can easily be arranged). Thus, adding interpreters cannot establish the inabilities needed for security.

The question is not "what functions can be computed?", but "given that I am a computa-tional object, what is my relationship to an already populated computational environment?". Let us call a set of computational objects coded in an insecure programming language "refer-ence level objects", and those which exist on top of a reference-level interpreter "interpreted objects". If the interpreter implements a secure language, then the interpreted objects are pro-tected from each other. Reference level objects, however, can simply ignore the interpreter and wreak havoc on the interpreted objects.

### 4.2. Ownership and trade

As software systems have evolved toward greater modularity, encapsulation of informa-tion and access have become more clean, uniform, and reliable. As has been discussed, en-capsulation in software serves the same crucial function as property rights in human affairs: it establishes protected spheres in which entities can plan the use of their resources free of inter-ference from unpredictable external influences. This enables entities to plan and act despite the limited, local nature of most knowledge; it thus permits more effective use of divided know-ledge, aiding the division of labor. The value of protected spheres and local knowledge has thus far been the sole motivation for giving software modules "property rights" through encapsulation.

In economic systems, property rights also enable economic entities to accumulate and con-trol the results of their efforts, providing the basis for an incentive system having the desirable evolutionary properties outlined in [1]. In agoric systems, encapsulation will begin to serve this function as well.

Agoric systems also require the encapsulation and communication of computational resources, such as a memory block or a processor time slice. This prevents the evolution of parasitic objects [I], confines the costs of inefficiency to inefficient objects and their customers, and (in suitable implementations) makes performance information available locally. Encapsulation and communication of resources correspond to ownership and voluntary transfer, the basis of trade.

A familiar systems programming construct which violates encapsulation of resources is the round-robin scheduler. In such a scheduler, the amount of processing power allocated to a process depends simply on the number of other processes. The processing power allocated to a given process will be reduced whenever some other process decides to spawn yet more processes. Under a round-robin scheduler, the processor is treated as a commons; given a diversity of interests, the usual tragedy is to be expected [26].

Artsy's paper on "The Design of Fully Open Computing Systems" (FOCS) [22] discusses an approach for an operating system design having the desirable properties specified above. Artsy's use of the term "fully open computing systems" corresponds to what would here be termed "extreme separation of mechanism and policy", where the mechanism is the support of protected transfer of ownership and the verification of ownership on access. All other resource allocation is then provided as user-level policy. Thus, schedulers and memory allocators are completely outside the secure operating system kernel and operate via an ownership-and-trade model. One can, for example, own and trade time-slices of a particular processor. Scheduling is performed at the user level by exchanging such commodities.

Starting from direct ownership of physical computational resources, more abstract models of ownership can be built. For example, a deadline scheduler can be viewed as follows: When a task is to be scheduled in a hard real-time application (*i.e.,* one that must meet real-time deadlines), it should be known beforehand how long it will take and by what time it must be done. When a process wishes to insure that it will be able to schedule a set of such tasks, it can purchase "abstract future time slices"—not specific time slices, but rights to a time slice of a certain duration within a certain period. Since this gives the seller of time slices greater flexibility with respect to other clients, such time slices should cost less than concrete ones. This is like a futures market, but with guaranteed availability—an honest seller of time slices will not obligate himself to sell time slices he may not be able to get. (See also [27].)

### 4.3. Resource ownership and performance modularity

The activity of a running program may be analyzed in terms of *competence* and *performance*. Competence refers to what a program can do given sufficient resources, but without explicit consideration of these resources. Competence includes issues of *safety*—what the program will not do, and *liveness*—whether the program will eventually do what it is supposed to, or will instead infinitely loop or deadlock. Performance refers to the resources the program will use, the efficiency with which it will use them, and the time it will take to produce results—precisely those issues ignored by competence. Both these issues have been the subject of formal analysis: the competence aspects of a programming language may be formal-

|  | Formal Analysis | Modularity |
|---|---|---|
| Competence, Safety and Liveness | Semantics, Correctness proofs | Object-oriented programming, Message passing |
| Performance, Efficiency | Complexity theory, Proofs of response time | Computational markets, Prices |

*Figure 4: Markets and performance modularity. Issues of program competence and performance can be dealt with using the conceptual tools of formal analysis and modularity. Computational markets provide leverage for modularizing performance issues like that of object-oriented programming for competence issues.*

ized as a programming language semantics and used to analyze safety properties via proofs of partial correctness and liveness properties via proofs of termination. The performance aspects of a program may be formally analyzed via complexity theory and proofs of response time (for real-time programming).

Formalization alone, however, is insufficient for dealing with these issues in large programs—a complex non-modular program in a formalized language will often resist formal (or informal) validation of many important properties; modularity is needed to make analysis tractable. Modularization proceeds by separating interface from implementation, allowing concern with what a module *does* to be somewhat decoupled from concern with *how it does it*. Object-oriented programming and abstract data types aid modularization of competence issues, with message protocols serving as an abstract interface for competence effects [28]. Similarly, computational markets will aid modularization of performance issues, with prices serving as an abstract interface for resource costs.

### 4.4. Currency

For a broad market to emerge from these foundations, a system must provide for ownership and trade not only of basic computational resources, but also of virtual, user defined resources. Such resources can serve as tokens for establishing a system of currency. Public key communications systems [29] enable implemention of a secure banking system; within a mutually trusted hardware subsystem, capability-based security plus unforgeable unique identifiers are sufficient for establishing a public key system without resorting to encryption [25].

Accounting mechanisms have been used in software to some extent. Old time-sharing systems are one of the more familiar models—a fact which may raise grave concerns about the desirability of agoric systems. But using an agoric system would not mean a return to the bad old days of begging for a grant of hundreds of dollars of computer time and storage to edit a medium-sized document late at night, or to perform some now-inexpensive computation. The cost of computers has fallen. It will continue to fall, and personal computers will continue to spread. Aside from overhead (which can be made small), accounting for the costs of computation will not make computation more expensive. Making human beings pay for computer time is not the goal of computational markets.

In agoric systems, objects will charge each other and the machine will charge the objects. Given low enough communications costs and the right sorts of demand, a personal computer could earn money for its owner by serving others, instead of remaining idle. A machine's owner need not pay to use it, since the internal charges and revenues all balance. In a stand-alone computer, currency will simply circulate, incurring a computational overhead but providing internal accounting information which can guide internal decisions.

Inside one machine, one could have the foundations establish an official currency system. No secure way has yet been found to do so between mutually distrustful machines on a network without relying on mutually-trusted, third-party machines serving as banks. In accord with the goal of uniformity, such banks are here suggested as the general model for transfer of currency [25,30]. These banks can maintain accounts for two parties; when party A transfers money to party B, the bank can verify for B that the money has been transferred. (The cost of verification provides an incentive for A and B to establish enough trust to make frequent verification unnecessary.) In this model, it is unnecessary and perhaps impossible to establish any one currency as standard. There will instead be a variety of local currencies with exchange rates among them; it has been argued that this will result in greater monetary stability, and hence in a more efficient market, than one based on a single currency [31].

## 4.5. Open problems

At the foundational level, many open issues remain. Actors and FCP seem to be clean, simple open-systems programming languages, but they have no evident mechanism for dealing with machine failure. Argus is an open-systems language able to deal with this problem, but only by directly providing distributed abortable transactions as a basic mechanism. While such transactions provide much leverage, they are quite complex. A promising line of investigation is the design of a language having the simplicity of Actors or FCP, but which provides *mechanisms* for failure-handling that enable user-level *policy* to support Argus-style transactions. Even more satisfying than such a design would be a demonstration that Actors or FCP already have sufficient mechanism.

More central to agoric systems is adequate resource accounting. There is as yet no open-systems language which provides for ownership and trade of basic computational resources while preserving semantic uniformity and supporting the emergence of charging and prices. It seems this has been accomplished in the realm of operating systems design [22], but unfortunately in a way which is not yet amenable to distributed systems. It would be exciting to apply Artsy's work to open-systems oriented operating systems like Mach [IV].

# 5. Agents and strategies

When a problem needs to be solved frequently, but no single solution is right in all situations, it is desirable to permit the testing and use of many solutions. To allow this freedom, one seeks to separate mechanism and policy, designing foundations that support a wide range of policies via general-purpose mechanisms.

Foundational mechanisms for ownership and trade of information and computational resources allow the choice of policy to be delegated to individual objects; these objects may in turn delegate their choices to other objects, termed *agents*. Even policies for such fundamental processes as processor scheduling and memory allocation can be so delegated. The following argues that agents at a higher level can accomplish adaptive automatic data structure selection, guide sophisticated code transformation techniques, provide for competition among business agents, and maintain reputation information to guide competition.

## 5.1. Resource allocation and initial market strategies

Systems programming problems such as garbage collection and processor scheduling have traditionally been addressed in the computational foundations, casting the architect in the role of omniscient central planner. In this approach, the architect imposes a single, system-wide solution based on global aggregate statistics, precluding local choice. In the market approach, however, these problems can be recast in terms of local negotiation among objects. Solutions in this framework also provide objects with price information, allowing them to make profitable use of the resulting flexibility.

This enables programmers to provide objects with specialized resource allocation strategies, but it need not force programmers to attend to this. Objects can delegate these strategic issues to business agents, and a programming environment can provide default agents when the programmer does not specify otherwise.

The companion paper "Incentive Engineering for Computational Resource Management" [III] describes and analyzes *initial market strategies* which, if followed by a set of business agents, result in distributed algorithms for allocation of processor time, memory space, and communication channels. Initial market strategies (whether these or others) will play a key role in establishing agoric systems: from a traditional programming perspective, they will provide initial policies for garbage collection and processor scheduling; from a market perspective, they will help provide initial resource prices and thus an environment in which more sophisticated entities can begin to operate. Thus, they will help bridge the gap between current practice and computational markets. As markets evolve, the scaffolding provided by initial market strategies may be largely or entirely replaced by other structures.

The initial strategies for processor scheduling are based on an auction in which bids can be automatically escalated to ensure that they are eventually accepted. The initial strategies for memory allocation and garbage collection are based on rent payment, with objects paying retainer fees to objects they wish to retain in memory; objects that are unwanted and hence unable to pay rent are eventually evicted, deallocating their memory space. These approaches raise a variety of issues (including the threat of strategic instabilities stemming from public goods problems) that are addressed in our companion paper. Together, these strategies provide a proof of concept (or at least strong evidence of concept) for the notion of decentralized allocation of computational resources.

Initial market strategies will provide a programmable system that generates price information, enabling a wide range of choices to be made on economic grounds. For example, processor and memory prices can guide decisions regarding the use of memory to cache recomputable results. Given a rule for estimating the future rate of requests for a result, one should cache the result whenever the cost of storage for the result is less than the rate of requests times the cost of recomputing the result (neglecting a correction for the overhead of caching and caching-decisions). As demand for memory in a system rises, the memory price will rise, and these rules should free the less valuable parts of caches. If the processing price rises, caches should grow. Thus, prices favor tradeoffs through trade.

## 5.2. Business location decisions

Price information can guide a variety of other choices. Many of these resemble business location decisions.

Main "core" memory is a high-performance resource in short supply. Disk is a lower performance resource in more plentiful supply. In an agoric system, core memory will typically be a high-rent (business) district, while disk will typically be a low-rent (residential) district. Commuting from one to the other will take time and cost money. An object that stays in core will pay higher rent, but can provide faster service. To the degree that this is of value, the object can charge more; if increased income more than offsets the higher rent, the object will profit by staying in core. Treating choice of storage medium as a business location problem takes account of considerations—such as the relative value of prompt service—that traditional virtual memory algorithms do not express.

Small objects would have an incentive to "car-pool" in disk-page sized "vehicles". But given the issues described in Section 3.5, a typical object buying resources on the market may occupy many pages. Instead of deciding whether it should be completely in or out of core, such an object might decide how many of its pages should be part of an in-core working set, perhaps relying on a traditional algorithm [32] to dynamically select the in-core pages.

The variety of types of memory also suggests a need for more flexibility than the traditional two-level approach provides. The many kinds of memory differ in many ways: consider fast RAM cache, write-once optical disk, and tape archived in multiple vaults. Memory systems differ with respect to:

- Latency
- Storage cost
- Access cost
- Reliability

- Transfer rate
- Locality structure
- Predictability of access time
- Security

Tradeoffs will change as technology changes. To be portable and viable across these changes, programs must be able to adapt.

Much has been written about the need to migrate objects in a distributed system in order to improve locality of reference [30,33,34]. Again, this resembles the problem of choosing a business location. Machines linked by networks resemble cities linked by highways. Different locations have different levels of demand, different business costs, and different travel and communications costs. Various traditional approaches correspond to:

- staying put and using the phone (as in Mach [VI] and the V kernel [35]),
- commuting to wherever the momentary demand is (as in Apollo [36]),
- moving only when there are no local customers (as in the Bishop algorithm [37]),
- coordinating multiple offices (as in Grapevine [38] and in [39]),
- and moving where labor costs are lower (load balancing, as in [40]).

If limited to any one of these methods, human societies would suffer terrible inefficiencies. One expects the same for large, diverse software systems. If a system's mechanisms support a range of policies, different objects can select different approaches.

The notion of location in a space is still rare in object-oriented programming (for an exception see [41]). All memory in an ideal von Neumann computer is effectively equidistant, and many real computers approximate this ideal, but in a widely distributed system, differing distances are of real importance. When objects are given an account of the costs of communicating and commuting, they gain a useful notion of distance for making economic decisions.

### 5.3. Business agents

In a market containing sophisticated, potentially malicious objects, how can simple objects hope to negotiate, compete, and survive? One answer would be to shelter simple, mutually-trusting objects within large, sophisticated objects, building the latter out of the former. This model, however, would preclude turning loose small objects as service-providers on the open market. Other means are required for giving small objects the market sophistication they need.

Just as delegation of tasks to other objects can enable a small, simple object to offer sophisticated services, so delegation can enable it to engage in sophisticated market behavior. In this work's terminology, an object can delegate competence-domain actions to a *subcontractor;* this corresponds to the normal practice of hierarchical decomposition, which originated with the subroutine. An object can likewise delegate performance-domain actions to an *agent;* this seems likely to be a normal practice in agoric systems. Simple objects then can make their way in a complex world by being born with service relationships to sophisticated agents (which themselves can be composed of simple objects, born with...). Initially, human decisions will establish these relationships; later, specialized agent-providing agents can establish them as part of the process of creating new economic objects. The initial market strategies mentioned in Section 5.1 could be provided by simple agents.

One might object that a simple object and its collection of agents together constitute a complex object. But these objects, though complex in the performance domain, can remain extremely simple in the competence domain. Further, large agents need not burden a simple object with enormous costs; in general a large number of objects would share the agents and their overhead. The object-and-agent approach thus can enable entities of simple competence to compete in the open market.

### 5.3.1. Data-type agents

In object-oriented programming, one can supply multiple implementations of an abstract data type, all providing the same service through the same protocol, but offering different performance tradeoffs [28]. An example is the lookup table, which may be implemented as an array, linked list, hash table, B-tree, associative memory, or as any of several other devices or data structures. In an object-oriented system, code which *uses* such an abstract data type is itself generally abstract, being independent of how the data type is implemented; this provides valuable flexibility. In contrast, code which *requests an instance* of such an abstract data type is usually less abstract, referring directly to a class which provides a particular implementation of that type. The resulting code embodies decisions regarding implementation tradeoffs in a relatively scattered, frozen form.

In a market, agents can unfreeze these decisions: instantiation requests can be sent to a data-type agent, which then provides a suitable subcontractor. In human markets, someone seeking a house can consult a real-estate agent. The real-estate agent specializes in knowing what is available, what tradeoffs are important, and what to ask clients regarding those tradeoffs. Similarly, a lookup table agent could know what lookup table implementations are available, what tradeoffs they embody, and (implicitly, through its protocol) what to ask clients regarding those tradeoffs (*e.g.,* a request might indicate "I will often be randomly indexing into the table"). The agent could also "ask questions" by providing a trial lookup table that gathers usage statistics: once a pattern becomes clear, the agent can transparently switch to a more appropriate implementation. Long term, sporadic sampling of usage patterns can provide a low-overhead mechanism for alerting the agent to needed changes in implementation.

An agent can do more. For example, the relative price of memory and processor time may vary with the time of day or with the state of technology; depending on the cost of different implementations and the cost of switching among them, a change may be profitable. Likewise, the table-user may desire faster responses; again, a change may be profitable.

If a newly-invented lookup table implementation is superior for some uses, it could be advertised (by its advertising agent) to prominent lookup table agents. "Advertising" could include paying these agents to test its performance under different patterns of use, enabling them to determine which of their clients could benefit from switching to it. The new table would soon be used by programs that were coded without knowledge of it, and which started running prior to its creation.

Unrelated agents can interact synergistically. Consider the case of a lookup table with distinct read and write ports and distributed users. As long as there are writers, this lookup table chooses to exist on only one machine (in order to preserve serializable semantics without the complexity of distributed updates). This implementation imposes substantial delays and communication costs on the readers: if all objects dropped access to its write port, the lookup table could transmit static copies of itself to all readers, lowering these costs. The table can represent this cost by charging an artificially high retainer fee for the write port, giving users

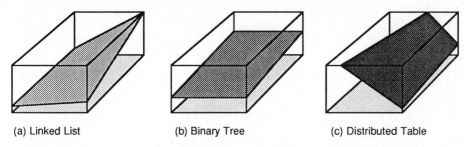

| (a) Linked List | (b) Binary Tree | (c) Distributed Table |

*Figure 5: Lookup table tradeoffs. Graphs (a), (b), and (c) show processing costs for hypothetical implementations of a lookup table serving multiple sites (see 5(d) below for graph axes). Each puts key-value associations, and gets the value associated with a given key. The average processing cost of a request depends on the mix of get and put operations, and the number of associations stored. Figure 5(a) shows a linked-list implementation which puts in constant time, but gets using a linear search. Figure 5(b) shows a balanced binary tree whose costs scale as the log of the number of associations. Both 5(a) and 5(b) are centralized data structures—a table exists at only one site and all requests must travel there, adding constant overhead. Figure 5(c) shows a distributed table, replicated at each client site: gets are inexpensive, requiring no external communication, but puts are costly, requiring locking, updating, and unlocking all copies of the table.*

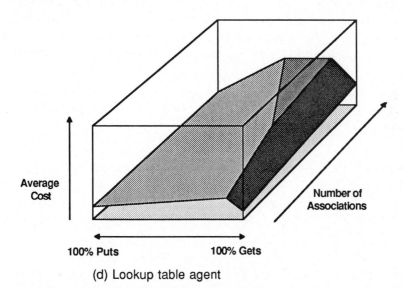

(d) Lookup table agent

*Figure 5(d): Lookup table agent. Given the above choices, clients with differing patterns of use should patronize different implementations. Figure 5(d) shows costs given that a client always makes the minimum-cost choice. An ideal lookup table agent can present this cost function (plus a small cost for expenses and profit margin), relieving the client of the need make this choice.*

an incentive to drop this capability and permit a shift to the less expensive implementation. This illustrates how local economic decisions can encourage appropriate performance tradeoffs involving such distinct aspects of the system as garbage collection, network traffic, and representation of data structures.

Given sufficiently powerful partial-evaluation agents [42], a data-type agent could offer to extend an object with a new protocol. For example, the user of a lookup table might frequently look up the values of the first N entries following a particular key. Rather than doing so by running a procedure using the existing protocol, it could offer to pay for partially evaluating the procedure with respect to the lookup table, and add a lookup-next-N request to the table's protocol. This would typically make servicing such requests more efficient; a portion of the resulting savings could paid as dividends to the object that invested in the partial evaluation.

### 5.3.2. Managers

Different agents of the same type will have different reputations and pricing structures, and they will compete with each other. An object must select which of these agents to employ. Just as an object may employ a lookup table agent to decide which lookup table to employ, so an object may employ an agent-selection agent to decide which agent to employ. Agent-selection agents are also in competition with each other, but this need not lead to an infinite regress: for example, an object can be born with a fixed agent-selection agent. The system as a whole remains flexible, since different objects (or versions of a single object) will use different agent-selection agents. Those using poor ones will tend to be eliminated by competition.

A generalization of the notion of an agent-selection agent is that of a manager. In addition to the functions already outlined, a manager can set prices, select subcontractors, and negotiate contracts. To select good agents and subcontractors, manager-agents will need to judge reputations.

### 5.3.3. Reputations

A reputation system may be termed *positive* if it is based on seeking objects expected to provide good service, and *negative* if it is based on avoiding those expected to provide bad service. Negative reputation systems fail if effective pseudonyms are cheaply available; positive reputation systems, however, require only that one entity cannot claim the identity of another, a condition met by the identity properties of actors [4,43] and public key systems [29]. Accordingly, computational markets are expected to rely on positive reputation systems.

It would seem that new objects could not acquire positive reputations ("Sorry, you can't get the job unless you show you've done it before."), but they need not have *given* good service to make one *expect* good service. For example, a new object can give reason to expect good service—thereby establishing a positive reputation—by posting a cash bond guaranteeing good performance. (This requires, of course, that both parties to the contract trust some third parties to hold the bond and to judge performance.) Despite the idea that software entities cannot make commitments [44], contracts with enforceable penalty clauses provide a way for them to do so.

The demand for reputation information will provide a market for reputation services, analogous to credit rating agencies, investment newsletters, Underwriters Laboratories, the Better Business Bureau, and *Consumer Reports*. When the correctness and quality of the service can be judged, it seems that an effective reputation service could work as follows. A reputation server approaches a service provider, offering money for service. (The server funds these purchases by selling information about the results.) The reputation agent has an incentive to appear to be a regular customer (to get an accurate sample), and regular customers have an incentive to appear to be reputation agents (to get high quality service). A restaurant reviewer has been quoted as saying "If someone claims to be me, he's not!" [45]. Given unforgeable identities, the best either can do is maintain anonymity. Service providers then have an incentive to provide *consistently* good service, since their reputation might be at stake at any time. This scenario generalizes to tests of reputation services themselves.

### 5.3.4. Compilation

Tradeoffs in compilation can often be cast in economic terms. For example, the best choice in a time-space tradeoff will depend on processor and memory costs, and on the value of a prompt result. Another tradeoff is between computation invested in transforming code *versus* that spent in running the code; this is particularly important in guiding the often computation-intensive task of partial evaluation.

Investment in code transformation is much like other investments in an economy: it involves estimates of future demand, and hence cannot be made by a simple, general algorithm. In a computational market, compilation speculators can estimate demand, invest in program transformations, and share in the resulting savings. Some will overspend and lose investment capital; others will spend in better-adapted ways. Overall, resources will flow toward investors following rules that are well-adapted to usage patterns in the system, thereby allocating resources more effectively. This is an example of the subtlety of evolutionary adaptation: nowhere need these patterns be explicitly represented.

Current programming practice typically sacrifices a measure of structural simplicity and modularity for the sake of efficiency. Some recent compilation technologies [42,46] can make radical, non-local transformations that change not only performance, but complexity measure. Use of such technology could free programmers to concentrate on abstraction and semantics, allowing the structure of the code to more directly express the structure of the problem. This can reduce the tension between modularity and efficiency.

As we later argue, computational markets will encourage the creation of reusable, high-quality modules adapted for composition into larger objects. The resulting composite objects will typically have components paying dividends to different investors, however, imposing internal accounting overhead. Again, there is a tension with efficiency, and again it can be reduced by means of compilation technology. Much compilation involves (invisibly) "violating" internal boundaries—compiling well-separated components into a complex, non-modular piece of code. In an agoric system, a compilation-agent can do the same, while also analyzing and compiling out the overhead of run-time accounting.

A *Pareto-preferred compiler* is one which performs this transformation so as to guarantee that some component will be better off and none will be worse off. This can be achieved even if the resulting division of income only approximates the original proportions, since the total savings from compilation will result in a greater total income to divide. The expectation of Pareto-preferred results is enough to induce objects to submit to compilation; since multiple results can meet this condition, however, room will remain for negotiation.

### 5.4. The scandal of idle time

Current resource allocation policies leave much to be desired. One sign of this is that most computing resources—including CPUs, disk heads, local area networks, and much more—sit idle most of the time. But such resources have obvious uses, including improving their own efficiency during later use. For example, heavily-used programs can be recompiled through optimizing compilers or partial evaluators; pages on disk can be rearranged to keep files contiguous; objects can be rearranged according to referencing structure to minimize paging [47], and so forth. In a computational market, a set of unused resources would typically have a zero or near-zero price of use, reflecting only the cost of whatever power consumption or maintenance could be saved by genuine idleness or complete shutdown. Almost any use, however trivial, would then be profitable. In practice, contention for use would bid up prices until they reflected the marginal value of use [5]. Idle time is a blatant sign of wasteful resource allocation policies; one suspects that it is just the tip of a very large iceberg.

Terry Stanley [48] has suggested a technique called "post-facto simulation" as a use of idle (or inexpensive) time. It enables a set of objects to avoid the overhead of fine-grained accounting while gaining many of its advantages. While doing real work, they do no accounting and make no attempt to adapt to internal price information; instead, they just gather statistics (at low overhead) to characterize the computation. Later, when processing is cheap and response time demands are absent (*i.e.,* at "night"), they simulate the computation (based on the statistics), but with fine-grained accounting turned on. To simulate the day-time situation, they do not charge for the overhead of this accounting, and proceed using simulated "day" prices. The resulting decisions (regarding choice of data structures, use of partial evaluation, *etc.*) should improve performance during future "days". This is analogous to giving your best real-time response during a meeting, then reviewing it slowly afterward: by considering what you should have done, you improve your future performance.

## 6. Agoric systems in the large

In describing the idea of market-based computation and some of its implications, this paper has implicitly focused on relatively isolated systems of software performing relatively conventional functions. The following examines two broader issues: how market-based computation could interact with existing markets for software, and how it could be relevant to the goal of artificial intelligence.

## 6.1. Software distribution markets

An agoric open system would provide a computational world in which simple objects can sell services and earn royalties for their creators. This will provide incentives that differ from those of the present world, leading to qualitative differences in software markets.

### 6.1.1. Charge-per-use markets

> Perhaps the central problem we face in all of computer science is how we are to get to the situation where we build on top of the work of others rather than redoing so much of it in a trivially different way.
>
> —R. W. Hamming, 1968 [49]

Consider the current software distribution marketplace. Producers typically earn money by charging for copies of their software (and put up with extensive illegal copying). Occasional users must pay as much for software as intense users. Software priced for intense users is expensive enough to discourage purchase by occasional users—even if their uses would be of substantial value to them. Further, high purchase prices discourage many potentially frequent users from trying the software in the first place. (Simply lowering prices would not be more efficient if this lowers revenues for the sellers: with lower expected revenue, less software would be written, including software for which there is a real demand.)

Now consider trying to build and sell a simple program which uses five sophisticated programs as components. Someone might buy it just to gain access to one of its components. How large a license fee, then, should the owners of those components be expected to charge the builder of this simple program? Enough to make the new program cost at least the sum of the costs of the five component programs. Special arrangements might be made in special circumstances, but at the cost of having people judge and negotiate each case. When one considers the goal of building systems from reusable software components, with complex objects making use of one another's services [50], this tendency to sum costs becomes pathological. The peculiar incentive structure of a charge-per-copy market may have been a greater barrier to achieving Hamming's dream than the more obvious technical hurdles.

In hardware markets, it can be better to charge for the use of a device than to sell a copy of it to the user:

> Why was [the first Xerox copier] so successful? Two thing contributed to the breakthrough, McColough says. . .technical superiority. . .and equally important, the marketing genius of the pricing concept of selling [the use of the copier], not machines. 'One aspect without the other wouldn't have worked,' he said. '. . .we couldn't sell the machines outright because they would have been too expensive.'
>
> —Jacobson and Hillkirk, 1986 [51]

Agoric systems will naturally support a charge-per-use market for software. In any market, software producers will attempt to extract substantial charges from high-volume users. With charge per use, however, the charges to be paid by high-volume users will no longer stand in the way of low-volume users; as a result, they will use expensive software that they could not afford today. At the same time, high-volume users will experience a finite marginal price for using software, rather than buying it and paying a zero marginal price for using it; they will cut back on some of their marginal, low-value uses. The overall benefit of numerous low-volume users making high-value use of the software will likely outweigh the loss associated with a few high-volume users cutting back on their low-value uses, yielding a net social benefit. It seems likely that some of this benefit will appear as increased revenues to software producers, encouraging increased software production.

In a charge-per-copy market, users face an incentive structure in which they pay nothing to keep using their present software, but must pay a large lump sum if they decide to switch to a competitor. A charge-per-use market will eliminate this artificial barrier to change, encouraging more lively competition among software producers and better adaptation of software to user needs.

By enabling small objects to earn royalties for their creators, charge-per-use markets will encourage the writing, use, and reuse of software components—to do so will finally be profitable. Substantial improvement in programming productivity should result; these improvements will multiply the advantages just described.

### 6.1.2. Hardware encapsulation

This charge-per-use scenario presents a major technical problem: it depends on the ability to truly protect software from illicit copying. True encapsulation would ensure this, but true encapsulation will require a hardware foundation that blocks physical attacks on security. Two approaches seem feasible: either keeping copies in just a few secure sites and allowing access to their services over a network, or developing a technology for providing users with local secure sites to which software can migrate.

In the limit of zero communication costs (in terms of money, delay, and bandwidth limitations), the disincentive for remote computation would vanish. More generally, lower communication costs will make it more practical for objects located on remote machines to offer services to objects on user machines. Remote machines can provide a hardware basis for secure encapsulation and copy protection—they can be physically secured, in a vault if need be. This approach to security becomes more attractive if software can be partitioned into public-domain front-ends (which engage in high-bandwidth interaction with a user), and proprietary back-ends (which perform sophisticated computations), and if bandwidth requirements between front- and back-ends can be minimized.

One system that might lend itself to this approach is an engineering service [13]. The user's machine would hold software for the representation, editing, and display of hardware designs. The back-end system—perhaps an extensive market ecosystem containing objects of diverse functionality and ownership—would provide computation-intensive numerical modeling of designs, heuristics-applying objects (perhaps resembling expert systems) for suggesting and evaluating modifications, and so forth.

Two disadvantages of separating front- and back-ends in this way are communications cost and response time. If hardware encapsulation can be provided on the local user's machine, however, software can migrate there (in encrypted form) and provide services on-site. Opaque boxes are a possible design for such secure hardware:

Imagine a box containing sensors and electronics able to recognize an attempt to violate the box's integrity [52]. In addition, the box contains a processor, dynamic RAM, and a battery. In this RAM is the private key of the manufacturer's public-key encryption key pair [29]; objects encrypted with the public key can migrate to the box and be decrypted internally. If the box detects an attempt to violate its physical integrity, it wipes the dynamic RAM (physically destructive processes are acceptable), deleting the private key and all other sensitive data. All disk storage is outside the box (fast-enough disk erasure would be too violent), so software and other data must be encrypted when written and decrypted when read. The box is termed *opaque* because no one can see its contents.

Internally, the opaque box would require encapsulation among software objects. This can be done by using a secure operating system [VI], by using capability hardware [53,54,55], or by demanding that objects be written in a secure programming language and either run under a secure interpreter or compiled by a secure compiler [IV,56]. Among other objects, the box would contain one or more branches of external banks, linked to them from time to time by encrypted communications; these banks would handle royalty payments for use of software.

Will greater hardware cost make opaque boxes uncompetitive for personal computer systems? If the added cost is not too many hundreds of dollars, the benefit—greater software availability—will be far greater, for many users. Opaque boxes can support a charge-per-use market in which *copies* of software are available for the cost of telecommunications. CD-ROMs full of encrypted software might be sold at a token cost to encourage use.

An intermediate approach becomes attractive if opaque boxes are too expensive for use as personal machines. Applications could be split into front and back-ends as above, but back-ends could run on any available opaque box. These boxes could be located wherever there is sufficient demand, and linked to personal machines via high-bandwidth local networks. People (or software) would find investment in opaque boxes profitable, since their processors would earn revenue. With high enough box-manufacturing costs, this approach merges into the remote-machine scenario; with low enough costs, it merges into the personal-machine scenario.

### 6.1.3. Inhibiting theft

As society embodies more and more of its knowledge and capabilities in software, the theft of this software becomes a growing danger. An environment that encourages the creation of large, capable, stand-alone applications sold on a charge-per-copy basis magnifies this problem, particularly when the stolen software will be used in places beyond the reach of copyright law.

A charge-per-use environment will reduce this problem. It will encourage the development of software systems that are composites of many proprietary packages, each having its security guarded by its creator. Further, it will encourage the creation of systems that are distributed over many machines. The division and distribution of functions will make the problem faced by a thief less like that of stealing a car and more like that of stealing a railroad. Traditional methods of limiting theft (such as military classification) slow progress and inhibit use; computational markets promise to discourage theft while speeding progress and facilitating use.

### 6.1.4. Integration with the human market

It has been shown how an agoric system would use price mechanisms to allocate use of hardware resources among objects. This price information will also support improved decisions regarding hardware purchase: if the market price of a resource inside the system is consistently above the price of purchasing more of the resource on the external market, then incremental expansion is advantageous. Indeed, one can envision scenarios in which software objects recognize a need for new hardware, lease room for it, and buy it as an investment.

It has been shown how objects in an agoric system would serve human needs, with human minds judging their success. Similarly, when objects are competent to judge success, they can hire humans to serve their needs—for example, to solve a problem requiring human knowledge or insight.

Conway's law states that "Organizations which design systems are constrained to produce systems which are copies of the communications structures of these organizations" (from [57] as quoted in [58]). If so, then software systems developed in a distributed fashion can be expected to resemble the organization of society as a whole. In a decentralized society coordinated by market mechanisms, agoric systems are a natural result.

### 6.2. The marketplace of mind

Artificial intelligence is unnecessary for building an agoric open system and achieving the benefits described here. Building such a system may, however, speed progress in artificial intelligence. Feigenbaum's statement, "In the knowledge lies the power", points out that intelligence is knowledge-intensive; the "knowledge acquisition bottleneck" is recognized as a major hindrance to AI. Stefik has observed [VII] that this knowledge is distributed across society; he calls for a "knowledge medium" in which knowledge contributed by many people could be combined to achieve greater overall intelligence.

Agoric systems should form an attractive knowledge medium. In a large, evolving system, where the participants have great but dispersed knowledge, an important principle is: "In the incentive structure lies the power". In particular, the incentives of a distributed, charge-per-use market can widen the knowledge engineering bottleneck by encouraging people to create chunks of knowledge and knowledge-based systems that work together.

Approaches based on directly buying and selling knowledge [VII,23] suffer from the peculiar incentives of a charge-per-copy market. This problem can be avoided by embodying knowledge in objects which sell knowledge-based services, not knowledge itself. In this way, a given piece of knowledge can be kept proprietary for a time, enabling producers to charge users fees that approach the value the users place on it. This provides an incentive for people to make the knowledge available. But in the long run, the knowledge will spread and competition will drive down the price of the related knowledge-based services—approaching the computational cost of providing them.

Agoric open systems can encourage the development of intelligent objects, but there is also a sense in which the systems themselves will become intelligent. Seeing this entails distinguishing between the idea of *intelligence* and the ideas of individuality, consciousness, and will. Consider the analogous case of human society.

It can be argued that the most intelligent system now known is human society as a whole. This assertion strikes some people as obvious, but others have a strong feeling that society should be considered less intelligent than an individual person. What might be responsible for these conflicting views?

The argument for the stupidity of society often focuses not on the achievements of society, but on its suboptimal structure or its slow rate of structural change. This seems unfair. Human brains are presumably suboptimal, and their basic structure has changed at a glacial pace over the broad time spans of biological evolution, yet no one argues that society is worse-structured than a brain (what would this mean?), or that its basic structure changes more slowly than that of a brain. Great intelligence need not imply optimal structure, and suboptimal structure does not imply stupidity.

Other arguments for the stupidity of society focus on the behavior of committees, or crowds, or electorates. This also seems unfair. Human beings include not only brains but intestines; our intelligence is not to be judged by the behavior of the latter. Not all parts need be intelligent for a system to be so. Yet other arguments focus on things individuals can do that groups cannot, but one might as well argue that Newton was stupid because he did not speak Urdu. A final argument for the stupidity of society focuses on problems that result when a few individuals who are thought to somehow *represent* society attempt to direct the actions of the vast number of individuals who actually *compose* society—that is, the problems of central planning, government, and bureaucracy. This statement of the argument seems an adequate refutation of it.

The argument for society's intelligence is simple: people of diverse knowledge and skills, given overall guidance by the incentives of a market system, can accomplish a range of goals which, if accomplished by an individual, would make that individual a super-human super-genius. The computer industry is a small part of society, yet what individual could equal its accomplishments, or the breadth and speed of its ongoing problem-solving ability?

Still, it is legitimate to ask what it means to speak of the "intelligence" of a diverse, distributed system. In considering an individual, one commonly identifies intelligence with the ability to achieve a wide range of goals through complex information processing. But in agoric systems, as in human society, the component entities will in general have diverse goals, and the system as a whole will typically have no goals [59]. Nonetheless, a similar concept of intelligence can be applied to individuals, societies, and computational markets.

Individuals taking intelligence tests are judged by their ability to achieve goals set by a test-giver using time provided for the purpose. Likewise, the intelligence of a society may be judged by its ability to achieve goals set by individuals, using resources provided for the purpose. In either case, the nature and degree of intelligence may be identified with a combination of the *range* of goals that can be achieved, the speed with which they can be achieved, and the efficiency of the means employed. By this measure, one may associate kinds and degrees of intelligence not only with individuals, but with corporations, with *ad-hoc* collections of suppliers and subcontractors, and with the markets and institutions that bring such collections together at need. *The idea of intelligence may thus be separated from the ideas of individuality, consciousness, and will.*

The notion of intelligence emerging from social interactions is familiar in artificial intelligence: Minsky [60] uses the society metaphor in his recent work on thinking and the mind; Kornfeld and Hewitt [61] use the scientific community as a model for programs incorporating due process reasoning [II]. Human societies demonstrate how distributed pieces of knowledge and competence can be integrated into larger, more comprehensive wholes; this process has been a major study of economics [8] and sociology [63]. Because these social processes (unlike those in the brain) involve the sometimes-intelligible interaction of visible, macroscopic entities, they lend themselves to study and imitation. This paper may thus be seen as proposing a form of multi-agent, societal approach to artificial intelligence.

## 7. The absence of agoric systems

Market-style software systems are a fairly obvious idea and have received some attention. However, in considering any fairly-obvious idea with (allegedly) great but unrealized potential, it is wise to ask why that potential has in fact not been realized. When an idea of this sort neither lends itself to formal proof nor to small, convincing demonstrations, the difficulty of making a case for it grows. Support from abstract arguments and analogies can be helpful, as can an examination of the practical issues involved. But in addition, it helps to see whether the idea has been tested and found wanting. Considering this major category of possible negative evidence is an aspect of due-process reasoning.

Why have agoric open systems not been implemented already? In part, because the software community has lacked an immediate, compelling need. Advances have been made, through better programming environments and methodologies (including the encapsulation and communication of information and access), and through tools for making larger structures visible to programmers [64]—all without building markets. These environments and methodologies have extended the programmer's conceptual span of control, enabling one mind or a few closely-coordinated, mutually-trusting minds to build ever larger and more complex programs. These advances have decreased the urgency of enabling extensive cooperation *without* mutual trust or extensive communications.

Another problem has been the scale-sensitivity of the market approach. In small systems, the overhead of accounting and negotiations is unjustified; further, incremental increases in scale have thus far been possible without markets. Robust service-trading objects must have a certain minimum complexity, or have access to trusted business-agents of a certain minimum complexity. The virtues of markets are greatest in large, diverse systems.

There has, perhaps, also been a cultural factor at work. Large, research-oriented computer networks have focused on academic and government work—that is, toward non-profit use. Further, the academic community already has an informal incentive structure that rewards the creators of useful software in an incremental way, in rough proportion to its usefulness. These reputation-based reward mechanisms facilitate the development of software systems that build on others' work; the differing incentives in the commercial community may be responsible for its greater tendency to build redundant systems from scratch.

These considerations seem sufficient to explain the lack of agoric systems today, while giving reason to expect that they will become desirable as computer systems and networks grow. In the large, open, evolving software systems of the future, the overhead of accounting will be less important than robustness and flexibility. Further, the development of automated programming systems will introduce "programmers" having (initially) a sharply limited ability to plan and comprehend. This will re-emphasize the problem of the "programmer's" span of conceptual control, and increase the need for mechanisms that strengthen localization and system robustness.

## 8. Conclusions

A central challenge of computer science is the coordination of complex systems. In the early days of computation, central planning—at first, by individual programmers—was inevitable. As the field has developed, new techniques have supported greater decentralization and better use of divided knowledge. Chief among these techniques has been object-oriented programming, which in effect gives property rights in data to computational entities. Further advance in this direction seems possible.

Experience in human society and abstract analysis in economics both indicate that market mechanisms and price systems can be surprisingly effective in coordinating actions in complex systems. They integrate knowledge from diverse sources; they are robust in the face of experimentation; they encourage cooperative relationships; and they are inherently parallel in operation. All these properties are of value not just in society, but in computational systems: markets are an abstraction that need not be limited to societies of talking primates.

This paper has examined many of the concrete issues involved in actually creating computational markets, from hardware and software foundations, to initial market strategies for resource management (chiefly in [III]), to the organization of systems of objects and agents able to interact in a market context. As yet, no obstacle to their realization has been found.

Distributed systems based on the charge-per-use sale of software services and computational resources promise a more flexible and effective software market, in which large systems will more often be built from pre-existing parts. With many minds building knowledge and competence into market objects, and with incentives favoring cooperation among these objects, the overall problem-solving ability of the system can be expected to grow rapidly.

On a small scale, central planning makes sense; on a larger scale, market mechanisms make sense. Computer science began in a domain where central planning made sense, and central planning has thus been traditional. It seems likely, however, that some modern computer systems are already large and diverse enough to benefit from decentralized market coordination. As systems grow in scale and complexity, so will the advantages of market-based computational systems.

## Appendix I. Issues, levels, and scale

This appendix explores how various computational issues change character from lower to higher levels of a system (in the sense described in Section 3.7). Agoric open systems can most easily be developed by building up from current systems—by finding ways to make a smooth transition from current programming practice to the practices appropriate to market ecosystems. (One aspect of this is dealt with in [III].) Understanding how issues will change from level to level will aid this process and minimize the chance of misapplying concepts from one level to problems on another level.

Higher levels of organization will raise issues not so much of system correctness as of system coherence. For example, while a sorting algorithm may be *correct* or *incorrect,* a large collection of software tools may be *coherent* or *incoherent*—its parts may work together well or poorly, even if all are individually correct. The notion of coherence presumes a level of complexity that makes it inapplicable to a sorting algorithm. Despite the differences between correctness and coherence, they have much in common: correctness can be seen as a formal version of coherence, one appropriate for small-scale objects. In this, as in many of the following issues, hard-edged criteria at lower levels of organization have soft-edged counterparts at higher levels.

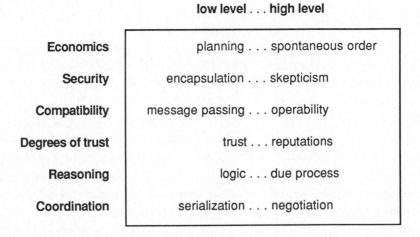

| | low level . . . high level |
| --- | --- |
| **Economics** | planning . . . spontaneous order |
| **Security** | encapsulation . . . skepticism |
| **Compatibility** | message passing . . . operability |
| **Degrees of trust** | trust . . . reputations |
| **Reasoning** | logic . . . due process |
| **Coordination** | serialization . . . negotiation |

*Figure 6: Changes in character of issues across levels.*

## I.1. Security

Alan Kay has characterized compatibility, security, and simplicity as essential properties for building open systems. For mutually untrusting objects to interact willingly, they must be secure. Encapsulation can provide security at a low level, as a formal property of computation. With this property, one can code an object so that the integrity of an internal data structure is guaranteed despite possible nonsense messages. Security at a high level involves skepticism and the establishment of effective reputation systems. Skepticism enables an object to continue reasoning coherently despite being told occasional lies.

Encapsulation—in this case, protection against tampering—is necessary for skepticism to work. Without encapsulation, a skeptical object's intellectual defenses could be overcome by the equivalent of brain surgery.

## I.2. Compatibility

Compatibility allows objects to be mutually intelligible, despite diverse origins. At a foundational level, it involves a shared message passing medium and mutual understanding of some protocol. Inside a small program written by a single programmer, objects can be carefully crafted so that any two that communicate will necessarily use the same protocol. Between large objects written by different people, or the same person at different times, checking for protocol agreement can frequently prevent disaster. For example, if an object is passed a reference to a lookup table when it is expecting a number, it may help to learn that "addition" will not be understood by the table before actually attempting it. Note that this itself relies on agreement on a basic protocol which provides a language for talking about other protocols.

In the Xerox Network System, clients and servers not only compare the type of protocol that they can speak, but the range of protocol versions that they understand [65]. If their ranges overlap, they then speak the latest mutually understood version. If their ranges do not overlap, they then part and go their separate ways. This is an example of bootstrapping from a mutually understood protocol to determine the intelligibility of other protocols. The developing field of interoperability [66] should soon provide many more.

Sophisticated objects should eventually have still broader abilities. Human beings, when faced with a novel piece of equipment, can often learn to make profitable use of unfamiliar capabilities. Among the techniques they use are experimentation, reading documentation, and asking a consultant. One may eventually expect computational analogues [67].

## I.3. Degrees of trust

Security is needed where trust is lacking, but security involves overhead; this provides an incentive for trust. At a low level, a single author can create a community of trusting objects. At an intermediate level trust becomes more risky because error becomes more likely. This encourages error-checking at internal interfaces, as is wise when a team of programmers (or one forgetful programmer) must assemble separately developed modules.

At higher levels, strategic considerations can encourage partial trust. A set of objects may make up a larger object, where the success of each depends on the success of all. Here, objects may trust each other to further their joint effort [68]. Axelrod's iterated prisoner's dilemma tournament [69] (see also [I]) shows another way in which strategic considerations can give rise to trust. One object can generally expect cooperative behavior from another if it can arrange (or be sure of) appropriate incentives.

In a simple iterated prisoner's dilemma game, this requires both having a long-term relationship and paying the overhead of noticing and reacting to non-cooperative behavior. Reputation systems within a community can extend this principle and lower the overhead of using it. Some objects can gather and sell information on another object's past performance: this both provides incentives for consistently good performance and reduces the cost of identifying and avoiding bad performers. In effect, reputation systems can place an object in an iterated relationship with the community as a whole.

The idea that encapsulation is needed at low levels for security, where we also expect complete trust seems to entail a conflict. But the function of encapsulation is to protect simple objects where trust is limited or absent (as it will be, between some pairs of objects). Complete trust makes sense among simple objects that are in some sense playing on the same team.

## I.4. Reasoning

Programming language research has benefited from the methodology of formalizing programming language semantics. A result is the ability to reason confidently (and mechanistically) about the properties of programs expressed in such languages. This can establish confidence in the correctness of programs having simple specifications. The logic programming community is exploring the methodology of transforming a formal specification into a logic program with the same declarative reading. The resulting logic program is not generally guaranteed to terminate, but if it does, it is guaranteed to yield a correct result, since the interpreter is a sound (though incomplete) theorem prover and the program is a sound theorem.

Deductive logic seems inadequate as a high-level model of reasoning, though there is much controversy about this. High level reasoning involves weighing pro and con plausibility arguments (due-process reasoning [II]), changing one's mind (non-monotonicity), believing contradictory statements without believing all statements, and so forth. There have been attempts to "fix" logic to be able to deal with these issues, but [70] argues that these will not succeed. A more appropriate approach to high level reasoning emphasizes coherence, plausibility, and pluralism instead of correctness, proof, and facts. (This does not constitute a criticism of logic programming: logic programming languages, like lambda-calculus languages, can express arbitrary calculations, including those that embody non-logical modes of reasoning.)

## I.5. Coordination

In order to coordinate activity in a concurrent world, one needs a mechanism for serialization. Semaphores [71] and serialized actors [IV,3,4] enable a choice between processes contending for a shared resource; these primitives in turn make possible more complex concurrency control schemes such as monitors [19] and receptionists [4], which allow the protected resource to interact with more than one process at a time. Monitors in turn have been used to build distributed abortable transactions (as in Argus, described elsewhere in this volume [V]), which support coherent computation in the face of failure by individual machines.

For very large distributed systems, transaction-based coordination requires too much consistency over too many participants. Dissemination models [38,39,72], and publication models [23,73] provide mechanisms that apply to larger scales.

The Colab is another project which has extended notions of coordination control. Colab is a project to build a collaborative laboratory—a multi-user interactive environment for supporting collaborative work [74]. In the Colab, a group of people work together on a set of data and sometimes contend for the right to modify the same piece of data. Initial attempts to deal with this by simply scaling up transactions proved unsuitable. Instead, *social-coordination* mechanisms were found, such as signals to indicate someone's interest in changing a piece of data. The applicability of these mechanisms is not human-specific, but should generalize to any situation in which there is often a significant investment in computation which would be thrown away by an aborted transaction.

An essential aspect of higher-level coordination mechanisms is negotiation. When allocating exclusive access to a resource for a millisecond, it often makes sense to rely on simple serialization. When allocating exclusive access for a year, it often makes sense to take greater care. One simple form of negotiation is an auction—a procedure in which the resource is allocated to the highest bidder. Hewitt in [75] explores Robert's Rules of Order as the basis for more sophisticated negotiation procedures.

Even sophisticated negotiation mechanisms will often rely on primitive serializers. In auctions, an auctioneer serializes bids; in Robert's Rules, the chair serializes access to the floor.

## I.6. Summary

This section has examined how a range of issues—security, compatibility, trust, reasoning, and coordination—may appear at different levels of market-based open systems. Certain themes have appeared repeatedly. Mechanisms at low levels often support those at higher levels, as (for example) high-level coordination mechanisms using simple serializers. Further, higher levels can inherit characteristics of lower levels, such as encapsulation and conservation laws.

Issues often blur at the higher levels—security and trust become intertwined, and may both depend on due-process reasoning. The bulk of this paper concentrates on low- and mid-level concerns which must be addressed first, but high-level issues all present a wealth of important research topics.

## Appendix II. Comparison with other systems

This section, and these papers, discuss and criticize many works. We wish to emphasize that *these* works have been chosen, not for their flaws, but for their value.

### II.1. The Xanadu hypertext publishing system

This paper has compared agoric systems to other systems for computation. Our first exposure to many of the central ideas of markets and computation, however, stems from our work with the Xanadu hypertext system [23]. Xanadu is a proposed on-line publishing medium for hypertext documents. A hypertext document differs from the normal notion of a document in that it contains *links,* connections between documents which readers can follow at the click of a mouse. Published documents thus form not a set of disconnected islands, but a web connected by references, quotes, criticisms, comments, and rebuttals.

How can a reader find a path in such an interconnected web? Rather than proposing that someone (somehow) create a single, official system index, the Xanadu project proposes support for decentralized indexing, and hence for pluralism. Any reader can author and publish a guide to any set of public documents. Other readers can then use this guide to sort material and orient themselves. Anyone can, of course, publish guides to other guides. Xanadu relies on the expectation that this activity will result in a spontaneous order—a richly-connected world of documents in which readers can find their way.

Why will indexing be done where needed? In part because readers will do much of the basic searching and sorting for themselves, and then publish the results (since publishing is easy). In addition, however, Xanadu provides a charge-per-read royalty arrangement to encourage publication of material for which there is a demand. Just as charge-per-use software will make it economical to assemble software from diverse components, so Xanadu's royalty arrangement is designed to encourage the assembly of documents from parts of other documents: if one document quotes another, a reader's royalty payments are split between them.

In Xanadu, documents are passive data. One way of conceiving of agoric systems is as a publishing medium for linked, active data.

### II.2. Knowledge medium

Mark Stefik's "Knowledge Medium" paper [VII] paints a visionary future in which AI systems, distributed across society, are able to communicate and share knowledge. In contrast, current expert systems are seen as isolated systems rebuilt from scratch each time. A knowledge medium would enable individual systems to specialize in encoding the knowledge most relevant to them, and would provide a market for the purchase of knowledge represented elsewhere. As a result, the process of encoding knowledge is expected to accelerate through division of labor and economies of scale.

This proposal is compatible with the agoric systems vision, but has a somewhat different emphasis. Stefik's paper emphasizes representing knowledge, communicating representations, and integrating representations together. While we certainly expect (and hope) that all this would occur in an agoric system, this work emphasizes the sale of knowledge-based services.

In Stefik's vision, a "knowledge provider" responds to a request by sending a representation of the knowledge it specializes in. The consumer is then faced with the task of relating this representation to its own. This problem would create a market for "knowledge integrators". In the model sketched in this paper, knowledge is "represented" by embodying it in objects that apply their knowledge to provide services. Consumers would then be integrating the *results* in order to provide further services.

Because of the copying problem, a market for services should be more effective than a market for representations. Once knowledge is transmitted, it will often spread without further rewarding its creators. This reduces the incentives for knowledge creation.

## II.3. Enterprise Net

Enterprise [VIII], by Malone, provides decentralized scheduling of tasks in a network of personal workstations by making use of market-like mechanisms. A *client* processor with a task to be scheduled broadcasts a request for bids to *contractor* processors. Available contractors respond with *bids;* these are evaluated by the client, which then sends the task to the best bidder. The client's request includes characteristics of the task which are pertinent in estimating its processing time. The best bidder is generally the contractor who responds with the earliest estimated completion time. This bidding protocol provides for decentralized decision making and enables clients to use their own criteria in evaluating candidate suppliers.

Compared to the agoric systems approach, Enterprise has several limitations. It assumes full mutual trust between clients and contractors, all working toward a common objective. It is also less flexible in the tradeoffs it can make—the system contains non-adaptable system parameters and uses no price mechanism. Lacking price signals, the system relies on prearranged, non-evolving rules to guide behavior. The inflexibility of such a system is illustrated by the following example.

Imagine two client tasks: a high-priority theorem proving task and a lower-priority fluid flow simulation task, and two server machines: a Vax 780 with an attached array processor and a Vax 750 without one. Both tasks prefer the 780 because it is faster, but the simulation task vastly prefers it because of the array processor; in comparison, the theorem prover is relatively indifferent. In Enterprise, both will try to get the 780, and the 780 will be allocated to the higher priority theorem prover. In an agoric system, however, the simulation task might offer only a trivial amount of money for the 750, resulting in a sufficiently lower market price that the theorem prover finds the bargain worth taking. Alternatively, if the theorem prover is already running on the 780, the simulation task could offer to pay it to migrate to the 750. This is but one example of the flexibility that market prices can bring to a system. Malone acknowledges that it may be useful to provide a price system within his framework.

## II.4. Malone's comparison of organizational structure

Malone [76] has also compared various organizational structures for coordinating communities of agents. A strong similarity between Malone's work and ours is the attempt to recognize parallel organizational forms in human societies and computer systems.

Malone sees markets as capable of providing efficient solutions to the problems of decentralized resource allocation in computer systems, as they have done in human organizations. He also maintains that factors existing in human societies which limit the optimality of markets can be excluded from software systems.

Transaction costs—such as expenses involved in trading on the market—limit the use of markets and encourage the use of other forms of human organization, such as hierarchies. These transaction costs increase in uncertain or complex markets. Traders must protect themselves from other opportunistic traders, usually by establishing contracts; negotiating such contracts (and living with their consequences) imposes important transaction costs.

Malone assumes that these costs will be absent from computer systems, arguing that "While non-opportunistic traders may be rare in human markets, there is no reason at all why computer programs cannot be constructed with [non-opportunistic] participants in a market-like organization." This may be so for non-evolving computational entities authored by an individual or team. In an open distributed system, however, the programs will themselves be authored by a diversity of people who will in fact have opportunistic motives with respect to each other; further, EURISKO-like systems [IX,77] may evolve software subject only to the constraint of market success. A system designed under the assumption of non-opportunistic participants can be effectively used only within limited contexts—roughly speaking, within a single firm.

## II.5. Harris, Yu, and Harris's market-based scheduling algorithm

Harris, Yu, and Harris have applied simulated markets to difficult factory scheduling problems. Although total optimality can be defined in this case, finding it is known to be NP-hard [78], and their initial results indicate that Pareto optimal schedules are very good by most conventional measures. In their approach, the requirements, constraints, and tradeoffs for scheduling an individual order are represented by a utility function. These utility functions can express many of the "arbitrary" constraints typical of a real factory, such as a requirement that one step follow another within a given time limit. By having these utility functions interact to set prices, a Pareto optimal solution is found relatively quickly by local hill climbing. "In less than a minute [this algorithm] can schedule an order requiring 150 processing steps over 90 resources" [78]. This system, while not allowing for evolution of scheduling strategies, demonstrates the value of a market model for directing resource allocation by computational means.

The representation language for expressing the preferences of an individual order are quite flexible, but less flexible than a general purpose programming language. This loss does confer certain advantages: opportunistic behaviors are impossible, and the algorithm can compose preferences via an efficient dynamic programming technique. Their algorithm thus creates a *computational market simulation*, rather than a *computational market;* it might find a role *within* a market by offering objects a low-overhead scheduling service, guided by external market prices.

## II.6. Sutherland's time sharing system

In "A Futures Market in Computer Time" [79], I. E. Sutherland describes a bidding mechanism (implemented in the medium of paper) that results in computer resources being allocated according to the users' priorities. Users compete for computer time by making bids for specific blocks of time, with the bidding currency being tokens which are assigned to users according to their relative priority. A bid can be pre-empted by a higher bid. Since higher priority users have more tokens to bid with, they are able to outbid the lower priority users. Being outbid, a user might then try for a "cheaper" block of time during a less desirable period of the day.

By having the price of a time period vary with demand, more efficient resource allocation is possible. There are, however, restrictions placed on the users—users cannot trade tokens or lower a bid—that limit the flexibility of this system.

## II.7. Connectionism and genetic algorithms

Two recent uses of spontaneous order principles in software are connectionism (also known as artificial neural systems or parallel distributed processing models) [80] and genetic algorithms [81]. The first draws its inspiration from models of how neural networks may operate, the second from genetically-based biological evolution. Both systems have shown impressive abilities to learn to recognize patterns in noisy data. Knowledge of these patterns does not have to be designed in *a priori* by some human designer. Rather, these systems are able to sift patterns from the data itself. Though this results in these systems "knowing" the pattern, it is nowhere explicitly represented—they do not know what patterns they know.

These systems and the agoric approach share certain similarities. All are spontaneous order systems engaging in distributed representation and adapting to changing circumstances in part by adjusting (and passing around) numeric weights. Some aspects of genetic algorithms are explicitly based on a market metaphor [82], and Barto proposes connectionist models based on networks of self-interested units [83].

All these systems learn (in part) by increasing numeric weights associated with components that have contributed to overall success. A problem that needs to be addressed by such a learning algorithm is the division of rewards when several components have together contributed to a joint success. Minsky writes:

> It is my impression that many workers in the area of 'self-organizing' systems and 'random neural nets' do not feel the urgency of this problem. Suppose that one million decisions are involved in a complex task (such as winning a chess game). Could we assign to each decision one-millionth of the credit for the completed task?. . .For more complex problems, with decisions in hierarchies. . .and with increments small enough to assure probable convergence, the running times would become fantastic.

Minsky wrote this in 1961 [84]. Despite the current progress of connectionism and genetic algorithms, he still considers this criticism essentially correct [85].

A capable learning system should be able to learn better credit assignment mechanisms. In an agoric system, when several objects are about to work together to produce some result, they can negotiate the division of profits and risk. Among simple objects, and early in the evolution of an agoric system, this negotiation might generally be handled by simple initial strategies that may be no more flexible than the "back propagation" [80] and "bucket-brigade" [81] algorithms employed by some connectionist and genetic-algorithm systems. As the system develops, market competition will reward objects which employ more sophisticated negotiating strategies that better reflect both the value derived from the various contributors, and what their competitors are offering.

Both connectionism and genetic algorithms try to *substitute* spontaneous order principles for design—individual, competing units within such systems are not large programs designed by conventional means. There is much to be gained both from design and evolution; the agoric systems approach has been designed to use the strengths of both.

## II.8. Summary

In summary, though the marketplace has often been used as a metaphor, it has generally not been used as a real model—these systems are not true computational markets. Attempts to copy patterns which have emerged in markets entail a loss of flexibility compared with using markets themselves. This criticism is analogous to the connectionist criticism of representationalist cognitive models [80]—that by attempting to model emergent patterns while discarding the foundations which made them possible, representationalist models are overly "brittle", sacrificing flexibility and learning ability.

## Acknowledgments

Since 1983, when we started exploring computational markets, many people have contributed their insights on these concepts. We thank the following for helpful suggestions on agoric systems and these papers: Agustin Araya, Yeshayahu Artsy, Jim Bennett, Peter Bishop, Daniel Bobrow, John Seely Brown, Andrew Cameron, Peter Deutsch, Mike Dixon, Tom Finholt, Mike Fischer, Bob Flegal, Felix Frayman, David Friedman, Milton Friedman, Stuart Greene, Roger Gregory, Robert Gruber, Eric Gullicson, Ken Haase, Robin Hanson, Jed Harris, Rich Hasha, Keith Henson, Karl Hess, Carl Hewitt, Chris Hibbert, Tad Hogg, Bernardo Huberman, Gene Hughes, Ted Kaehler, Ken Kahn, Kirk Kelley, Scott Kim, Bill Kornfeld, David Lindbergh, Pattie Maes, Thomas Malone, John McCarthy, Diana Merry, Marvin Minsky, Ted Nelson, Gayle Pergamit, Alan Perlis, Chris Peterson, Harry Pyle, Jim Rauen, Jonathan Rees, Ramana Rao, Phil Salin, Allan Schiffman, Ehud Shapiro, Jeff Shrager, Randy Smith, Terry Stanley, Mark Stefik, Richard Steiger, Debbie Tatar, Eric Tribble, Dave Ungar, Steve Witham, Chee Yu, and Frank Zdybel.

For providing the ideas which inspired this work, we thank Carl Hewitt, Marvin Minsky, Ted Nelson, Doug Lenat, Robert Axelrod, Richard Dawkins, and most especially Friedrich Hayek.

For having arranged to make this research possible, we thank Jonathan Schmidt, Vic Poor, Charlie Smith, Mark Stefik, the Datapoint Technology Center, the Foresight Institute, the MIT Artificial Intelligence Laboratory, the Stanford Artificial Intelligence Laboratory, and the Xerox Palo Alto Research Center.

Mark S. Miller dedicates his contributions to these papers to his uncle

### Henry I. Boreen

who started him on the road to intelligence.

## References

Papers referenced with roman numerals can be found in the present volume:

Huberman, Bernardo (ed.), *The Ecology of Computation* (Elsevier Science Publishers/North-Holland, 1988).

[I] Miller, Mark S., and Drexler, K. Eric, "Comparative Ecology: A Computational Perspective", this volume.

[II] Hewitt, Carl, "Offices are Open Systems", this volume.

[III] Drexler, K. Eric, and Miller, Mark S., "Incentive Engineering for Computational Resource Management", this volume.

[IV] Kahn, Kenneth, and Miller, Mark S., "Language Design and Open Systems", this volume.

[V] Liskov, Barbara, "Guardians and Actions: Linguistic Support for Robust, Distributed Programs", this volume.

[VI] Rashid, Richard, "From RIG to Accent to Mach: The Evolution of a Network Operating System", this volume.

[VII] Stefik, Mark, "The Next Knowledge Medium", this volume.

[VIII] Malone, Thomas W., Fikes, R. E., and Howard, M. T., "Enterprise: A Market-Like Task Scheduler for Distributed Computing Environments", this volume.

[IX] Lenat, Douglas B., and Brown, John Seely, "Why AM and EURISKO Appear to Work", this volume.

[1] Popper, Karl R., *Objective Knowledge: An Evolutionary Approach* (Oxford University Press, London, 1972).

[2] Hayek, Friedrich A., *The Counter-Revolution of Science: Studies on the Abuse of Reason* (Liberty Press, Indianapolis, 1979).

[3] Clinger, Will, *Foundations of Actor Semantics* (MIT, Cambridge, MA, May 1981) MIT AI-TR-633.

[4] Agha, Gul, *Actors: A Model of Concurrent Computation in Distributed Systems* (MIT Press, Cambridge, MA, 1986).

[5] Alchian, Armen A., and Allen, William R., *University Economics* (Wadsworth, Belmont, CA, 1968, Second Edition).

[6] Hayek, Friedrich A., *The Constitution of Liberty* (University of Chicago Press, Chicago, 1960) p.156.

[7] Smith, Adam, *An Inquiry into the Nature and Causes of The Wealth of Nations* (University of Chicago Press, Chicago, 1976) p.531.

[8] Hayek, Friedrich A., "Competition as a Discovery Procedure", in: *New Studies in Philosophy, Politics, Economics and the History of Ideas* (University of Chicago Press, Chicago, 1978) p.179–190.

[9] Hayek, Friedrich A., "Economics and Knowledge", from: *Economica, New Series*

(1937), Vol. IV, pp.33–54; reprinted in: Hayek, Friedrich A., (ed.), *Individualism and Economic Order* (University of Chicago Press, Chicago, 1948).

[10] Hayek, Friedrich A., *New Studies in Philosophy, Politics, Economics and the History of Ideas* (University of Chicago Press, Chicago, 1978) p.71.

[11] Drexler, K. Eric, "Molecular Engineering: An Approach to the Development of General Capabilities for Molecular Manipulation", in: *Proceedings of the National Academy of Science USA* (Sept. 1981) Vol. 78, No.9, pp.5275–5278.

[12] Drexler, K. Eric, "Rod Logic and Thermal Noise in the Molecular Nanocomputer", in: *Proceedings of the Third International Symposium on Molecular Electronic Devices* (Elsevier Science Publishers / North Holland, 1987).

[13] Drexler, K. Eric, *Engines of Creation* (Anchor Press / Doubleday, Garden City, New York, 1986).

[14] Coase, R. H., "The Nature of the Firm", in: *Economica, New Series* (1937), Vol. IV, pp.386–405; reprinted in: Stigler, G. J., and Boulding, K. E., (eds.), *Readings in Price Theory* (Richard D. Irwin, Inc., Chicago, 1952).

[15] Williamson, Oliver, *Markets and Hierarchies: Analysis and Anti-Trust Implications* (Free Press, New York, 1975).

[16] Malone, Thomas W.; Yates, JoAnne; and Benjamin, Robert I., "Electronic Markets and Electronic Hierarchies", in: *Communications of the ACM* (June 1987) Vol.30, No. 6, pp.484–497.

[17] Smith, Vernon L., "Experimental Methods in the Political Economy of Exchange", in: *Science* (10 October 1986) Vol.234, pp.167–173.

[18] Star, Spencer, "TRADER: A Knowledge-Based System for Trading in Markets", in: *Economics and Artificial Intelligence First International Conference* (Aix-En-Provence, France, September 1986).

[19] Hoare, C.A.R., *Communicating Sequential Processes* (Prentice-Hall, New York, 1985).

[20] INMOS Limited, *Occam Programming Manual* (Prentice-Hall International, London, 1984).

[21] Shapiro, Ehud, (ed.), *Concurrent Prolog: Collected Papers* (MIT Press, Cambridge,

MA, 1987) in press.

[22] Artsy, Yeshayahu, and Livny, Miron, *An Approach to the Design of Fully Open Computing Systems* (University of Wisconsin / Madison, March 1987) Computer Sciences Technical Report #689.

[23] Nelson, Theodor, *Literary Machines* (published by author, version 87.1, 1987, available from Project Xanadu, 8480 Fredricksburg #8, San Antonio, TX 78229. Available as hypertext on disk from Owl International, 14218 NE 21st St., Bellevue, WA 98007. 1981).

[24] Granovetter, Mark, "The Strength of Weak Ties", in: *American Journal of Sociology* (1977) Vol. 78, pp.1360–1380.

[25] Miller, Mark S., Bobrow, Daniel G., Tribble, Eric Dean, and Levy, Jacob, "Logical Secrets", in: Shapiro, Ehud, (ed.), *Concurrent Prolog: Collected Papers* (MIT Press, Cambridge, MA, 1987) in press.

[26] Hardin, Garrett, "The Tragedy of the Commons", in: *Science* (13 December 1968) Vol. 162, pp.1243–1248.

[27] Kurose, James F., Schwartz, Mischa, and Yemini, Yechiam, "A Microeconomic Approach to Decentralized Optimization of Channel Access Policies in Multiaccess Networks", in: *Proceedings of the Fifth International Conference on Distributed Computing Systems* (IEEE, Denver CO, May 1985) pp.70–77.

[28] Goldberg, Adele, and Robson, Dave, *Smalltalk-80: The Language and its Implementation* (Addison-Wesley, Reading MA, 1983).

[29] Rivest, R., Shamir, A., and Adelman, L., "A Method for Obtaining Digital Signatures and Public-Key Cryptosystems", in: *Communications of the ACM* (Feb. 1978) Vol. 21, No. 2, pp.120–126.

[30] Tanenbaum, Andrew S., and van Renesse, Robbert, "Distributed Operating Systems", in: *ACM Computing Surveys* (ACM, New York, December 1985) Vol. 17, No. 4, pp.419–470.

[31] Hayek, Friedrich A., *Denationalisation of Money* (The Institute of Economic Affairs, Westminster, London, 1978, Second Edition).

[32] Denning, Peter J., "The Working Set Model for Program Behavior", in: *Communications of the ACM* (May 1968) Vol 2, No. 5, pp.323–333.

[33] Artsy, Y., Chang, H-Y, and Finkel, R.,

*Processes Migrate in Charlotte* (University of Wisconsin / Madison, August 1986) Computer Sciences Technical Report #655.

[34] Artsy, Y., and Finkel, R., "Simplicity, Efficiency, and Functionality in Designing a Process Migration Facility", in: *Proceedings of the Second Israel Conference on Computer Systems and Software Engineering* (IEEE, Tel-Aviv, Israel, May 1987) 3.1.2, pp.1–12.

[35] Cheriton, D.R., "The V Kernel: A Software Base for Distributed Systems", in: *IEEE Software* (April 1984) 1, 2, pp.19–42.

[36] Leach, P.J., Levine, P.H., Douros, B.P., Hamilton, J. A., Nelson, D.L., and Stumph, B.L., "The Architecture of an Integrated Local Network", in: *IEEE Journal on Selected Areas in Communication* (IEEE, November 1983) SAC-1, 5, 842–857.

[37] Bishop, Peter B., *Computers with a Large Address Space and Garbage Collection* (MIT, Cambridge, MA, May 1977) MIT/LCS/TR-178.

[38] Birrell, Andrew D.; Levin, Roy; Needham, Roger M.; and Schroeder, Michael D., "Grapevine: an Exercise in Distributed Computing", in: *Communications of the ACM* (April 1982) Vol. 25, No. 4.

[39] Terry, Douglas Brian, *Distributed Name Servers: Naming and Caching in Large Distributed Environments* (Xerox PARC, February 1985) CSL-85-1.

[40] Barak, A., and Shiloh, A., "A Distributed Load-Balancing Policy for a Multicomputer" in: *Software Practice and Experience* (September 1985) 15, pp.901–913.

[41] Shapiro, Ehud, "Systolic Programming: A Paradigm for Parallel Processing", in: *Proceedings of the International Conference on Fifth Generation Computer Systems* (1984) pp.458–471.

[42] Kahn, Kenneth, *A Partial Evaluator of Lisp Written in a Prolog Written in Lisp Intended to be Applied to the Prolog and Itself which in turn is Intended to be Given to Itself Together with the Prolog to Produce a Prolog Compiler* (University of Uppsala, Sweden, 1983) UPMAIL Tech. Report No. 17.

[43] Theriault, D., *Issues in the Design and Implementation of Act 2* (MIT AI Lab, Cambridge, MA., 1983) AI-TR-728.

[44] Winograd, Terry, and Flores, Fernando, *Understanding Computers and Cognition* (Ablex, Norwood, NJ, 1986).

[45] Witham, Steve, *personal communication* (1987).

[46] Safra, S., and Shapiro, Ehud, "Meta-Interpreters For Real", in: *Proceedings, IFIP-86* (1986) pp.271–278.

[47] Stamos, James W., *A Large Object-Oriented Virtual Memory: Grouping Strategies, Measurements, and Performance* (Xerox PARC, Palo Alto, CA, May 1982) SCG-82-2.

[48] Stanley, Terry, *personal communication* (1987).

[49] Hamming, R. W., "One Man's View of Computer Science", in: Ashenhurst, Robert L., and Graham, Susan, (eds.), *ACM Turing Award Lectures: The First Twenty Years 1966–1985* (Addison-Wesley, Reading, MA, 1987) pp.216.

[50] Cox, Brad J., *Object Oriented Programming: An Evolutionary Approach* (Addison-Wesley, Reading, MA, 1986) pp.26–28.

[51] Jacobson, Gary, and Hillkirk, John, *Xerox: American Samurai* (Macmillan, New York, 1986).

[52] Chaum, David, "Design Concepts for Tamper Responding Systems", in: *Advances in Cryptology: Proceedings of Crypto '83* (Plenum Press, NY, 1984) pp.387–392.

[53] Levy, Henry M., *Capability-Based Computer Systems* (Digital Press, Bedford, MA, 1984).

[54] Gehringer, Edward F., *Capability Architectures and Small Objects* (UMI Research Press, Ann Arbor, MI, 1982).

[55] Organick, Elliott I., *A Programmer's View of the Intel 432 System* (McGraw-Hill, New York, 1983).

[56] Rees, Jonathan A., and Adams, Norman I., IV, "T: a Dialect of Lisp or, Lambda: The Ultimate Software Tool", in: *Proceedings of the 1982 ACM Symposium on Lisp and Functional Programming* (August 1982).

[57] Conway, M.E., "How Do Committees Invent?", in: *Datamation* (April 1968) 14, 4, pp.28–31.

[58] Brooks, Frederick P., Jr., *The Mythical Man Month* (Addison-Wesley Publishing Company, Reading, MA, 1975) pp.111.

[59] Hayek, Friedrich A., "Cosmos and Taxis" in: *Law, Legislation and Liberty, Vol. 1: Rules and Order,* (University of Chicago Press, Chicago, 1973) pp.35–54.

[60] Minsky, Marvin, *The Society of Mind*

(Simon and Schuster, New York, 1986).

[61] Kornfeld, William A., and Hewitt, Carl, "The Scientific Community Metaphor", in: *IEEE Transactions on Systems, Man, and Cybernetics* (IEEE, 1981) SMC-11, pp.24–33.

[63] March, J. G., "Footnotes to Organizational Change", in: *Administrative Science Quarterly* (1981) 26, pp.563–577.

[64] Barstow, David R., Shrobe, Howard E., and Sandewall, Erik, (eds.), *Interactive Programming Environments* (McGraw-Hill, New York, 1984).

[65] Xerox, *Courier: The Remote Procedure Call Protocol* (Xerox Corp, Stamford CT, 1982) p.5.

[66] Rao, Ramana Balusu, *Toward Interoperability and Extensibility in Window Environments via Object-Oriented Programming* (MIT Press, 1987) submitted as Masters Thesis.

[67] Shrager, Jeff, and Klahr, David, "Instructionless Learning about a Complex Device: The Paradigm and Observations", in: *Int. J. Man-Machine Studies* (1986) 25, pp.153–189.

[68] Dawkins, Richard, *The Selfish Gene* (Oxford University Press, New York, 1976).

[69] Axelrod, Robert, *The Evolution of Cooperation* (Basic Books, New York, 1984).

[70] McDermott, Drew, "A Critique of Pure Reason", to appear in: Levesque, Hector, (ed.), *Computational Intelligence* (National Research Council of Canada, August or September, 1987).

[71] Dijkstra, E. W., "Co-operating Sequential Processes", in: Genuys, F., (ed.), *Programming Languages* (Academic Press, New York, 1968) pp.43–112.

[72] Demers, Alan, Greene, Dan, Hauser, Carl, Irish, Wes, Larson, John, Shenker, Scott, Sturgis, Howard, Swinehart, Dan, and Terry, Doug, "Epidemic Algorithms for Replicated Database Maintenance", in: *Proceedings of the Sixth Annual ACM Symposium on Principles of Distributed Computing* (ACM, Vancouver, British Columbia, Canada, August 10–12, 1987) pp.1–12.

[73] Hanson, Robin, *Toward Hypertext Publishing: Issues and Choices in Database Design* (draft available from Foresight Institute, Palo Alto, CA, 1987).

[74] Stefik, Mark, Foster, Gregg, Bobrow, Daniel G., Lahn, Kenneth, Lanning, Stan, and

Suchman, Lucy, "Beyond the Chalkboard: Computer Support for Colaboration and Problem Solving in Meetings", in: *Communications of the ACM* (January 1987) Vol. 30, No. 1, pp.32–47.

[75] Hewitt, Carl, "Robert's Rules of Order" (in press).

[76] Malone, Thomas W., "Organizing Information Processing Systems: Parallels Between Human Organizations and Computer Systems", in: Zacharay, W., Robertson, S., and Black, J., (eds.), *Cognition, Computation, and Cooperation* (Ablex Publishing Corp., Norwood, NJ, 1986).

[77] Lenat, Douglas B., "The Role of Heuristics in Learning by Discovery: Three Case Studies", in: Michalski, Ryszard S., Carbonell, Jaime G., and Mitchell, Tom M. (eds.), *Machine Learning: An Artificial Intelligence Approach* (Tioga Publishing Company, Palo Alto, CA, 1983) pp.243–306.

[78] Harris, Jed, Yu, Chee, Harris, Britton, *Market Based Scheduling* (1987) in preparation.

[79] Sutherland, I.E., "A Futures Market in Computer Time", in: *Communications of the ACM* (June 1968) Volume 11, Number 6.

[80] McClelland, James L., Rumelhart, David E., and PDP Research Group, *Parallel Distributed Processing* (MIT Press, Cambridge, MA, 1986) Volumes 1 and 2.

[81] Holland, John H., Holyoak, Keith J., Nisbett, Richard E., and Thagard, Paul R., *Induction: Processes of Inference, Learning, and Discovery* (MIT Press, Cambridge, MA, 1986).

[82] Holland, John H., Holyoak, Keith J., Nisbett, Richard E., and Thagard, Paul R., *Induction: Processes of Inference, Learning, and Discovery* (MIT Press, Cambridge, MA, 1986) pp.72–75, 79.

[83] Barto, Andrew G., "Game Theoretic Cooperativity in Networks of Self-Interested Units", in: Denker, John S. (ed.), *Neural Networks for Computing* (American Institute of Physics, New York, 1986) pp.41–46.

[84] Minsky, Marvin, "Steps Toward Artificial Intelligence", in: Feigenbaum, Edward A., and Feldman, Julian, (eds.), *Computers and Thought* (Robert E. Krieger, Malabar, FL, 1981) pp.406–450.

[85] Minsky, Marvin, *personal communication* (1987).

The Ecology of Computation
B.A. Huberman (editor)
© Elsevier Science Publishers B.V. (North-Holland), 1988

# Enterprise:
# A Market-like Task Scheduler for
# Distributed Computing Environments

Thomas W. Malone, Richard E. Fikes*, Kenneth R. Grant**, and Michael T. Howard***
*MIT*

This paper describes a system for sharing tasks among personal workstations connected by a local area network. The system, called Enterprise, is based on the metaphor of a market: processors send out "requests for bids" on tasks to be done and other processors respond with bids giving estimated completion times that reflect machine speed and currently loaded files. Enterprise includes a simple scheduling protocol that assigns tasks to the best machine available at run-time (either remote or local).

The paper also summarizes simulations of this protocol in a wide variety of situations (e.g., different processor speeds, system loads, and message delay times). The protocol is found to provide substantial performance improvements over processing tasks on the machines at which they originate even in the face of relatively large message delays and relatively inaccurate estimates of processing times. The benefits from pooling tasks among machines are found to be largely realized with a relatively small number of machines (about 5 to 10), and adding more machines has very little additional benefit.

With the rapid spread of personal computer networks and the increasing availability of low cost VLSI processors, the opportunities for massive use of parallel and distributed computing are becoming more and more compelling ([Jon80]; [Gaj85]; [Dav 81b]; [Ens81]; [Ber82]; [Bir82]). One of the fundamental problems that must be solved by all such systems is the problem of how to schedule tasks on processors. This problem is, of course, a well-known one in traditional operating systems and scheduling theory, and there are a number of mathematical and software techniques for solving it in both single and multi-processor systems (e.g., [Dei84]; [Con67]; [Jon80]; [Lam68]; [Kle81]; [Sto77]; [Sto78]; [Wit80]; [Vnt81]; [Tan85]; [Cho79]; [Ni81]).

Almost all the traditional work in this area, however, deals with centralized scheduling techniques, where all the information is brought to one place and the decisions are made there. In highly parallel systems, where the information used in scheduling and the resulting actions

---

*     Intellicorp, Mountain View, CA.
**    Now at Oracle Corp., Belmont, CA.
***  Now at Datext, Inc., Woburn, MA.

are distributed over a number of different processors, there may be substantial benefits from developing decentralized scheduling techniques. For example, when a centralized scheduler fails, the entire system is brought to a halt, but systems that use decentralized scheduling techniques can continue to operate with all the remaining nodes. Furthermore, much of the information used in scheduling is inherently distributed and rapidly changing (e.g., momentary system load). Thus, decentralized scheduling techniques can "bring the decisions to the information" rather than having to constantly transmit the information to a centralized decision maker. Because of these advantages, a growing body of recent work has begun to explore such decentralized scheduling techniques in more detail (e.g., [Sta85]; [Sin85]; [Liv82]; [Eag86a]; [Eag86b]; [Wan85]; [Mal83]; [Ni85]; [Lar82]; [Smi80]; [Cho79]; [Bry81]; [Sta84]; [Ten81a]; [Ten81b]; [SRC85]; see [Sta85] and [Wan85] for useful reviews).

In this paper we describe a prototype system called Enterprise that uses a particular kind of decentralized scheduling technique: a market-like "bidding" mechanism to assign tasks to processors (see [Far72]; [Smi80]; [Sin85]; [Far73]; [Sta84]). Such techniques are remarkably flexible in terms of the kinds of factors they can take into account: job characteristics, processor capacities and speeds, current network loading and current locations of data and related tasks (e.g., see [Sta84]). The Enterprise system uses a simple and effective bidding protocol, called the Distributed Scheduling Protocol (DSP), and we summarize simulation results that explore the behavior of this protocol in a wide variety of situations. These simulations and a variety of other approaches to decentralized scheduling are described in more detail elsewhere [Mal87].

## OVERVIEW OF THE ENTERPRISE SYSTEM

A traditional philosophy used in designing systems based on local area networks is to have dedicated personal workstations which remain idle when not used by their owners, and dedicated special purpose servers such as file servers, print servers, and various kinds of data base servers ([Bir82], [Bog80], [Sch84]). A system like Enterprise that schedules tasks on the best processor available at run time (either remote or local) enables a new philosophy in designing such distributed systems. In this new philosophy, personal workstations are still dedicated to their owners, but during the (often substantial) periods of the day when their owners are not using them, these personal workstations become general purpose servers, available to other users on the network. "Server" functions can migrate and replicate as needed on otherwise unused machines (except for those such as file servers and print servers that are required to run on specific machines). Thus programs can be written to take advantage of the maximum amount of processing power and parallelism available on a network at any time, with little extra cost when there are few extra machines available.

*System Architecture*

The Enterprise system schedules and runs processes on personal workstations connected by a local area network. It is implemented in Interlisp-D and runs on Xerox 1100 series Scientific Information Processors connected with an Ethernet. It provides facilities for: (1) communicating between processes on different machines, (2) scheduling tasks on the best available machines (either remote or local), and (3) writing programs with subtasks to be performed remotely.

As shown in Figure 1, the Enterprise system provides these facilities in three layers of software. The first layer provides an Inter-Process Communication (IPC) facility by which different processes, either on the same or different machines, can send messages to each other. When the different processes are on different machines, the IPC protocol uses internetwork datagrams called PUPs (see [Bog80]) to provide reliable non-duplicated delivery of messages over a "best efforts" physical transport medium such as an Ethernet [Met76]. Enterprise uses a pre-existing protocol that is highly optimized for remote procedure calls ([Bir84], [Tho83]) in which messages are passed to remote machines as procedure calls on the remote machines. This IPC may be used for any asynchronous message passing between processes.

The next layer of the Enterprise system is the Distributed Scheduling Protocol (DSP) which, using the IPC, locates the best available machine to perform a task (even if the best machine for a task turns out to be the one on which the request originated). If the IPC guarantees that messages are received in the order they are sent, then some redundant processing will be avoided, but the DSP does not require this guarantee.

The top layer of the Enterprise system is a Remote Process Mechanism, which uses both DSP and IPC to create processes on different machines that can communicate with each other. Using the same programming language constructs as those already used for local processes, this layer allows programmers to create, delete, and query the status of processes running on remote machines.

The most novel part of the Enterprise system is the Distributed Scheduling Protocol, so we will devote the rest of this paper to describing its definition, implementation, and performance.

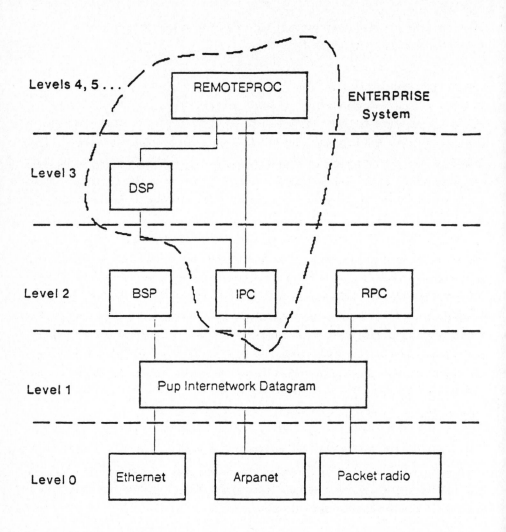

**Figure 1**

Protocol layers used in the Enterprise system

## THE DISTRIBUTED SCHEDULING PROTOCOL

The Distributed Scheduling Protocol (DSP) is based on the metaphor of a market (similar to the contract net protocol of Smith and Davis ([Smi80]; [Smi81]; [Dav83]; see [Mal87] for a review of a variety of other scheduling approaches). The contract net protocol is a very general protocol for distributing tasks in a network of heterogenous processors based on whatever task specific criteria are provided by the system designer. Its "announcement, bid, award" sequence allows for mutual selection of clients and contractors; that is, contractors choose which clients to serve and clients choose which contractors to use.

In order to achieve any particular scheduling objective with such a system, however, specific selection criteria must be developed. The most important way in which DSP differs from the contract net protocol is by specializing the selection criteria to two primary dimensions: (1) contractors select clients' tasks in the order of numerical *task priorities*, and (2) clients select contractors on the basis of *estimated completion times* (from among the contractors that satisfy the minimum requirements to perform the job). We will see below how this simple specialization of the generalized contract net protocol allows us to make connections to a variety of optimality results from traditional scheduling theory, including those about minimizing mean flow times, and to do detailed evaluations of the effect of numerous factors on scheduling performance.

Figure 2 illustrates the steps in the Distributed Scheduling Protocol:

(1) *Request*
   The client broadcasts a "request for bids" that includes the (numerical) priority of the task, any special requirements, and a summary description of the task that allows contractors to estimate its processing time.

(2) *Response*
   Idle contractors respond with "bids" giving their estimated completion times. Busy contractors respond with "acknowledgements" and add the request to their queues (in order of priority). When a busy contractor becomes idle, it submits a bid for the next request on its queue and waits for a response from the client.

(3) *Evaluation of bids and task assignment*
   (a) If more than one bid has been received when the client evaluates bids, the task is sent to the best bidder and cancel messages are sent to the other bidders. The

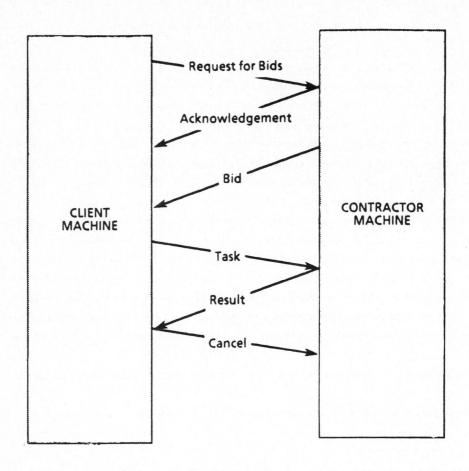

**Figure 2**

Messages in the Distributed Scheduling Protocol

length of time to wait before evaluating bids is a parameter that is set depending on the message delay time.

(b) If no bids have been received when the client evaluates bids, the task is sent to the first subsequent bidder.

(4) *Cancellation and reassignment*

(a) If a later bid is "significantly better" than the best early one, the client cancels the task on the early bidder and sends the task to the later bidder. The criterion for deciding whether a late bid is "significantly better" is a parameter, the effect of which is examined in the simulations below.

(b) If the later bid is not significantly better (or if the task has side-effects and cannot be restarted), the client sends a cancel message to the later bidder.

(5) *Return results*

When a contractor finishes a task, it returns the result to the client. When a client receives the result of a task, it broadcasts a "cancel" message so that all the contractors can remove the request from their queues.

A detailed description of the messages needed to perform these steps is included in the Appendix.

*Estimating processing times.* As just described, DSP requires estimates of processing time for each task. In many cases, it is not possible to make these estimates with great accuracy. However, since DSP only uses this information to do rank ordering (e.g., of bids from different contractors), only rough estimates are needed. In some cases, historical processing times for similar jobs might provide a basis for making more precise estimates, possibly using parameters such as the size of the input files. Our simulation studies below include an examination of the consequences of making these estimates very poorly.

*Estimating priorities.* DSP also requires a numerical priority for each task. We consider below several ways of assigning these priorities in order to achieve various global scheduling objectives. In our use of the prototype system and in our simulations, we simply use estimated processing time as the priority, with shortest processing times having highest priority.[1]

*Source-initiative vs. server-initiative scheduling.* Before considering how DSP is implemented in Enterprise, it is useful to view DSP in terms of a distinction between two general approaches to distributed scheduling ([Wan85], [Eag86a], [Eag86b]): (1) *source-initiative*, in which the node at which a task arises determines where to send it, and (2) *server-initiative*, in which server nodes select the tasks they will process. Using this distinction, Eager, Lazowska, and Zahorjan [Eag86a] found that a source-initiative approach outperformed a server-initiative approach at light to moderate system loads, but that a server-initiative approach was preferable at high system loads.

DSP is, in a sense, a hybrid of these two approaches. Strictly speaking, DSP is a source-initiative approach since sources (clients) must first broadcast a task description ("request for bids") before servers (contractors) ever know about a task. In lightly loaded networks, several bids from idle servers will be submitted immediately and the source will choose the best one (e.g., the one from the fastest processor). When all servers are busy, however, the servers simply store task requests until a server becomes free. Then the server takes the initiative in submitting a bid on the highest priority outstanding request (e.g., the task with the shortest estimated processing time). Thus, DSP shifts naturally between being primarily source-initiative at light loads to being primarily server-initiative at heavy loads.


## IMPLEMENTATION OF THE DISTRIBUTED SCHEDULING PROTOCOL

The DSP process, as we have just described it, is intended to be general enough to apply to almost any distributed scheduling situation. In this section, we describe how we adapted it for use in our situation where: (1) Processing times are not always known in advance; (2) Processors and communications are sometimes unreliable; (3) Tasks that originate at one workstation may be processed either at that workstation or at another one; and (4) Different workstations may be "owned" by different people.

*Estimating processing times*

In the prototype Enterprise implementation, the summary description of a task that is included in the "request for bids" message consists of: (a) the estimated processing time for the task on a "standard" processor (in our case a Xerox 1100 processor), and (b) the names and lengths of the files that must be loaded before the processing can begin. The estimated processing time for a task is supplied by the programmer, or if no estimate is supplied, a default value is used.

In order to compute a bid, a contractor adjusts the estimated processing time to account for the contractor's own speed relative to a "standard" processor, and then adds the file loading time for all the required files that are not already loaded on the contractor's machine. File loading time is estimated as being proportional to file length.

*Unreliable processors and communications*

In addition to the messages involved in the bidding cycle, clients periodically query the contractors to which they have sent tasks about the status of the tasks. If a contractor fails to respond to a query (or any other message in the DSP), the client assumes the contractor has failed. Failures might result from hardware or software malfunctions or from a person preempting a machine for other uses. In any case, unless the task description specifically prohibits restarting failed tasks, the client automatically reschedules the task on another machine. Similarly, if a contractor fails to receive periodic queries from one of its clients, the contractor assumes the client has failed and the contractor aborts that client's task.

Since a task can be restarted several times during its lifetime (e.g., because of processor failures or because of a late bid improvement), there can be different "incarnations" of the same process [Nel81]. Because messages can sometimes be delayed or lost, confusions might result from messages referring to earlier incarnations of a current task. To prevent such confusions, each incarnation of a task is assigned a task identifier that is guaranteed to be unique across time and space. In order to do this, a timestamp of the most recent "milestone event" in the life of the process is included in the task identifier. Milestone events are the sending of either a request for bids or a task message concerning the task. Both these events render obsolete all previous DSP messages concerning the task. Before responding to DSP messages about a particular task, therefore, both clients and contractors check to be sure the message concerns the most recent incarnation of the task. (These task identifiers serve the same purpose as the call identifiers used by Birrell and Nelson [Bir84]).

In view of the benefits described below from using "late bid improvement" rescheduling in lightly loaded systems (as ours was), and in view of the unpredictable delays in message transmission, the Enterprise system implements a variation of the DSP protocol in which the first bid for a task is always accepted, rather than waiting any fixed time to evaluate bids. Then if a later bid is significantly better, the task is rescheduled.

*Adding machines to the bidding network*

The Enterprise implementation assumes that the owners of idle workstations voluntarily put their machines into a mode where the machines respond to requests for bids from the network. Shoch and Hupp [Sho82] describe an alternative mechanism for locating and activating idle machines on a network without their owners' intervention.

*The "remote or local" decision*

Any program that creates a new process in Enterprise must specify whether the process is (1) required to be run on the local machine, (2) required to be run on a remote machine, or (3) may be run either remotely or locally depending on where the process is expected to complete soonest. If the process is required to be run locally, DSP is not involved at all. If the process is required to be run remotely, the first bid for the task is accepted as just described.

Finally, if the process may be scheduled either remotely or locally, the client accepts the first bid except that its own bid is not processed until a specified interval has elapsed. (Otherwise, the client's own bid would presumably always be the first one.) Since contractor machines are assumed to be processing tasks for only one user at a time, the client machine's own bid is also inflated by a factor that reflects the current load on the client machine. Human users of a processor can express their willingness to have tasks scheduled locally by setting either of these two parameters: (a) the delay period before processing local bids, and (b) the factor by which local bids are inflated.

*"Gaming" the system*

If people supply their own estimates of processing times for their tasks and these time estimates are also used to determine priority, there is a clear incentive for people to bias their processing time estimates in order to get higher priority. To counteract this incentive, the current implementation of Enterprise has an "estimation error tolerance" parameter. If a task takes significantly longer than it was estimated to take (i.e., more than the estimation error tolerance), the contractor aborts the task and notifies the client that it was "cut off." This cutoff feature prevents the possibility of a few people or tasks monopolizing an entire system.

## GLOBAL SCHEDULING OBJECTIVES
## IN THE DISTRIBUTED SCHEDULING PROTOCOL

One of the advantages of DSP is that it separates the *policy* decisions about how priorities are assigned from the *mechanism* of actually scheduling tasks according to these priorities (e.g., [Cof73], [Lam68]). Traditional schedulers for centralized computing systems often use *list scheduling* as a basis for layering the design of a system (e.g., [Cof73]). In this approach, one level of the system sequences jobs according to their order in a priority list while the policy decisions about how priorities are assigned are made at a higher level in the system (see [Lam68]). DSP allows precisely the same kind of separation of policy and mechanism. The DSP protocol itself is concerned only with sequencing jobs according to priorities assigned at some higher level. By assigning these priorities in different ways, the designers of distributed systems can achieve different global objectives. For example, it is well known that in systems of identical processors with all jobs available at the same time, the average waiting time of jobs is minimized by doing the shortest jobs first [Con67]. Thus, in this case, by assigning priorities in order of job length, completely decentralized decisions based on priority would result in a globally optimal sequencing of tasks on processors.

Of course, the performance of real systems is affected, not only by the order in which tasks are processed on different machines, but also by the communication overhead involved in such activities as bidding and assigning tasks. We consider one aspect of this overhead-- communication delay--in our simulations. In the remainder of this section, we discuss several different ways of assigning priorities to achieve different possible objectives.

*Optimality results for mean flow time and maximum flow time.* Traditional scheduling theory (e.g., [Con67]) has been primarily concerned with minimizing one of two objectives: (1) the average flow time of jobs ($F_{ave}$)--the average time from availability of a job until it is completed, and (2) the maximum flow time of jobs ($F_{max}$)--the time until the completion of the last job. Minimizing $F_{max}$ also maximizes the utilization of the processors being scheduled [Cof73]. The most general forms of both these problems are NP-complete ([Bru74], [Iba77]), so much of the literature in this field has involved comparing scheduling heuristics in terms of bounds on computational complexity and "goodness" of the resulting schedules relative to optimal schedules (e.g., [Dav81a], [Jaf80]).

A number of results suggest the value of using two simple heuristics, shortest processing time first (SPT) and longest processing time first (LPT), to achieve the objectives $F_{ave}$ and $F_{max}$, respectively. For example, consider the use of these two heuristics in cases where all jobs are available at the same time and their processing times are known exactly. In these cases, if all the processors are identical, then SPT exactly minimizes $F_{ave}$ [Con67] and LPT is guaranteed to produce an $F_{max}$ that is no worse than 4/3 of the minimum possible value [Gra69]. If some processors are uniformly faster than others, then the LPT heuristic is guaranteed to produce an $F_{max}$ no worse than twice the best possible value [Gon77]. Results regarding these heuristics are also known for cases where all jobs are available at the same time but their exact processing times are not known in advance. Instead the processing times have certain random distributions (e.g., exponential) with different expected values for different jobs. In these cases, if the system contains identical processors on which preemptions and sharing are allowed, then SPT and LPT exactly minimize the expected values of $F_{ave}$ and $F_{max}$, respectively, ([Web82], [Gla79]). Finally, in cases where the jobs are not all available at the same time but instead arrive randomly and have exponentially distributed processing times, if the processors are identical and allow preemption, then LPT exactly minimizes $F_{max}$ [Van81]. Even though SPT has not, to our knowledge, been shown to exactly minimize $F_{ave}$ in systems where jobs arrive randomly, the above results suggest that it is at least likely to be a good heuristic in this case.

*Other scheduling objectives.* DSP can also be used to achieve many other possible objectives besides the traditional ones of minimizing mean or maximum flow time for independent jobs. For example:

(1) *Parallel heuristic search.* Many artificial intelligence programs use various kinds of heuristics for determining which of several alternatives in a search space to explore next. For example, in a traditional "best first" heuristic search, a heuristic evaluation function is employed at each step in the search to select the most promising alternative to be explored next [Nil80]. If such a heuristic evaluation function is used to set priorities for the tasks to be scheduled by DSP, then contractors can use this information to select the tasks on which they will bid. When each contractor becomes free, it will bid on the most promising available task as rated by the heuristic evaluation function.

Thus, instead of having only one processor working on only the single most promising alternative at a time, a system with $n$ processors can be always exploring the $n$ most promising alternatives. Furthermore, if different processors have different capabilities, then clients will choose processors that are best suited (i.e., have shortest estimated processing times) for their tasks.

The DSP protocol can also, of course, be used in heuristic searches in a more straightforward way to assign a fixed set of subtasks to processors. For example, Singh and Genesereth's ([Sin85]) system uses a bidding protocol to assign deduction steps to distributed processors. Their use of the protocol appears to be minimizing $F_{max}$ by giving highest priority to the most costly tasks.

(2) *Arbitrary market with priority points.* Another obvious use of DSP is to assign each human user of the system a fixed number of priority points in each time period. Users (or their programs) can then allocate these priority points to tasks in any way they choose to reflect their preferences for faster response times on some jobs than others. For example,

users might assign more priority points to "interactive" tasks for which they are actively waiting and fewer priority points to "background" tasks for which their need is less urgent. (See [Sut68] for a similar--though non-automated--scheme, and Mendelson ([Men85]) for a related analysis aimed at determining, not micro-level priorities, but macro-level chargeback policies ).

(3) *Incentive market with priority points.* If the personal computers on a network are assigned to different people, then a slight modification of the arbitrary market in (2) can be used to give people an incentive to make their personal computers available as contractors. In this modified scheme, people accumulate additional priority points for their own later use every time their machine acts as a contractor for someone else's task.

## SIMULATIONS OF THE DISTRIBUTED SCHEDULING PROTOCOL

In many real distributed scheduling environments, including our motivating example of workstations on a network, minimizing the mean flow time of independent jobs is likely to be the primary scheduling objective. Unfortunately, as we noted above, the problem of scheduling tasks to meet this objective is usually NP-hard, and other analytic results about the effects of sequencing strategies (other than random) are quite scarce. It is therefore appropriate to rely heavily on simulations to investigate strategies for achieving this objective. In this section, we summarize the results of a series of simulation studies we reported elsewhere [Mal87] that investigate the performance of DSP in a variety of situations.

**Simulation parameters**

*Priorities.* Since we assume that the scheduling objective is to minimize the mean flow time of jobs, priorities in all simulations were determined according to the shortest processing time first (SPT) heuristic.

*Processor speeds.* Ten different configurations of machines on the network were defined. In all configurations, a total of 8 units of processing power was available, but in different cases this was achieved in different ways: a single machine of speed 8; or 8 machines of speed 1; or 1 machine of speed 4 and 2 machines of speed 2; etc. We will denote different network configurations below by a sequence of the machine speeds they contain (e.g., "422").

*Job loads.* For all the simulations, jobs were assumed to be independent of each other and suitable for processing on any machine in the network. The job arrivals were assumed to be a Poisson process and the amount of processing in each job was assumed to be exponentially distributed (with a mean of 60 time units on a processor of speed 1). System utilization was defined as the expected amount of processing requested per time interval divided by the total amount of processing power in the system, and three different levels of system utilization (0.1, 0.5, and 0.9) were simulated.

*Accuracy of job processing time estimates.* In addition to the actual amount of processing in each job, the jobs also included an estimated amount of processing for each job (i.e., the estimate a user might have made of how long the job would take). These estimates are used to determine job priorities and estimated completion times. In order to examine extreme cases, these estimates were either perfect (0 percent error) or relatively inaccurate (+/- 100 percent error). In the case of inaccurate estimates, the errors were uniformly randomly distributed over the range.

*Communications delays.* In order to simulate "pure" cases of the different scheduling mechanisms, most of our simulations treat communication among machines as perfectly reliable and instantaneous. In real situations where communication delays are negligible relative to job processing times, this assumption of instantaneous communications is appropriate.

In other simulations, designed to explore the effect of communication delays, we assumed constant delays for the transmission of all messages. The values for message delay that were simulated were equivalent to 0%, 5%, 10%, and 15% respectively of the average job processing time. The simulations include only the effect of message delays; they do not include any other factors such as processing overhead needed to transmit and receive messages.

Even though, as we will see below, the effect of increasing communication delays is quite linear, the results cannot be obtained by simply adding the total message delay time per job (the delay required for 4 messages) to the results for no delays. This simple approach does not work because it neglects the time saved by having the announcements of waiting jobs already queued at processors that are busy when the jobs are first announced.

*Restarting after late bids.* In most of the simulations of DSP, late bids are never accepted no matter how much of an improvement they are over the earlier bids (i.e., step (4a) is not included in the algorithm). In one series of simulations, designed to test the effect of this parameter, a range of values for this "late bid improvement" parameter is investigated.

## Simulation methods

In order to increase the power of comparisons between different simulations at the same utilization level, the variance reduction technique called *common random numbers* was used (see [Law82a], pp. 350-354). In this technique, the same sequence of random numbers is used to generate jobs in each of the different simulations. Each simulation was run until a 90 percent confidence interval could be computed with a width of less than 15 percent of the estimated mean. The number of jobs required ranged from 1200 jobs in some of the simulations for system utilization of 0.1 to over 75,000 jobs in some of the simulations for system utilization of 0.9 (see [Mal87] for more details).

## Simulation results

*Relative effects of system load, processor speeds, and accuracy of processing time estimates*

We first investigated the results of DSP scheduling with a variety of system loads, network configurations, and accuracies of processing time estimates. In order to focus on the effect of these factors, message delays were kept constant (at 0), and late bids were never accepted, no matter how much better they were (i.e., the "late bid improvement" parameter was effectively infinite). Figure 3 shows the effect of system load for a typical configuration (1 machine of speed 4 and 4 machines of speed 1). Similar results were obtained for the other configurations. Figure 4 shows the effect of processor speed configuration holding constant both system load (at 50% utilization) and accuracy of processing time estimates (at 0% error). These figures show that both system load and processor speed configuration have a major impact on mean flow time (as much as a factor of 4 for the range of conditions we studied), while the accuracy of processing time estimates does not appear to be a major factor in performance (at most a difference of about 15% between perfect estimates and estimates with errors of up to 100%).

Figure 4 shows that the effect of dividing the same amount of processing power into more and more processors is almost linear and that the number of processors used has a much greater impact on flow time than the maximum range of processor speeds. Even if we restrict our attention to the first part of the graph where the number of processors ranges from 1 to 4, we see that this makes a difference of approximately a factor of 3 in flow time, while changing from a configuration with identical processors to one with a speed range of a factor of 4 makes only about a 12 percent difference in flow time.

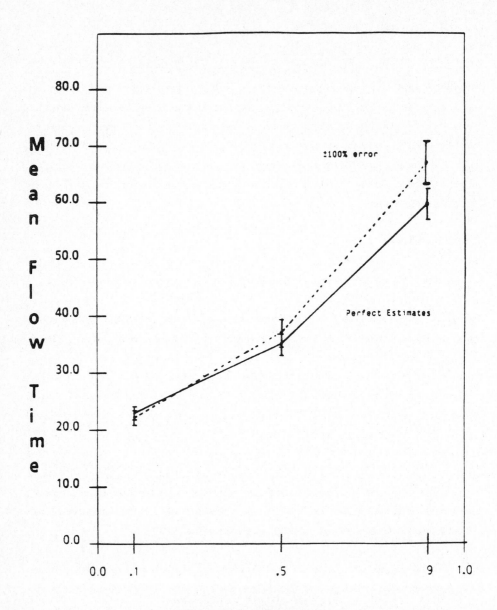

**System Utilization**

**Figure 3**

Effect on mean flow time of system utilization and accuracy of processing time
estimates (for DSP with network configuration 41111)

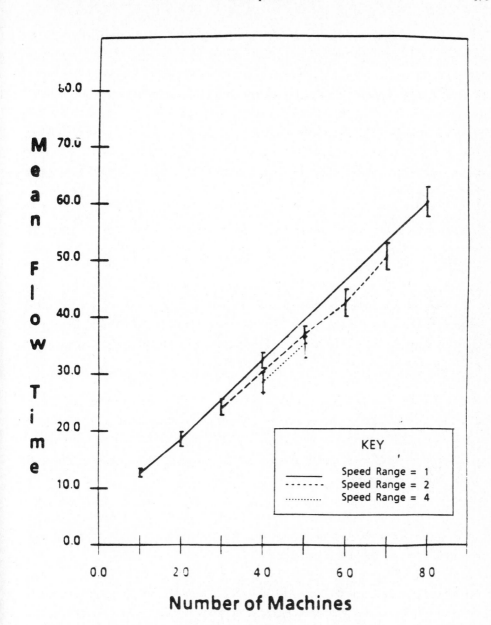

**Figure 4**

Effect on mean flow time of network configuration
(number of machines and maximum range of processor speeds).
For DSP, 50% system utilization, perfect estimates of processing times,
total processing capacity fixed at 8.

*Increasing the size of the bidding network while keeping overall utilization constant*

The results we have just seen all involve configurations in which the total amount of processing power in the network is constant (a total of 8 processing units), but divided among processors in different ways. From the point of view of a network designer, another relevant question is how many processors to combine in one bidding network, that is, how many processors to group together for the purpose of sharing tasks. To answer this question, we assume that the speed of each processor and the overall utilization remain constant and then consider the effect of adding processors to the network.

Since simple ways of analytically computing the effects of sequencing are not known, we use the results of the DSP simulations to estimate the effect of (shortest processing time first) sequencing in networks with different numbers of identical machines. Then these estimates are adjusted analytically to refer to networks in which all the machines have the same speed (speed 1). Since the simulations for a machine of speed 8 and one of speed 1 are identical except for the time units, we can make this adjustment, by simply scaling time units. If $W_{N,s}$ is the mean flow time for a network with N identical machines of speed s, then a network with N machines of speed s' would have a mean flow time of $W_{N,s'} = (s/s')W_{N,s}$.

These results are shown in Figure 5. It is clear that pooling work from several processors can, indeed, have a significant impact on flow time. This effect, however, is very dependent on the system utilization. There is essentially no benefit at low utilizations; at moderate utilizations, there is very little additional benefit after about 4 machines, and even for heavy utilizations, most of the benefits have been exhausted by about 8 machines.

It is important to realize that this result is quite general. The shape of the curves shown in the figure does not depend on processor speeds or average job processing times; changes in these factors merely change the scale of the vertical axis.

The implication of this result for system design is quite important. It suggests that there can be significant benefits from pooling work generated by different machines in a network but that there is no need to have large numbers of machines all on the same bidding network. In many situations, several separate networks of 8 - 10 processors each should perform as well, from the point of view of reducing mean flow time, as a single network including all the processors together.

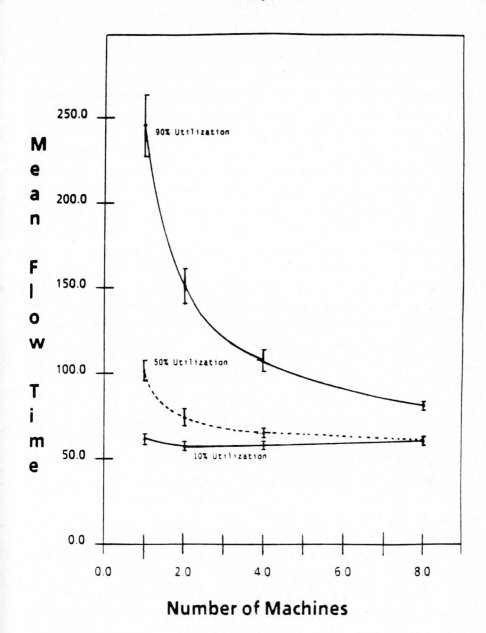

**Figure 5**

Effect on mean flow time of adding processing capacity
while keeping overall utilization constant
(for DSP with perfect processing time estimates
and identical machines of speed 1)

*Effects of message delays*

One of the possible problems with pooling work from several machines (even if only a few machines are involved) is that the message delays required for scheduling and for transferring results back and forth might overwhelm the flow time benefits obtained from pooling. Figure 6 compares the results of pooling jobs by network scheduling to the results of processing all jobs locally on the machines at which they originate. The configurations simulated were chosen from our total set of configurations to represent the situation in which the least benefit would result from pooling (only two identical machines) and the situations in which the most benefit would result (the maximum number of total machines or the maximum range of processor speeds).

The results in Figure 6 show that pooling of work can, in fact, be beneficial, even when message delays are quite substantial. With moderate loads (50%) and large numbers of processors, pooled scheduling is superior to strictly local processing even when message delays exceed 20% of the average job processing time! Even in the configuration where pooling has the least benefit (two identical machines), pooled scheduling is preferred at moderate loads up to about the point where message delays exceed 5% of the average job processing time.

*Effects of "late bid improvement" parameter*

Figure 7 shows the effect of varying the amount of improvement required in "late" bids before jobs will be cancelled on the machines to which they were originally sent and restarted on the late bidding machine. If we let $t_E$ be the estimated completion time in the earlier bid, $t_L$ be the estimated completion time in the late bid, and t be the time at which the late bid is evaluated, then the "improvement" is $i = 1 - (t_L - t)/(t_E - t)$. Late bids must exceed some criterion parameter $i_0$ before they will be accepted.

We have simulated the configuration in which this factor could make the most difference (the configuration with the maximum range of processor speeds). The most improvement possible for a single job in this situation is 0.75 (if a processor of speed 4 becomes available immediately after a bid has been awarded to a processor of speed 1). Therefore, setting $i_0$ at 0.75 or greater will result in no rescheduling.

As Figure 7 shows, at low utilizations performance is improved by rescheduling for any improvement at all, no matter how small, but at moderate utilizations, performance is made slightly worse by this strategy. In both cases, the optimal setting for $i_0$ appears to be somewhere in the range of 0.4 to 0.6. At moderate utilizations, the maximum benefit from using this

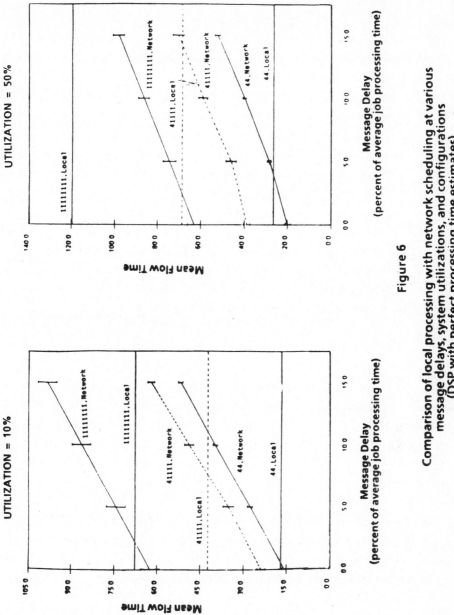

**Figure 6**

Comparison of local processing with network scheduling at various
message delays, system utilizations, and configurations
(DSP with perfect processing time estimates)

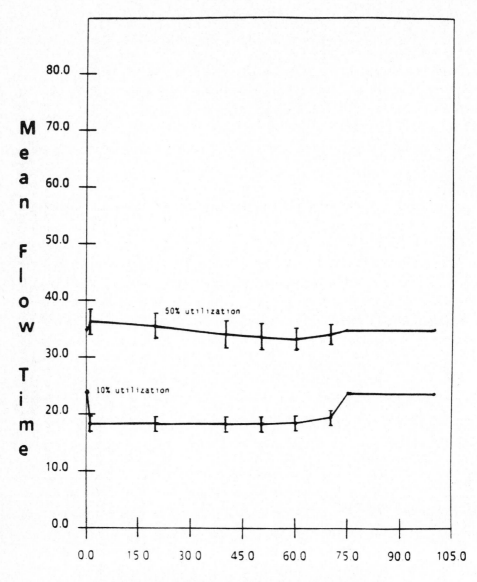

**Figure 7**

Effect on mean flow time of various settings
for "late bid improvement" criterion, $i_0$
(DSP with perfect estimates of processing time.
Network configuration 41111)

parameter appears to be about 5 percent, while at low utilizations using this parameter may result in overall flow time improvements on the order of 20 to 25 percent. This result is sensible since the only cost of rescheduling is the processing time "wasted" on the first processor, and with low utilization, this processing time is plentiful anyway. As utilizations increase, the cost of "wasting" time on the first processor to which a job is assigned increases and the potential benefit from using this parameter becomes negligible.

## CONCLUSION

Any designer of a parallel processing computing system, whether the processors are geographically distributed or not, must solve the problem of scheduling tasks on processors. In this paper, we presented a simple heuristic method for solving this problem and summarized simulations of its performance in a wide variety of situations. This scheduling heuristic is particularly suited to a decentralized implementation in which separate decisions made by a set of geographically distributed processors lead to a globally coherent schedule. Our results were encouraging about the desirability of this and similar heuristics in such a situation: (1) substantial performance improvements result from sharing tasks among processors in systems with more than light loads; (2) in many cases, these benefits are still present even when message delay times are as much as 5 to 20 percent of the average task processing time; (3) in many cases, the additional benefits from pooling tasks among more than 8 or 10 machines are small; and (4) large errors in estimating task processing times cause little degradation in scheduling performance.

The Enterprise system shows how this approach can allow users of personal workstations on a network to easily take advantage of the maximum amount of processing power and parallelism available on the network at any time, with little extra cost when there are few extra machines available.

## Acknowledgements

The first part of this work was performed while three of the authors (Malone, Fikes, and Howard) were at the Xerox Palo Alto Research Center. The work has been supported by the Xerox Palo Alto Research Center, the Xerox University Grants Program, and the Center for Information Systems Research, MIT.

The authors would like to thank Michael Cohen, Randy Davis, Larry Masinter, Mike Rothkopf, Vineet Singh, Henry Thompson, Bill van Melle, and an anonymous referee for helpful comments. They would also like to thank Rodney Adams and--especially--Debasis Bhaktiyar for running many of the simulations whose results are reported here.

## Footnote

1 Strictly speaking, this approach only makes sense in systems with "uniform processors", that is where the processing times on all processors are proportional, but with some processors faster than others. In this case, processing time estimates can be made in terms of processing times on a "standard speed processor." All our simulations are of such "uniform processor" systems and the machines on which the prototype system was implemented were close enough to having this characteristic that the assumption was a useful simplification.

## Appendix

Table 1 summarizes the message formats used in the Distributed Scheduling Protocol. The message definitions use a modified form of BNF specification. Nonterminal symbols are enclosed by angle brackets ("< >"), terminal symbols are written without delimiters, ellipses ("...") are used to indicate lists containing an arbitrary number of 0 or more terms, and square brackets ("[ ]") indicate comments.

## Table 1

### DSP Message Formats

| | | |
|---|---|---|
| \<DSPmessage\> | → | \<requestforbids\> \| \<bid\> \| \<acknowledgement\> \| \<task\> \| \<result\> \| \<query\> \| \<status\> \| \<bump\> \| \<cancel\> \| \<cutoff\> |
| \<requestforbids\> | → | (REQUESTFORBIDS \<taskID\> priority \<earliestStartTime\> \<requirements\> \<taskSummary\>) |
| \<bid\> | → | (BID \<taskID\> \<startTime\> \<completionTime\>) |
| \<acknowledgement\> | → | (ACK \<taskID\>) |
| \<task\> | → | (TASK \<taskID\> priority \<taskSummary\> taskDescription) |
| \<result\> | → | (RESULT \<taskID\> \<resultStatus\> \<runtime\> result) |
| \<query\> | → | (QUERY \<taskID\>) |
| \<status\> | → | (STATUS \<taskstatus\> \<startTime\> \<completionTime\>) |
| \<bump\> | → | (BUMP \<startTime\> \<completionTime\>) |
| \<cancel\> | → | (CANCEL \<taskID\>) |
| \<cutoff\> | → | (CUTOFF \<taskID\> \<runtime\>) |
| \<taskID\> | → | (hostName taskName taskCreationTime lastMilestoneTime) |
| \<taskCreationTime\> | → | systemTime |
| \<lastMilestoneTime\> | → | systemTime |
| \<earliestStartTime\> | → | systemTime |
| \<startTime\> | → | systemTime |
| \<completionTime\> | → | systemTime |
| \<resultStatus\> | → | NORMAL \| ERROR |
| \<runtime\> | → | (elapsedTime machineType) |
| \<taskstatus\> | → | LOCAL \| BIDDING \| SCHEDULED \| DELIVERED \| RUNNING \| NORMAL \| ERROR \| DELETED \| CUTOFF |
| \<requirements\> | → | (\<requirement\> ... \<requirment\>) |
| \<requirement\> | → | REMOTE \| REMOTEORLOCAL \| (HOSTS \<hostName\> ...\<hostName\>) \| [other terms to be added] |
| \<taskSummary\> | → | (\<summaryterm\> ... \<summaryterm\>) |
| \<summaryterm\> | → | ( TIME timeEst) \| (FILES \<fileDescriptionList\>) \| [other terms to be added] |
| \<fileDescriptionList\> | → | \<fileDescription\> \| \<fileDescription\> \<fileDescriptionList\> |
| \<fileDescription\> | → | (fileName fileCreationDate fileLoadTimeEst) |

# References

[Ber82]     Berhard, R. Computing at the speed limit. *IEEE Spectrum*, July 1982, 26-31.

[Bir84]     Birrell, A. D., and Nelson, B. J. Implementing remote procedure calls. *ACM Transactions on Computer Systems*, 1984, 2(1), 39-59.

[Bir82]     Birrell, Andrew D., Levin, Roy, Needham, Roger M., Schroeder, Michael D., Grapevine: An Excercise in Distributed Computing. *Communications of the ACM*, 25(4), April 1982.

[Bog80]     Boggs, David R., Shoch, John F., Taft, Edward A., Metcalfe, Robert M., Pup: An Internetwork Architecture. *IEEE Transactions on Communications*, COM-28, (4), April 1980.

[Bru74]     Bruno, J., Coffman, E. G., & Sethi, R. Scheduling independent tasks to reduce mean finishing time. *Communications of the ACM*, 1974, 17, 382-387.

[Bry81]     Bryant, R., & Finkel, R. A stable distributed scheduling algorithm. *Proceedings of the Second International Conference on Distributed Computer Systems*, April 1981.

[Cho79]     Chow, Y. and Kohler, W. Models for dynamic load balancing in a heterogeneous multiple processor system. *IEEE Transaction on Computers*. May 1979, C-18.

[Cof73]     Coffman, Edward G., Jr., and Denning, Peter J., *Operating Systems Theory*. Prentice-Hall, Inc., Englewood Cliffs, New Jersey, 1973.

[Con67]     Conway, R. W., Maxwell, W. L., Miller, L. W. *Theory of Scheduling*. Addison-Wesley Publishing Company, Reading, Massachusetts, 1967.

[Dav81b]    Davies, D., Holler, E., Jensen, E., Kimbleton, S., Lampson, B., LeLann, G., Thurber, K., and Watson, R. *Distributed systems-Architecture and implementation: Lecture notes in computer science, vol. 105*. New York: Springer-Verlag, 1981.

[Dav83]     Davis, R., and Smith, R. G., Negotiation as a Metaphor for Distributed Problem Solving. *Artificial Intelligence*, Volume 20 Number 1, January 1983.

[Dei84]     Deitel, H. M. *An Introduction to Operating Systems*. Reading, Mass.: Addison Wesley, 1984.

[Eag86a]    Eager, D. L., Lazowska, E. D., & Zahorjan, J. A comparison of receiver-initiated and sender-initiated adaptive load sharing. *Performance Evaluation*, 6, 1986, 53-68.

[Eag86b]    Eager, D. L., Lazowska, E. D., & Zahorjan, J. Adaptive load sharing in homogeneous distributed systems. *IEEE Transactions on Software Engineering*, vol. SE-12, 1986 (May), 662-675.

[Ens81]     Enslow, P. What is a distributed data processing system?. *Computer*, vol. 11, June 1980.

[Far72]     Farber, D. J. and Larson, K. C. The structure of the distributed computing system-- Software. In J. Fox (Ed.), *Proceedings of the Symposium on Computer-Communications Networks and Teletraffic*, Brooklyn, NY: Polytechnic Press, 1972, pp. 539-545.

[Far73]    Farber, D., et al. The distributed computer system. *Proceedings of the 7th Annual IEEE Computer Society International Conference*, February 1973.

[Gaj85]    Gajski, D aand Peir, J. Essential Issues in Multiprocessor Systems. *IEEE Computer*, June 1985, pp. 9-27.

[Gla79]    Glazebrook, K. D. Scheduling tasks with exponential service times on parallel processors. *Journal of Applied Probability*, 1979, 16, 685-689.

[Gon77]    Gonzales, T., Ibarra, O. H., and Sahni, S. Bounds for LPT schedules on uniform processors, *SIAM Journal of Computing*, 1977, 6, 155-166 (as cited by [Jaffee]).

[Gra69]    Graham, R. L. Bounds on multiprocessing timing anomalies. *SIAM Journal of Applied Mathematics*, 1969 (March), 17, 416-429 (summarized in Coffman and Denning, pp. 100-106.).

[Iba77]    Ibarra, O. H. and Kim, C. E. Heuristic algorithms for scheduling independent tasks on nonidentical processors. *Journal of the ACM*, 1977 (April), 24, 280-289.

[Jaf80]    Jaffe, J. M. Efficient scheduling of tasks without full use of processor resources. *Theoretical Computer Science*, 1980, 12, 1-17.

[Jon80]    Jones, A. K., and Schwarz, P. Experience Using Multiprocessor Systems - A Status Report. *Computing Surveys*, Volume 12, Number 2, June 1980.

[Kle81]    Kleinrock, L., and Nilsson, A. On optimal scheduling algorithms for time-shared systems. *Journal of Association of Computing Machinery*, 28, 3, pp. 477-486, July 1981.

[Lam68]    Lampson, B. W. A scheduling philosophy for multiprocessing systems. *Communications of the ACM*, 1968 (May), 11, 347-359.

[Lar82]    Larsen, R., McEntire, P., and O'Reilly, J. *Tutorial: Distributed control.* Silver Spring, MD: IEEE Computer Society Press, 1982.

[Law82a]   Law, A. M., & Kelton, W. D. *Simulation modeling and analysis.* New York: McGraw-Hill, 1982a.

[Liv82]    Livny, M., & Melman, M. Load balancing in homogeneous broadcast distributed systems. *Proceedings of the Computer Network Performance Symposium*, Maryland, 1982.

[Mal83]    Malone, T., Fikes, R., Howard, M., *Enterprise: A market-like task scheduler for distributed computing environments.* Working paper, Xerox Palo Alto Research Center, Palo Alto, CA, October, 1983 (Also available as CISR WP#111, Center for Information Systems Research, Massachusetts Institute of Technology, Cambridge, MA, October, 1983).

[Mal87]    Malone, T.W., Fikes, R.E., Grant, K.R. & Howard, M.T. *Market-like task scheduling in distributed computing environments.* Massachusetts Institute of Technology, Sloan School of Management Working Paper #1785-86, May 1986.

[Men85]    Mendelson, H. Pricing computer services: Queueing effects. *Communications of the ACM*, 28,3, March 1985.

[Met76]    Metcalfe, R. M., and Boggs, D. R., Ethernet: distributed packet switching for local computer networks. *Communications of the ACM*, 19 (7), July 1976.

[Nel81]    Nelson, B. J. Remote Procedure Call. Xerox Palo Alto Research Center, CSL-81-9, May 1981.

[Ni81]     Ni, L. M., & Hwang, K. Optimal load balancing strategies for a multiple processor system. *Proceedings of the 10th International Conference on Parallel Processing*, August 1981, pp. 352-357.

[Ni85]     Ni, L. M., Xu, C. W., & Gendreau, T. B. A distributed drafting algorithm for load balancing. *IEEE Transactions on Software Engineering*, 1984 (October), *SE-11*, (No. 10), 1153-1161.

[Nil80]    Nilsson, N. J. Principles of Artificial Intelligence. Palo Alto, CA: Tioga Publishing Co., 1980.

[Sch84]    Schroeder, M., Birrell, A., and Needham, R. Experience With grapevine: The Growth of a Distributed System. *ACM Transaction on Computer Systems*, 1984, 2(1), 3-23.

[Sho82]    Shoch, John F., Hupp, Jon A., The WORM Programs - Early Experience with a Distributed Computation. *Communications of the ACM*, 25(3), March 1982.

[Sin85]    Singh, V. & Genesereth, M. A variable supply model for distributing deductions. *Proceedings of the International Joint Conference on Artificial Intelligence*, August 1985, Los Angeles, CA.

[Smi80]    Smith, R. G., The Contract Net Protocol: High-Level Communication and Control in a Distributed Problem Solver  IEEE Transactions on Computers  Volume C-29 Number 12, December 1980.

[Smi81]    Smith, R. G. and Davis, R., Frameworks for Cooperation in Distributed Problem Solving. *IEEE Transactions on Systems, Man, and Cybernetics*, Volume SMC-11 Number 1, January 1981.

[Sta84]    Stankovic, J. and Sidhu, I. An adaptive bidding algorithm for processes, clusters and distributed groups. In *Proceedings of the Fourth Interational Conference on Distributed Computing Systems*, May 1984.

[Sta85]    Stankovic, J. An application of bayesian decision theory to decentralized control of job scheduling. *IEEE Transactions of Conputers*, 1985, *C-34*, 2, pp. 117-130.

[SRC85]    Stankovic, J., Ramaritham, K., and Cheng, S. Evaluation of a flexible task scheduling algorithm for distributed hard real-time systems. *IEEE Transactions on computer*, C-34, *12*, December 1985.

[Sto78]    Stone, H. and Bokhari, S. Control of distributed processes. *Computer*, vol. 11, pp. 97-106, July 1978.

[Sut68]    Sutherland, I. E. A futures market in computer time. *Communications of the ACM*, 1968 (June), 11, 449-451.

[Tan85]    Tantawi, A. & Towsley, D. Optimal static load balancing in distributed computer systesm. *Journal of the ACM*, 1985, *32*, 445-465.

[Ten81a]    Tenney, R., Strategies for distributed decisionmaking. *IEEE Transactions on Systems, Man and Cybernetics*, vol. SMC-11, pp. 527-538, August 1981.

[Ten81b]    Tenney, R. and Sandel, Jr., N.  Structures for distributed decisionmaking. *IEEE Transactions on Systems, Man and Cybernetics*, vol. SMC-11, pp. 517-527, August 1981.

[Tho83]    Thompson, H.  Remote Procedure Call.  Unpublished documentation for Interlisp-D system, Xerox Palo Alto Research Center, Palo Alto, CA; January, 1983.

[Van81]    Van der Heyden, L.  Scheduling jobs with exponential processing and arrival times on identical processors so as to minimize the expected makespan. *Mathematics of Operations Research*, 1981, 6, 305-312.

[Vnt81]    Van Tilborg, A. M., & Wittie, L. D.  Distributed task force scheduling in multi-microcomputer networks. *Proceedings of the National Computer Conference*, 1981, 50, 283-289.

[Wan85]    Wang, Y. T., & Morris, R. J. T.  Load sharing in distributed systems. *IEEE Transactions on Computer Systems*, vol. C-34, 1985 (March), 204-217.

[Web82]    Weber, R. R.  Scheduling jobs with stochastic processing requirements on parallel machines to minimize makespan or flowtime. *Journal of Applied Probability*, 1982, 19, 167-182.

[Wit80]    Wittie, L. and van Tilborg, A.  MICROS, A distributed operationg system for micronet, A reconfigurable network computer. *IEEE Transactions on Conputing*, vol. C-29, December 1980.

The Ecology of Computation
B.A. Huberman (editor)
© Elsevier Science Publishers B.V. (North-Holland), 1988

# From RIG to Accent to Mach: The Evolution of A Network Operating System

Richard F. Rashid
Computer Science Department
Carnegie-Mellon University
Pittsburgh, Pa. 15213

## 1. Background

Mach is a multiprocessor operating system kernel currently under development at Carnegie-Mellon University. In addition to binary compatibility with Berkeley's current UNIX 4.3 bsd release, Mach provides a number of new facilities not available in 4.3, including:

- Support for tightly coupled and loosely coupled general purpose multiprocessors.

- An internal symbolic kernel debugger.

- Support for transparent remote file access between autonomous systems.

- Support for large, sparse virtual address spaces, copy-on-write virtual copy operations, and memory mapped files.

- Provisions for user-provided memory objects and pagers.

- Multiple threads of control within a single address space.

- A capability-based interprocess communication facility integrated with virtual memory management to allow transfer of large amounts of data (up to the size of a process address space) via copy-on-write techniques.

- Transparent network interprocess communication with preservation of capability protection across network boundaries.

As of July 1987, Mach runs on most uniprocessor VAX architecture machines: VAX 11/750, 11/780, 11/785, 8200, 8600, 8650, MicroVAX I, and MicroVAX II. Mach also runs on three multiprocessor VAX machines, the four (11/780 or 11/785) processor VAX 11/784 with 8 MB of shared memory the VAX 8300 (with up to 4 processors) and VAX 8800. Mach has been ported to the IBM RT PC, the SUN 3, the 16 processor Encore MultiMax and a 26 processor Sequent Balance 21000. The current version of the system includes all of the features listed above and is in production use by CMU researchers on a number of projects including a multiprocessor speech recognition system called Agora [6] and a project to build parallel production systems.

Mach is the logical successor to CMU's Accent [17, 18] kernel -- an operating system designed to support a large network of uniprocessor scientific personal computers. The design and implementation of Accent was in turn based on experiences gained during the development of the University of Rochester's RIG system [3, 15], a message-based network access machine. Both RIG and Accent have seen considerable use over the years. RIG provided a variety of functions including terminal support and remote file access within the Rochester environment until early this year when the last RIG machine was removed from service. Accent continues in use at CMU as the basic operating system for a network of 150 PERQ workstations and has seen commercial use in printing and publishing workstations as well as engineering design systems. As a third generation network operating system Mach, benefits from the lessons learned in over ten years of design, implementation and use of RIG and Accent. This paper summarizes the lessons of those systems and their impact on the design and implementation of Mach.

## 2. The Evolution of Accent from RIG

Implementation of RIG began in 1975 on an early version of the Data General Eclipse mini-computer. The first usable version of the system came on-line in the fall of 1976. Eventually the Rochester network included several RIG Eclipse nodes as network servers and a number of Xerox Altos acting as RIG client hosts. RIG provided clients network file services, ARPANET access, printing services and a variety of other functions. Active development continued well into the 1980's but obsolescence of its Data General Eclipse and Xerox Alto hardware base eventually dictated its demise in the Spring of 1986.

### 2.1. The RIG Design

The basic system structuring tool in RIG was an interprocess communication (IPC) facility which allowed RIG processes to communicate by sending packets of information between themselves. RIG's IPC facility was defined in terms of two basic abstractions: *messages* and *ports*.

A RIG port was defined to be a kernel-provided queue for messages and was referenced by a global identifier consisting of a dotted pair of integers ⟨*process number.port number*⟩. A RIG port was protected in the sense that it could only be manipulated directly by the RIG kernel, but it was unprotected in the sense that any process could send a message to a port. A RIG port was tied directly to the RIG abstraction of a *process* -- a protected address space with a single thread of program control.

A RIG message was composed of a header followed by data. Messages were of limited size and could contain at most two scalar data items or two array objects. The type tagging of data in messages was limited to a small set of simple scalar and array data types. Port identifiers could be sent in messages only as simple integers which would then be interpreted by the destination process.

Due largely to the hardware on which it was implemented, RIG did not allow either a paged virtual memory or an address space larger than $2\uparrow16$ bytes. RIG did, however, use simple memory mapping techniques to move data [3]. The largest amount of data which could be transferred at a time was 2K bytes.

## 2.2. Problems with RIG

The RIG message passing architecture was originally intended more as a means for achieving modular decomposition (much like Brinch-Hansen's RC4000) rather than as the basis for a distributed system. It was discovered early on, though, that RIG's message passing facility could be adapted as the communication base for a network operating system. Unfortunately, as RIG became heavily used for networking work at Rochester a number of problems with the original design became apparent:

* **Protection**

    The fact that ports were represented as global identifiers which could be constructed and used by any process implied that a process could not limit the set of processes which could send it a message. To function correctly, each process had to be prepared to accept any possible message sent to it from any potential source. A single errant process could conceivably flood a process or even the entire system with incoherent messages.

* **Failure notification**

    Another difficulty with global identifiers was that they could be passed in messages as simple integers. It was therefore impossible to determine whether a given process was potentially dependent on another process. In principle any process could store in its data space a reference to any other process. The failure of a machine or a process could therefore not be signaled back to dependent processes automatically. Instead, a special process was invented which ran on each machine and was notified of process death events. Processes had to explicitly register their dependencies on other processes with this special "grim reaper" process in order to receive event-driven notifications.

* **Transparency of service**

    Because ports were tied explicitly to processes, a port defined service could not be moved from one process to another without notifying all parties. Transparent network communication was also compromised by this naming scheme. A port identifier was required to explicitly contain the network host identifier as part of its process number field. As the system expanded from one machine to one network to multiple interconnected networks this caused the port identifier to expand in size -- usually resulting in considerable reimplementation work.

● **Maximum message size**

The limited size of messages in RIG resulted in a style of interprocess interaction in which large data objects (such as files) had to be broken up into chunks of 2K bytes or less. This constraint impacted on the efficiency of the system (by increasing the amount of message communication) and on the complexity of client/server interactions (e.g., by forcing servers to maintain state information about open files).

## 2.3. The evolution of RIG

CMU's Spice [9] distributed personal workstation project provided an opportunity to effectively "redo" a RIG-like system taking into account that system's limitations. The result was the Accent operating system kernel for the PERQ Systems Corporation PERQ computer.

The Accent solution to the problems present in the RIG design was based on two basic ideas:

1. **Define ports to be capabilities as well as communication objects.**

By providing processes with capabilities to ports rather than a global identifier for them[1], it was possible to solve at one time the problems of protection, failure notification and transparency:

   ● Protection in Accent is provided by allowing processes access only to those ports for which they have been given capabilities.

   ● Processes can be notified automatically when a port disappears on which those processes are dependent because the kernel now has complete knowledge of which processes have access to each port in the system. There is no hidden communication between processes.

   ● Transparency is complete because the ultimate destination of a message sent to a port is unknown by the sender. Thus transparent intermediary processes can be constructed which forward messages between groups of processes without their knowledge (either for the purpose of debugging and monitoring or for the purpose of transparent network communication).

2. **Use virtual memory to overcome limitations in the handling of large objects.**

---

[1]An idea borrowed from Forest Baskett's DEMOS system [5].

The use of a large address space (a luxury not possible in the design of RIG) and copy-on-write memory mapping techniques permits processes to transmit objects as large as they can directly access themselves. This allows processes such as file servers to provide access to large objects (e.g., files) through a single message exchange -- drastically reducing the number of messages sent in the system [10].

The first line of Accent code was written in April 1981. As late as May 1986 Accent was still in use at CMU on a network of 150 PERQ workstations. In addition to network operating system functions such as distributed process and file management, window management and mail systems, several applications were built using Accent. These included research systems for distributed signal processing [11], distributed speech understanding [6] and distributed transaction processing [19]. Four separate programming environments were implemented -- CommonLisp, Pascal, C and Ada -- including language support for an object-oriented remote procedure call facility [13]. Accent is still in use at CMU and elsewhere today, although the role it plays within the Department of Computer Science has diminished with as PERQ workstations have been replaced with MicroVAX II, SUN 3 and IBM RT PC systems.

# 3. The Accent Design

Accent is organized around the notion of a protected, message-based interprocess communication facility integrated with copy-on-write virtual memory management. Access to all services and resources, including the process management and memory management services of the operating system kernel itself, are provided through Accent's communication facility. This allows completely uniform access to such resources throughout the network. It also implies that access to kernel provided services is indistinguishable from access to process provided resources (with the exception of the interprocess communication facility itself).

### 3.1. Interprocess communication

The Accent interprocess communication facility is defined in terms of abstractions which, as in RIG, are called *ports* and *messages*.

The *port* is the basic transport abstraction provided by Accent. A port is a protected kernel object into which messages may be placed by processes and from which messages may be removed. A port is logically a finite length queue of messages sent by a process. Ports may have any number of senders but only one receiver. Access to a port is granted by receiving a message containing a port capability (to either send or receive).

Ports are used by processes to represent services or data structures. For example, the Accent window manager uses a port to represent a window on a bitmap display. Operations on a window are requested by a client process by sending a message to the port representing that window. The window manager process then receives that message and handles the request. Ports used in this way can be thought of as though they were capabilities to objects in a object oriented system(Jones78). The act of sending a message (and perhaps receiving a reply) corresponds to a cross-domain procedure call in a capability based system such as Hydra [2] or StarOS [12].

A *message* consists of a fixed length header and a variable size collection of typed data objects. Messages may contain both port capabilities and/or imbedded pointers as long as both are properly typed. A single message may transfer up to $2\uparrow32$ bytes of by-value data.

Messages may be sent and received either synchronously or asynchronously. A software interrupt mechanism allows a process to handle incoming messages outside the flow of normal program execution.

Figure 3-1 shows a typical message interaction. A process A sends a message to a port P2. Process A has send rights to P2 and receive rights to a port P1. At some later time, process B which has receive rights to port P2 receives that message which may in turn contain send rights to port P1 (for the purposes of sending a reply message back to process A). Process B then (optionally) replies by sending a message to P1.

Should port P2 have been full, process A would have had the option at the point of sending the message to: (1) be suspended until the port was no longer full, (2) have the message send operation return a port full error code, or (3) have the kernel accept the message for future transmission to port P2 with the proviso that no further message can be sent by that process to P2 until the kernel sends a message to A telling it the current message has been posted.

### 3.2. Virtual memory support
Accent provides a $2\uparrow32$ byte paged address space for each process in the system and a $2\uparrow32$ byte paged address space for the operating system kernel. Disk pages and physical memory can be addressed by the kernel as a portion of its $2\uparrow32$ byte address space. Accent maintains a virtual memory table for each user process and for the operating system kernel. The kernel's address space is paged and all user process maps are kept in paged kernel memory. Only the kernel virtual memory table, a small kernel stack, the PERQ screen, I/O memory and those

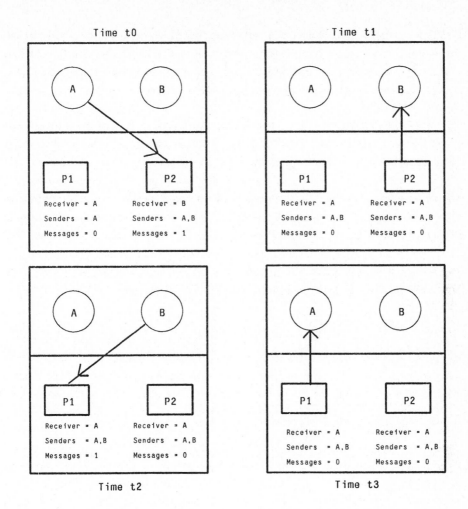

**Figure 3-1:** Typical message exchange

PASCAL modules required for handling the simplest form of page fault need be locked in physical memory, although in practice parts of the kernel debugger and symbol tables for locked modules are also locked to allow analysis of system errors. The total amount of kernel code and symbol table information locked is 64K bytes [10].

Whenever large amounts of data (the threshold is a system compile-time constant normally set at 1K bytes) are transmitted in a message, Accent uses memory mapping techniques rather than data copying to move information from one process to another within the same machine. The semantics of message passing in Accent imply that all data sent in a message are logically copied from one address space to another. This can be optimized by the kernel by mapping the sent data copy-on-write in both the sending and receiving processes.

Figure 3-2 shows a process A sending a large (for example 24 megabyte) message to a port P1. At the point the message is posted to P1, the part of A's address space containing the message is marked copy-on-write -- meaning any page referenced for writing will be copied and the copy placed instead into A's virtual memory table. The copy-on-write data then resides in the address space of the kernel until process B receives the message. At that point the data is removed from the address space of the kernel. By default, the operating system kernel determines where in the address space of B the newly received message data is placed. This allows the kernel to minimize memory mapping overhead. Any attempt by either A or B to change a 512 byte page of this copy-on-write data results in a copy of that page being made and placed into that process' address space.

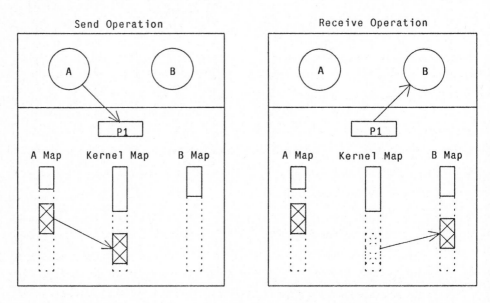

**Figure 3-2:** Memory mapping operations during message transfer

### 3.3. Network communication

The abstraction of communication through ports permits the distinction between access to local and remote resources to be completely invisible to a client process. In addition, Accent exploits the integration of memory management and IPC to provide a number of options in the handling of virtual memory, including the ability to allow memory to be sent copy-on-reference across a network. Each entry of an Accent virtual memory table maps a contiguous region of process virtual memory to a contiguous portion of an Accent *memory object*. A memory object is the basic unit of secondary storage in Accent. Memory objects can be contiguous physical memory (as used for the PERQ screen or I/O buffers) or a randomly addressed disk file. A memory object can also be backed not by disk or main memory, but by a process through a port. Initial references to a page of data mapped to a port are trapped by the kernel and a request for the necessary data is forwarded in a message on that port. This feature allows processes to provide the system with virtual memory that they themselves maintain (either locally or over a network connection to another machine). In this way network communication servers can provide copy-on-reference network transmission of pages in a large message.

## 4. Key Implementation Issues in Accent

Many of the implementation decisions made in Accent were based on experiences with RIG. Nevertheless, the addition of virtual memory and capability management to the RIG design made it unclear how the RIG experiences would extrapolate to the Accent environment.

### 4.1. IPC Implementation

The actual implementation of the message mechanism relied on several assumptions about the use of messages:

- the average number of messages outstanding at any given time per process would be small,

- the number of port capabilities needed by a process could vary from two to several hundred, and

- the use of simple messages (meaning messages which contained port capabilities only in their header and which contained less than a few kilobytes) would so dominate complex messages that simple messages would be an important special case.

Each of these assumptions had held true for RIG [4, 15]. It was hoped that although Accent provided a substantially different application environment than RIG, the RIG experiences would provide a reasonable prediction of Accent performance.

Given these expectations, the implementation was optimized for anticipated common cases, including:

- The assumption that there would seldom be more than one message waiting for a process at a time led to an implementation in which messages are queued in per-process rather than per-port queues.

- To allow large numbers of ports per process and fast lookup, port capabilities are represented as indexes into a global port record array stored in kernel virtual memory. Port access is protected through the use of a bitmap of process access rights kept per port (the number of processes is much less than the number of ports).

- The assumption that simple messages would be an important special case led to the addition of a field to the message header so that user processes can indicate whether or not a message is simple and thus allow special handling by the kernel.

These usage assumptions did in fact prove true for Accent. Table 4-1 demonstrates the properties of Accent message passing as measured during an active day of use.

| | |
|---|---|
| 1.01 | Average probes to requested message |
| 33.42 | Average port rights held per process |
| 14.38 | Average ports owned per process |
| 0.094 | Ratio of complex to simple messages |

**Table 4-1:** Message use statistics

## 4.2. Virtual Memory Implementation

The lack of sophisticated virtual memory management in RIG (and in fact in nearly all message-based systems of that era) meant that Accent could not benefit from previous experience with virtual memory use resulting from message operations. Instead, the design of Accent's virtual memory implementation grew out of simple assumptions based purely on intuition. These initial assumptions influenced the design of the Accent virtual memory implementation:

- process maps had to be compact, easy to manipulate and support sparse use of a process address space,

- the number of contiguously mapped regions of the address space would be reasonably small, and

• large amounts of memory would frequently be passed copy-on-write in messages.

The Accent process virtual memory map is maintained as a two-level indirect table terminating in linked lists of entries (see Figure 4-1). Each entry on the linked list maps a contiguous portion of process virtual memory into contiguous regions of Accent memory objects. The map is organized so that large portions can be validated, invalidated or copied without having to modify the linked lists of map entries. This is accomplished by having valid, copy-on-write and write-protect bits at each level of the table. During lookup, these bits are "ored" together. Thus all of memory can be efficiently made copy-on-write by just setting the copy-on-write bits of valid entries in level one of the process map table. Figure 4-1 illustrates the translation of a virtual address to an offset within a memory object.

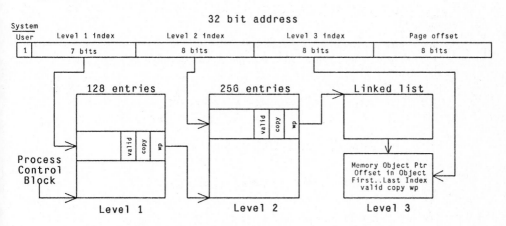

**Figure 4-1:** Mapping a virtual address in Accent

Physical memory in Accent is used as a cache of secondary storage. There are no special disk buffers. Access to all information (e.g., files) is through message passing (and subsequent page faulting if necessary).

This scheme is flexible enough to be used internally by the kernel to remap portions of its own address space. An entire process virtual memory map, for example, is copied in a fork operation without physically copying the map by using Accent's copy-on-write facility. To reduce map manipulation overheads, changes caused by copy-on-write updates are recorded first in a virtual to physical address translation table (kept in physical memory) and are not incorporated into a process map until the relevant page must be written out to secondary storage.

Copy-on-write access to memory objects is provided through the use of *shadow* memory objects which reflect page differences between a copied object and the object it shadows (which could in turn be a shadow). Disk space for newly created pages or pages written copy-on-write is allocated on an as-needed basis from a special paging area. No disk space is ever allocated to back up a process address space unless the paging algorithms need to flush a dirty page. See figure 4-2.

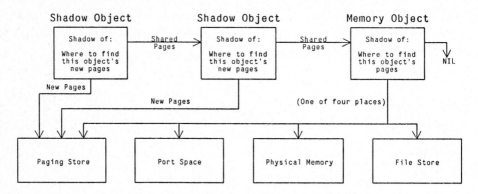

**Figure 4-2:**   An example of memory object shadowing

Most shadow memory objects are small (under 32 pages). Most large shadows contain only a few pages of data different from the objects they shadow. These facts led to an allocation scheme in which small shadows are allocated contiguously from the paging store and larger shadows use a page map and are allocated as needed.

Overall, the basic assumptions about the use of process address space in Accent appear to hold true. The typical user process table:

- is between 1024 and 2048 bytes in size,

- contains 34-70 mapping entries, and

- maps a region of virtual memory approximately eight megabytes in extent (in PERQ PASCAL each separately compiled module occupies a distinct 128K byte region of memory) and about one to two megabytes in size.

Although all memory is passed copy-on-write from one process to another, the number of copy-on-write faults is typically small. A typical PASCAL compile/link/load cycle, for example, requires only slightly more than one copy-on-write fault per second. Clearly most of the data passed by copy in Accent is read and not written. The result is that the logical advantages of copy-on-write are obtained with costs similar to that of mapped shared memory [7].

### 4.3. Programming issues

One of the problems with message based systems has traditionally been the fact that existing programming languages do not support their message semantics. In RIG, a special remote procedure call function was provided called "Call" [14] which took as its arguments a message identifier, a process-port identifier, and operation arguments along with their type information. One of the early decisions in the implementation of Accent was to define all interprocess message interfaces in terms of a high-level specification language. The properties of ports allow them to be viewed as object references. The interprocess specification language is defined in terms of operations on objects. Subsystem specifications in this language are compiled by a program called Matchmaker into remote procedure call stubs for the various programming languages used in the system -- currently C, PASCAL, ADA and Common LISP. The result is that all interprocess interfaces look to the programmer as though they were procedural interfaces in each of these languages. In PASCAL, for example, the interface procedure for writing a string to a window of the screen would look like:

WriteString(window,string-to-be-written)

All Matchmaker specified calls take as their first argument the port object on which the operation is to be performed. The remote procedure call stub then packages the request in a message, sends it to the port, and waits for a reply message (if necessary). Initial access to server ports is accomplished either through inheritance (by having the parent process send port rights to its children) or by accessing a name server process (a port for which is typically passed to a process by inheritance). A complete description and specification of Matchmaker can be found in [13].

Matchmaker's specification language allows both synchronous and asynchronous calls as well as the specification of timeouts and exception handling behavior. It supports both by-value and by-value-result parameters. It allows types to be defined as well as the specification of their bit packing characteristics in the message. For the server process, Matchmaker produces routines which allow incoming messages to be decoded and server subroutines automatically invoked with the proper arguments.

The support provided by Matchmaker is similar to some of the features which have been introduced in modern languages for managing multiple tasks such as the ADA rendezvous mechanism [1]. Matchmaker, however, supports a number of different programming languages and provides a much greater range of options for synchronous and asynchronous behavior in a distributed environment.

Despite the obvious simplicity of simple "remote procedure call" style interfaces, a suprizingly high percentage of network operating system interfaces take advantage of the asynchronous form of Matchmaker interfaces. Of 225 system interfaces:

- 170 (approximately 77 percent) are synchronous,

- 45 (approximately 19 percent) are asynchronous and

- 10 (approximately 4 percent) represent exceptions.

Runtime statistics show that over 50 percent of messages actually sent during normal system execution are sent as part of asynchronous Matchmaker specified operations -- normally due to the behavior of I/O subsystems (such as handlers for the PERQ keyboard and display) or basic system servers (such as network protocol servers).

Matchmaker server interfaces account for approximately 10 percent of the total network operating system code -- roughly 75.5k bytes out of 757k bytes. For the Accent kernel itself, the Matchmaker interface is 10280 bytes out of approximately 115k bytes. Runtime costs are considerably less. During a PASCAL compilation, for example, less than 2 percent of CPU time is due to Matchmaker interface overheads.

## 4.4. Key Statistics[2]

### 4.4.1. Hardware and basic system performance of Accent

Table 4-2 compares the relative performance of PERQ and VAX-11/780 CPUs. Timings were performed in PASCAL on the PERQ and in C on a VAX running UNIX 4.1bsd.

PASCAL programs written for the PERQ range in overall speed from 1/5 to 1/3 the speed of comparable programs on the VAX 11/780, depending on whether 16-bit or 32-bit operations

---

[2]A more detailed performance analysis of Accent from which this data was taken can be found in [10].

predominate. In fairness to the PERQ hardware, the underlying microengine is much faster than the PASCAL timings in table 4-2 would indicate. Microcoded operations often run as fast as or faster than equivalent VAX 11/780 assembly language. Note, for example, the relative speeds of the microcoded context switch and kernel trap operations. Moreover, instruction sets better tuned to the PERQ hardware, such as the Accent CommonLisp instruction set, run at speeds closer to 50 percent of the VAX. Nevertheless, for the purpose of gauging the performance of the Accent kernel code, which is written in PASCAL and makes heavy use of 32-bit arithmetic, pointer chasing and packed field accessing, the CPU speed of a PERQ is about 1/5 that of a VAX 11/780.

| Perq | Vax | Ratio | Operation |
|---|---|---|---|
| 2300ns | 720ns | .31 | Tick (32-bit stack local) |
| 12us | 4us | .25 | Simple loop (16-bit integer) |
| 20us | 3us | .17 | Simple loop (32-bit integer) |
| 35us | 20us | .57 | Null procedure call/return |
| 75us | 25us | .33 | Procedure call with 2 arguments |
| 80us | 400us | 5.00 | Context switch |
| 132us | 264us | 2.00 | Null kernel trap |
| 30s | 9s | .30 | Baskett Puzzle Program (16-bit) |
| 50s | 10s | .20 | Baskett Puzzle Program (32-bit) |

**Table 4-2:** Comparison of Perq and Vax-11/780 operation times
For executing kernel code, a Perq CPU
is about 1/5 of a Vax-11/780.

### 4.4.2. IPC Costs

Table 4-3 shows the costs of various forms of message passing in Accent. As was previously described, Accent distinguishes between *simple* and *complex* messages to improve performance of common message operations. Simple messages are defined to be those with less than 960 bytes of in-line data that contain no pointers or port references (other than those in the message header). Other messages are considered complex. The times for complex messages listed in the table were measured for messages containing one pointer to 1024 bytes of data. The observed ratio of simple to complex messages in Accent is approximately 12-to-1.

The average number of messages per second observed during periods of heavy standard version use (e.g., compilation) is less than 30. There were 67378 simple messages and 4279

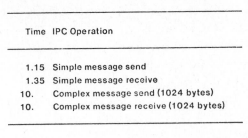

| Time | IPC Operation |
|------|---------------|
| 1.15 | Simple message send |
| 1.35 | Simple message receive |
| 10. | Complex message send (1024 bytes) |
| 10. | Complex message receive (1024 bytes) |

**Table 4-3:** IPC operation times in milliseconds

complex messages sent during one measurement of three hours of editing, network file access, and text formatting, an average of less than eight per second [10].

### 4.4.3. Accessing file data

One of the reasons for the relatively low message rate of message exchange in Accent is the heavy reliance on virtual memory mapping techniques for transferring large amounts of data in messages. A process making a request for a large file typically receives the entire file in a single message sent back from a file server process. As a result, all file access in Accent is mediated through the memory management system. There are no separate file buffers maintained by the system or special operations required for file access versus access to other forms of process mapped memory. By contrast, in RIG the same operation would have required as many message exchanges between client and server as there were pages in the file.

Table 4-4 shows the costs associated with reading a 56K byte file under UNIX 4.1bsd on a VAX 11/780 with a 30 millisecond average access time Fujitsu disk and under the standard version of Accent with a 30 millisecond average access time MAXSTORE drive.

The measured cost of a file access in Accent as shown in table 4-4 is due, in part, to the cost of a disk write to update the file access time. This disk write is unbuffered in Accent and thus is included in the file request time. The Unix disk write associated with an open is buffered and is excluded from the open/close time.

Accent file access speed is limited by the basic fault time of about four milliseconds (see table 4-5), the average number of consecutive file pages on a disk track and the cost of making new VP entries. Its page size is only 512 bytes, in contrast to 1024 bytes for 4.1bsd and 4096 or 8192 for 4.2bsd.

| System | Time | Operation |
|--------|------|-----------|
| Accent | 66 | Request file from server |
| UNIX 4.1 | 5-10 | Open/close |
| Accent | 5-10 | Read a page (512 bytes) |
| UNIX 4.1 | 16-18 | Read a page (1024 bytes) |
| UNIX 4.2 | 16-18 | Read a page (4096 bytes) |

**Table 4-4:** File access times in milliseconds

Accent file reading performance is comparable
to that of Unix4.1bsd. File reading performance
is dominated by the disk blocking factor.

Once mapped, file access in Accent ranges from somewhat faster than 4.1bsd to slightly slower, depending on the locality of file pages. 4.2bsd file access [16] is considerably faster than either 4.1bsd or Accent. This increase in speed appears to be due almost entirely to the larger (typically 4096 byte) file page size. The actual number of disk I/O operations per second under 4.2 is almost identical to 4.1, about 50-60 per second, and appears to be bounded by the rotational speed of the disk (60 revolutions per second).

### 4.4.4. Fault handling and copy-on-write

Table 4-5 summarizes the results from test programs that caused 100,000 instances of a variety of memory fault types. It shows the average total times required to handle single faults.

| Total | Type of fault |
|-------|---------------|
| 0.623 | Null fault |
| 3.355 | Read fault, zero fill |
| 3.704 | Write fault, zero fill |
| 3.760 | Read fault, memory fill, small file |
| 4.504 | Read fault, memory fill, large file |
| 3.833 | Write fault, CopyOnWrite copy |

**Table 4-5:** Fault handling times in milliseconds

Overall, the costs of copy-on-write memory management are nearly identical to that of by-reference memory mapping. Less than 0.01 percent of the total time associated with an entire rebuilding of the operating system and user programs from source is used to handle copy-on-write faults [10].

# 5. Mach: Adapting Accent to Multiprocessors

Accent went beyond demonstrating the feasibility of the message passing approach to building a distributed system. Experience with Accent showed that a message based network operating system, properly designed, can compete with more traditional operating system organizations. The advantages of this approach are system extensibility, protection and network transparency.

By the fall of 1984, however, it became apparent that, without a new hardware base, Accent would eventually follow RIG into oblivion. Hastening this process of electronic decay was Accent's inability to completely absorb the ever growing body of UNIX developed software both at CMU and elsewhere -- despite the existence of a "UNIX compatibility" package.

Mach was conceived as an Accent-like operating system which would provide complete UNIX compatibility. It was also designed to better accommodate the kind of general purpose shared-memory multiprocessors which appear to be on their way to becoming the successors to traditional general purpose uniprocessor workstations and timesharing systems.

## 5.1. The design of Mach

The design of Mach differs from that of Accent in several crucial ways:

- The Accent notion of a process, which like RIG is an address space and single program counter, was split into two new concepts:

  1. a *task*, which is the basic unit of resource allocation including a paged address space, protected access to system resources (such as processors, ports and memory), and

  2. a *thread*, which is the basic unit of CPU utilization.

- A facility for handling a form of structured sharing of read/write memory between tasks in the same family tree was added to allow finer granularity synchronization than could be achieved with a kernel provided mechanism.

- The Mach IPC facility was further simplified. This came about as the logical result of using thread mechanisms to handle some forms of asynchrony and error handling (much as was done in the V Kernel [8]).

• The notion of memory object was generalized to allow general purpose user-state external pager tasks to be built.

These design modifications are a consequence of handling shared-memory multiprocessor architectures. Accent provided no tool for fine grain synchronization or lightweight processes. Both are important for effective use of multiprocessor cycles in a variety of applications.

Despite these changes, the basic features which allowed Accent to provide uniform access to both local and network resources are still in place. This allows networks of multiprocessors or of multiprocessors and uniprocessors to be built using the same basic system abstractions. As in Accent, operations on all Mach objects other than messages are performed by sending messages to ports which are used to represent them. For example, the act of creating a task or thread returns access rights to the port which represents the new object and which can be used to manipulate it. A thread can suspend another thread by sending a suspend message to that thread's *thread port*, even across a network boundary.

Tasks are related to each other in a tree structure by task creation operations. Virtual memory may be marked as inheritable to a task's children. Memory regions may be inherited read-write, copy-on-write or not at all. A standard UNIX fork operation, for example, takes the form of a task with one thread creating a child task with a similar single thread of control and all its memory shared copy-on-write.

The notions of multiple threads of control within a task and limited sharing between task allows Mach to provide three levels of synchronization and communication: fine grain, intra-application interprocess communication and inter-application interprocess communication.

Fine grain communication is performed on memory shared either within a task or between related tasks. Mach provides a library to support synchronization on shared memory to avoid the cost of kernel trap operations on short-term locks. Network read/write shared memory is not provided by the kernel, but is potentially implementable by a user-state process acting as an external object pager (see discussion of object pagers below).

Intra-application inter-thread communication is performed using the standard Send and Receive ports primitives but can be implemented more efficiently in the presence of shared libraries and memory. By the nature of the abstractions, threads can ignore the difference between intra-application communication and inter-application communication.

Inter-application communication requires the intervention of the Mach kernel to provide protection. As in Accent, large amounts of data in messages may be mapped copy-on-write from one address space to another rather than copied. Data forwarded in messages over the network can be transmitted on reference rather than all at once at the discretion of the network server.

## 5.2. Implementation

### 5.2.1. Virtual memory modifications

While system analysis indicated that the basic Accent virtual memory scheme worked well, it also demonstrated that the data structure used to represent an Accent process map -- a two-level indirect table terminated in linked lists of mapping descriptors -- was unnecessarily complicated. Because nearly all operations on maps are sequential and maps seldom get very large, Mach implements task address maps as simple ordered lists of mapping descriptors. Each descriptor maps a range of virtual addresses to a range of bytes in a memory object. The only non-sequential operation -- lookup events due primarily to memory faults -- is sped by the use of hints based on previous lookup requests.

Another innovation of Mach over Accent is in the use of *sharing maps* to represent read/write shared regions between tasks. A Mach mapping descriptor may point either directly to a memory object (which can then only be shared copy-on-write) or indirectly to memory objects through a sharing map. A sharing map is simply an address map which maps a range of virtual addresses shared by at least two task address maps. All operations on tasks maps in a shared range of addresses are performed through indirection on sharing maps.

Overall, the Mach data structures are simpler, more compact and more expressive than those of Accent. A Mach address map can be thought of as a simple run-length encoding of a process address space. A typical UNIX-style process can be expressed in less than 100 bytes.

### 5.2.2. Mach IPC

The introduction of the notion of tasks and threads into Mach necessitated some changes to Accent's basic IPC facility. Port access rights in Mach are owned by a task. All threads within a task may therefore send or receive messages on that task's ports. The availability of threads to manage asynchronous activities simplified handling of software interrupts. Moreover, several message options, such as message priorities and the ability to preview the contents of a message before it had to be received, had been found to be largely unused for their intended purpose in Accent and have been removed.

### 5.2.3. Managing hardware diversity

Mach was intended from the outset to handle a wide diversity of both uniprocessor and multiprocessor hardware. For example, Mach provides a task memory sharing and a thread memory sharing model for multiprocessor memory synchronization. This allows Mach to support both multiprocessors which support full memory sharing with cache consistency as well as machines with only partial sharing or explicit memory caching. In practice, the system already is configured to handle a wide range of uniprocessor and multiprocessor VAX configurations. The same binary kernel image is used on both uniprocessor and multiprocessor systems.

Mach also handles another form of diversity. Messages, because they contain tagged data, are transformed from one machine data format to another by network servers. Properly typed Matchmaker interfaces allow programs written on an RT PC to communicate with VAX applications despite different byte ordering, data packing and data format conventions. There are, however, limits on this form of machine independence. For example, no attempt is made to preserve precision of floating point numbers converted from one form to another.

### 5.2.4. Confronting UNIX

One mechanism for ensuring Mach's survival in the face of a flood of UNIX based software is to make certain that it is compatible with an existing UNIX environment. This was achieved by building Mach to allow UNIX 4.3bsd system calls to be handled in much the same way they would be handled in a completely native system. The Mach kernel effectively supplants the basic system interface functions of the UNIX 4.3bsd kernel: trap handling, scheduling, multiprocessor synchronization, virtual memory management and interprocess communication. 4.3bsd functions are provided by kernel-state processes which are scheduled by the Mach kernel and share communication queues with it. Work is now underway to remove non-Mach UNIX functionality from kernel-state and provide these services through user-state processes.

## 6. Conclusions

The evolution of network operating systems from RIG through Mach was, in a sense, driven by the evolution of distributed computer systems from small networks of minicomputers in the middle 1970s to large networks of personal workstations and mainframes in the early 1980s to networks of uniprocessor and multiprocessor systems today. Not suprisingly, the basic software primitives of Mach -- task, thread, port, message and memory object -- parallel the hardware abstractions which characterize modern distributed systems -- nodes, processors, network channels, packets and primary and secondary memory. Experiences, both good and bad, with RIG and Accent have played an important role in determining the exact definition of the Mach mechanisms and their implementation.

## 7. Acknowledgements

In addition to anything the author may have done, the heroes of the RIG kernel development were Gene Ball and Ilya Gertner. Jerry Feldman was in large part responsible for the initial RIG design and the system's name. The Accent development team included George Robertson and Gene Ball as well as the author. Keith Lantz and Sam Harbison made notable contributions to the design. Mary Shaw contributed the name. Others contributed greatly to Accent's evolution: particularly Doug Philips, Jeff Eppinger, Robert Sansom, Robert Fitzgerald, David Golub, Mike Jones and Mary Thompson. Matchmaker could not have come into existence without the aid of Mary Thompson, Mike Jones, Rob MacLachlin and Keith Wright. Mach was the brainchild of many including Avie Tevanian, Mike Young and Bob Baron. Dario Giuse came up with the name.

# References

[1]     Department of Defense.
        *Preliminary Ada Reference Manual*
        1979.

[2]     Almes, G. and G. Robertson.
        An Extensible File System for Hydra.
        In *Proc. 3rd International Conference on Software Engineering*. IEEE, May, 1978.

[3]     Ball, J.E., J.A. Feldman, J.R. Low, R.F. Rashid, and P.D. Rovner.
        RIG, Rochester's Intelligent Gateway: System overview.
        *IEEE Transactions on Software Engineering* 2(4):321-328, December, 1976.

[4]     Ball, J.E., E. Burke, I. Gertner, K.A. Lantz and R.F. Rashid.
        Perspectives on Message-Based Distributed Computing.
        In *Proc. 1979 Networking Symposium*, pages 46-51. IEEE, December, 1979.

[5]     Baskett, F., J.H. Howard and J.T. Montague.
        Task Communication in DEMOS.
        In *Proc. 6th Symposium on Operating Systems Principles*, pages 23-31. ACM,
            November, 1977.

[6]     Bisiani, R., Alleva, F., Forin, A. and R. Lerner.
        Agora: A Distributed System Architecture for Speech Recognition.
        In *International Conference on Acoustics, Speech and Signal Processing*. IEEE, April,
            1986.

[7]     Bobrow, D.G., Burchfiel, J.D., Murphy, D.L. and Tomlinson, R.S.
        TENEX, a paged time sharing system for the PDP-10.
        *Communications of the ACM* 15(3):135-143, March, 1972.

[8]     Cheriton, D.R. and W. Zwaenepoel.
        The Distributed V Kernel and its Performance for Diskless Workstations.
        In *Proc. 9th Symposium on Operating Systems Principles*, pages 128-139. ACM,
            October, 1983.

[9]     Spice Project.
        *Proposal for a joint effort in personal scientific computing*.
        Technical Report , Computer Science Department, Carnegie-Mellon University, August,
            1979.

[10]    Fitzgerald, R. and R. F. Rashid.
        The integration of Virtual Memory Management and Interprocess Communication in
            Accent.
        *ACM Transactions on Computer Systems* 4(2):, May, 1986.

[11]    Hornig, D.A.
        *Automatic Partitioning and Scheduling on a Network of Personal Computers*.
        PhD thesis, Department of Computer Science, Carnegie-Mellon University, November,
            1984.

[12]    Jones, A.K., R.J. Chansler, I.E. Durham, K. Schwans and S. Vegdahl.
        StarOS, a Multiprocessor Operating System for the Support of Task Forces.
        In *Proc. 7th Symposium on Operating Systems Principles*, pages 117-129. ACM,
             December, 1979.

[13]    Jones, M.B., R.F. Rashid and M. Thompson.
        MatchMaker: An Interprocess Specification Language.
        In *ACM Conference on Principles of Programming Languages*. ACM, January, 1985.

[14]    Lantz, K.A.
        *Uniform Interfaces for Distributed Systems.*
        PhD thesis, University of Rochester, May, 1980.

[15]    Lantz, K.A., K.D. Gradischnig, J.A. Feldman and R.F. Rashid.
        Rochester's Intelligent Gateway.
        *Computer* 15(10):54-68, October, 1982.

[16]    McKusick, M.K., W.N. Joy, S.L. Leach and R.S. Fabry.
        A Fast File System for UNIX.
        *ACM Transactions on Computer Systems* 2(3):181-197 , August, 1984.

[17]    Rashid, R.F. and G. Robertson.
        Accent: A Communication Oriented Network Operating System Kernel.
        In *Proc. 8th Symposium on Operating Systems Principles*, pages 64-75. ACM,
             December, 1981.

[18]    R.F. Rashid.
        *The Accent Kernel Interface Manual.*
        Technical Report , Department of Computer Science, Carnegie-Mellon University,
             January, 1983.

[19]    Spector, A.Z. et al.
        Support for Distributed Transactions in the TABS Prototype.
        In *Proceedings of the Fourth Symposium on Reliability in Distributed Software and
             Database Systems*, pages 186-206. October, 1984.

The Ecology of Computation
B.A. Huberman (editor)
© Elsevier Science Publishers B.V. (North-Holland), 1988

# Incentive Engineering
# for Computational Resource Management

K. Eric Drexler

MIT Artificial Intelligence Laboratory,
545 Technology Square, Cambridge, MA 02139*

Mark S. Miller

Xerox Palo Alto Research Center,
3333 Coyote Hill Road, Palo Alto, CA 94304

Agoric computation [I,II] will require market-compatible mechanisms for the allocation of processor time and storage space. Recasting processor scheduling as an
auction process yields a flexible priority system. Recasting storage management as
a system of decentralized market negotiations yields a distributed garbage collection
algorithm able to collect unreferenced loops that cross trust boundaries. Algorithms
that manage processor time and storage in ways that enable both conventional computation and market-based decision making will be useful in establishing agoric
systems: they lie at the boundary between design and evolution. We describe such
algorithms in some detail.

## 1. Introduction

In the agoric model of computation [II], market mechanisms—prices and negotiations—
coordinate the activity of objects. As in existing markets, these mechanisms will allocate
resources in a decentralized fashion, guided by local knowledge and decisions rather than by
central planning and direction. Through selective rewards, markets will encourage the evolution of useful and efficient objects.

This model raises questions at several levels, ranging from foundations (how can hardware and software support secure market mechanisms?) to high-level emergent properties
(how will evolved computational markets behave?). Here we focus on a question at an intermediate level, asking how the basic computational resources of processor capacity and data
storage can be managed in a market-compatible fashion, given suitable foundations. We first
examine objectives and constraints for decentralized resource management, and then describe
a promising set of *initial market strategies*. These are algorithms that can help seed a system

---

* Visiting Scholar, Stanford University. Box 60775, Palo Alto, CA 94306

with a workable initial set of objects. Initial market strategies (or *initial strategies,* for short), must be compatible with current programming practice and (when widely used) must provide an environment in which resources typically have prices that reflect costs—that is, an environment in which other objects can make economic decisions that make sense.

## 1.1. The role of initial market strategies

Agoric systems will evolve from lesser to greater complexity. To begin evolving, they will need a comparatively simple structure from which to build. The role of initial market strategies is to serve as a sort of scaffolding: they must support the right things and have the right general shape, but they must also be replaceable as construction proceeds. Though they must embody sound engineering principles, they need not themselves be architectural wonders.

For computation to occur, storage and processing power must be allocated and managed— functions that existing algorithms handle [1,2]. To get a computational market started, we will need initial strategies that also enable market-based decision making. To enable conventional computation, the use of an initial strategy by a set of objects must ensure the reliable scheduling of processes and allocation and deallocation of storage. To enable globally-sensible, market-based decision making, the use of an initial strategy by a set of objects must provide an environment in which the *price* of using an object reflects the real *cost* of that use.

These initial market strategies, however, *cannot* use price information to guide their own actions. To behave reliably in a conventional computational sense, they must pursue their goals regardless of cost. If resource prices are to make economic sense, however, objects at some level (perhaps contracting with systems of initial-strategy objects) must be willing to forgo or delay actions which will cost more than their estimated worth. Initial market strategies exist to provide an environment in which more advanced market strategies can function and evolve (even evolving to replace the initial strategies themselves).

Initial programming environments can provide initial market strategies as default parts of object definitions. Though initial strategies will perform functions ordinarily handled by an operating system or language environment, they need not be foundational or uniform across a system. The foundational mechanisms of agoric systems will delegate decisions regarding processor scheduling and storage management to unprivileged objects, enabling them to follow diverse policies. Initial strategies will simply provide policies that work, until better policies emerge.

The initial market strategies described here are intended to serve two purposes: first, to provide a proof-of-concept (or at least evidence-of-concept) for the feasibility of decentralized resource management meeting the constraints we describe; and second, to provide a point of departure for further work—a set of ideas to criticize and improve upon. For several of our choices, straightforward alternatives can likely be found. Many will prove superior.

Throughout the present discussion, "object" should be considered a scale-independent notion: an object should frequently be regarded as a large, running program, such as an expert system or on-line database. Large objects may or may not be themselves composed of objects, and objects in general need not incorporate any notion of class hierarchy or inheritance.

Some of the following algorithms have relatively high overhead and are not proposed for use with small objects; large objects might use conventional algorithms for fine-grained internal resource management.

## 1.2. Auction-based processor scheduling

Most objects will need only a fraction of the service of a processor, hence we expect rental to emerge as a major means of acquiring processor time. Since objects will frequently be able to trade off processor use against storage requirements, communications use, or service quality, processor time will have a price relative to these other resources. This price will vary from processor to processor and from moment to moment. If an agoric system is open, extensible, and uses real currency, and if machine owners are alert, then the long-term average price of processor time in the system will reflect the external market price of adding more processors to the system—if it were much higher, the owners could profit by adding processors; if it were much lower, they could profit by removing and selling them.

Since the demand for processor time is apt to fluctuate rapidly, proper incentives will require rapidly fluctuating prices. This can be arranged by auctioning each slice of processor time to the highest-bidding process. The urgency of a task can be reflected in the size of its bid. Auctions can also be used to schedule other resources allocated on a time-slice by time-slice basis, such as communication channels. Again, fluctuating prices can provide incentives for delaying less urgent tasks, leveling loads, and so forth.

In discussing the allocation of processing resources, we describe the allocation of raw processor time. Some objects in an agoric system might not purchase time this way, but might instead purchase interpretation services on a similar (or very different) basis. A system that can provide a market in raw processor time can serve as a foundation for more sophisticated services of this sort.

## 1.3. Rent-based storage management

Because storage needs will frequently be transient, we expect that rental from owners will emerge as a major means of holding storage. As with processor time, storage will have a price relative to other resources, and this price will vary across different media, locations, and times. As with processors, the long-term average price of storage in the system will reflect the external market price of adding more storage to the system, if owners are alert to opportunities for profit. We discuss allocation of raw storage space here, but a system that can provide a market in raw space can serve as a foundation for more sophisticated storage services.

The basic idea of our initial strategy and the emergent garbage collection algorithm is as follows:

- Landlords own storage space.
- They charge other objects rents at a rate determined through auction.
- Referenced objects (*consultants*) charge referencing objects (*clients*) retainer fees, using these to pay their rent (and the retainer fees charged by *their* consultants).
- When objects fail to pay rent they are evicted (that is, garbage collected).

These arrangements provide a natural way to free storage from unproductive uses. If an object cannot or will not pay its rent, then some other object must be bidding more for the available space (if no object was bidding for the space, its price would be zero). Since an object's income (and hence rent-paying ability) reflects the value placed on the object by its users, eviction of non-paying objects will typically improve the overall usefulness of the contents of storage.

Frequently-used consultants will be able to pay their rent out of their usage fees. Rarely-used (but referenced) consultants can charge their clients retainer fees adequate to cover their rent (and that of any consultants they themselves retain). In these relationships, pointers are bi-directional: a consultant also knows its clients. Unreferenced objects will be unable to earn usage fees or charge retainer fees; they will be unable to pay, and will be evicted, thereby accomplishing garbage collection (or forcing migration to a fixed-entry-price archive). This is the basis of the *market sweep* approach to garbage collection.

Rent-based storage management also allows a generalization of pointer types. Some systems distinguish between the traditional *strong pointers* and *weak pointers* [3]. A strong pointer retains a referenced object regardless of the cost: it represents an unbounded commitment to maintaining access. A weak pointer maintains access as long as the object has not been garbage collected, but does not itself cause the object to be retained. Weak pointers are an existing step toward economic storage management: they represent a small value placed on access—in effect, an infinitesimal value. This suggests a generalization in which an object will pay only a bounded amount for continued access to an object. This may be termed a *threshold pointer*. Thresholds may be set in various ways, for example, by limiting the total retainer fee that will be paid, or the total fee that will be paid in a given time period. When multiple threshold pointers reference an object, their strengths add; thus, they integrate information about the demand for retaining the object in a given region of storage. (As we will see, however, any situation in which a consultant asks retainer fees from multiple clients presents a challenge in incentive engineering—why should a client pay, if others will do so instead?)

Differing rents in differing media give objects an incentive to migrate to the most cost-effective locations. If clients offer a premium for fast service and demand service frequently, a consultant might best be located in RAM; if slow service is adequate and demand is low, a consultant might best be located on disk, or on a remote server. Caching decisions can thus be treated as a business location problem.

Rent-based storage management solves a standing problem of distributed garbage collection. Consider a loop of objects, each pointing to the next, each on a different company's machine, and all, collectively, garbage. Garbage collection could be accomplished by migrating objects to collapse the loop onto one machine, thus making its unreferenced nature locally visible [4]. But what if the companies don't fully trust one another? By sending the representation of an object to an untrusted machine, the algorithm would allow encapsulation to be violated, giving away access to critical objects and resources. With rent-based storage management, however, migration is unnecessary: since unreferenced loops have no net income but still must pay rent, they go broke and are evicted.

The problem of unreferenced loops crossing trust boundaries highlights the lack of a notion of payment-for-service in traditional approaches to storage management. Introducing this notion seems essential when hardware and data are separately owned. In its absence, distributed systems will be subject to problems in which one person (or entity) forces the retention of another's storage but has no incentive to free it.

As suggested earlier, we do not expect explicit rental arrangements to be economical for very small objects. The appropriate minimum scale is an open question; the ultimate test of answers to this question will be market success.

## 1.4. Design constraints

As we have noted, initial market strategies must satisfy various constraints, which fall into two classes. First, they must result in a programmable system; this can most easily be guaranteed by ensuring that they meet the familiar constraints that have evolved in systems programming practice. Second, they must result in a system with market incentives, making possible the evolution of the new programming practices expected in agoric open systems.

Systems programming constraints often guarantee some property regardless of cost—for example, guaranteeing that referenced objects will be retained. Sound market incentives require that all resources used be paid for, since to do otherwise in an evolving system would foster parasitism. These two constraints would seem to be in conflict. To resolve this, we introduce the notion of the *well-funded object*. An object is well-funded if it has immediate access to ample funds to pay for the computations it spawns. A well-funded object might typically represent a human user and fund some computations serving that user. These computations are required to satisfy traditional systems programming constraints only so long as the well-funded object remains solvent, that is, so long as the user is willing to pay their cost.

The chief systems-programming constraint in processor scheduling is that processes be scheduled—that is, that there be a way to arrange bidding such that a well-funded process can be guaranteed non-starvation and hence eventual execution. The chief market-compatibility constraints in processor scheduling are that processor prices fluctuate to adjust demand to the available supply, that objects be able to make scheduling decisions based on price information, and that opportunities for malicious strategies be limited—for example, that a process not be able to force a high price on a competing process while avoiding that high price itself.

Several systems-programming constraints are important in storage management. First, non-garbage—everything reachable by a chain of strong pointers leading from a well-funded object—must not be collected. Second, garbage—everything that is unreferenced and cannot induce other objects to reference or pay it—should eventually be collected. Finally, overhead costs should be reasonable: bookkeeping storage per object should be bounded and the computational burden of the algorithms should scale roughly linearly (at most) with the number of objects.

Market-compatibility constraints are also important in storage management. Objects should manage retainer-fee relationships such that there is an incentive for clients to pay retainers, lest there be an incentive to shirk. A consultant's total retainer fees (which amount to a price for its availability) should reflect real storage costs, to provide non-initial-strategy clients with a reasonable basis for decisions. Finally, objects should not require unbounded cash reserves to avoid improper garbage collection.

Non-initial-strategy objects need not themselves meet system-programming constraints, since they are free to act in any manner that furthers their market success. They will still typically require reasonable computational costs, smooth interaction with other strategies, and bounded cash reserves. A complex market-level object, however, will be unlikely to point strongly at an object having unpredictable or uncontrollable costs. It must therefore be prepared for such consultants to go away. It may also spawn low-priority processes; some of these may never run.

How can a complex object be prepared for loss of access? Current practice already provides many examples of objects able to deal with the unexpected unavailability of objects they use. Programs are frequently prepared for the breaking of inter-machine or inter-process connections, or for the inability to open an expected file. Files are commonly updated so that they are in a recoverable state even if they should suffer the sudden loss of the updater. Argus provides abortable transactions and exception handling [III]. Additional recovery mechanisms can be expected among complex objects in a market environment.

# 2. Processor scheduling

This section describes initial market strategies for both sellers and buyers. In processor scheduling, we will term the time-seller (or agent for the seller) an *auction house,* and a time-buyer (or agent for a buyer) a *bidder*. A system may have any number of competing sellers.

## 2.1. Auctioning processor time: the escalator algorithm

A standard approach to scheduling processes uses a "first-come, first-served" queue. A newly-ready process always joins the tail of the queue, and the processor always runs the process at the head of the queue. This ensures that each process will eventually run (regardless of processor demand), guaranteeing what is known as *non-starvation* or *fairness*. This mechanism does not enable market trade-offs among the needs of different processes, however. A natural approach to doing so is the "highest-bid, first-served" queue. This corresponds to auctioning time-slices, with the queue corresponding to an auction house. Naïvely applied, this would lead to disaster: if the market price of the processor stays above a process's posted bid, the process will never run, and hence never learn that it needs to raise its bid. This defines a central problem in auctioning processor time.

### 2.1.1. Auction-house initial strategies

A basic question in an auction-based strategy is the nature of the auction: kinds include the double auction, English auction, Dutch auction, and first-price and second-price sealed-bid auctions [5,6]. In a double auction, sellers offer lower and lower prices while buyers offer higher and higher prices until they meet. In the familiar English auction, buyers bid higher and higher prices until the process plateaus; the seller accepts the highest bid. In a Dutch auction, a seller offers lower and lower prices until a buyer claims the item at the present price. In a first-price sealed-bid auction, fixed bids are submitted, and the highest is accepted; in a second-price sealed-bid auction, the highest is accepted, but the highest bidder pays the amount bid by the second-highest.

These auction institutions have differing applicability to the sale of time slices. The double, English, and Dutch auctions (at least in naïve implementations) require that processes be active while bidding for the very processor they need in order to be active—a major problem. Sealed-bid auctions avoid this problem, but they fail to guarantee non-starvation: if the processor price remains above what a process has bid, it will never be scheduled—and if the process is never scheduled, it cannot raise its bid. Thus, auctioning processor time is a bit like trying to auction wakeup pills to a sleeping crowd.

The approach explored here will be a variant of a sealed-bid auction, but the choice between first- and second-price forms remains. In laboratory experiments with human bidders, second-price sealed-bid auctions are known to give results similar to those of English auctions, and both lead to efficient markets (as does the double auction) [5,6]. In the English auction, the winning bidder pays only slightly more than the second-highest bidder; a second-price sealed-bid auction yields a similar result directly. Dutch and first-price sealed-bid auctions lead to less efficient markets.

First-price sealed-bid auctions give an incentive to guess what the next-highest bid will be, and to bid just slightly more. This strategic guessing serves no useful purpose in a market system. Second-price auctions give an incentive to consider only the question: "At what given price would my best decision change from 'buy' to 'don't-buy'?" This is the price one should bid, since bidding any other price might result in buying (or not buying) when one should not. Estimating this price means estimating actual value, which serves a decidedly useful purpose in the market system.

We have selected a variant of a second-price, sealed-bid auction for our initial market strategy. It may be called an *escalating-bid auction*.

This system may be visualized as an auction house full of escalators (admittedly a strange image). A process enters the auction by placing a bid on one of the escalators—the greater the bid, the greater the initial height. Each escalator rises at a different rate, raising its bids at that rate. (A special stationary escalator holds fixed bids.) Together, the initial bid and escalation rate are a form of priority. A processor always runs the highest-bidding process. A house rule sets a maximum allowable initial bid—you can get on only at (say) the first five floors.

Each auction house owns or leases a processor, or a certain fraction of its operating time. Escalator data structures make the highest bid readily available (*i.e.*, each escalator is a priority queue). Each non-stationary escalator is characterized by a rate of escalation, escalationRate, measured in currency units per time unit. At a time t, the value of a bid of zero initial value placed on an escalator at time timeOfBid is simply escalationRate $\times$ (t - timeOfBid). A non-zero initial bid of value initialBid is assigned a virtual bid-time, timeOfBid, equal to

t - (initialBid / escalationRate), and entered accordingly. Thus, each non-stationary escalator is marked with a fixed escalationRate and holds a current list of bids, sorted in time-
OfBid order. Each bid includes its timeOfBid, a suspended process, and access to an expense account. The stationary escalator is a special case; instead of a timeOfBid it records a
fixed initialBid. (A negative initialBid is acceptable on a moving escalator. We assume that
two idle processes are entered with zero bids on the stationary escalator to avoid accepting a
negative bid-value; the first always stands ready to run, at the price set by the second.)

To place a bid on an escalator, one sends a suspended process, an initial bid, and access to
an expense account from which the auction house is to withdraw money. When the bid is
placed, the auction house immediately withdraws from the expense account enough funds to
cover the worst-case cost of handling that bid.

At the beginning of each time slice, the auction house examines the top bid on each escalator, taking the highest bid among them (and promoting its follower) while noting the second-
highest bid (taking into account the newly-promoted bid). It then charges the high bidder the
amount of the second-highest bid, and gives the high bidder a slice of processor time. If the
highest bidder's expense account fails to cover the (escalated) bid, however, it is removed
without running, and a bid equaling the balance of its expense account is entered for this bidder on the stationary escalator.

The escalating-bid auction seems well suited to the processor scheduling problem. It
avoids the sleeping-bidder problem and it ensures that a processor can accept a bid at any
time—crucial, when the commodity to be sold is as perishable as time itself.

### 2.1.2. Bidder initial strategies

A sufficient initial strategy for a bidder is simply to place a zero bid on the fastest escalator
backed by the bidder's own expense account. Note that, among initial-strategy bidders, the
escalator algorithm reduces to a round-robin scheduler. In a slight variation, a negativeinitial-
Bid can be placed to ensure a delay of at least ( -initialBid/escalationRate) until the bidder
next runs.

### 2.1.3. Analysis

In an open system, where total processor capacity and demand will be responsive to market forces, the market price of time on a processor will be bounded. Accordingly, a bid placed
on any non-stationary escalator will eventually grow large enough to ensure that it is accepted.
Thus, non-starvation would be ensured.

Where too much of the demand is unresponsive to price, other conditions are necessary to
ensure non-starvation, such as limiting the maximum initial bid, maxInitialBid, to some
fixed value (the "fifth floor") as suggested above. Consider a process Z with a bid on a moving escalator. Z will either run or have its bid escalated past maxInitialBid within a fixed
time; at that time, only a finite number of other processes can have bids higher than Z's, and if
Z is riding the *fastest* escalator, no new process can be scheduled to run ahead of it. Thus, the
auction house guarantees non-starvation to any process that follows the strategy of always

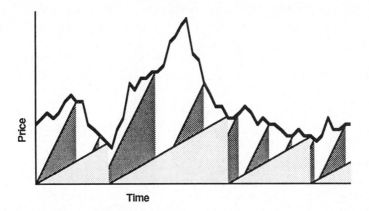

**Price**

**Time**

*Figure 1: Escalating bids. The jagged line above represents a hypothetical processor price history. The series of light triangles below represents the bid-history of a process that repeatedly reschedules itself with a zero initial bid; the dark triangles represent that of a similar process using a faster escalator. The processor price history reflects the bids of numerous other processes.*

entering a bid on the fastest escalator.

The relationship among bids, prices, and rates of use is simple in certain illustrative cases. Assume a stable price for time-slices, equal to $P$, and an escalator that raises bids at a rate $R$ per time slice; an object that repeatedly reschedules itself after running by placing a zero initial bid on this escalator will receive a fraction of the processor time roughly equal to $R/P$. Consider an auction house in which a fixed number of processes repeatedly run and reschedule themselves, placing bids with zero initial values and a fixed distribution across the various escalators; assume further that bids are numerous enough and uniform enough to make second-highest bids approximately equal to highest bids. There will then be a steady-state price for a time-slice (with small fluctuations); this price will equal the sum over the escalators of the number of bids on each times the amount of escalation during a time-slice. (This quantity equals the per-time-slice increase in the sum of the bids, and all the money bid is eventually spent on processor time.) Non-zero initial bids will have an effect roughly like that of different escalation rates, and fluctuating rates of bid-placement will cause fluctuations in processor price.

Given fluctuating prices (see Figure 1), faster escalation rates will result in higher average costs per time slice. If scheduled at random times, rapidly-escalating bids will strike the market-price line at nearly random times (random sampling would hold strictly if escalation were infinitely fast). As may be seen, slowly escalating bids are unable to strike the price line at the top of sharp price peaks; they are more likely to strike the down-side of price troughs. Figure 1 also illustrates how a strategy of re-bidding at zero on an escalator after every run will, on the average, use more time-slices during broad troughs than during broad peaks, yielding a cost per time slice that is lower than the average cost; conversely, bids placed on fast escalators will pay a higher than average cost.

The overhead of the escalator algorithm is modest and insensitive to the number of bids being escalated. Assume N is the number of bids on an escalator and M is the number of escalators. Placing or removing a bid is then an operation taking a time proportional to $\log(N)$, given a suitable choice of escalator data structure (a priority queue). Finding the highest and second-highest bids by searching the top bids is an operation taking a time proportional to M.

### 2.1.4. Variations

The simplest auction-house initial strategy provides a fixed set of escalators, as described; more complex strategies could create and delete escalators to suit bidder demand. Other extensions would allow bidding for multiple time-slices as a block (up to some maximum size), or enable refunding payment on unused portions of a time slice (and starting the next full time-slice early). Where multiple processors are equally accessible, a single auction house could serve them all. Finally, the owner of a processor could run an auction procedure for a fraction of the available time slices and an entirely different procedure (perhaps some form of futures market for real-time scheduling) in another.

As described, the simplest bidder initial strategy is to schedule a zero bid on the fastest escalator. A more complex strategy might use a fast escalator only for fast service at a (likely) higher price, or slower escalators for slower service, at a (likely) lower price. A positive initial bid on a slow escalator can speed service while still giving better odds of running at a low price than does a bid on a fast escalator. Tasks of strictly limited value (which need not be completed) can be scheduled on the stationary escalator; they will run only if the price of processor time falls low enough. A regularly-scheduled rebidding agent can be used to implement a very broad class of strategies, taking into account new information from bid to bid.

There are several open issues in this approach to processor scheduling. These include finding procedures for:

- choosing maxInitialBid (where this parameter is needed),
- choosing the numbers and rates of escalators, and
- charging for bid-record storage.

In addition to solving the sleeping-bidder problem peculiar to process scheduling, the escalator algorithm provides a low-overhead auction procedure for allocating other resources that are naturally divided into time slices. For example, parameters for a bidding strategy could be part of a packet traversing a network, enabling the packets to bid for access to communication channels.

### 2.2. Expense accounts

We have described initial market strategies for the relationship between owners and bidders; we also need strategies among bidders, to ensure that they can pay for processing time. Since bidders typically need processing time in order to satisfy external requests, the initial market strategy should follow the dynamic structure of relationships created by request messages from client objects to their consultants.

When a client requests service from a consultant, we assume the client will pay to satisfy the request. We need an initial strategy that enables consultants to charge and clients to pay, all with a minimum of programmer attention (the following strategy does, however, require that objects distinguish between request and response messages). The *initial* strategy should itself provide neither profit nor loss, and hence should simply require that consultants charge for their operating costs, and that clients pay for them. This initial market strategy must (as always) interact smoothly with other strategies. The initial strategy must accommodate clients wishing to monitor charges or limit payments, and consultants wishing to charge less or more than their expenses (*e.g.*, to promote a new service or to collect royalties).

The initial strategy is as follows: Each process draws operating expenses from its *current expense account*. A client includes access to its current expense account in each outgoing request. The consultant then uses this account as its current expense account while satisfying the request. This strategy is identical to the protocol specified in the Act 2 language [7] for passing *sponsors*. Like expense accounts, these give bounded access to processor time [8].

In a set of objects following this initial market strategy, all computation serving an external request will be paid for by the account contained in that request. Since no computation will be cut off while that account remains solvent, well-funded computations will be completed.

In variations on this strategy, a consultant may charge according to whatever policy it wishes, since it is free to draw funds from the incoming account and to use a different account to pay for its computation. If a consultant requires a minimum sum to complete a computation, it can ensure access to this sum by transferring it to a new account at the outset.

A client may limit its payments to a consultant by sending a new account with the request and placing a limited sum in that account. This is like a threshold pointer, in that the client limits its liability at the risk of cutting off valid computation.

A client may monitor its payments to a consultant by sending a *shadow account* which passes charges through to an actual account while remembering their sum. When the consultant finishes, the client recovers the record of the total charges and shuts down the shadow account. This enables clients to accumulate cost information to guide further requests.

## 3. Storage management

In rent-based storage management, we again must specify strategies both for the relationships between buyers and sellers (here, renters and landlords) and for the relationships among renters (in their roles as clients and consultants). The latter are complex.

### 3.1. Renting memory: the rental-auction algorithm

In a fully competitive market for storage space, a landlord (having many competitors) will maximize revenue by seeking full storage utilization, setting its rental price at a level at which supply equals demand (the *market-clearing rate*). An auction-based initial market strategy can approximate this rather well.

A landlord maintains (or uses) an auction house which keeps two data structures, a *bid list* and a *drop list*. The bid list records requests for blocks of storage; each request is associated with an object, a desired quantity of storage (limited to a maximum request, maxBlockRequest, of perhaps 1% of total local storage), and a price—per unit of memory, per of unit of time—bid for acquiring it (bidPrice). Bids are accompanied by deposits to cover handling charges. The drop list records already-leased blocks of storage, each associated with an object, a block size, and a unit rental price at which the object would prefer to release it (dropPrice). The lists are ordered by bidPrice and dropPrice respectively. A running total is kept of the amount of wasted space.

We consider the bid list to also contain an infinite number of bids at zero rental price for atomic blocks of storage to be allocated to a *free memory sponge* object. The sponge will be allocated memory only when no one has any use for free storage; any memory so allocated is entered on the drop list with a zero price. In a mature agoric open system, the demand for memory space should be enormous at low enough prices. With a charge-per-use policy, there is no bound to the amount of software that would migrate to a machine offering a zero storage price; storage of debugging traces and caching of calculated results would likewise expand at a zero storage price. Therefore, one would not expect to see a zero price or see any memory allocated to the sponge.

Fresh unheld space becomes available at the beginning of operations, when space is vacated, when objects are evicted for nonpayment of rent, or when more memory is purchased and added to the system. The auction house then accepts bids from the top of the bid-list, highest bidPrice first. It continues allocating blocks to bidders until it encounters a bid for a block larger than the remaining unheld space. This bid is shelved, the allocation process stops, and the price of this unsuccessful bid is taken as the rental price of storage for all objects during the next time segment.

If, as expected, the blocks requested total more than the storage available, then the maximum unallocated storage will be smaller than maxBlockRequest. If this is 1% of the total, storage utilization will be at least 99%. For example, consider a computer with ten megabytes of main memory and a memory management unit that maps addresses in 1kilobyte blocks. Memory to be allocated and traded would consist of integral numbers of these 1kilobyte blocks (which can be mapped arbitrarily, hence we can ignore fragmentation). One percent of 10 megabytes is 100 kilobytes, so this is maxBlockRequest and the largest amount that can be wasted by the above procedure. We assume that any object needing a block bigger than 100 kilobytes can afford the trouble of acquiring it 100 kilobytes at a time.

When a new bid is placed, its bidPrice is compared to the highest bidPrice on the bid list. If it is lower, it is placed on the bid list; if it is equal to or greater than the highest bidPrice and equal to or less than the lowest dropPrice on the drop list, then it is accepted if it requests a block that can be allocated from unheld space, and otherwise is placed on the bid list. If it is greater than the lowest dropPrice, then room may be freed for it.

In this case, the auction house attempts to identify enough space to accommodate the new bidder, starting with the unheld storage and then proceeding to the held blocks lowest on the drop list. Objects responsible for identified blocks are asked to vacate them or to set a higher dropPrice. On vacating, renters are refunded the unused portion of their rent money. This process stops when (1) enough space has been freed, or (2) a block is encountered having a drop price equal to or greater than the bidPrice of the new bidder. In case (1), the new bidder receives storage space and is placed on the drop list at a dropPrice of its choosing; in case (2), the new bidder is placed at the head of the bid list. In either case, the rental price of storage becomes the bidPrice of the highest unsuccessful bidder.

To guarantee that resources used will be paid for (and avoid incentives for the evolution of parasitic software), landlords must require payment for a rent period in advance. This payment should cover the cost of the next billing cycle and include a deposit to cover the cost of deallocating memory and of any special services specified in the lease agreement, such as erasure of vacated space (a sort of cleaning deposit). Rental rates will fluctuate during a rent period, with the length of a rent period varying as the inverse of the average rental rate.

Landlords can accept lease agreements of varying lengths, requiring varying amounts of pre-paid rent to allow objects to tune their storage management overhead. They can likewise agree to provide a period of advance notice before collecting rent, giving the renter time to raise money, find alternative storage, or close out its affairs.

A more complex strategy would offer prompt storage allocation (from pre-emptable cache or unheld storage), charging a premium for this service. Alternatively, this and other services could be provided by renters subletting space in their blocks. A useful service would allow a renter to split off a piece of its storage block and post a new drop-list entry for it, allowing the sale of portions of allocated blocks without the overhead of the auction house procedure.

## 3.2. The market-sweep algorithms

An initial market strategy for renters is to get space by placing high (perhaps escalating) bids, and to keep it by paying whatever is necessary, so long as funds hold out. The challenge is to have funds hold out while the renter should stay, and eventually run out when the renter should vacate. Since a consultant must pay its rent in order to serve referencing clients, the initial market strategy follows the referencing structure among consultants and their clients. This structure is a directed graph containing cycles and changing over time. As a result, these strategies are more complex than those above.

A consultant must not be evicted if can be reached through a chain of strong pointers starting from a well-funded object (*i.e.,* non-garbage must not be collected). Many objects will pay their rent out of fees charged for their services, but some objects—though never before used—may be of great value in rare contingencies: consider an object that contains plans for coping with the next terrestrial asteroid impact. Objects that are needed but rarely used must survive by charging their clients retainer fees; an initial strategy must assume this worst case.

A system based on retainer fees must avoid several problems. In one approach, objects would, when charged rent, send *alert messages* to their clients, asking for the needed sum; these clients would do likewise until a solvent object was found to pay the bill. This system has low capital costs, requiring little cash on hand, but it leads to an explosion of circulating alert messages, and hence to unacceptable transaction costs. In an alternative approach, objects would keep enough cash on hand to cover worst-case rent and retainer fees. This system has minimal transaction costs per rent period, but in the absence of information on worst-case rents and fees, capital requirements are unbounded and garbage collection would be indefinitely postponed.

For a system to be acceptable, transaction and capital costs must both be bounded. Transactions should require on the order of one message per pointer per rent cycle, capital required should be some fixed multiple of per-cycle expenses, and the per-cycle retainer fees paid by a client should be reasonably related to the rent paid by its dependent consultants.

Satisfying these constraints proves to be difficult. The component algorithms of the market-sweep approach include the following:

• The *dividend algorithm,* an initial market strategy which provides incentives to pay retainer fees to an object and provides it with estimates of future use. It has strategic properties which should make it useful in contexts outside storage management.

• The *retainer-fee algorithm,* an elementary algorithm for billing clients. This provides for cash flow in normal circumstances.

• The *alert algorithm,* which provides for fast cash flow when needed to prevent improper eviction. It is an initial strategy aimed at guaranteeing systems programming constraints, but it involves a race which can fail given a sufficiently unfavorable combination of cash reserves, rental notice period, message-passing speed, and message path length.

• The *base-demand algorithm,* which provides estimates of future cash requirements to minimize the need for alerts. It is essentially heuristic, aimed at tuning reserves and estimating costs. As a cost-estimater, it can underestimate the drop in retainer charges that will occur when a new client points into a cyclic reference structure.

### 3.2.1. The dividend algorithm

Raising money by simply dividing the total retainer charge equally among several directly-pointing clients won't work; it suffers from the classic public-goods problem: each client has an incentive to shirk, as long as another will pay. To pay to retain a consultant while a competitor uses it without paying is an evolutionarily unstable strategy—clients following it will lose in price competition. Multiple clients can pretend to be single clients (and thus cut their liability) by pointing via a middleman (Figure 2). To make simple retainer-charging schemes of this sort work would require peculiar and uneconomical limitations on object interactions, such as (somehow) preventing one object from serving as a middleman for another, or preventing a consultant from offering service to new clients.

A better alternative is for the consultant to collect a large enough surcharge *per use* to compensate all clients (or their heirs and assigns) for their earlier retainer payments. This approach converts retainer-payment into a form of investment, to be repaid through dividends raised by imposing a per-use surcharge. To make such investment attractive, dividends must be propor-

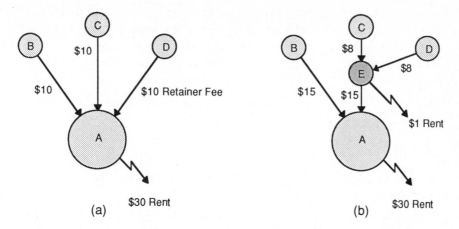

**Figure 2: Client conspiracy.** *Straight arrows represent clients pointing to consultants; they are labeled with the corresponding retainer fee payments; crooked arrows represent rent payments. (a) shows the charges if a consultant's liabilities are split equally among its clients; (b) shows how C and D can reduce their payments by pointing through a forwarder, E.*

tional to the amounts invested, and must include compensation for the risk that a consultant may in reality be used seldom (or not at all), yielding few or no dividends.

This raises the problem of estimating a consultant's future use rate (or use probability). The lower the expected use rate, the higher the per-use charges and dividends must be to compensate clients for their investment. These use-rate estimates must somehow reflect the client's own judgment, lest clients be unwilling or too-willing to pay.

Future use rates for a consultant could be estimated using the sum, average, or median of future use rates estimated and reported by its clients. But why should these reports be accurate? Mechanisms which yield estimates proportional to the sum or average are clearly unstable: if all clients share equally in retainer payments, high-use-rate clients should estimate an infinite use rate, to drive the per-use surcharge for dividend payments to zero; low-use-rate clients should estimate a zero rate, to maximize their dividends. Use of the median mechanism throws away information (*e.g.*, a single high-use-rate client among several low-use-rate clients will have no effect on the estimate); this presumably leads to wasteful strategic behavior.

Another approach would be to accept bids for the privilege of investing, with the winning bidder asking the smallest surcharge-and-dividend per future use. This approach is stable, since payment is voluntary and will typically be justified at some level of dividend, but it fails to integrate market information effectively. Instead, it encourages clients to give a falsely-high impression of their future use rates, to drive down others' bids and hence their own future usage charges. Thus, the prospective bidder must guess others' actions based on what may be actual disinformation. Further, the special role of the low bidder encourages messy strategic behavior.

One would like an algorithm for collecting retainer payments and paying dividends that has better properties. Ideally, it should give clients an incentive to report accurate use estimates, enabling a synthesis of estimates made by those in the best position to know; further, it should provide incentives for simple strategic behavior in typical situations, and it should be insensitive to issues of entity definition—to whether one treats a buying club as an object or as a collection of objects.

### 3.2.1.1. Description

This section provides a brief, abstract description of the dividend algorithm in its simplest form. Later sections describe its operation more informally, analyze its properties, and describe a slight modification that yields a more practical version.

Definitions of variables

$R$ = a retainer-seeking object (the consultant)

$t$ = an index specifying a time at which $R$ collects retainer fees

$F_t$ = the total fee required by $R$ at time $t$

$C_j$ = a client of $R$

$m$ = the number of clients referencing object $R$

$N_{jt}$ = the reported estimate of number of future uses of $R$ by $C_j$

$S_{jt} = F_t N_{jt} / \sum_{i=1}^{m} N_{it}$ = the share of $F_t$ requested of $C_j$

$P_{jt}$ = the amount actually paid by $C_j$ (is $\leq S_{jt}$)

$N'_{jt} = N_{jt} P_{jt} / S_{jt}$ = the "effective" reported estimate of future uses

$F'_t$ = the total amount actually collected by $R$ at $t$, $= \sum_{i=1}^{m} P_{it}$

$D_{jt}$ = the "dividend sum" at $t$ for $C_j$

$A_{jt} = P_{jt} / \sum_{i=1}^{m} N'_{it} = F'_t N'_{jt} / \left( \sum_{i=1}^{m} N'_{it} \right)^2$ = the amount to be added to the dividend sum

$n_{jt}$ = the actual number of future uses by $C_j$, counting from time $t$

$E_{jt}$ = the expected net cost of future uses (resulting from actions *at time t*)

$L_t$ = time since $R$ last collected retainer fees

$W$ = time weighting factor (for the time-weighted version of the dividend algorithm)

The dividend algorithm proceeds as follows: at time $t$, object $R$ has clients $C_i (i = 1$ to $m)$ and seeks a total retainer fee $F_t$. For each client $C_j$, $R$ maintains a dividend sum $D_{jt}$, created and initialized as zero when $C_j$ first pointed at $R$. At time $t$, $R$ asks each client $C_j$ for a number $N_{jt}$. $R$ then asks each $C_j$ for an amount of money

$$S_{jt} = F_t N_{jt} / \sum_{i=1}^{m} N_{it} \, .$$

From $C_j$, $R$ receives (after using charging algorithms described in the next section) an amount $P_{jt}$. Then, R replaces each $N_{jt}$ (as needed) with $N'_{jt} = N_{jt}P_{jt}/S_{jt}$, and (in the unweighted form of the dividend algorithm) sets

$$D_{jt} = D_{j(t-1)} + A_{jt}, \text{ where } A_{jt} = P_{jt}\Big/\sum_{i=1}^{m} N'_{it}.$$

When R is used between times $t$ and $t+1$ (by any object, whether among $C_i$ or not), R collects a surcharge equal to

$$\sum_{i=1}^{m} D_{it},$$

(plus an amount to cover actual service costs, profits, and so forth—these charges are ignored in the following, since they have no effect on rent and retainer strategies). R then pays a dividend equal to $D_{it}$ to each client $C_i$.

### 3.2.1.2. Basic analysis

Clients evolved under competitive pressures will tend to act so as to minimize the expected net costs of their actions. These costs may be analyzed as follows.

Assume that client $C_j$ first paid a retainer fee to R at time $t = T_1$. For a client $C_j$, total expected costs and paybacks are a function of $F_t$, $N_{it}$, and $P_{it}$ (for $i = 1$ to m, and $t = T_1$ to $\infty$). The analysis of expected costs may be simplified by noting how payments are mediated though the dividend sum $D_j$. Let us represent a sum over $i = 1$ to m, $i \neq j$ as

$$\sum_{i \neq j} X_i.$$

The cost to $C_j$ of using R at a time $T_2$ is

$$\sum_{i \neq j} D_{it} = \sum_{t=T_1}^{T_2} \sum_{i \neq j} A_{it}.$$

Payback at the time of use by another (at time $T_2$) is

$$D_{jt} = \sum_{t=T_1}^{T_2} A_{jt}.$$

Since these costs and paybacks are a simple sum of contributions from different times, distinct contributions can be identified from each time. Thus one can isolate the consequences to $C_j$ that result from retainer-payment actions (by $C_j$ and others) at any given time: these consequences are independent of retainer-payment actions at other times. This simplifies the analysis of optimal strategies. The net cost to $C_j$ *resulting from actions at time t* (represented as $E_{jt}$) is simply (1) the immediate cost of paying the retainer fee, plus (2) the net surcharge per $C_j$'s own use (resulting from the other clients' increments to the dividend sum at time t multiplied by the future number of uses by $C_j$), minus (3) the dividends from each of the other clients' uses (resulting from $C_j$'s own increment to the dividend sum at time t multiplied by the total future number of uses by others). This is

$$E_{jt} = P_{jt} + \Big(\sum_{i \neq j} A_{it}\Big) n_{jt} - A_{jt}\Big(\sum_{i \neq j} n_{it}\Big),$$

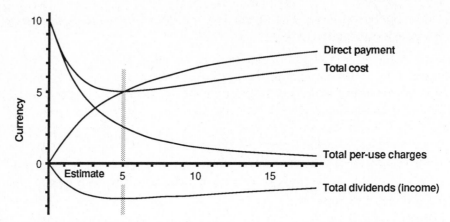

*Figure 3: Dividends and incentives. Assume that client $C_j$ will make five future uses of object R, while its other clients together will make a total of five uses. Differing usage estimates $N'_{jt}$ will then incur long-run costs shown above, assuming that R charges a retainer fee of ten currency units, and that the other clients' estimates sum to five. Note that $C_j$'s total cost is minimized by reporting a correct estimate of its own future use.*

$$= F'_t \left(\sum_{i=1}^{m} N'_{it}\right)^{-1} \left[n_{jt} + N'_{jt}\left(1 - \sum_{i=1}^{m} n_{it}/\sum_{i=1}^{m} N'_{it}\right)\right].$$

Considered as a function of $n_{jt}$, this has a minimum at

$$N'_{jt\,(optimal)} = \frac{2\,n_{jt} + \left(\sum_{i\neq j} n_{it} - \sum_{i\neq j} N'_{it}\right)}{1 + \left(\sum_{i\neq j} n_{it} / \sum_{i\neq j} N'_{it}\right)}.$$

### 3.2.1.3. Analysis of incentives

The above equation implies that if

$$\sum_{i\neq j} N'_{it} = \sum_{i\neq j} n_{it},$$

then the optimum value of $N'_{jt}$ for client $C_j$ to submit equals $n_{jt}$. That is, if other clients are making accurate predictions of their future usage, then one can minimize costs by accurately predicting one's own usage. Cost allocation is uniform, with desirable incentives. After removal of a fixed sum to cover R's expenses, all charges are redistributed among the clients in a zero-sum game. If all clients accurately estimate their own usage, then each client's net charges are strictly proportional to its usage. This provides a level playing field for large and small entities, avoiding perverse incentives. Since $N'_{jt\,(optimal)} = n_{jt}$, and since $n_{jt}$ represents real uses, pooling or splitting demand among objects can make no strategic difference.

If other clients suffer from a systematic bias in their usage estimates, this benefits those that estimate their own use correctly. All the inaccurate clients can be modeled as one large, inaccurate client which (by hypothesis) is in an environment in which the remaining client(s) make correct estimates. Accordingly, its inaccuracy is suboptimal, causing losses. As this is a zero-sum game, those losses accrue to the accurate estimators.

But if a client knows that other clients are systematically submitting inaccurate estimates of their future usage, *and* knows the direction of their bias, it can bias its own estimate to improve its expected earnings. The direction of optimal bias—whether in the same or opposite direction to the others' bias—depends on additional knowledge of the relative magnitudes of the usage rates involved. It should be rare for a client to have all this knowledge. In a typical round, a client submits a number, then pays a request. It has no direct way to infer others' estimates or their actual future usage rates.

If others' total estimates are known to mistakenly equal zero, $C_j$'s formally optimal value of $N_{jt}^i$ is zero, driving the future charge per use to infinity, and giving infinite expected dividend revenue to $C_j$ (assuming demand for $R$ is truly independent of its surcharge!). However, consideration of the real relation between price and demand will give different results, in which $R$ is in price competition both with $R$'s competitors and with any alternative copies of $R$, and in which the client-investor $C_j$ must be viewed as a co-provider of $R$'s service. Further, if $R$ (or the creator of $R$) expects future uses from yet-unaccounted-for clients, then self-investment (by acting as a virtual client) makes economic sense. This would raise the effective total of others' estimates above zero.

In addition to the price-sensitivity of demand, the fixed transaction costs of paying retainer fees modify these conclusions somewhat, giving low-rate users an incentive not to participate in the process. If enough do not, the resulting underestimate of usage will give a positive return on investment to the clients that do, covering their transaction costs. A full analysis of optimal behavior seems likely to be complex.

### 3.2.1.4. Adding a time horizon

A major problem remains with this form of the algorithm: the magnitude of the dividend accounts grows steadily over time, without bound. There is no equilibrium cost per use, given finite estimates $N_{jt}^i$ by the clients, even given provision of an identical service to identical clients at a uniform rate. If clients expect an unbounded number of future uses, the algorithm becomes indeterminate regarding allocation of retainer shares to clients, refunds of invested sums become infinitesimal, and full payback of invested sums is indefinitely postponed. It therefore makes sense to investigate a broader family of dividend algorithms.

Consider a consultant $R$ that (according to contract) will be in existence only until a time $T$. The above algorithm may be applied, and retains all its properties, given that the clients notice that their uses will (of necessity) cease at time $T$. This would continue to hold if $R$ were immediately replaced with a new instance of itself having all dividend accounts initialized to zero. Clients could continue receiving service, but their optimal values of $N_{jt}^i$ before $T$ would take account only of expected uses before $T$. The same analysis would hold if $R$ simply zeroed its accounts at $T$, again according to contract.

In general, a consultant $R$ can announce a policy in which all dividend accounts are to be multiplied by a time-dependent factor $w(t)$; in the above case, this factor is one before $T$ and zero afterwards. Since expected costs and resulting strategic decisions are dependent only on expectations, actions, and policies in the current time period, a different weighting function could be announced for each period.

Assume that each client $C_j$ will use $R$ (counting from the present time $t$) at times $\tau_{j1}, \tau_{j2}, \tau_{j3} \ldots$. Represent the weighting function applied to the dividend sums (relative to the present time period $t$) as $w_t(\tau)$. The net cost to $C_j$ resulting from actions at time $t$ is then

$$E_{jt} = P_{jt} + \left( \sum_{i \neq j} A_{it} \right) \sum_{k=1}^{\infty} w_t(\tau_{jk}) - A_{jt} \left( \sum_{i \neq j} \sum_{k=1}^{\infty} w_t(\tau_{ik}) \right)$$

But this is simply the original expression for $E_{jt}$ with the substitution

$$n_{jt} = \sum_{k=1}^{\infty} w_t(\tau_{jk}).$$

Hence the analysis proceeds as before, but with sums of time-weighted uses replacing sums of uses; the previous analysis becomes a special case in which all weights are unity.

This immediately makes available a family of strategies sharing desirable properties. A simple member of the family is $w(t) = \exp(-Wt)$, where $W$ is non-negative. This may be implemented in approximate form to create an initial-strategy dividend algorithm in which, in each round, $R$ sets

$$D_{jt} = D_{j(t-1)} \exp(-WL_t) + A_{jt}.$$

For a uniform rate of use equal to $U_j$ (the time-average of $dn_{jt}/dt$), the optimal value of $N_{jt}$ is approximately $U_j/W$; this is exact, in the limit of short time periods $L_t$. As we shall see, $W$ should *not* be set based on time-value-of-money considerations. Though the function is exponential, it does not represent compound interest.

This algorithm retains the stability and incentive properties of the first algorithm described. In addition, it yields a stable cost per use, given stable total retainer fees and usage-rates. Charges per use are still equal for all users, if all users estimate their usage correctly. Further, this algorithm asks clients for estimates of usage in an (effectively) bounded time interval—that is, it asks them for an estimate they may plausibly be able to make.

The parameter $W$ can be heuristically tuned subject to the constraint that it be non-negative. In general, it should perhaps be tuned to make

$$\sum_{i=1}^{m} N_{it}' \approx 1.$$

This would change the sense of what is being estimated from the number of future uses to the probability of use within a bounded time interval. An object $R$ may at any time announce that future estimates will be entered into new dividend accounts subject to a new function $w(t)$, so long as it pays dividends that result from summing the results of the new accounts with the results of the old accounts (which must be updated according to the old algorithm). This maintains all the incentive properties described above and allows retuning of $W$ in a fair way, at the expense of additional overhead.

This algorithm allows a natural way to account for the time value of money, which may be important, since objects recover their investments only after a delay. If all clients submit low estimates, then all will receive greater dividends when R is used; this corresponds to receiving a return on their investment. For example, if they all bias their estimates by assuming a slightly greater value of W than R uses in its calculations, then the result will be as if they receive a certain rate of interest while their investments are repaid. (This holds on the average, assuming that actual use rates match expected use rates.) If different objects seek different rates of return, strategic considerations become more complex. Time-value-of-money considerations should be small in systems open to the external market, because market interest rates measured in percent per year are tiny per day or second. Long-run interest rates will equilibrate in a connected open system—investment will move toward higher rates, driving them down.

### 3.2.1.5. Accounting costs

A remaining problem with this algorithm is that R must maintain a dividend account for every client ever charged a retainer. This may be corrected in a way that demonstrates a generally-applicable principle for lowering accounting overhead.

What is important to the incentive structure of an algorithm (in the absence of risk-averseness considerations, as is appropriate with small enough sums of money) is not that *actual costs* have a certain magnitude, but that *average costs* do so. Random variations in actual expenses and payments make no difference if the amounts are small and the averages are correct. Accordingly, with proper attention to these points and to conservation of currency, charges and payments may be rounded or made on a statistical basis.

In the present case, we seek a principled way to cut off payments to former clients, cutting short the long, exponential tail of the dividend account. This can be done by freezing the magnitude of the account when it reaches a small-enough level, and then giving the account a suitable half-life for total deletion (using decisions based on random numbers to give a certain probability of deletion per unit time). This leaves the expected payback in all future periods unchanged, but makes the expected cost of maintaining the account asymptotically approach zero.

### 3.2.1.6. Circulation of usage estimates

Leaving aside the small correction for the time value of money, an estimate $N'_{jt}$ may be interpreted as indicating a rate of use equal to $W N'_{jt}$. The quantity

$$W \sum_{i=1}^{m} N'_{it}$$

is then R's total expected rate of use, which R can use in estimating the rate at which it will use its own consultants, thereby propagating usage information through the system. The dividend algorithm thus provides local incentives for the combination and propagation of accurate estimates of future service demand, perhaps making possible sophisticated heuristics for anticipatory resource allocation—heuristics that reflect global conditions through purely local interactions. A conservative initial market strategy, however, might be to base usage estimates initially on some global average of initial-object-usage rates, and later on actual experience.

### 3.2.1.7. Open problems: the dividend algorithm

Several open problems are associated with the dividend algorithm. These include selecting an appropriate value of W and choosing an initial usage estimate in the absence of prior history.

A particularly interesting problem is the exploration of strategies which rapidly propagate future-usage estimates though a network of objects. If R's clients report increases in their expected usage, then R very likely has good reason to report increases in its expected usage of its consultants. General rules for revising these estimates must be stable in the presence of cyclic reference structures, and stable in the presence of clever, self-interested participants.

### 3.2.2. Normal money flow: the retainer-fee algorithm

The retainer-fee algorithm is the basic strategy for collecting funds to cover an object's rent and retainer-fee obligations. We earlier described initial market strategies as a sort of scaffolding for building a market. We expect the dividend algorithm just described to be scaffolding of a sort that eventually becomes a structural member; the retainer-fee and other initial-strategy algorithms for storage management seem like scaffolding of a sort one expects to be replaced as the construction proceeds. They raise fewer issues of incentives and strategic stability and are intended chiefly to ensure adequate money flow on a heuristic basis.

The retainer-fee algorithm proceeds as follows. In a given cycle each renter-object R has a number of clients, numberOfClients, and a current balance, currentBalance; it calculates (as discussed below) a desiredBalance (a target cash reserve) and a balanceReserve to be set aside for certain classes of payment. The latter is chosen such that the expected expenses for the next rent cycle can be paid without dipping into the reserve. Section 3.2.4, on the base demand algorithm, will explain how these expenses are estimated.

When asked to pay rent, R first calculates a total retainer fee $F_t$ by calculating the amount (if any) by which its currentBalance falls short of its desiredBalance. R then charges each of its clients a retainer fee $S_{jt}$ calculated through the dividend algorithm. (To this is added a surcharge, not counted in the dividend algorithm, to cover the billing cost; from an incentive perspective, this surcharge simply adds to the transaction costs discussed in the section on the dividend algorithm.) Clients pay these charges from their available funds, if they can. The dividend algorithm provides incentives to pay, since shortfalls will make $N'_{jt} < N_{jt}$.

If all clients pay in full, then R achieves a balance equaling its desiredBalance and is finished. If any fail to pay in full within a fixed time limit, those clients that paid their shares are asked for the remaining sum by iterating the retainer fee and dividend algorithms on these clients, using the values of $N_{jt}$ they reported in the first round, and defining $F_t$ as the remaining sum to be collected. This maintains the incentive structure of the dividend algorithm.

Since this process always eliminates a client from consideration, it can be iterated (counting the first round) no more than numberOfClients times. Given the addition of a billing charge, the maximum un-reimbursed message cost at any time is numberOfClients times the cost per message, hence the cash on hand needed to follow this protocol is strictly bounded and may be covered by a fixed per-client deposit.

If iteration of this request process fails to produce enough money to prevent an improper eviction, further measures must be taken. These are the subject of the alert algorithm.

### 3.2.2.1. Open problems: the retainer fee algorithm

Two open problems related to the retainer-fee algorithm involve essentially heuristic choices of parameters. One is the choice of how much cash to keep on hand to meet cash-flow contingencies, another is the choice of the length of a pre-paid rent period. An initial market strategy for the former is presented below as the base-demand algorithm. The latter depends on (at least) the cost of storage rental, the cost of processing rent requests, and the likelihood (as a function of time) that one should vacate storage.

Generation scavenging [9] and the Lieberman-Hewitt garbage collection algorithm [1] both rely on the insight that objects have a high infant mortality—that a good predictor of the longevity of an object is its age. Both check new objects more frequently, thereby collecting more garbage with less effort and cost. Our initial strategy can do likewise simply by pre-paying rent for longer times as the renter ages.

### 3.2.3. Special money flow: the alert algorithm

If the retainer-fee algorithm fails to produce enough money to prevent R's eviction, R sends each of its clients an alert message. Strong pointing fundamentally means responding to alert messages appropriately: other money-handling procedures can fail, but (with caveats about execution time, notice, and rent periods) an unbroken chain of correct alert-processing objects leading back to a well-funded object will suffice to retain R in storage.

The idea of the alert process is to send requests for funds as far up and out through the chain of client relationships as is needed to find an object able to supply ample money. Failure to collect the needed money is assumed to imply that no solvent entity is willing to pay for continued storage of the renter, which may therefore be garbage-collected.

An algorithm for accomplishing this is described in Figures 4 and 5, and code implementing it is listed in the appendix to this paper. Recipients of alert messages first seek funds through application of the retainer-fee algorithm, then send further alert messages if needed. Propagation of alert messages in endless loops is avoided by giving each a unique identifier; objects refuse all but the first alert message with a given identifier.

All alert messages seek the full funds needed to satisfy the original alerter, plus enough to compensate the participating objects for their handling costs. This enables them to maintain a balance (the alertReserve) adequate to process further alert messages. Maintaining an alert-Reserve is like keeping a quarter for use in emergencies. Should you ever need to use it, you should use that phone call not only to take care of the emergency, but also to request a new quarter.

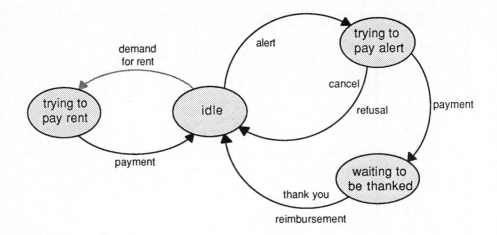

**Figure 4: State transitions of the alert algorithm.** *Ellipses represent an object's states; labels on arrows show which messages may cause it to change to another state. All states and messages are shown in Figure 5 except the demand-for-rent message (here drawn in grey).*

When a client pays the requested amount, the recipient sends *cancel* messages to its other clients, informing them that payment is no longer necessary. Due to asynchrony, however, multiple clients may pay before being cancelled. Further, a payment propagating down a chain of client-consultant references may be met by a corresponding cancellation propagating up the same chain. When a consultant finds it has received an unnecessary payment, it reimburses the payer-client. If the payer itself had merely passed the payment down, then it needs to pass the reimbursement up to *its* payer-client; thus, it needs to remember which client paid it. Since we require bounded storage costs for the algorithm, the payer needs to know when it can forget this knowledge. This occurs when the payer is reimbursed or thanked for payment— when an alert payment is actually used for rent, thank you messages propagate back up the path the payment came from. This algorithm allows a client to process only a single alert message at a time (another source of potential delay). A client must have enough storage to queue up one message per consultant, and enough cash on hand to send one message per client, hence the resources required to follow this protocol are strictly bounded.

From the perspective of the dividend algorithm, the alert process may be viewed as another iteration of the retainer-fee request cycle. Accordingly, objects that are prepared to pay alert-message requests promptly will have a competitive advantage over those that are not.

### 3.2.3.1. Open problems: the alert algorithm

The greatest problem with this alert-message mechanism is the time it requires. Even in the parallel-processing case, the time needed is proportional to the distance from a distressed to a solvent object. In the sense of guaranteeing non-collection of non-garbage objects, it works in the worst case only under the idealized assumption that alert processing times are negligible in

| States — Messages | Trying to pay rent (alertID, alertQ, count) | Trying to pay alert (alertID, alertQ, count, alerter) | Waiting to be thanked (alertID, alertQ, payer) | Idle |
|---|---|---|---|---|
| **Alert** (alertID, alerter, amount) | Send refusal to alerter | | | If can pay amount, pay it; else alert clients, become "trying to pay alert" |
| *If alert IDs differ:* | If can pay amount, pay it; else place on alertQ | | | |
| **Cancel** (alertID) | Ignore cancel (payment is coming) | Cancel clients; process next alert, or idle | Ignore cancel (reimbursement is coming) | Ignore cancel |
| *If alert IDs differ:* | If for alert on alertQ, dequeue and ignore alert; else ignore cancel | | | |
| **Thank you** (alertID) | Error | Error | Thank payer; process next alert or idle | Ignore thank you |
| *If alert IDs differ:* | Ignore thank you | | | |
| **Reimbursement** (alertID, check) | Error | Error | Reimburse payer; process next alert or idle | Accept reimbursement |
| *If alert IDs differ:* | Accept reimbursement | | | |
| **Payment** (alertID, check, payer) | Pay rent, thank payer, cancel other clients, process next alert or idle | Pay alert, cancel other clients, wait to be thanked | Reimburse payer | Reimburse payer |
| *If alert IDs differ:* | Reimburse payer | | | |
| **Refusal** (alertID) | If all clients have refused, liquidate self | If all clients have refused, refuse alert, process next alert or idle | Ignore refusal | Ignore refusal |
| *If alert IDs differ:* | Ignore refusal | | | |

***Figure 5: Alert algorithm states and messages.*** *Columns represent possible object states (with state variables); rows represent messages (with arguments). Rows are split according to whether the* alertID *in a received message matches that remembered in the state variable. If so, the message concerns the same alert. The first four messages propagate from consultants to clients; the last two, from clients to consultants.*

comparison to rent pay periods. In practice, this algorithm's range of effectiveness will depend on the real times involved. The outstanding open problem is to develop an algorithm which avoids these delay problems in ensuring that non-garbage objects receive the money they need, or to develop clear (preferably locally-computable) bounds on the correctness of the alert algorithm—that is, to characterize when the algorithm is guaranteed to work.

### 3.2.4. Cost estimation: the base-demand algorithm

Given the overhead of the alert-message mechanism, one would prefer to minimize its use. To do so requires forestalling emergencies by making sound, conservative estimates of future cash needs. Further, if most objects maintain substantial cash reserves, alert messages need not propagate far to reach a source of funds.

A renter might seek to determine its cash needs for the next cycle by multiplying the last cycle's expenses by a safety margin. Though initially plausible, this approach is unstable in the presence of cyclic client-consultant relationships: objects request money to build up safety margins, and these requests become expenses for their clients; when propagated around a loop, safety-margin multipliers cause an exponential explosion in the cash reserves and requests.

The essential idea of the base-demand algorithm is to circulate estimated-cost information to aid planning, and to do so independently of the more irregular and opportunistic circulation of money. This algorithm operates in parallel with the retainer-fee and alert algorithms just described.

With its first retainer request, R forwards to each client R's rentalPeriod (the interval until the end of R's next rent period) and a baseDemandShare equal to R's totalBase-Demand times $S_{jt}$. When R is newly created or retains no consultants, R's totalBase-Demand equals R's rent per unit time; otherwise it equals R's rent per unit time plus the sum of the baseDemandShares reported by R's consultants. Each renter stores a table of its consultant's baseDemandShares and rentalPeriods. A consultant's *demand chunk* is defined as the product of the consultant's reported rent period and baseDemandShare.

A candidate standard for the adequacy of a desiredBalance is that it call for enough cash on hand to eliminate shortfalls during any rent period, in a steady-state system. This requires determining an upper bound for the rent and retainer requests that may arrive and adding the resulting value to the alertReserve discussed above. One such upper bound consists of R's totalBaseDemand times R's rent period, to account for average expenses, plus the sum of all R's consultants' demand chunks, to account for a worst-case peak in demand (in which, for example, a set of long-period renters all charge retainer fees during one of R's shorter rent periods).

### 3.2.4.1. Analysis

The dynamic behavior of this system may be visualized in terms of a physical model in which each object's rent obligations are a source of "demand flux lines." When a new renter is introduced in a system with uniform rent periods, the demand-flux lines stemming from its

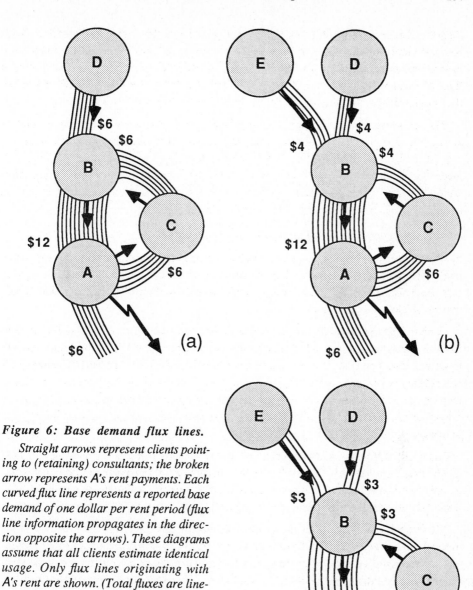

**Figure 6: Base demand flux lines.**

Straight arrows represent clients pointing to (retaining) consultants; the broken arrow represents A's rent payments. Each curved flux line represents a reported base demand of one dollar per rent period (flux line information propagates in the direction opposite the arrows). These diagrams assume that all clients estimate identical usage. Only flux lines originating with A's rent are shown. (Total fluxes are linear superpositions of individual fluxes.)

6(a) shows the equilibrium state of A's flux lines when A is charged $6 rent. 6(b) shows a non-equilibrium state that results after E begins pointing at B, splitting its fee-payment with D and C (which has not yet propagated the change). 6(c) shows the new equilibrium, approached asymptotically in this looped case.

rent extend one consultant-to-client step per rent period until they end in a non-retained funds source—that is, in an entity that pays its obligations out of earnings, capital, and so forth. Where a retained consultant has several clients, the bundle of lines splits but conserves total flux. When an established renter disappears, its associated flux lines suffer a wave of termination, propagating at the same speed.

Figure 6 illustrates several states in a system before and after a new client begins pointing at a looped structure. Where pointing relationships loop, but some pointers enter from the outside (as shown), a certain fraction of demand-flux escapes in each circuit of the loop. This gives the total demand flux an exponential settling behavior in which the equilibrium total-BaseDemand values accurately predict per-cycle expenses. (Non-uniform rent periods change the speed with which lines propagate, but do not change the essential dynamics.)

### 3.2.4.2. Open problems: the base-demand algorithm

The base-demand algorithm propagates base demand information at an awkwardly slow rate, particularly in the presence of cyclic structures. This can sometimes make emergency cash demands (and resort to the alert algorithm) unavoidable. Better heuristics for determining cash on hand would be desirable.

With the present algorithm, objects in cyclic structures will also report biased cost numbers. In a modified version of the situation shown in Figure 6, if D's estimated use of B is arbitrarily low, then B may report an arbitrarily high base demand estimate to E, although E will actually be charged no more than the sum of A, B, and C's rent. This results in B appearing less competitive than it is. This bias is unpleasant, but at least has stable consequences: if E does decide to retain B, it will be favorably surprised, and hence will have no incentive to immediately reverse its decision.

Many of the problems of this algorithm result from objects participating in cyclic structures of which they are unaware. Finding cycles by propagating full referencing information would violate the privacy of the objects involved. An open problem is to determine how little information about reference structure can be revealed while still alleviating the above problems.

There are also problems with the incentive structure of this algorithm. Information on base demand can be viewed as an indication of the expected storage surcharge for using a consultant. Objects therefore have an incentive to attempt to gain clients by deviating from the algorithm and understating costs. This is similar to the "low-balling" problem in cost-plus contracts—companies may knowingly provide a low estimate of costs while a contractor is being selected; overruns occur later, after enough time and money have been invested in the project to prevent clients from easily switching. A more market-like alternative for estimating future costs might provide rewards and penalties that would avoid this peculiar incentive.

### 3.3. Applications

How practical are these algorithms for storage management? They are substantially more complex than typical garbage collection algorithms, but this complexity need not be visible to a programmer—it presents a simple interface. In terms of computational resources, though, they are substantially more expensive than typical garbage collection algorithms; this restricts their applicability. One would not use them to allocate and free cons cells in a Lisp system, but one could use them to allocate and free space for large objects—even Lisp systems themselves—which might use conventional garbage collection internally.

In general, algorithms like these will make less sense when objects are small, simple, short-lived, and mutually trusting. They will make more sense when objects are large enough to make their storage costs worth considering (in the sense of "worth the overhead of computing costs and making tradeoffs"). They will make more sense when objects are complex enough to make economic decisions, and long-lived enough for the cost of making those decisions to be amortized over a significant storage time. Finally, some form of market-based storage management seems necessary if objects coded by different groups for different purposes are to make efficient use of machine resources and each other.

Some of the flaws of these algorithms become unimportant if the consequence of evicting an object is merely clearing a copy of it from a local cache or migrating it to a different machine or a different form of long-term storage. If failure to pay rent does not destroy an object, then delays in alert processing can no longer threaten program correctness. Further, large objects are more often candidates for migration than for deletion. Information of the sort circulated by the dividend and base-demand algorithms can help to tune local working-sets of objects in distributed open systems.

# 4. Initial strategies for trust

Many of the above algorithms make strategic sense only if one object can trust another object to follow them. For example, there are direct financial incentives to embezzle funds or misreport earnings by violating the dividend algorithm, and there are market-share incentives to produce falsely low cost estimates by violating the base-demand algorithm. Further, improper market intelligence (who is using what services?) can be gleaned by comparing alert-ID values arriving via different consultants. Thus, one needs what may be called initial strategies for trust.

The simplest strategy is for an object to trust whatever existing objects it is initially instructed to trust. This need not lead to great inflexibility or put a great burden on the programmer. Standard initial market strategies for resource management can be provided by a programming environment. In one kind of implementation, a wide range of objects will use instances of the same, small set of initial-strategy objects; these objects will recognize and trust each other, and will be able to interact with other objects in ways that do not assume trust. (Unforgeable identities are an essential foundation for trust.) Thus, use of standard initial strategies can itself be an initial strategy for trust.

Other means of building trust are discussed in [II]. They include creating or noticing situations having the characteristics of indefinitely-iterated prisoner's dilemma games [10] (see also the discussion in [I]), use of posted bonds, use of positive-reputation systems, and use of behavior-certification agencies.

## 5. Probabilistic cash flows

As noted in the discussion of accounting overhead in the dividend algorithm, the incentive structure of an algorithm (in the absence of risk aversion) is determined by its average *expected* payoffs, which can deviate from its actual payoffs on any given occasion. This principle has general applicability.

### 5.1. Processor accounting

The overhead of the escalator algorithm may be acceptable at the scale of, say, tasks in the Mach operating system [IV], but not at the finer-grained level of Mach threads, Actor tasks [11], or FCP processes [V]. Scheduling of light-weight processes like these might best be handled by a simple round-robin scheduler, which itself buys time through an auction house. How might these light-weight processes be charged so as to subject them to price incentives and compensate the round-robin process for the time it buys—all at low overhead? One approach is to use probabilistic charging: at random, uniformly-distributed times (a Poisson process with mean interarrival time $T$), note which light-weight process is currently running and charge its sponsoring account $T$ times the current price of processor time. On the average, the round-robin process receives the market price for time; on the average, each light-weight process pays it. And yet on a typical occasion, a light-weight process will run without being charged, and hence without accounting overhead.

### 5.2. Gambling

A different kind of probabilistic cash flow is gambling, wagering money on a chance event. This too has its place.

Consider an object which has just received an alert message asking for more money than it can pay or raise though retainer-fee requests. Sending an alert message may be expensive, in terms of direct communication costs and costs imposed on clients. It is an elementary result of decision analysis [12] that when $X\%$ more money has over $X\%$ more utility, for some value of $X$ (which requires that the utility-*vs.*-money curve somewhere be concave upwards) there exists a fair bet (or one with a small "house percentage") that is rationally worth taking. This can be the case both in alert processing and elsewhere in an agoric system.

To illustrate the principle (albeit with absurd numbers), assume that an object has a balance of $50 and receives an alert message demanding $100. Assume further that the object has 10 clients, and that transmitting an alert costs $1 per message. If the object simply alerts its clients and then pays its bill, it will pay a total of $110. If, however, the object gambles the $50 in a fair bet on a double-or-nothing basis, its expected net payment will be half the net payment that will result if the gamble is won $(1/2 \times \$50)$ plus half the net payment that will result if the gamble is lost, $(1/2 \times (\$50 + \$100 + \$10))$. This equals $105, for an expected savings of $5. Similar bets can be profitable, so long as the house percentage amounts to less than $5. Thus, gambling might profitably be made part of a market strategy for alert processing.

One can predict that market forces will favor the emergence of rational gambling in agoric systems. To provide gambling services, one expects to see lottery objects with substantial cash reserves. These will accept payments of X units of currency with a request for a greater sum Y, and return Y with a probability slightly less than X/Y.

## 5.3. Insurance

Another (and more respectable) form of gambling is insurance, or risk pooling. This can be based on a form of trust that will arise naturally in an agoric system.

A set of objects sharing a single program (code, script, class) is like a set of organisms sharing a single genome. It is an elementary result of evolutionary theory [13] that the genes of such organisms (in, say, a colony) will be selected for complete altruism among "individuals". And indeed, colonial polyps often share digestive tracts, and thus all their food.

Objects sharing a script can likewise (with full trust) offer to share cash reserves, in effect insuring one another against temporary shortages and expensive alert processing. In insurance terms, the shared incentives of these objects eliminate the problem of "moral hazard", that is, of insured entities taking uneconomic risks because "the insurance company will pay for any losses". Here, objects care as much about the "insurance company" as about themselves (more accurately, "evolutionary pressures will favor those objects which behave in a manner that can be regarded as 'caring' in this way"). Objects of types which abuse this mechanism to prevent proper garbage collection will in general have higher costs and lose in price competition. This is a case in which Hofstader's "superrationality" [14] and Genesereth's "common behavior assumption" [15] will apply.

# 6. Conclusions

This paper has explored mechanisms for the allocation of processor time and storage that are compatible both with programming practice and with market mechanisms. Processor scheduling through an auction process yields a flexible, decentralized priority system, allowing a variety of strategies that make tradeoffs involving the speed, certainty, and cost of service. Storage can be managed through auctioning of rental space and decentralized networks of client-consultant relationships. This yields a distributed garbage collection algorithm able both to collect unreferenced loops that cross trust boundaries and to accumulate rough price information to guide economic decisions regarding, for example, local caching in distributed systems.

Some of these algorithms (*e.g.*, for processor scheduling) have per-decision costs comparable to those of non-market mechanisms in current use; others have costs that are much greater. In general, these costs will be acceptable for objects of sufficient size and processes of sufficient duration. The question of the appropriate scale at which to apply market mechanisms can be addressed by additional study but will best be addressed by experience in actual computational markets. The proposals made here can doubtless be improved upon; they are merely intended to illustrate some of the issues involved in incentive engineering for computational markets, and to provide a starting point for discussion and design. Any advances toward lower costs, greater effectiveness, and better incentive structures will shift tradeoff points in favor of finer-grained application of market mechanisms.

Even heavy overhead costs would leave intact a solid case for market mechanisms in computation. This case rests on the value of doing the right thing (or something like it) with some overhead costs, rather than doing something blatantly wrong with polished efficiency. And when finding the right thing to do requires cooperation, competition, and freewheeling experimentation, the value of decentralized systems with market accountability becomes very great indeed.

## Appendix: code for the alert algorithm

The alert algorithm is the most procedurally intricate of the initial strategies described here, hence it is the one least suited to description in English. It is documented here by code written in the programming language FCP [V,16]; this code has not been run. To facilitate object-oriented programming, we are using a form of syntactic sugar known as "keyword terms" [17]. A keyword term can be distinguished from the familiar positional term by use of curly braces instead of parentheses. The arguments of a keyword term are identified by the keyword to the left of the colon instead of by position. All unmentioned keywords are considered to be associated with unbound variables. The keyword term "foo{KTerm but bar:a, baz:b}" is identical to the keyword term "KTerm" except that "bar" is associated with "a" and "baz" is associated with "b". Keyword terms can be efficiently translated into positional terms.

```
% mem
  % Alert

    % Not idle
mem([Msg | Self], State) :-
    alert{alertID:ID, alerter:Alerter} = Msg,
    state{stateName:SName, alertID:ID} = State,
    SName =\= idle |
    Alerter = [refusal{alertID:ID}],
    mem(Self?, State).

    % IDs differ
mem([Msg | Self], State) :-
    alert{alertID:ID1} = Msg,
    state{stateName:SName, alertID:ID2} = State,
    SName =\= idle,
    ID1 =\= ID2 |
    tryToPayAlert(Msg, Self, NewSelf, State,
        NewState),
    mem(NewSelf?, NewState?).

    % Idle

    % alertQ empty
mem([Msg | Self], State) :-
```

```
    alert{} = Msg,
    state{stateName:idle, alertQ:[]} = State |
    tryToPayAlert(Msg, Self, NewSelf, State,
        NewState),
    mem(NewSelf?, NewState?).


    % alertQ non-empty
mem(Self, State) :-
    state{stateName:idle, alertQ:[AlertMsg |
        AlertMsgs], clients:Clients} = State |
    alert{alertID:ID, alerter:Alerter, amount:Amount} =
        AlertMsg,
    alertClients(Clients, alert{AlertMsg but
        alerter:Self1}, NumClients, NewClients),
    NewState = state{State but
        stateName:tryingToPayAlert, alertID:ID,
        alertQ:AlertMsgs, count:NumClients?,
        clients:NewClients?},
    merge(Self?, Self1?, NewSelf),
    mem(NewSelf?, NewState?).

    % Cancel

    % Trying to pay rent
mem([cancel{alertID:ID} | Self], State) :-
```

```
state{stateName:tryingToPayRent, alertID:ID} =
      State |
mem(Self?, State).
```

## % Trying to pay alert

```
mem([cancel{alertID:ID} | Self], State) :-
    state{stateName:tryingToPayAlert, alertID:ID,
          clients:Clients} = State |
    cancelClients(Clients, cancel{alertID:ID},
          NewClients),
    NewState = state{State but stateName:idle,
          clients:NewClients},
    mem(Self?, NewState?).
```

## % Waiting to be thanked

```
mem([cancel{alertID:ID} | Self], State) :-
    state{stateName:waitingToBeThanked, alertID:ID}
          = State |
    mem(Self?, State).
```

## % Ids differ

```
mem([cancel{alertID:ID1} | Self], State) :-
    state{stateName:SName, alertID:ID2, alertQ:Q} =
          State,
    SName =\= idle,
    ID1 =\= ID2 |
    forgetAlert(Q?, ID1, NewQ),
    NewState = state{State but alertQ:NewQ?},
    mem(Self?, NewState?).
```

## % Idle

```
mem([cancel{} | Self], State) :-
    state{stateName:idle, alertQ:[]} = State |
    mem(Self?, State).
```

## % Thank you

## % Trying to pay rent

```
mem([Msg | Self], State) :-
    thankYou{alertID:ID} = Msg,
    state{stateName:tryingToPayRent, alertID:ID} =
          State |
    error(Msg),
    mem(Self?, State).
```

## % Trying to pay alert

```
mem([Msg | Self], State) :-
    thankYou{alertID:ID} = Msg,
    state{stateName:tryingToPayAlert, alertID:ID} =
          State |
    error(Msg),
    mem(Self?, State).
```

## % Waiting to be thanked

```
mem([Msg | Self], State) :-
    thankYou{alertID:ID} = Msg,
    state{stateName:waitingToBeThanked, alertID:ID,
          payer:Payer} = State |
    Payer = [Msg],
    NewState = state{State but stateName:idle},
    mem(Self?, NewState?).
```

## % Ids differ

```
mem([thankYou{alertID:ID1} | Self], State) :-
    state{stateName:SName, alertID:ID2} = State,
    SName =\= idle,
    ID1 =\= ID2 |
    mem(Self?, State).
```

## % Idle

```
mem([thankYou{} | Self], State) :-
    state{stateName:idle} = State |
    mem(Self?, State).
```

## % Reimbursement

## % Trying to pay rent

```
mem([Msg | Self], State) :-
    reimbursement{alertID:ID} = Msg,
    state{stateName:tryingToPayRent, alertID:ID} =
          State |
    error(Msg),
    mem(Self?, State).
```

## % Trying to pay alert

```
mem([Msg | Self], State) :-
    reimbursement{alertID:ID} = Msg,
    state{stateName:tryingToPayAlert, alertID:ID} =
          State |
    error(Msg),
    mem(Self?, State).
```

## % Waiting to be thanked

```
mem([Msg | Self], State) :-
    reimbursement{alertID:ID} = Msg,
    state{stateName:waitingToBeThanked, alertID:ID,
          payer:Payer} = State |
    Payer = [Msg],
    NewState = state{State but stateName:idle},
    mem(Self?, NewState?).
```

## % Ids differ

```
mem([Msg | Self], State) :-
    reimbursement{alertID:ID1, check:Check} = Msg,
    state{alertID:ID2} = State,
    ID1 =\= ID2 |
    deposit(Check?, State?, NewState),
    mem(Self?, NewState?).
```

## % Idle

```
mem([Msg | Self], State) :-
    reimbursement{check:Check} = Msg,
    state{stateName:idle} = State
          |
    deposit(Check?, State?, NewState),
    mem(Self?, NewState?).
```

## % Payment

## % Trying to pay rent

```
mem([Msg | Self], State) :-
    payment{alertID:ID, check:Check, payer:Payer} =
          Msg,
```

```
state{stateName:tryingToPayRent, alertID:ID,
    clients:Clients} = State |
payRent(Check?, State?, State1),
Payer = [thankYou{alertID:ID} | Payer1],
creditPayer(Payer1, Check?, State1?, State2),
cancelClients(Clients, cancel{alertID:ID},
    NewClients),
NewState = state{State2 but stateName:idle,
    clients:NewClients},
mem(Self?, NewState?).
```

### % Trying to pay alert

```
mem([Msg | Self], State) :-
payment{alertID:ID, check:Check, payer:Payer} =
    Msg,
state{stateName:tryingToPayAlert, alertID:ID,
    alerter:Alerter, clients:Clients} = State |
creditPayer(Payer, Check?, State?, State1),
Alerter = [payment{Msg but payer:Self1}],
cancelClients(Clients, cancel{alertID:ID},
    NewClients),
NewState = state{State1? but
    stateName:waitingToBeThanked,
    payer:Payer, clients:NewClients},
mem(Self?, NewState?).
```

### % Waiting to be thanked

```
mem([Msg | Self], State) :-
payment{alertID:ID, check:Check, payer:Payer} =
    Msg,
state{stateName:waitingToBeThanked, alertID:ID}
    = State |
Payer = [reimbursement{alertID:ID,
    check:Check}],
mem(Self?, State).
```

### % Ids differ

```
mem([Msg | Self], State) :-
payment{alertID:ID1, check:Check, payer:Payer}
    = Msg,
state{stateName:SName, alertID:ID2} = State,
SName =\= idle,
ID1 =\= ID2 |
Payer = [reimbursement{alertID:ID,
    check:Check}],
mem(Self?, State).
```

### % Idle

```
mem([Msg | Self], State) :-
payment{alertID:ID, check:Check, payer:Payer} =
    Msg,
state{stateName:idle} = State |
Payer = [reimbursement{alertID:ID,
    check:Check}],
mem(Self?, State).
```

### % Refusal

### % Trying to pay rent

#### % count = 0

```
mem(Self, State) :-
state{stateName:tryingToPayRent, count:0} =
    State |
liquidate(Self, State).
```

#### % count > 0

```
mem([refusal{alertID:ID} | Self], State) :-
state{stateName:tryingToPayRent, alertID:ID,
    count:Count} = State,
Count > 0 |
NewCount := Count - 1,
NewState = state{State but count:NewCount?},
mem(Self?, NewState?).
```

### % Trying to pay alert

#### % count = 0

```
mem(Self, State) :-
state{stateName:tryingToPayAlert, alertID:ID,
    count:0, alerter:Alerter} = State |
Alerter = [refusal{alertID:ID}],
NewState = state{State but stateName:idle},
liquidate(Self, NewState?).
```

#### % count > 0

```
mem([refusal{alertID:ID} | Self], State) :-
state{stateName:tryingToPayAlert, alertID:ID,
    count:Count} = State,
Count > 0 |
NewCount := Count - 1,
NewState = state{State but count:NewCount?},
mem(Self?, NewState?).
```

### % Waiting to be thanked

```
mem([refusal{alertID:ID} | Self], State) :-
state{stateName:waitingToBeThanked, alertID:ID}
    = State |
mem(Self?, State).
```

### % Ids differ

```
mem([refusal{alertID:ID1} | Self], State) :-
state{stateName:SName, alertID:ID2} = State,
SName =\= idle,
ID1 =\= ID2 |
mem(Self?, State).
```

### % Idle

```
mem([refusal{} | Self], State) :-
state{stateName:idle} = State |
mem(Self?, State).
```

## % Other predicates

### % tryToPayAlert

```
tryToPayAlert(AlertMsg, Self, NewSelf, State,
        NewState) :-
    alert{amount:Amount} = AlertMsg,
    collectRetainer(Amount?, State?, State1, Check,
        Ok),
    tryToPayAlert1(Ok?, Check?, AlertMsg, Self,
        NewSelf, AlertsForQ),
    state{alertQ:Q} = State1?,
    append(AlertsForQ?, Q?, NewQ),
    NewState = state{State1? but alertQ:NewQ?}.

tryToPayAlert1(true, Check, AlertMsg, Self, NewSelf,
        []) :-
    alert{alertID:ID, alerter:Alerter} = AlertMsg,
    Alerter = [payment{alertID:ID, check:Check,
        payer:Self1}],
    merge(Self?, Self1?, NewSelf).

tryToPayAlert1(false, Check, AlertMsg, Self,
        NewSelf, [Alert]).
```

### % alertClients

```
alertClients([], AlertMsg, 0, []) :-
    alert{alerter:[]} = AlertMsg.
```

```
alertClients([Client | Clients], AlertMsg, NumClients,
        [NewClient | NewClients]) :-
    alert{alerter:Alerter} = AlertMsg,
    Client = [alert{AlertMsg but alerter:Alerter1} |
        NewClient?],
    alertClients(Clients, alert{AlertMsg but
        alerter:Alerter2}, NCMinus1, NewClients),
    NumClients := 1 + NCMinus1,
    merge(Alerter1?, Alerter2?, Alerter).
```

### % cancelClients

```
cancelClients([], CancelMsg, []).

cancelClients([Client | Clients], CancelMsg,
        [NewClient | NewClients]) :-
    Client = [CancelMsg | NewClient?],
    cancelClients(Clients, CancelMsg, NewClients).
```

### % forgetAlert

```
forgetAlert([], ID, []).

forgetAlert([AlertMsg | Q], ID, Q) :-  `
    alert{alertID:ID, alerter:[]} = AlertMsg | true.

forgetAlert([AlertMsg | Q], ID1, [AlertMsg | NewQ?]) :-
    alert{alertID:ID2} = AlertMsg,
    ID1 =\= ID2 |
    forgetAlert(Q, ID1, NewQ).
```

## Acknowledgments

Note: see the paper "Markets and Computation: Agoric Open Systems" in this book [II] for general discussion, acknowledgments, and comparison with other work.

## References

Papers referenced with roman numerals can be found in the present volume:

Huberman, Bernardo (ed.), *The Ecology of Computation*
(Elsevier Science Publishers/North-Holland, 1988).

[I]  Miller, Mark S., and Drexler, K. Eric,
     "Comparative Ecology: A Computational
     Perspective", this volume.

[II]  Miller, Mark S., and Drexler, K. Eric,
     "Markets and Computation: Agoric Open
     Systems", this volume.

[III]  Liskov, Barbara, "Guardians and Actions:
     Linguistic Support for Robust, Distributed
     Programs", this volume.

[IV]  Rashid, Richard F., "From RIG to Accent to
     Mach: The Evolution of a Network Operating
     System", this volume.

[V]  Kahn, Kenneth, and Miller, Mark S.,
     "Language Design and Open Systems", this

volume.

[1]  Lieberman-Hewitt Algorithm: Lieberman,
     Henry, and Hewitt, Carl, "A Real-Time
     Garbage Collector Based on the Lifetimes of
     Objects", in: *Communications of the ACM*
     (June 1983) 26, 6, pp.419-429.

[2]  Quarterman, John S., Silbershatz, Abraham,
     Peterson, James L., "4.2BSD and 4.3BSD as
     Examples of the UNIX System", in: *ACM
     Computing Surveys* (December 1985) Vol. 17
     No. 4 pp.379–418.

[3]  Rees, Jonathan A., and Adams, Norman I.,
     IV, "T: a Dialect of Lisp or, Lambda: The
     Ultimate Software Tool", in: *Proceedings of*

the *1982 ACM Symposium on Lisp and Functional Programming* (August 1982).

[4] Bishop, Peter B., *Computers with a Large Address Space and Garbage Collection* (MIT, Cambridge, MA, May 1977) MIT/LCS/TR-178.

[5] Smith, Vernon L., "Experimental Methods in the Political Economy of Exchange", in: *Science* (10 October 1986) Vol. 234, pp.167–173.

[6] Friedman, Daniel, "On the Efficiency of Experimental Double Auction Markets", in: *American Economic Review* (March 1984) Vol. 24, No. 1, pp. 60-72.

[7] Theriault, D., *Issues in the Design and Implementation of Act 2* (MIT AI Lab, Cambridge, MA., 1983) AI-TR-728.

[8] Kornfeld, William A., "Using Parallel Processing for Problem Solving" (MIT AI Lab, Cambridge, MA, 1979) MIT-AI-561.

[9] Ungar, David Michael, *The Design and Evaluation of a High Performance Smalltalk System* (MIT Press, Cambridge, MA, 1987).

[10] Axelrod, Robert, *The Evolution of Cooperation* (Basic Books, New York, 1984).

[11] Agha, Gul, *Actors: A Model of Concurrent Computation in Distributed Systems* (MIT Press, Cambridge, MA, 1986).

[12] Raffia, Howard, *Decision Analysis: Introductory Lectures on Choices under Uncertainty* (Addison-Wesley, Reading, MA, 1970).

[13] Dawkins, Richard, *The Selfish Gene* (Oxford University Press, New York, 1976).

[14] Hofstadter, Douglas R., "Dilemmas for Superrational Thinkers, Leading Up to a Luring Lottery", in: *Metamagical Themas: Questing for the Essence of Mind and Pattern* (Basic Books, New York, 1985) pp. 739-755.

[15] Genesereth, M. R., Ginsberg, M. L., and Rosenschein, J. S., *Cooperation without Communication* (1984) HPP Report 84-41.

[16] Shapiro, Ehud, (ed.), *Concurrent Prolog: Collected Papers* (MIT Press, Cambridge, MA, 1987) in press.

[17] Hirsh, Susan, Kahn, Kenneth M., and Miller, Mark S., *Interming: Unifying Keyword and Positional Notations* (Xerox PARC, Palo Alto, CA, 1987) in press.

The Ecology of Computation
B.A. Huberman (editor)
Elsevier Science Publishers B.V. (North-Holland), 1988

# Guardians and Actions: Linguistic Support for Robust, Distributed Programs

BARBARA LISKOV and ROBERT SCHEIFLER
Massachusetts Institute of Technology

An overview is presented of an integrated programming language and system designed to support the construction and maintenance of distributed programs: programs in which modules reside and execute at communicating, but geographically distinct, nodes. The language is intended to support a class of applications concerned with the manipulation and preservation of long-lived, on-line, distributed data. The language addresses the writing of robust programs that survive hardware failures without loss of distributed information and that provide highly concurrent access to that information while preserving its consistency. Several new linguistic constructs are provided; among them are atomic actions, and modules called guardians that survive node failures.

Categories and Subject Descriptors: C.2.4 [**Computer-Communication Networks**]: Distributed Systems—*distributed applications*; *distributed databases*; D.1.3 [**Programming Techniques**]: Concurrent Programming; D.3.3 [**Programming Languages**]: Language Constructs—*abstract data types*; *concurrent programming structures*; *modules, packages*; D.4.5 [**Operating Systems**]: Reliability—*checkpoint/restart*; *fault-tolerance*; H.2.4 [ **Database Management**]: Systems—*distributed systems*; *transaction processing*

General Terms: Languages, Reliability

Additional Key Words and Phrases: Atomicity, nested atomic actions, remote procedure call

## 1. INTRODUCTION

Technological advances have made it cost effective to construct large systems from collections of computers connected via networks. To support such systems, there is a growing need for effective ways to organize and maintain *distributed programs*: programs in which modules reside and execute at communicating, but geographically distinct, locations. In this paper we present an overview of an integrated programming language and system, called ARGUS, that was designed for this purpose.

A preliminary version of this paper appeared in the Conference Record of the Ninth Annual Symposium on Principles of Programming Languages, January 1982 [18].
This research was supported in part by the Advanced Research Projects Agency of the Department of Defense, monitored by the Office of Naval Research under contract N00014-75-C-0661, and in part by the National Science Foundation under grant MCS 79-23769.
Authors' address: Laboratory for Computer Science, Massachusetts Institute of Technology, 545 Technology Square, Cambridge, MA 02139.

Reprinted from *ACM Transactions on Programming Languages and Systems*, Vol. 5, No. 3, July 1983, pp. 381-404.

Distributed programs run on *nodes* connected (only) via a communications network. A node consists of one or more processors, one or more levels of memory, and any number of external devices. Different nodes may contain different kinds of processors and devices. The network may be long haul or short haul, or any combination, connected by gateways. Neither the network nor any nodes need be reliable. However, we do assume that all failures can be detected as explained in [15]. We also assume that message delay is long relative to the time needed to access local memory and therefore that access to nonlocal data is significantly more expensive than access to local data.

The applications that can make effective use of a distributed organization differ in their requirements. We have concentrated on a class of applications concerned with the manipulation and preservation of long-lived, on-line data. Examples of such applications are banking systems, airline reservation systems, office automation systems, database systems, and various components of operating systems. In these systems, real-time constraints are not severe, but reliable, available, distributed data is of primary importance. The systems may serve a geographically distributed organization. Our language is intended to support the implementation of such systems.

The application domain, together with our hardware assumptions, imposes a number of requirements:

*Service.* A major concern is to provide continuous service of the system as a whole in the face of node and network failures. Failures should be localized so that a program can perform its task as long as the particular nodes it needs to communicate with are functioning and reachable. Adherence to this principle permits an application program to use replication of data and processing to increase availability.

*Reconfiguration.* An important reason for wanting a distributed implementation is to make it easy to add and reconfigure hardware to increase processing power, decrease response time, or increase the availability of data. It also must be possible to implement logical systems that can be reconfigured. To maintain continuous service, it must be possible to make both logical and physical changes *dynamically*, while the system continues to operate.

*Autonomy.* We assume that nodes are owned by individuals or organizations that want to control how the node is used. For example, the owner may want to control what runs at the node, or to control the availability of services provided at the node. Further, a node might contain data that must remain resident at that node; for example, a multinational organization must abide by laws governing information flow among countries. The important point here is that the need for distribution arises not only from efficiency considerations, but from political and sociological considerations as well.

*Distribution.* The distribution of data and processing can have a major impact on overall efficiency, in terms of both responsiveness and cost-effective use of hardware. Distribution also affects availability. To create efficient, available systems while retaining autonomy, the programmer needs explicit control over the placement of modules in the system. However, to support a reasonable degree of modularity, changes in the location of modules should have limited, localized effects on the actual code.

*Concurrency.* Another major reason for choosing a distributed implementation is to take advantage of the potential concurrency in an application, thereby increasing efficiency and decreasing response time.

*Consistency.* In almost any system where on-line data is being read and modified by ongoing activities, there are consistency constraints that must be maintained. Such constraints apply not only to individual pieces of data, but to distributed sets of data as well. For example, when funds are transferred from one account to another in a banking system, the net gain over the two accounts must be zero. Also, data that is replicated to increase availability must be kept consistent.

Of the above requirements, we found consistency the most difficult to meet. The main issues here are the coordination of concurrent activities (permitting concurrency but avoiding interference) and the masking of hardware failures. Thus, to support consistency we had to devise methods for building a reliable system on unreliable hardware. Reliability is an area that has been almost completely ignored in programming languages (with the exception of [22, 25, 28]). Yet our study of applications convinced us that consistency is a crucial requirement: an adequate language must provide a modular, reasonably automatic method for achieving consistency.

Our approach is to provide *atomicity* as a fundamental concept in the language. The concept of atomicity is not original with our work, having been used extensively in database applications [4–6, 8–10]. However, we believe the integration into a programming language of a general mechanism for achieving atomicity is novel.

The remainder of the paper is organized as follows. Atomicity is discussed in the next section. Section 3 presents an overview of ARGUS. The main features are *guardians*, the logical unit of distribution in our system, and atomic *actions*. Section 4 illustrates many features of the language with a simple mail system. The final section discusses what has been accomplished.

## 2. ATOMICITY

Data consistency requires, first of all, that the data in question be resilient to hardware failures, so that a crash of a node or storage device does not cause the loss of vital information. Resiliency is accomplished by means of redundancy. We believe the most practical technique using current technology is to keep data on stable storage devices [15].[1] Of course, stable storage, in common with any other technique for providing resiliency, cannot guarantee that data survive all failures, but it can guarantee survival with extremely high probability.

Data resiliency only ensures data survival in a quiescent environment. Our solution to the problem of maintaining consistent distributed data in the face of concurrent, potentially interfering activities, and in the face of system failures such as node crashes and network disruptions while these activities are running, is to make activities *atomic*.

The state of a distributed system is a collection of data objects that reside at various locations in the network. An activity can be thought of as a process that

---

[1] We need merely assume that stable storage is accessible to every node in the system; it is not necessary that every node have its own local stable storage devices.

attempts to examine and transform some objects in the distributed state from their current (initial) states to new (final) states, with any number of intermediate state changes. Two properties distinguish an activity as being atomic: indivisibility and recoverability. By *indivisibility* we mean that the execution of one activity never appears to overlap (or contain) the execution of any other activity. If the objects being modified by one activity are observed over time by another activity, the latter activity will either always observe the initial states or always observe the final states. By *recoverability* we mean that the overall effect of the activity is all-or-nothing: either all of the objects remain in their initial state, or all change to their final state. If a failure occurs while an activity is running, it must be possible either to complete the activity or to restore all objects to their initial states.

## 2.1 Actions

We call an atomic activity an *action*. An action may complete either by *committing* or by *aborting*. When an action aborts, the effect is as if the action had never begun: all modified objects are restored to their previous states. When an action commits, all·modified objects take on their new states.

One simple way to implement the indivisibility property is to force actions to run sequentially. However, one of our goals is to provide a high degree of concurrency. The usual method of providing indivisibility in the presence of concurrency, and the one we have adopted, is to guarantee *serializability* [6]; namely, actions are scheduled in such a way that their overall effect is as if they had been run sequentially in some order. To prevent one action from observing or interfering with the intermediate states of another action, we need to synchronize access to shared objects. In addition, to implement the recoverability property, we need to be able to undo the changes made to objects by aborted actions.

Since synchronization and recovery are likely to be somewhat expensive to implement, we do not provide these properties for all objects. For example, objects that are purely local to a single action do not require these properties. The objects that do provide these properties are called *atomic objects*, and we restrict our notion of atomicity to cover only access to atomic objects. That is, atomicity is guaranteed only when the objects shared by actions are atomic objects.

Atomic objects are encapsulated within *atomic abstract data types*. An abstract data type consists of a set of objects and a set of primitive operations; the primitive operations are the only means of accessing and manipulating the objects [21]. Atomic types have operations just like normal data types, except that the operations provide indivisibility and recoverability for the calling actions. Some atomic types are built in, while others are user defined. ARGUS provides, as built-in types, atomic arrays, records, and variants, with operations nearly identical to those on the normal arrays, records, and variants provided in CLU [20]. In addition, objects of built-in scalar types, such as characters and integers, are atomic, as are structured objects of built-in immutable types, such as strings, whose components cannot change over time.

Our implementation of (mutable) built-in atomic objects is based on a fairly simple locking model. There are two kinds of locks: read locks and write locks. Before an action uses an object, it must acquire a lock in the appropriate mode.

The usual locking rules apply: multiple readers are allowed, but readers exclude writers, and a writer excludes readers and other writers. When a write lock is obtained, a *version* of the object is made, and the action operates on this version. If, ultimately, the action commits, this version will be retained, and the old version discarded. If the action aborts, this version will be discarded, and the old version retained. For example, atomic records have the usual component selection and update operations, but selection operations obtain a read lock on the record (not the component), and update operations obtain a write lock and create a version of the record the first time the action modifies the record.

All locks acquired by an action are held until the completion of that action, a simplification of standard two-phase locking [9]. This rule avoids the problem of *cascading* aborts: if a lock on an object could be released early, and the action later aborted, any action that had observed the new state of that object would also have to be aborted.

Within the framework of actions, there is a straightforward way to deal with hardware failures at a node: they simply force the node to crash, which in turn forces actions to abort. As was mentioned above, we make data resilient by storing it on stable storage devices. Furthermore, we do not actually copy information to stable storage until actions commit. Therefore, versions made for a running action and information about locks can be kept in volatile memory. This volatile information will be lost if the node crashes. If this happens, the action must be forced to abort. To ensure that the action will abort, a standard two-phase commit protocol [8] is used. In the first phase, an attempt is made to verify that all locks are still held, and to record the new state of each modified object on stable storage. If the first phase is successful, then in the second phase the locks are released, the recorded states become the current states, and the previous states are forgotten. If the first phase fails, the recorded states are forgotten and the action is forced to abort, restoring the objects to their previous states.

Turning hardware failures into aborts has the merit of freeing the programmer from low-level hardware considerations. It also reduces the probability that actions will commit. However, this is a problem only when the time to complete an action approaches the mean time between failures of the nodes. We believe that most actions will be quite short compared to realistic mean time between failures for hardware available today.

It has been argued that indivisibility is too strong a property for certain applications because it limits the amount of potential concurrency [14]. We believe that indivisibility is the desired property for most applications, *if* it is required only at the appropriate levels of abstraction. ARGUS provides a mechanism for *user-defined* atomic data types. These types present an external interface that supports indivisibility but that can offer a great deal of concurrency as well. We do not present our mechanism here; user-defined atomic types are discussed in [30].

## 2.2 Nested Actions

So far we have presented actions as monolithic entities. In fact, it is useful to break down such entities into pieces; to this end we provide hierarchically structured, *nested* actions. Nested actions, or subactions, are a mechanism for coping with failures, as well as for introducing concurrency within an action. An action may contain any number of subactions, some of which may be performed sequentially, some concurrently. This structure cannot be observed from outside; that is, the overall action still satisfies the atomicity properties. Subactions appear as atomic activities with respect to other subactions of the same parent. Subactions can commit and abort independently, and a subaction can abort without forcing its parent action to abort. However, the commit of a subaction is conditional: even if a subaction commits, aborting its parent action will abort it. Further, object versions are written to stable storage only when top-level actions commit.

Nested actions aid in composing (and decomposing) activities in a modular fashion. This allows a collection of existing actions to be combined into a single, higher level action, and to be run concurrently within that action with no need for additional synchronization. For example, consider a database replicated at multiple nodes. If only a majority of the nodes need to be read or written for the overall action to succeed, this is accomplished by performing the reads or writes as concurrent subactions, and committing the overall action as soon as a majority of the subactions commit, even though some of the other subactions are forced to abort.

Nested actions have been proposed by others [4, 10, 26]; our model is similar to that presented in [23]. To keep the locking rules simple, we do not allow a parent action to run concurrently with its children. The rule for read locks is extended so that an action may obtain a read lock on an object provided every action holding a write lock on that object is an ancestor. An action may obtain a write lock on an object provided every action holding a (read or write) lock on that object is an ancestor. When a subaction commits, its locks are inherited by its parent; when a subaction aborts, its locks are discarded.

Note that the locking rules permit multiple writers, which implies that multiple versions of objects are needed. However, since writers must form a linear chain when ordered by ancestry, and actions cannot execute concurrently with their subactions, only one writer can ever actually be executing at one time. Hence, it suffices to use a stack of versions (rather than a tree) for each atomic object. On commit, the top version becomes the new version for the parent; on abort, the top version is simply discarded. Since versions become permanent only when top-level actions commit, the two-phase commit protocol is used only for top-level actions. A detailed description of locking and version management in a system supporting nested actions is presented in [23].

In addition to nesting subactions inside other actions, it is sometimes useful to start a new top action inside another action. Such a "nested" top action, unlike a subaction, has no special privileges relative to its parent; for example, it is not able to read an atomic object modified by its parent. Furthermore, the commit of a nested top action is not relative to its parent; its versions are written to stable storage, and its locks are released, just as for normal top actions. Nested top actions are useful for benevolent side effects. For example, in a naming system a name lookup may cause information to be copied from one location to another, to speed up subsequent lookups of that name. Copying the data within a nested top action ensures that the changes remain in effect even if the parent action aborts.

## 2.3 Remote Procedure Call

Perhaps the single most important application of nested actions is in masking communication failures. Logical nodes (described in Section 3) in ARGUS communicate via messages. We believe that the most desirable form of communcation is the paired send and reply: for every message sent, a reply message is expected. In fact, we believe the form of communication that is needed is *remote procedure call*, with *at-most-once* semantics, namely, that (effectively) either the message is delivered and acted on exactly once, with exactly one reply received, or the message is never delivered and the sender is so informed.

The rationale for the high-level, at-most-once semantics of remote procedure call is presented in [16] (see also [29]). Briefly, we believe the system should mask from the user low-level issues, such as packetization and retransmission, and that the system should make a reasonable attempt to deliver messages. However, we believe the possibility of long delays and of ultimate failure in sending a message cannot and should not be masked. In such a case, the communication would fail.[2] The sender can then cope with the failure according to the demands of the particular application. However, coping with the failure is much simpler if it is guaranteed that in this case the remote procedure call had no effect.

The all-or-nothing nature of remote procedure call is similar to the recoverability property of actions, and the ability to cope with communication failures is similar to the ability of an action to cope with the failures of subactions. Therefore, it seems natural to implement a remote procedure call as a subaction: communication failures will force the subaction to abort, and the caller has the ability to abort the subaction on demand. However, as mentioned above, aborting the subaction does not force the parent action to abort. The caller is free to find some other means of accomplishing its task, such as communicating with some other node.

## 2.4 Remarks

In our model, there are two kinds of actions: subactions and top-level actions. We believe these correspond in a natural way to activities in the application system. Top-level actions correspond to activities that interact with the external environment, or, in the case of nested top actions, to activities that should not be undone if the parent aborts. For example, in an airline reservation system, a top-level action might correspond to an interaction with a clerk who is entering a related sequence of reservations. Subactions, on the other hand, correspond to internal activities that are intended to be carried out as part of an external interaction; a reservation on a single flight is an example.

Not all effects of an action can be undone by aborting that action, since a change to the external environment, for example, printing a check, cannot be undone by program control alone. But as long as all effects can be undone, the user of our language does not need to write any code to undo or compensate for the effects of aborted actions.

---

[2] For example, the system would cause the communication to fail if it is unable to contact the remote node. We believe the system, and not the programmer, should take on this kind of responsibility, because the programmer would find it very difficult to define reasonable timeouts.

Before doing something like printing a check, the application program should make sure that printing the check is the right thing to do. One technique for ensuring this is to break an activity into two separate, sequential top-level actions. All changes to the external environment are deferred to the second action, to be executed only if the first action is successful. Such a technique will greatly decrease the likelihood of actions having undesired effects that cannot be undone.

The commit of a top-level action is irrevocable. If that action is later found to be in error, actions that compensate for the effects of the erroneous action (and of all later actions that read its results) must be defined and executed by the user. Compensation must also be performed for effects of aborted actions that cannot be undone. Note that, in general, there is no way that such compensation could be done automatically by the system, since extrasystem activity is needed (e.g., cancelling already issued checks).

Given our use of a locking scheme to implement atomic objects, it is possible for two (or more) actions to *deadlock*, each attempting to acquire a lock held by the other. Although in many cases deadlock can be avoided with careful programming, certain deadlock situations are unavoidable. Rather than having the system prevent, or detect and break, deadlocks, we rely on the user to time out and abort top-level actions. These timeouts generally will be very long, or will be controlled by someone sitting at a terminal. Note that such timeouts are needed even without deadlocks, since there are other reasons why a top action may be too slow (e.g., contention).

A user can retry a top action that aborted because of a timeout or crash, but ARGUS provides no guarantee that progress will be made. ARGUS will be extended if needed (e.g., by raising the priority of a top action each time it is repeated [27] or by using checkpoints [10]).

## 3. LINGUISTIC CONSTRUCTS

In this section we describe the main features of ARGUS. The most novel features are the constructs for implementing guardians, the logical nodes of the system, and for implementing actions, as described in the previous section. To avoid rethinking issues that arise in sequential languages, we have based ARGUS on an existing sequential language. CLU [17, 20] was chosen because it supports the construction of well-structured programs through abstraction mechanisms and because it is an object-oriented language, in which programs are naturally thought of as operating on potentially long-lived objects.

### 3.1 Overview

In ARGUS, a distributed program is composed of a group of *guardians*. A guardian encapsulates and controls access to one or more resources, for example, databases or devices. A guardian makes these resources available to its users by providing a set of operations called *handlers*, which can be called by other guardians to make use of the resources. The guardian executes the handlers, synchronizing them and performing access control as needed.

Internally, a guardian contains data objects and processes. The processes execute handlers (a separate process is spawned for each call) and perform background tasks. Some of the data objects, for example, the actual resources, make up the *state* of the guardian; these objects are shared by the processes. Other objects are local to the individual processes.

A guardian runs at a single node but can survive crashes of this node (with high probability). Thus, the guardians themselves are resilient. A guardian's state consists of *stable* and *volatile* objects. Resiliency is accomplished by writing the stable objects to stable storage when a top action commits; only those objects that were modified by the committing action need be written. The probability of loss of volatile objects is relatively high, so these objects must contain only redundant information if the system as a whole is to avoid loss of information. Such redundant information is useful for improving efficiency, for example, an index into a database for fast access.

After a crash of the guardian's node, the language support system recreates the guardian with the stable objects as they were when last written to stable storage. A process is started in the guardian to recreate the volatile objects. Once the volatile objects have been restored, the guardian can resume background tasks and can respond to new handler calls.

Guardians allow a programmer to decompose a problem into units of tightly coupled processing and data. Within a guardian, processes can share objects directly. However, direct sharing of objects between guardians is not permitted. Instead, guardians must communicate by calling handlers, and the arguments to handlers are passed by value: it is impossible to pass a reference to an object in a handler call. This rule ensures that objects local to a guardian remain local, and thus ensures that a guardian retains control of its own objects. It also provides the programmer with a concept of what is expensive: local objects are close by and inexpensive to use, while nonlocal objects are more expensive to use. A handler call is performed using a message-based communication mechanism. The language implementation takes care of all details of constructing and sending messages (see [11]).

Guardians are created dynamically. The programmer specifies the node at which a guardian is to be created; in this way individual guardians can be placed at the most advantageous locations within the network. The (name of the) guardian and (the names of) its handlers can be communicated in handler calls. Once (the name of) a guardian or one of its handlers has been received, handler calls can be performed on that guardian. Handler calls are location independent, however, so one guardian can use another without knowing its location. In fact, handler calls will continue to work even if the called guardian has changed its location, allowing for ease of system reconfiguration.

Guardians and handlers are an abstraction of the underlying hardware of a distributed system. A guardian is a logical node of the system, and interguardian communication via handlers is an abstraction of the physical network. The most important difference between the logical system and the physical system is reliability: the stable state of a guardian is never lost (to a very high probability), and the at-most-once semantics of handler calls ensures that the calls either succeed completely or have no effect.

## 3.2 Guardian Structure

The syntax of a guardian definition is shown in Figure 1.[3] A guardian definition implements a special kind of abstract data type whose operations are handlers.

---

[3] In the syntax, optional clauses are enclosed with [ ], zero or more repetitions are indicated with { }, and alternatives are separated by |.

name **= guardian** [*parameter-decls*] **is** *creator-names*
                                                **handles** *handler-names*
{*abbreviations*}
Fig. 1.   Guardian structure.          ([**stable**] *variable-decls-and-inits*)
                                       [**recover** *body* **end**]
                                       [**background** *body* **end**]
                                       {*creator-handler-and-local-routine-definitions*}
                                       **end** *name*

The name of this type, and the names of the handlers, are listed in the guardian header. In addition, the type provides one or more creation operations, called *creators*, that can be invoked to create new guardians of the type; the names of the creators are also listed in the header. Guardians may be *parameterized*, providing the ability to define a class of related abstractions by means of a single module. Parameterized types are discussed in [17, 20].

The first internal part of a guardian is a list of abbreviations for types and constants. Next is a list of variable declarations, with optional initializations, defining the guardian state. Some of these variables can be declared as **stable** variables; the others are volatile variables.

The stable state of a guardian consists of all objects *reachable* from the stable variables; these objects, called stable objects, have their new versions written to stable storage by the system when top-level actions commit. ARGUS, like CLU, has an object-oriented semantics. Variables name (or refer to) objects residing in a heap storage area. Objects themselves may refer to other objects, permitting recursive and cyclic data structures without the use of explicit pointers. The set of objects reachable from a variable consists of the object that variable refers to, any objects referred to by that object, and so on.[4]

Guardian instances are created dynamically by invoking creators of the guardian type. For example, suppose a guardian type named *spooler* has a creator with a header of the form

*create* = **creator**(*dev*: *printer*) **returns** (*spooler*)

When a process executes the expression

*spooler*$*create*(*pdev*)

a guardian object is created at the same physical node where the process is executing and (the name of) the guardian is returned as the result of the call.[5] Guardians can also be created at other nodes. Given a variable *home* naming some node,

*spooler*$*create*(*pdev*) @ *home*

creates a guardian at the specified node.

When a creator is invoked, a new guardian instance is created, and any initializations attached to the variable declarations of the guardian state are executed. The body of the creator is then executed; typically, this code will finish

---

[4] In languages that are not object oriented, the concept of reachability would still be needed to accommodate the use of explicit pointers.
[5] As in CLU, the notation *t*$*op* is used to name the *op* operation of type *t*.

initializing the guardian state and then return the guardian object. (Within the guardian, the expression **self** refers to the guardian object.)

Aside from creating a new guardian instance and executing state-variable initializations, a creator has essentially the same semantics as a handler, as described in the next section. In particular, a creator call is performed within a new subaction of the caller, and the guardian will be destroyed if this subaction or some parent action aborts. The guardian becomes permanent (i.e., survives node crashes) only when the action in which it was created commits to the top level. A guardian cannot be destroyed from outside the guardian (except by aborting the creating action). Once a guardian becomes permanent, only the guardian can destroy itself, using a **destroy** primitive.

The **recover** section runs after a crash. Its job is to recreate a volatile state that is consistent with the stable state. This may be trivial, for example, creating an empty cache, or it may be a lengthy process, for example, creating a database index.

After a crash, the system recreates the guardian and restores its stable objects from stable storage. Since updates to stable storage are made only when top-level actions commit, the stable state has the value it had at the latest commit of a top-level action before the guardian crashed. The effects of actions that had executed at the guardian prior to the crash, but had not yet committed to the top level, are lost, and the actions are aborted.

After the stable objects have been restored, the system creates a process in the guardian to first execute any initializations attached to declarations of volatile variables of the guardian state and then execute the **recover** section. This process runs as a top-level action. Recovery succeeds if this action commits; otherwise, the guardian crashes, and recovery is retried later.

After the successful completion of a creator, or of the **recover** section after a crash, two things happen inside the guardian: a process is created to run the **background** section, and handler invocations may be executed. The **background** section provides a means of performing periodic (or continuous) tasks within the guardian; examples are given in Section 4. The **background** section is not run as an action, although generally it creates top-level actions to execute tasks, as explained in Section 3.4.[6]

## 3.3 Handlers

Handlers (and creators), like procedures in CLU, are based on the termination model of exception handling [19]. A handler can terminate in one of a number of conditions: one of these is considered to be the "normal" condition, while others are "exceptional" and are given user-defined names. Results can be returned in both the normal and exceptional cases; the number and types of results can differ among conditions. The header of a handler definition lists the names of all exceptional conditions and defines the number and types of results in all cases. For example,

*files_ahead_of* = **handler**(*entry_id*: *int*) **returns** (*int*)
                                              **signals** (*printed*(*date*))

---

[6] A process that is not running as an action is severely restricted in what it can do. For example, it cannot call operations on atomic objects or call handlers without first creating a top-level action.

might be the header of a spooler handler used to determine how many requests are in front of a given queue entry. Calls of this handler either terminate normally, returning an integer result, or exceptionally in condition *printed* with a date result. In addition to the named conditions, any handler can terminate in the *failure* condition, returning a string result; failure termination may be caused explicitly by the user code, or implicitly by the system when something unusual happens, as explained further below.

A handler executes as a subaction. As such, in addition to returning or signaling, it must either commit or abort. We expect committing to be the most common case, and, therefore, execution of a **return** or **signal** statement within the body of a handler indicates commitment. To cause an abort, the **return** or **signal** is prefixed with **abort**.

Given a variable *x* naming a guardian object, a handler *h* of the guardian may be referred to as *x.h*. Handlers are invoked using the same syntax as for procedure invocation, for example,

*x.h*("read", 3, *false*)

However, whereas procedures are always executed locally within the current action, and always have their arguments and results passed by *sharing*,[7] handlers are always executed as new subactions, usually in a different guardian, and always have their arguments and results passed by value.

Let us examine a step-by-step description of what the system does when a handler is invoked:

(1) A new subaction of the calling action is created.
(2) A message containing the arguments is constructed. Since part of building this message involves executing user-defined code (see [11]), message construction may fail. If so, the subaction aborts and the call terminates with a *failure* exception.
(3) The system suspends the calling process and sends the message to the target guardian. If that guardian no longer exists, the subaction aborts, and the call terminates with a *failure* exception.
(4) The system makes a reasonable attempt to deliver the message, but success is not guaranteed. The reason is that it may not be sensible to guarantee success under certain conditions, such as a crash of the target node. In such cases, the subaction aborts, and the call terminates with a *failure* exception. The meaning of such a failure is that there is a very low probability of the call succeeding if it is repeated immediately.
(5) The system creates a process and a subaction (of the subaction in step (1)) at the receiving guardian to execute the handler. Note that multiple instances of the same handler may execute simultaneously. The system takes care of locks and versions of atomic objects used by the handler in the proper manner, according to whether the handler commits or aborts.
(6) When the handler terminates, a message containing the results is constructed, the handler action terminates, the handler process is destroyed, and the message is sent. If the message cannot be sent (as in step (2) or (4) above),

---

[7] Somewhat similar to passing by reference. See [17].

the subaction created in step (1) aborts, and the call terminates with a *failure* exception.

(7) The calling process continues execution. Its control flow is affected by the termination condition as explained in [19]. For example,

*count*: *int* := *spool.files__ahead__of(ent)* % normal return
    **except when** *printed(at: date)*: ...    % exceptional returns
        **when** *failure(why: string)*: ...
    **end**

Since a new process is created to perform an incoming handler call, guardians have the ability to execute many requests concurrently. Such an ability helps to avoid having a guardian become a bottleneck. Of course, if the guardian is running on a single-processor node, then only one process will be running at a time. However, a common case is that in executing a handler call another handler call to some other guardian is made. It would be unacceptable if the guardian could do no other work while this call was outstanding.

The scheduling of incoming handler calls is performed by the system. Therefore, the programmer need not be concerned with explicit scheduling, but instead merely provides the handler definitions to be executed in response to the incoming calls. An alternative structure for a guardian would be a single process that multiplexed itself and explicitly scheduled execution of incoming calls. We think our structure is more elegant, and no less efficient since our processes are cheap: creating a new process is only slightly more expensive than calling a procedure.

As was mentioned above, the system does not guarantee message delivery; it merely guarantees that, if message delivery fails, there is a very low probability of the call succeeding if it is repeated immediately. Hence, there is no reason for user code to retry handler calls. Rather, as mentioned earlier, user programs should make progress by retrying top-level actions, which may fail because of node crashes even if all handler calls succeed.

### 3.4 In-Line Actions

Top-level actions are created by means of the action statement

**enter topaction** *body* **end**

This causes the *body* to execute as a new top-level action. It is also possible to have an in-line subaction:

**enter action** *body* **end**

This causes the *body* to run as a subaction of the action that executes the **enter**.

When the body of an in-line action completes, it must indicate whether it is committing or aborting. Since committing is assumed to be most common, it is the default; the qualifier **abort** can be prefixed to any termination statement to override this default. For example, an in-line action can execute

**leave**

to commit and cause execution to continue with the statement following the **enter** statement; to abort and have the same effect on control, it executes

**abort leave**

Falling off the end of the *body* causes the action to commit.

### 3.5 Concurrency

The language as defined so far allows concurrency only between top actions originating in different guardians. The following statement form provides more concurrency:

**coenter** {*coarm*} **end**

where

coarm ::= armtag [**foreach** decl-list **in** iter-invocation]
      body

armtag ::= **action** | **topaction**

The process executing the **coenter**, and the action on whose behalf it is executing, are suspended; they resume execution after the **coenter** is finished.

A **foreach** clause indicates that multiple instances of the coarm will be activated, one for each item (a collection of objects) yielded by the given iterator invocation.[8] Each such coarm will have local instances of the variables declared in the *decl-list*, and the objects constituting the yielded item will be assigned to them. Execution of the **coenter** starts by running each of the iterators to completion, sequentially, in textual order. Then all coarms are started simultaneously as concurrent siblings. Each coarm instance runs in a separate process, and each process executes within a new top-level action or subaction, as specified by the *armtag*.

A simple example making use of **foreach** is in performing a write operation concurrently at all copies of a replicated database:

```
coenter
   action foreach db: db_copy in all_copies(···)
      db.write(···)
   end
```

This statement creates separate processes for the guardian objects yielded by *all_copies*, each process having a local variable *db* bound to a particular guardian. Each process runs in a newly created subaction and makes a handler call.

A coarm may terminate without terminating the entire **coenter** either by falling off the end of its *body* or by executing a **leave** statement. As before, **leave** may be prefixed by **abort** to cause the completing action to abort; otherwise, the action commits.

A coarm also may terminate by transferring control outside the **coenter** statement. Before such a transfer can occur, all other active coarms of the **coenter** must be terminated. To accomplish this, the system forces all coarms that are not yet completed to abort. A simple example where such early termination is useful is in performing a read operation concurrently at all copies of a replicated database, where a response from any single copy will suffice:

```
coenter
   action foreach db: db_copy in all_copies(···)
      result := db.read(···)
      exit done
   end except when done: ... end
```

---

[8] An iterator is a limited kind of coroutine that provides results to its caller one at a time [17, 20].

Once a read has completed successfully, the **exit** will commit the read and abort all remaining reads. The aborts take place immediately; in particular, it is not necessary for the handler calls to finish before the subactions can be aborted. (Such aborts can result in *orphan* handler processes that continue to run at the called guardians and elsewhere. We have developed algorithms for dealing with orphans, but they are beyond the scope of this paper.)

There is another form of **coenter** for use outside of actions, as in the **background** section of a guardian. In this form the *armtag* can be **process** or **topaction**. The semantics is as above, except that no action is created in the **process** case.

## 3.6 Program Development and Reconfiguration

ARGUS, like CLU, provides separate compilation of modules with complete type checking at compile time (see [17]). Separate compilation is performed in the context of a program library, which contains information about abstractions (e.g., guardian types).

Before creating a guardian at a node, it is first necessary to load the code of that guardian at that node. Once the code image has been loaded, any number of guardians of that type can be created at that node. It is also possible to load a different code image of the same guardian type at the node, and then create guardians that run that code.

To build a code image of a guardian definition, it is necessary to select implementations for the data, procedural, and iteration abstractions that are used, but not for other guardian abstractions. In other words, each guardian is linked and loaded separately. In fact, each guardian is independent of the implementation of all other guardians, because our method of communicating data values between guardians is implementation independent (see [11]). A guardian is also independent of all abstractions except for those it actually uses. New abstractions can be added to the library, and new implementations can be written for both old and new abstractions, without affecting any running guardian.

Guardians are constrained to communicate with other guardians only via handlers whose types were known when the guardian was compiled. Communication via handlers of unknown type is not sensible; the situation is exactly analogous to calling a procedure of unknown type. Of course, a guardian or handler argument of known type but unknown value can be very useful. We *do* provide this: guardians and handlers can be used as arguments in local procedure calls and in handler calls.

Compile-time type checking does *not* rule out dynamic reconfiguration. By receiving guardians and handlers dynamically in handler calls, a guardian can communicate with new guardians as they are created or become available. For example, the ARGUS system contains a distributed *catalog* that registers guardians and handlers according to their type. The catalog would respond to a request for printer guardians by returning all guardians of type "printer" that previously had been registered.

In many applications it will be necessary to change the implementations of running guardians. We are investigating a replacement strategy that permits new implementations to be provided for running guardians without affecting the users of these guardians [2]. This system also allows for certain kinds of changes in guardian type (e.g., additional handlers).

## 4. A SIMPLE MAIL SYSTEM

In this section we present a simple mail system, designed somewhat along the lines of Grapevine [1]. This is a pedagogical example: we have chosen inefficient or inadequate implementations for some features, and have omitted many necessary and desirable features of a real mail system. However, we hope it gives some idea of how a real system could be implemented in ARGUS.

The interface to the mail system is quite simple. Every user has a unique name (*user__id*) and a mailbox. However, mailbox locations are hidden from the user. Mail can be sent to a user by presenting the mail system with the user's user__id and a *message*; the message will be appended to the user's mailbox. Mail can be read by presenting the mail system with a user's user__id; all messages are removed from the user's mailbox and are returned to the caller. For simplicity, there is no protection on this operation: any user may read another user's mail. Finally, there is an operation for adding new users to the system, and there are operations for dynamically extending the mail system.

All operations are performed within the action system. For example, a message is not really added to a mailbox unless the sending action commits, messages are not really deleted unless the reading action commits, and a user is not really added unless the requesting action commits.

The mail system is implemented out of three kinds of guardians: mailers, maildrops, and registries. *Mailers* act as the front end of the mail system: all use of the system occurs through calls of mailer handlers. To achieve high availability, many mailers are used, for example, one at each physical node. All mailers would be registered in the catalog for dynamic lookup. A *maildrop* contains the mailboxes for some subset of users. Individual mailboxes are not replicated, but multiple, distributed maildrops are used to reduce contention and to increase availability, in that the crash of one physical node will not make all mailboxes unavailable. The mapping from user__id to maildrop is provided by the *registries*. Replicated registries are used to increase availability, in that at most one registry need be accessible to send or read mail. Each registry contains the complete mapping for all users. In addition, registries keep track of all other registries.

Two built-in atomic types are used in implementing the mail system: *atomic__array* and *struct*. Atomic arrays are one-dimensional and can grow and shrink dynamically. Of the array operations used in the mail system, *new* creates an empty array, *addh* adds an element to the high end, *trim* removes elements, *elements* iterates over the elements from low to high, and *copy* makes a complete copy of an array. A read lock on the entire array is obtained by *new*, *elements*, and *copy*, and a write lock is obtained by *addh* and *trim*. Structs are immutable (hence atomic) records: new components cannot be stored in a struct object once it has been created. However, the fact that a struct is immutable does not prevent its component objects from being modified if they are mutable.

The mailer guardian is presented in Figure 2. Each mailer is given a registry when created; this registry is the mailer's stable reference to the entire mail system. The mailer also keeps a volatile reference, representing the "best" access

```
mailer = guardian is create
    handles send_mail, read_mail, add_user,
            add_maildrop, add_registry, add_mailer

reg_list = atomic_array[registry]
msg_list = atomic_array[message]

stable some: registry      % stable reference to some registry
best: registry             % volatile reference to some registry
recover
    best := some           % reassign after a crash
end

background
    while true do
        enter topaction
            regs: reg_list := best.all_registries()
            coenter
                action foreach reg: registry in reg_list$elements(regs)
                    reg.ping()         % see if it responds
                    best := reg        % make it best
                    exit done          % abort all others
                end except when done: end
            end except when failure(*): end
            sleep(···)      % some amount of time
        end
    end

create = creator(reg: registry) returns (mailer)
    some := reg
    best := reg
    return(self)
end create

send_mail = handler(user: user_id, msg: message) signals (no_such_user)
    drop: maildrop := best.lookup(user)
    resignal no_such_user
    drop.send_mail(user, msg)
end send_mail

read_mail = handler(user: user_id) returns (msg_list) signals (no_such_user)
    drop: maildrop := best.lookup(user)
    resignal no_such_user
    return(drop.read_mail(user))
end read_mail

add_user = handler(user: user_id) signals (user_exists)
    drop: maildrop := best.select(user)
    resignal user_exists
    regs: reg_list := best.all_registries()
    coenter
        action
            drop.add_user(user)
        action foreach reg: registry in reg_list$elements(regs)
            reg.add_user(user, drop)
        end
end add_user

add_maildrop = handler(home: node)
    drop: maildrop := maildrop$create() @ home
    regs: reg_list := best.all_registries()
    coenter
        action foreach reg: registry in reg_list$elements(regs)
            reg.add_maildrop(drop)
        end
end add_maildrop

add_registry = handler(home: node)
    new: registry := best.new_registry(home)
    regs: reg_list := best.all_registries()
    coenter
        action foreach reg: registry in reg_list$elements(regs)
            reg.add_registry(new)
        end
end add_registry

add_mailer = handler(home: node) returns (mailer)
    m: mailer := mailer$create(best) @ home
    return(m)
end add_mailer

end mailer
```

Fig. 2. Mailer guardian.

path into the system. The **background** code periodically polls all registries; the first to respond is used as the new best registry.

A mailer performs a request to send or read mail by first using the best registry to look up the maildrop for the specified user and then forwarding the request to that maildrop. A mailer adds a new user by first calling the registry *select* handler to make sure the user is not already present and to choose a maildrop; then, concurrently, the new user/maildrop pair is added to each registry, and the new user is added to the chosen maildrop. A maildrop (or registry) is added by creating the maildrop (or registry) and then concurrently adding it to all registries. A new mailer is created with the current best registry for its stable reference.

Figure 3 shows the registry guardian. The state of a registry consists of an atomic array of registries together with a *steering list* associating an array of users with each maildrop. When a registry is created, it is given the current steering list and an array of all other registries, to which array it adds itself. The *lookup* handler uses linear search to find the given user's maildrop. The *select* handler uses linear search to check if a user already exists, and then chooses some existing maildrop. The *add__user* handler uses linear search to find the specified maildrop and then appends the user to the associated user list. The *add__user, add__maildrop,* and *add__registry* handlers perform no error checking because correctness is guaranteed by the mailer guardian.

The maildrop guardian is given in Figure 4. The state of a maildrop consists of an atomic array of mailboxes; a mailbox is represented by a struct containing a user__id and an atomic array of messages. A maildrop is created with no mailboxes. The *add__user* handler is used to add a mailbox. Note that this handler does not check to see if the user already exists since the mailer will have already performed this check. The *send__mail* and *read__mail* handlers use linear search to find the correct mailbox. When the mailbox is found, *send__mail* appends a message to the end of the message array; *read__mail* first copies the array, then deletes all messages, and, finally, returns the copy. Both handlers assume the user exists; again, the mailer guarantees this.

Now that we have all of the pieces of the mail system, we can show how the initial configuration of the mail system is created:

*reg*: *registry* := *registry*$*create*(*reg__list*$*new*( ), *steer__list*$*new*( )) @ *home* 1
*m*: *mailer* := *mailer*$*create*(*reg*) @ *home* 2

where *reg__list* and *steer__list* are defined as in the registry. The resulting mailer can then be placed in the catalog and used to add maildrops and users, as well as more registries and mailers.

Finally, we show a simple use of the mail system, namely, sending a message to a group of users, with the constraint that the message be delivered either to all of the users or to none of them:

```
enter action
   coenter
      action foreach user: user__id in user__group("net")
         m.send__mail(user, msg)
      end except when no__such__user, failure(*):     % ignore failure string
               abort leave
            end
   end
```

```
registry = guardian is create
                    handles lookup, select, all_registries, ping,
                            add_user, add_maildrop, new_registry,
                            add_registry
reg_list  = atomic_array[registry]
steer_list = atomic_array[steering]
steering  = struct[users: user_list,    % users with mailboxes
                   drop: maildrop]       % at this maildrop
user_list = atomic_array[user_id]
stable regs: reg_list        % all registries
stable steers: steer_list    % all users and maildrops
create = creator(rlist: reg_list, slist: steer_list) returns (registry)
    reg_list$addh(rlist, self)     % add self to list
    regs := rlist
    steers := slist
    return(self)
    end create

lookup = handler(user: user_id) returns (maildrop) signals (no_such_user)
    for steer: steering in steer_list$elements(steers) do
        for usr: user_id in user_list$elements(steer.users) do
            if usr = user then return(steer.drop) end
            end
        end
    signal no_such_user
    end lookup

select = handler(user: user_id) returns (maildrop) signals (user_exists)
    for steer: steering in steer_list$elements(steers) do
        for usr: user_id in user_list$elements(steer.users) do
            if usr = user then signal user_exists end
            end
        end
    return(···)     % choose, for example, maildrop with least users
    end select

all_registries = handler( ) returns (reg_list)
    return(regs)
    end all_registries

ping = handler( )
    end ping

add_user = handler(user: user_id, drop: maildrop)
    for steer: steering in steer_list$elements(steers) do
        if steer.drop = drop
            then user_list$addh(steer.users, user)     % append user
                return
            end
        end
    end add_user

add_maildrop = handler(drop: maildrop)
    steer: steering := steering${users: user_list$new( ),
                                   drop: drop}
    steer_list$addh(steers, steer)
    end add_maildrop

new_registry = handler(home: node) returns (registry)
    reg: registry := registry$create(regs, steers) @ home
    return(reg)
    end new_registry

add_registry = handler(reg: registry)
    reg_list$addh(regs, reg)
    end add_registry
end registry
```

Fig. 3.   Registry guardian.

```
maildrop = guardian is create
                    handles send__mail, read__mail, add__user
box__list = atomic__array[mailbox]
mailbox = struct[mail: msg__list,      % messages for
                 user: user__id]       % this user
msg__list = atomic__array[message]
stable boxes: box__list := box__list$new( )
create = creator( ) returns (maildrop)
   return(self )
   end create
send__mail = handler(user: user__id, msg: message)
   for box: mailbox in box__list$elements(boxes) do
      if box.user = user
         then msg__list$addh(box.mail, msg)      % append message
              return
         end
      end
   end send__mail
read__mail = handler(user: user__id) returns (msg__list)
   for box: mailbox in box__list$elements(boxes) do
      if box.user = user
         then mail: msg__list := msg__list$copy(box.mail)
              msg__list$trim(box.mail, 1, 0)      % delete messages
              return(mail)
         end
      end
   end read__mail
add__user = handler(user: user__id)
   box: mailbox := mailbox${mail: msg__list$new( ),
                           user: user}
   box__list$addh(boxes, box)
   end add__user
end maildrop
```

Fig. 4. Maildrop guardian.

The message is sent to all users simultaneously. A nonexistent user or a failure to send a message transfers control outside the **coenter**, forcing termination of all active coarms; the outer action is then aborted, guaranteeing that none of the messages is actually delivered.

### 4.1 Remarks

One obvious problem with the mailers as implemented is that, if the best registry for a mailer goes down, the mailer effectively goes down as well, since every task the mailer performs (including choosing a new *best* registry) requires communication with that registry. A better implementation might be for each mailer to have stable and volatile references to multiple registries, and for mailer handlers to try several registries (sequentially) before giving up.

Close examination of the mail system reveals places where the particular choice of data representation leads to less concurrency than might be expected. For example, in the maildrop guardian, since both *send__mail* and *read__mail* modify the message array in a mailbox, either operation will lock out all other operations on the same mailbox until the executing action commits to the top level. Even worse, since both *send_mail* and *read_mail* read the mailbox array, and *add_user* modifies that array, an *add_user* operation will lock out all operations on all mailboxes at that maildrop. In the registry guardian, an *add_user* operation will lock out *lookup* operations on all users with mailboxes at the given maildrop, and an *add_maildrop* operation will lock out all *lookup* operations.

In a traditional mail system this lack of concurrency might be tolerable, but there are other, similar systems where it would not be acceptable. What is needed are data types that allow more concurrency than do atomic arrays. For example, an associative memory that allowed concurrent insertions and lookups could replace the mailbox array in maildrops and the steering list in registries; a queue with a "first-commit first-out" semantics, rather than a "first-in first-out" semantics, could replace the message arrays in maildrops. Such types can be built as user-defined atomic types, although we do not present implementations here.

The concurrency that *is* built in to the mail system can lead to a number of deadlock situations. For example, in the registry guardian, any two concurrent *add_user* or *add_registry* requests will almost always deadlock, and two *add_maildrop* requests can deadlock by modifying registries in conflicting orders. Some of these deadlocks would disappear if data representations allowing more concurrency were used. For example, the use of a highly concurrent associative memory for the steering list would allow all *add_maildrop* requests to run concurrently, as well as all *add_user* requests for distinct users. Other deadlocks can be eliminated simply by reducing concurrency. To avoid deadlocks between *add_registry* requests, all *new_registry* calls could be made to a distinguished registry, and *new_registry* could obtain a write lock on the registry list before creating the new registry.

It may be argued that the strict serialization of actions enforced by the particular implementation we have shown is not important in a real mail system. This does not mean that actions are inappropriate in a mail system, just that the particular granularity of actions we have chosen may not be the best. For example, if an action discovers that a user does (or does not) exist, it may not be important that the user continues to exist (or not to exist) for the remainder of the overall action. It is possible to build such "loopholes" through appropriately defined abstract types. As another example, it might not be important for all registries to have the most up-to-date information, provided they receive all updates eventually. In particular, when adding a user, it may suffice to guarantee that all registries eventually will be informed of that user. This could be accomplished by keeping appropriate information in the stable state of one of the registries, and using a background process in that registry to (eventually) inform all other registries.

## 5. SUMMARY AND CONCLUSIONS

ARGUS has two main concepts: guardians and actions. Guardians maintain local control over their local data. The data inside a guardian are truly local; no other guardian has the ability to access or manipulate the data directly. The guardian provides access to the data via handler calls, but the actual access is performed inside the guardian. It is the guardian's job to guard its data in three ways: by synchronizing concurrent access to the data, by requiring that the caller of a handler have the authorization needed to do the access, and by making enough of the data stable so that the guardian as a whole can survive crashes without loss of information.

While guardians are the unit of modularity, actions are the means by which distributed computation takes place. A top-level action starts at some guardian. This action can perform a distributed computation by making handler calls to other guardians; those handler calls can make calls to still more guardians; and so on. Since the entire computation is an atomic action, it is guaranteed that the computation is based on a consistent distributed state and that, when the computation finishes, the state is still consistent, assuming in both cases that user programs are correct.

ARGUS is quite different from other languages that address concurrent or distributed programs (e.g., [3, 7, 12, 24]). Those languages tend to provide modules that bear a superficial resemblance to guardians, and some form of communication between modules based on message passing. For the most part, however, the modules have no internal concurrency and contain no provision for data consistency or resiliency. Indeed, the languages completely ignore the problem of hardware failures. In the area of communication, either a low-level, unreliable mechanism is provided, or reliability is ignored, implying that the mechanism is completely reliable, with no way of actually achieving such reliability.

Although a great many details have been omitted, we hope enough of the language has been described to show how ARGUS meets the requirements stated in the introduction. Consistency, service, distribution, concurrency, and extensibility are all well supported in ARGUS. However, there are two areas that are not well supported. One is protection. Guardians could check for proper authorization before performing requests, for example, by requiring principal IDs as arguments to handler calls. But, there is no way within the language to express constraints as to where and when guardians may be created. For example, the owner of a node may wish to allow a particular guardian to be created at that node but disallow that guardian from creating other guardians at the node. These kinds of protection issues are under investigation.

Another area that may need work is support for scheduling. Within a guardian a separate process is automatically created for each handler call. This structure provides no direct support for scheduling incoming calls. If one wanted to give certain incoming calls priority over others, this could be done explicitly (by means of a shared monitorlike [13] object). If one wanted certain incoming calls to take priority over calls currently being executed, this could be done (very awkwardly) by programming handlers to relinquish control periodically. However, if one wanted to make priorities global to an entire node, rather than just within a single guardian, there would be no way to accomplish this in ARGUS. We are not convinced that priorities are required frequently enough to justify any additional mechanism. We prefer to adopt a "wait-and-see" attitude, although we are investigating priority mechanisms.

Supporting atomic activities as part of the semantics of a programming language imposes considerable implementation difficulties. We have completed a preliminary, centralized implementation of the language, ignoring difficult problems such as lock propagation and orphan detection. We are working on a real, distributed implementation. At this point it is unclear how efficient such an implementation can be.

The approach to resiliency taken in ARGUS represents an engineering compromise given the current state of hardware. If ultrareliable hardware does become practical, it may no longer be necessary to compensate for hardware failures in software. This would simplify the structure of guardians since stable objects and the recover section would no longer be needed. Furthermore, the implementation of ARGUS would become more efficient.

However, regardless of advances in hardware, we believe atomic actions are necessary and are a natural model for a large class of applications. If the language/system does not provide actions, the user will be compelled to implement them, perhaps unwittingly reimplementing them with each new application, and may implement them incorrectly. For some applications, actions simply may be a convenient tool, not a strictly necessary one. We believe that actions can be implemented efficiently enough that they will be used in applications even when they are not strictly necessary. We expect to get a much more realistic idea of the strengths and weaknesses of the language once the distributed implementation is complete and we can run applications.

## ACKNOWLEDGMENTS

The authors gratefully acknowledge the contributions made by members of the ARGUS design group, especially Maurice Herlihy, Paul Johnson, and Bill Weihl. The paper was improved by the comments of the referees and many others.

## REFERENCES

1. BIRRELL, A.D., LEVIN, R., NEEDHAM, R.M., AND SCHROEDER, M.D.   Grapevine: An exercise in distributed computing. *Commun. ACM 25*, 4 (Apr. 1982), 260–274.
2. BLOOM, T.   Dynamic Module Replacement in a Distributed Programming Environment. Ph.D. dissertation, Laboratory for Computer Science, Massachusetts Inst. of Technology, Cambridge, Mass., to appear.
3. BRINCH HANSEN, P.   Distributed processes: A concurrency programming concept. *Commun. ACM 21*, 11 (Nov. 1978), 934–941.
4. DAVIES, C.T.   Data processing spheres of control. *IBM Syst. J. 17*, 2 (1978), 179–198.
5. DAVIES, C.T., JR.   Recovery semantics for a DB/DC system. In Proceedings, ACM 73: Annual Conference, Aug. 1973, pp. 136–141.
6. ESWARAN, K.P., GRAY, J.N., LORIE, R.A., AND TRAIGER, I.L.   The notions of consistency and predicate locks in a database system. *Commun. ACM 19*, 11 (Nov. 1976), 624–633.
7. FELDMAN, J.A.   High level programming for distributed computing. *Commun. ACM 22*, 6 (June 1979), 353–368.
8. GRAY, J.N.   Notes on data base operating systems. In *Lecture Notes in Computer Science*, vol. 60: *Operating Systems, An Advanced Course*, R. Bayer, R.M. Graham, G. Seegmüller (Eds.). Springer-Verlag, New York, 1978, pp. 393–481.
9. GRAY, J.N., LORIE, R.A., PUTZOLU, G.F., AND TRAIGER, I.L.   Granularity of locks and degrees of consistency in a shared data base. In *Modeling in Data Base Management Systems*, G.M. Nijssen (Ed.). Elsevier North-Holland, New York, 1976.
10. GRAY, J., MCJONES, P., BLASGEN, M., LINDSAY, B., LORIE, R., PRICE, T., PUTZOLU, F., AND TRAIGER, I.   The recovery manager of the System R database manager. *Comput. Surv. (ACM) 13*, 2 (June 1981), 223–242.

11. HERLIHY, M., AND LISKOV, B.   A value transmission method for abstract data types. *ACM Trans. Program. Lang. Syst. 4*, 4 (Oct. 1982), 527–551.
12. HOARE, C.A.R.   Communicating sequential processes. *Commun. ACM 21*, 8 (Aug. 1978), 666–677.
13. HOARE, C.A.R.   Monitors: An operating system structuring concept. *Commun. ACM 17*, 10 (Oct. 1974), 549–557.
14. LAMPORT, L.   Towards a theory of correctness for multi-user data base systems. Rep. CA-7610-0712, Massachusetts Computer Associates, Wakefield, Mass., Oct. 1976.
15. LAMPSON, B., AND STURGIS, H.   Crash recovery in a distributed data storage system. Xerox PARC, Palo Alto, Calif., Apr. 1979.
16. LISKOV, B.   On linguistic support for distributed programs. In Proceedings, IEEE Symposium on Reliability in Distributed Software and Database Systems, Pittsburgh, Pa., July 1981, pp. 53–60.
17. LISKOV, B., ATKINSON, R., BLOOM, T., MOSS, E., SCHAFFERT, J.C., SCHEIFLER, R., AND SNYDER, A.   *Lecture Notes in Computer Science*, vol. 114: *CLU Reference Manual*. Springer-Verlag, New York, 1981.
18. LISKOV, B., AND SCHEIFLER, R.   Guardians and actions: Linguistic support for robust, distributed programs. In Conference Record of the 9th Annual ACM Symposium on Principles of Programming Languages, Albuquerque, N.M., Jan. 25–27, 1982, pp. 7–19.
19. LISKOV, B., AND SNYDER, A.   Exception handling in CLU. *IEEE Trans. Softw. Eng. SE-5*, 6 (Nov. 1979), 546–558.
20. LISKOV, B., SNYDER, A., ATKINSON, R., AND SCHAFFERT, C.   Abstraction mechanisms in CLU. *Commun. ACM 20*, 8 (Aug. 1977), 564–576.
21. LISKOV, B., AND ZILLES, S.N.   Programming with abstract data types. In Proceedings, ACM SIGPLAN Conference on Very High Level Languages. *SIGPLAN Notices* (ACM) *9*, 4 (Apr. 1974), 50–59.
22. LOMET, D.   Process structuring, synchronization, and recovery using atomic actions. In Proceedings of an ACM Conference on Language Design for Reliable Software. *SIGPLAN Notices* (ACM) *12*, 2 (Mar. 1977).
23. MOSS, J.E.B.   Nested Transactions: An Approach to Reliable Distributed Computing. Ph.D. dissertation and Tech. Rep. MIT/LCS/TR-260, Laboratory for Computer Science, Massachusetts Inst. of Technology, Cambridge, Mass., 1981.
24. PRELIMINARY ADA REFERENCE MANUAL.   *SIGPLAN Notices* (ACM) *14*, 6 (June 1979), pt. A.
25. RANDELL, B.   System structure for software fault tolerance. *IEEE Trans. Softw. Eng. SE-1*, 2 (June 1975), 220–232.
26. REED, D.P.   Naming and Synchronization in a Decentralized Computer System. Ph.D. dissertation and Tech. Rep. MIT/LCS/TR-205, Laboratory for Computer Science, Massachusetts Inst. of Technology, Cambridge, Mass., 1978.
27. ROSENKRANTZ, D.J., STEARNS, R.E., AND LEWIS, P.M., II.   System level concurrency control for distributed database systems. *ACM Trans. Database Syst. 3*, 2 (June 1978), 178–198.
28. SHRIVASTAVA, S.K., AND BANATRE, J.P.   Reliable resource allocation between unreliable processes. *IEEE Trans. Softw. Eng. SE-4*, 3 (May 1978), 230–240.
29. SPECTOR, A.Z.   Performing remote operations efficiently on a local computer network. *Commun. ACM 25*, 4 (Apr. 1982), 246–260.
30. WEIHL, W., AND LISKOV, B.   Specification and implementation of resilient, atomic data types. Computation Structures Group Memo 223, Laboratory for Computer Science, Massachusetts Inst. of Technology, Cambridge, Mass., Dec. 1982.

Received November 1981; revised September 1982; accepted November 1982

The Ecology of Computation
B.A. Huberman (editor)
© Elsevier Science Publishers B.V. (North-Holland), 1988

# Language Design and Open Systems

Kenneth M. Kahn
Mark S. Miller

Knowledge Systems Area
Intelligent System Laboratory
Xerox Palo Alto Research Center

## Abstract

We argue that a distributed implementation of a programming language brings flexibility and uniformity to the programming of open systems. We define an *open system* to be a large collection of computational services that use each other without central coordination, trust, or complete knowledge of each other. For a distributed language to be well-suited for programming of such open systems it should not rely upon global constructs. It should be possible to securely encapsulate servers with state. It must deal with the non-determinism and asynchrony of the world and other computations. It should localize errors and failures. And it should be possible to reprogram despite continuous operation.

We discuss why nearly all of today's programming languages and their straight forward extensions are inadequate as a foundation upon which to program large-scale open systems. We describe two major exceptions: actor languages and concurrent logic programming languages. We attempt to show why these languages are good for writing programs which both provide services and take advantage of services offered by others in a manner that scales from basic computation steps to very large distributed systems. We argue that actor languages and concurrent logic programming languages are really very similar, despite very different origins and conceptual models. We examine ways in which actor languages and concurrent logic programming languages differ in their suitability for open systems.

# 1   Open Systems

We anticipate a future in which large collections of diverse computations use each other without central coordination, trust, or complete knowledge of each other. These collections of computations change as computations offer new services, discontinue old services, and connections between services change. These services differ in their capabilities, owners, authors, and purposes. They cannot be centrally administered since they cross organizational (and even national) boundaries. Some of these services such as a compiler or a symbolic integrator are purely computational. Others services such as airline seating systems and banking systems interact with the surrounding world.

Hewitt [1] calls such collections of interlinked services *open systems* and characterizes them as having:

- *Concurrency* due to simultaneous influx of information.

- *Asynchrony* due to temporally partially ordered demands by the external environment and the communication delays in communication between computations.

- *Decentralized control* to avoid bottlenecks in communication and to facilitate the participation of a large number of organizations.

- *Inconsistent information* from multiple sources maintained by independent components.

- *Arms-length relationships* due to security and reliability concerns.

- *Continuous operation* despite component failures.

# 2   Programming Support

Very few languages have been designed to support large decentralized collections of cooperating services. Nearly all programming languages were designed for describing tightly coordinated computations. In a few languages, these computations are executable on multi-processors. Actor languages, concurrent logic programming languages, and Argus [2] are among the few designed to support both tightly coordinated, possibly parallel, computations as well as largely independent cooperating computations.

Current practice today is to introduce remote procedure calls (RPC) into languages enabling the calling of procedures in other address spaces and in other languages [3]. The semantics of remote procedure calls, however, typically differ from that of ordinary procedure calls. The mechanism restricts the types of data that can be exchanged to the common subset that most languages accept. RPC does not support the transmission of shared, mutable data structures. RPC only implements call by value, *i.e.*, only copies of values are passed to the remote procedure.[1] Most programming languages are based upon call by sharing or call by reference.

The semantic differences between local and remote procedure calls interfere with program analysis and transformation by both programmers and programs. Programs are more complex because they need to use two different forms of procedures calls. In the best case the remote calls form a special case of the usual procedure calls. But even then it is difficult to modify programs to change between using local and remote services. Consider a program using a service provided locally whose protocol makes use of capabilities which RPC cannot support. Such a program is difficult to modify to make use of a remote service instead. In the other direction, a program using a remote service does so in an impoverished manner. The remote service can be replaced with a local one. Significant modification, however, is typically necessary to extend the protocol in useful ways that are not possible using RPC.

The synchronous call/return control of remote procedure calls matches well the control structures of most languages but uses resources inefficiently. A response from a remote service typically has a long latency or turnaround time. The process that made the remote procedure call suspends computation waiting for a response. Often the computation could do something useful instead of waiting. Various constructs for supporting remote asynchronous message sending have been proposed, but these constructs tend to be very difficult to use in languages designed around traditional control constructs.

In summary, we currently have rich protocols between programs in the same address space and limited protocols between programs in different address spaces, due to the inability of RPC to pass mutable data structures. Furthermore, the control structures in use today are acceptable for communication between processes sharing the same processor since while one waits the other is computing. It is inadequate when inter-processor communication is involved.

One approach attacks these problems at the operating system level and not at the language level. A good example of this is the Mach distributed operating system [4]. It implements ports for communication, threads of computation corresponding to processes sharing the same address space, and tasks corresponding to separate address spaces. Programs in any language running under Mach communicate by sending messages to ports. Ports can be used to represent remote references. Since ports can be passed in messages these programs can communicate with a rich protocol. Mach provides a good set of abstractions for "gluing" together different services.

# 3   Advantages of a Uniform Foundation

We believe that operating systems like Mach provide good support for open systems at a coarse granularity. A distributed implementation of a properly designed programming language can provide the same support in a uniform manner at a much finer

---

[1] In Lisp terminology, RPC preserves *equal*-ness and not *eq*-ness of arguments.

granularity. In both cases, programs using services provided by programs participating in the same distributed implementation use local and remote services in the same way. The underlying computational model of Mach or a good distributed language captures the use of local and remote services in a uniform manner.

A distributed operating system is not a programming language. Only a programming language can provide a uniform notation for describing how services are defined and interact. An instance of a distributed language consists of a set of nodes all implementing the same language kernel. Entities are referred to in a uniform manner independent of which nodes defined or created them. A distributed language gives the programmer flexibility in putting computations along the local/remote spectrum. Programs need not change as they switch between using services they define and using functionally equivalent services of others. Distributed languages change the meaning of locality. Currently, the criterion for locality of data is the same address space while for control the criterion is the same processor. In a distributed language locality is a spectrum that has no semantic import. If a distributed language supports any control of locality, it is only for performance and not for correctness. This transparency between local and remote computation means that a program developed on a uni-processor will work in a parallel computer or a distributed network of computers.[2]

# 4 Examples – Actors and FCP

In this section we present two families of distributed languages suitable for open systems programming. The first family is the actor languages which were designed giving high priority to open systems concerns. These languages take the macroscopic view of computation and services and shrink it down to apply to computation at all scales. The other family of languages is concurrent logic programming languages which evolved from efforts to extend logic programming to give concurrency control to programmers.

## 4.1 Actors

The definition of the actor model can be phrased in terms of individual atomic actors. We are frequently concerned with the relationship among much larger scale entities. A very powerful aspect of the actor model is that systems of actors can themselves be modeled by actor theory. In particular, the properties that concern us with here apply fully between arbitrary disjoint configurations of actors. Representation of objects with changeable state is important to the implementation of uniform open systems. It is desirable to use abstractions which permit one to ignore machine boundaries, and object-oriented systems can accomplish this. In a diverse open system, it is also important to be able to represent arbitrary pieces of software and hardware which, in the general case, must be treated as objects with state. Actor systems can do this in a natural and uniform fashion [5].

---

[2] A synchronization bug may not manifest itself in the uni-processor implementation.

A concrete example is an airline seating system. If there is only one seat left, and two people attempt to reserve it, only one will succeed. The situation is inherently a non-deterministic race [6]. The response of the airline seating system to any one user will be not only a function of that user's input, but also of its own internal state, which is subject to modification as a result of interactions with other users. A capable system has to be able to deal with this, even when the number and identity of the users changes as the system runs.

A possible concrete realization of the actor model is as follows. A non-primitive actor consists of a script and a set of references to other actors (its acquaintances). The set of acquaintances constitute the actor's state. The script is code that determines what the actor does on receiving a message (the script is frequently a collection of methods). Let us call the receipt of a message and the actor's ensuing internal computation an event. Computation consists of a partial causal order of events. During an event, the accessible actors are:

- the receiving actor,

- the acquaintances of the receiving actor,

- the acquaintances of the incoming message,

- any new actors created during the event.

The actions a non-primitive actor can take during an event consist of:

- Creating new actors, whose acquaintances must be selected from the accessible actors – these typically are either "continuations" or new messages;

- Sending an accessible actor as a message to another accessible actor;

- Becoming one of the accessible actors.

These laws restrict all information flow between actors to be message passing. Information cannot flow, for example, by side effects to shared environments.

Primitive actors can perform arbitrary internal computation (like addition and actor creation), as long as they respect these locality laws [6]. Actors are able to express data, procedural, and control abstractions. Actors are concurrent analogues of the closures of Scheme which they inspired [7]. Actors differ in their implicit concurrency, in their ubiquity (in most actor languages everything, including messages, is an actor), and in their uniformity (all behavior is defined as responses to messages).

Computation typically proceeds by processing and scheduling pending events. A worker (*e.g.* a processor on a network) contains a queue of pending events. A pending event consists of a message and its receiver. A worker engages in computation by picking a pending event out of this queue, and executing the event specified. Among the actions specified by the script of the receiver of the event is a set of new message sending events. Part of processing the current event is to schedule these new pending events on the queue of some worker.

Each actor has a queue of incoming messages directed to its em mail address. Actors continuely wait for messages to appear. The script of the actor is applied to the messages in the order they arrive. The mail system serializes concurrent communications. The serialization of messages happens at the primitive level invisible to actors.

## 4.2   Flat Concurrent Prolog

A representative of the concurrent logic programming family of languages is Flat Concurrent Prolog (FCP). This language evolved from an attempt to extend Prolog with concurrency control. It is a new logic programming language which replaces the backtracking search mechanism of Prolog with communicating concurrent processes [8].

As in Prolog, a program in FCP is a collection of Horn clauses. A Horn clause is a logical implication of the form $\forall x_1, \ldots, x_k | A_0 \leftarrow A_1 \wedge A_2 \wedge \ldots \wedge A_n$ where the $A$'s are atomic formulas. $n$ and $k$ can be 0. There are no variables occurring in the $A$'s other than $x_1$ through $x_k$.

In FCP (and Prolog) clauses have the syntax: $A_0$ :- $A_1, A_2, \ldots, A_n$. and variables are normally denoted by symbols beginning with an upper case letter.

FCP and Prolog programs can be read declaratively as sets of logical implications. A single clause reads as "for all $x_1$ through $x_k$, $A_0$ is true if $A_1$ through $A_n$ are all true". A clause in which $n$ is zero is read as "for all $x_1$ through $x_k$, $A_0$ is true". Clauses in Prolog can also be read procedurally as "to solve a goal matching $A_0$, solve the subgoals $A_1$ through $A_n$ *in that order*".

FCP extends the syntax of clauses by adding the commit operator "|". There is exactly one commit operator per clause. The consequent $A_0$ of a clause is called the *head*, the conjunction of atomic formulas before the commit operator, the *guard*, and the conjunction of formulas after the commit operator, the *body*.

An FCP clause $H$ :- $G_1, \ldots, G_m | B_1, \ldots, B_n$. has a process or behavioral reading which says, "a process matching H, can be reduced to the system of processes $B_1$ through $B_n$ if the guard processes $G_1$ through $G_m$ successfully terminate". FCP treats atomic formulas as processes, whereas Prolog treats them as procedure calls. A process can *commit* with a clause if the process unifies with the head of the clause and the guard successfully terminates.

An FCP procedure is a collection of clauses for the same predicate. It is interpreted as "to reduce a process, replace the process by the system of processes in the body of one of the clauses which can commit". When more than one clause can commit one is chosen arbitrarily. When no clauses can commit then the computation fails. Unlike Prolog, FCP cannot backtrack or search for all solutions. Correct FCP implementations are sound but incomplete theorem provers (as is also the case for pure Prolog).

FCP is based upon implicit *and-parallelism*. And-parallelism is the concurrent execution of FCP processes. It is called and-parallelism since the set of active processes corresponds to a conjunction of atomic formulas which must be true for the query to be true.

A consequence of implicit and-parallelism is that FCP programs are highly concurrent. A consequence of that is that there is a need to synchronize FCP processes. FCP extends unification with a dataflow annotation which enables programmers to express when a process is ready to reduce. The dataflow annotation is a "?" at the end of variable name indicating that that occurrence of the variable is *read-only*. A process is forced to suspend it can reduce only by binding a read-only occurrence of a variable with a value. Efficient implementations of FCP associate suspended processes with the variables which caused the suspension. No attempts are made to reduce a suspended process. A suspended process need only be activated when the variables it is waiting for are bound. One can think about the read-only annotation as a dataflow declaration saying "do not use this occurrence of the variable until some other process running concurrently gives it a value". From the point of view of the declarative reading, the read-only annotations are ignored (and the commits are treated as conjunctives).

Shapiro and Takeuchi [9] describe a concurrent logic programming technique for defining actors or servers. An FCP server is defined as a recurrent process which has arguments implementing its state variables. It also has arguments which are variables shared with other processes used for communication. The service is typically suspended waiting for requests on its input channels. When a request comes in it spawns processes to service the request and a process to service further requests possibly with different state variables.

Services defined in this manner have a logical reading. Predicates define permissible message histories from a given initial state. The message histories are the streams of incoming requests and the state variables are the other arguments of the predicate. An open question is whether this reading of FCP descriptions of servers is valuable.

This programming technique has been captured by high level programming abstractions in Mandala [10], Vulcan [11], and POOL [12]. These are actor languages implemented on top of different concurrent logic programming languages. FCP has been used to implement Vulcan, an actor language based upon unification. An open research question is how well suited actor languages are for implementing FCP.

As an illustration of the power of these abstractions consider the following program which implements a simple bank account using the object-oriented abstractions of Vulcan.

```
/* declare the state variables of accounts */
class(account,[Balance, Name, Number,...]).

deposit(Amount) -->
        /* increase the balance for a deposit */
        new Balance is Balance + Amount.

balance(Balance).       /* report current balance */

withdraw(Amount) -->
```

```
        Amount > Balance
        ifTrue reportOverdrawn(Name, ...)
        ifFalse new Balance is Balance - Amount.
```

The program is translated automatically into the following FCP program using the object-oriented programming technique of Shapiro and Takeuchi.

```
account([deposit(Amount) | NewAccount], Balance, Name, Number,...) :-
        /* spawn two processes: one to do the addition */
        plus(Balance, Amount, NewBalance),
        /* and another to begin processing of subsequent messages */
        account(NewAccount?, NewBalance?, Name, Number,...).
account([balance(Balance) | NewAccount], Balance, Name, Number,...) :-
        /* unify answer with balance; process subsequent messages */
        account(NewAccount?, Balance, Name, Number,...).
account([withdraw(Amount) | NewAccount], Balance, Name, Number,...) :-
        /* if the balance is not less than the amount */
        Balance >= Amount |
        /* spawn two processes: one to do the subtraction */
        diff(Balance, Amount, NewBalance),
        /* and another to begin processing of subsequent messages */
        account(NewAccount?, NewBalance?, Name, Number,...).
account([withdraw(Amount) | NewAccount], Balance, Name, Number,...) :-
        Balance < Amount |
        reportOverdrawn(Name, Balance, Amount,...),
        account(NewAccount?, Balance, Name, Number,...).
```

This program describes how a recurrent process should behave as messages are put on its input stream. If the process has multiple users then the standard programming technique in FCP is to set up merge processes which non-deterministically (but fairly) combine the requests on multiple streams into the stream being consumed by the recurrent process. In this way, the program performs correctly when the same account receives concurrent requests. Accounts and their users can be distributed when the program is run under a distributed implementation of FCP.

# 5   Language Design Principles

In this section we present a list of criteria that any distributed language for open systems *must* satisfy. We then present a list of criteria that such languages *should* satisfy. Subsequently we explore in detail each of these criteria and how well actor, concurrent logic programming, and other languages satisfy them.

## 5.1   Criteria for Distributed Languages for Open Systems

To support programming of large collections of interlinked independent services a distributed language must:

- Be able to define servers which are immune from the misbehavior of others,

- Be able to survive hardware failure,

- Be able to serialize simultaneous events,

- Be able to securely encapsulate entities with state,

- Be able to dynamically create and connect services,

- And finally, it must not rely upon global constructs.

The above properties which are necessary for building robust servers are the immunity from the misbehavior of others, the survivability, and the security. For building open systems consisting of interacting independent robust servers the properties for dynamic creation of servers, concurrency, synchronization, and dynamic connectivity are needed.

A distributed language is much more effective in supporting large-scale distributed computations if it also has the properties listed below. These properties are not strictly necessary at the distributed language level since higher levels of language can provide them.

- Can reprogram running programs,

- Can use foreign services not implemented in the distributed language,

- Can define services which can be used by foreign computations,

- Is based upon computational principles which scale,

- Supports the expression of very highly concurrent programs,

- Supports small-scale programming well.

## 5.2   Global Constructs

Many programming languages rely upon global centrally maintained constructs. Examples are the global binding environments in Common Lisp and many other languages, the global database of clauses in Prolog, and the sharing of named Smalltalk [13] classes like "Object". The usefulness of these language constructs is limited to the execution of programs in non-shared language kernels. The difficulty of supporting these constructs grows as the number of users of a distributed language grows. The cost of making a change is prohibitive if many nodes need to reflect the change atomically. Also, anyone can change the definition of a shared object such as the class "Object" in Smalltalk in such a way that all programs using that class are broken.

The most serious shortcoming of centrally administered structures is that any change may be overridden by another change under the control of someone else. Changing a global variable is clearly pointless, if immediately afterward someone else changes the variable to some other value.

It may be sensible to have globally accessible structures if there is control and coordination of those who modify these structures. A distributed name server like Grapevine [14] maintains a dynamic table by only guaranteeing that updates will *eventually* be reflected on all nodes. While useful, this is not the same concept of a global environment that one finds in programming languages.

The actor model and actor languages have been carefully designed to rely only upon local or scoped programming constructs. In contrast, FCP relies upon a global association of predicate names to predicates. The Logix programming system for FCP addresses this by introducing modules. Unless explicitly exported, predicate names are local to a module. This leaves the smaller (but still intolerable) problem of a global association of module names and modules.

At Xerox PARC, we are developing a language called "Lexical FCP" which introduces lexical scoping to FCP. We expect this to provide a principled way of defining and using modules in which all names are scoped. Our approach is modeled on that achieved in the T dialect of Scheme [15].

## 5.3   Immunity from the Misbehavior of Other Servers

Software errors need to be localized to the program responsible. For example, it is not reasonable for a service to break because it received a malformed request. Instead, the sender should be held responsible. The language should support the construction of "bullet-proof" services, *i.e.*, services whose reliability depends only upon its internal workings and the correct behavior of services it uses, and not upon correct behavior by its clients.

A distributed implementation of a language has to be very robust. All failures or errors must be localized or the entire system could crash. A large-scale open system cannot crash and be restarted. Its operation must be continuous. Consider the controlling system of a power plant. Its performance can be enhanced if it is able to interact with other services. For example, it could better anticipate power usage by communicating with a weather service, with neighboring power plants, and so on. Despite such (weak) interdependencies a nuclear reactor should be in no danger of melting because the weather service crashes.

Several languages are defined to enter undefined states if certain errors occur. Common Lisp, for example, distinguishes between signaling an error and "it is an error". Many semantic models of programs represents errors with "bottom" indicating an undefined state. These practices are unacceptable in a open systems framework. If an error occurs in one process in a large open system, it is unreasonable for all processes to become undefined. The languages and semantic models need to define what happens to processes sharing data with other processes which encounter errors.

Actor languages have been designed in which every request message contains a *customer*. Normally the customer is sent any results from processing the embedded message. When instead an error is detected, a message is sent to the customer describing the problem. This keeps the errors localized and makes actors robust in the face of malformed requests. Additionally, it provides a convenient mechanism for describing what actions should be taken upon error detection.

The computational model of FCP has no notion of errors and a failure is a failure of the entire system of computations from which there is no way to proceed. Fortunately, there are several FCP programming techniques which remedy the situation. The Logix operating system defines a fail-safe meta-interpreter and a corresponding efficient source-to-source transformation. The creator of a computation running under such a meta-interpreter is signaled when the computation fails. It is also possible to write fail-safe servers in FCP which simply recur to process remaining messages upon the receipt of a bad message. This interferes with the logical reading of a server as a predicate defining permissible message histories since any message is acceptable (even though it is ignored).

These techniques do not assign responsibility to the sender of the malformed message. To remedy this we are exploring a programming technique called *merge filters* which filters out inappropriate messages as they are merged into the stream of messages being consumed by the server.

## 5.4 Surviving Hardware Failure

Neither actor nor concurrent logic programming languages currently deal with hardware failure. Transaction-oriented systems like Argus [2] do address this issue. An important area of research is to explore how such ideas can be incorporated into actor and concurrent logic programming languages.

## 5.5 Arbitration between Concurrent Inputs

Many parts of open systems connect with the external world. Programs must deal with the concurrency of the real world. A banking system, for example, faces simultaneous access to accounts from different automated teller machines. Concurrency also arises in the communication between different computations when the communication time is large relative to the speed of processing. The programming language needs to deal with concurrent events and arbitrate between simultaneous accesses.

The underlying computation model of the language must accommodate non-determinism. Functional programming and rewrite systems, for example, usually have the Church-Rosser property. Computations satisfying this property return the same results independent of which path is followed to the solution. Input is modeled as a stream which cannot be asked if it is *currently* empty. This means that strictly functional programs are not capable of responding to requests as they arrive on multiple streams. The Church-Rosser property is inherently incompatible with the programming of open systems which are in continuous operation and interact with the surrounding (non-deterministic) environment. Quasi-functional languages deal with this shortcoming by adding a non-deterministic stream merger primitive. This sacrifices the major strength of functional programming – its attractive semantics based upon mathematical functions [16]. Output is no longer a function of the input.

Actors hide arbitration in the mail system. An actor processes messages in the order in which they arrive.

FCP is a non-deterministic language with committed choice. The basic commitment operation in FCP is used to express "don't care" non-determinism – that the correct operation of the program does not depend upon which choice is taken. The basic reduction cycle of FCP does this arbitration at a very fine granularity. This permits a large degree of flexibility in dealing with several messages arriving concurrently. One could give priority to certain messages or channels. One could detect branches in the partial ordering of messages sent and process each branch concurrently [17].

## 5.6   Evolvability

All programming systems support changes to program sources and their recompilation or re-execution. A distributed language, in addition, needs a way of reprogramming executing programs. Consider a service which is being used by several other programs and needs to be modified. The difficult problem is how to maintain references to the service during its recompilation. A few languages support dynamic code linking of executing programs. Dynamic linking of names to objects supports evolvability at the price of reliance upon global names. It is possible to modify running programs without relying upon global names as demonstrated by the T dialect of Scheme [15] and actor systems. They do this by making lexical environments explicit manipulable entities, thereby giving the programmer control over the scope of the dynamic linking.

Occam [18] and CSP [19], languages designed for large-scale parallel computing, suffer from their inability to dynamically construct communication networks. Dataflow languages are also so restricted. These languages do not allow the transfer of access to a server since communication channels cannot be passed between processes. This is a fundamental shortcoming that cannot be alleviated within the language without sacrificing encapsulation [20].

The language in which programs are written needs to evolve as well. Incompatible changes are much harder to propagate over a distributed language implementation than is the case with non-distributed languages. Computations are spread out over different nodes and it is very difficult to atomically spread language changes between these nodes while programs are running. This situation makes us favor layered languages with a small distributed kernel. The advantage of this is that a small kernel changes much less frequently than a large language. Concurrent logic programming languages, Scheme, and actor languages have small kernels and missing functionality is provided by programs and layers written in the language. This is in contrast to languages like Common Lisp and Ada that are large and not well layered. Common

Lisp, for example, provides hundreds of functions and macros to aid in tasks ranging from list manipulation to output formatting to maintaining tables. They are defined to be part of the Common Lisp language rather than letting them evolve as library packages.

Two relatively new techniques for adding functionality to very small but powerful languages are meta-programming and partial evaluation. The Logix system illustrates well their usefulness [21,22]. Logix is an operating system written in FCP. FCP appears to lack capabilities which are essential for building systems. The FCP language does not support interrupts, failure control, or program debugging capabilities. These are provided instead at higher levels of language through the programming of *enhanced meta-interpreters*. Enhanced meta-interpreters provide these and many other extra capabilities to the programs which they meta-interpret. This means that programs which do not need such capabilities pay no performance penalty for their existence. Meta-programming allows the set of capabilities available to evolve since they are implemented solely in terms of the distributed kernel language. Partial evaluation makes this technique practical by optimizing away the levels of interpretation. It transforms programs to be run under a meta-interpreter into programs which are executed without meta-interpretation.

An actor, after processing a message, "becomes" another (possibly identical) actor to process the remaining (and future) messages sent to its mail address. All communications sent to the old actor now are forwarded to the new one. This is the basic building block for reprogramming running programs.

Similarly, a recurrent process in FCP by convention spawns a process of the same sort to process subsequent messages. It can instead spawn a different process thus "becoming" a different recurrent process.

Both actors and FCP have the needed building blocks for reprogramability. In both cases, servers can change arbitrarily. The capability to change a server need never spread beyond the creator of the server.

Actor and concurrent logic programming languages are able to dynamically create and connect services. In actors, the connection is accomplished by mutual references to services. In FCP, it is typically done by active processes mediating mutual references to logic variables. For example, common programming practice in FCP is to create networks of *merge* processes. These processes non-deterministically, but fairly, combine requests on two streams into a third stream. A server need only respond to requests on one stream. The network of merge processes producing that stream can be modified as new clients appear and old ones disappear.

## 5.7   Strict Data Encapsulation

Strict encapsulation is the ability to define servers in which access to their internals and the ability to update them is restricted by program control. Actor languages, concurrent logic programming languages, and many other languages support strict encapsulation. Languages like Smalltalk, Prolog, C, and Common Lisp do not provide such a (negative) capability.[3] Common Lisp structures and objects are not encapsulated. The Common Lisp language does not provide a way to access the internals of a function closure; implementations, however, are permitted to, and typically do, have primitives which violate closure encapsulation.

Good software engineering practice respects module boundaries. The enforcement of this respect ranges from good programming hygiene, to social mechanisms, to language restrictions. Module boundaries prevent hidden dependencies between parts of programs so that modules can be modified independently, so long as they maintain their external interface. Many modern programming languages support module boundaries while allowing debuggers and other programming tools to violate them.

This weak form of encapsulation is inadequate for large-scale open systems. As systems get larger the goals and purposes of the providers of services diverge. Programs can depend upon services offered by systems in different organizations, corporations, or even countries. *Many services could not be offered if they were required to trust their clients.* A bank cannot trust its customers to leave account information unmodified. An airline needs to protect its seating and reservation systems from customer modifications. And so on. Most services need the protection that strict encapsulation provides against competitors, thieves, terrorists, and mischievous hackers.

Much good work on functional programming, dataflow languages, rewriting systems, and logic programming languages (without concurrency control or committed choice operators) has demonstrated the conceptual leverage from computational models that avoid mutual references to objects with state. Program transformation, debugging, and analysis are greatly simplified by avoiding side-effects. Such programs are often well-suited for parallel or distributed execution. These formalisms however are limited in the kinds of applications they are capable of supporting. Many applications need to reflect changes in shared entities or resources. Examples are the number of seats left on a flight, the current balance of a bank account, a database, the files queued and waiting for printing, and so on.

Servers implemented as recurrent processes are securely encapsulated since the only means of interaction with them is by putting messages on their input channels. FCP processes themselves are safe from manipulation or inspection since they are not program accessible. Concurrent logic programming is unique in providing a base which retains the conceptual leverage normally lost in supporting mutual references to objects with states while providing the equivalent functionality via recurrent processes.[4]

Actors are securely encapsulated since they can only be accessed via message passing. There are no primitive messages to which all actors must respond although there are standardized protocols in common use.

---

[3]These languages differ in the extent to which they could feasibly be modified to provide encapsulation. Smalltalk, for example, violates encapsulation only in order to provide programming tools like inspectors and debuggers. This could instead be provided by use of a debugging meta-interpreter without changing the essential character of the language. In contrast C permits programmers to manipulate pointer address explicitly and could not be modified to respect object boundaries.

[4]Concurrent quasi-functional languages can use similar techniques [16].

## 5.8 Unencapsulated Entities

In many actor languages all entities are encapsulated and all interactions are by requests to their external interfaces. In such languages a user of an object cannot detect whether that object is really a "Trojan horse". Consider a service which computes some mathematical function according to some proprietary algorithm. If the numbers the client sends can be actors which report back the tests and operations performed on them, then the secrecy of the algorithm can be compromised. The concurrent logic programming languages support immutable encapsulated entities called terms which are open to inspection by anyone. A service can tell if a number is a term, for example, and deal with it safe in the knowledge that it is only what it appears to be. Some actor languages support both actors and unencapsulated values at the price of uniformity [6].

Trojan horses are possible in the actor model since there is no way to know anything about an actor except by message sending. An actor behaving like a number, but reporting back about messages it receives, is indistinguishable from an ordinary number. In FCP, terms are used as a concise description of immutable unencapsulated entities. Message protocols typically require terms when information is being passed that need not maintain local state. The basic unification mechanism of FCP is used to inspect and manipulate terms. When local state or security is needed then streams to recurrent processes are used.

## 5.9 Interoperability

Interoperability is the ability of programs written in one system to use services written in another. Despite the advantages of joining a large collection of nodes executing the same distributed language, it is naive to expect that all services will be written in this language. The distributed language will not have completely removed the need for remote procedure calls or Mach-like facilities. Use of a distributed language enables large collections of processors to support a uniform computational substrate. Mach-like facilities are needed for communication between these large collections. A good distributed language needs to be able to support computations that use foreign services. It also should support the writing of services that can be used by foreign computations.

A service running in a different language (or in the same language but not on a node of the same distributed implementation) can be modeled as a configuration of actors. It may be that the protocol with this remote service is very impoverished since it is not capable of accepting any references to actors. Communication may be limited to sending copies of actors corresponding to primitive datatypes like numbers and strings. References to customers cannot be used in protocols when communicating with foreign services incapable of using actor mail addresses. These problems can be alleviated if local computations and the foreign service run under the same instance of a distributed operating system like Mach. This is because one can pass references to actors as Mach ports.

FCP can model a foreign service as a recurrent process, again with a limited protocol. The Logix operating system does this to provide low-level services such as a keyboard handler. It is more difficult to arrange things so that an FCP server is available to "outsiders". The difficulties stem from the fact that FCP protocols rely heavily upon logic variables. This resembles the problem that actor protocols typically rely upon customers. Distributed operating systems like Mach, however, support continuations which are similar to actor customers. None have been designed to support the unification of logic variables that FCP requires. The problem is even more difficult to solve because FCP requires that unification of several logic variables happen atomically. This is primarily a concern for the theory underlying FCP since, in practice, server protocols very rarely rely upon atomic unification.

# 6   Choice of Distributed Language Matters!

Criteria for comparing non-distributed programming languages include ease and conciseness of program expression, availability of efficient implementations, simplicity, ease of program analysis, modification and transformation (both manual and automatic), familiarity, standardization, ease of learning, and ease of extensibility. Languages cannot, however, be compared in any absolute sense on the basis of their abilities because all non-trivial programming languages are Turing equivalent – they can simulate each other.

Distributed languages can be compared using more absolute criteria. A distributed language must deal with on-going computations. For example, consider a language which does not provide strict encapsulation. One can implement (simulate) another language with strict encapsulation on top of it. Entities implemented in the language with strict encapsulation can be made safe from each other. The problem is that the entities written in the base language can violate the implementation of those in the layer on top. In general, if a language does not enforce certain restrictions, then it is impossible to enforce those restrictions between any on-going computations and computations implemented in a higher level of software that may enforce the restrictions. Such restrictions, for example, those that support security and safety, can be critical for the success of many applications. These restrictions can be thought of as "negative capabilities" which cannot be attained by simulation.

Another case of where the Turing equivalence of languages does not apply is dealing with the non-determinism of the real world. An application may require that requests from two different sources be serviced fairly. The language needs to be able to express that if a request is coming in from one of the sources, to service it, and if, requests are coming in from both services, to non-deterministically choose one and then the other. Functional and re-write languages with the Church-Rosser property compute the same results independent of the timing of requests. This is because requests are modeled as streams which cannot be detectably empty and then subsequently contain any messages. These languages are unable to support programs which need to react to the non-determinism of the world (and other programs) in an on-going fashion.

The non-determinism of the real world requires committed choice. [23] The real world cannot in general undo a choice and try another as if nothing happened. The "don't know" non-determinism of Prolog is inadequate for dealing with the committed-choice non-determinism of the world. After dispensing money from an automated teller machine, the system cannot backtrack and get the money back. The ATM must make a committed choice.

## 6.1   Scaling of Principles

It is very desirable that a distributed language be based upon constructs and principles that scale to very large systems. The language should have no gratuitous discontinuities as the scale of computation changes. An object reference, for example, should behave and mean the same regardless of whether the object referred to is local or remote. An implementation needs to treat the cases differently but it should maintain semantic uniformity at the language level.

Actors are a good example of a concept that scales. The actor concept takes a model of large-scale distributed computation and scales it down to basic computational steps. Various laws and theorems have been developed describing the locality, causality and ordering of events in an actor system. These laws apply to actors of any size or complexity. These laws apply equally well to individual actors as to disjoint collections of actors.

Actor configurations nest in the sense that the meaning of an actor configuration is the same as the joining of all disjoint subconfigurations. Another example of a language construct exhibiting nesting are processes in CSP [19]. A collection of CSP processes is a CSP process. Languages based upon constructs which nest are better suited for programming in the large because they retain the same ways of thinking and analysis for both small and large applications.

A different aspect of scalability is the avoidance of programming constructs which do not work well at large scales. Many useful programming constructs for building small applications do not scale. Global name spaces, for example, are common partly because they facilitate programming-in-the-small, rapid prototyping, and exploratory programming. Commonly used debugging tools violate encapsulation and assume that nothing of relevance is occurring simultaneously. Search-oriented programming abstractions as those found in Prolog can dramatically increase the conciseness and efficiency of certain applications but does not scale.

An important open research question is whether these useful programming constructs and tools have to be sacrificed because they do no scale to large distributed systems. Sometimes, one needs to weigh the advantages of scalability and uniformity against the advantages of small-scale tools and abstractions. Sometimes, programming systems provide the advantages of both. The T programming environment, for example, permits one to program with the convenience of global definitions, without the semantic difficulties. The FCP debugging tools of Logix are another example. They are based upon enhanced meta-interpretation [21]. A debugging meta-interpreter can be built so that only the creator of a server is given the capability to debug it.

The computational principles and constructs underlying a programming language should apply at levels ranging from basic computational steps to complex negotiations between large collections of servers. This is an ideal which no language can achieve. Actors achieve it because all the actor laws apply equally well between individual actors as between disjoint collections of actors. Communication between overlapping configurations can happen either via message passing or via shared actors. The utility of the actor laws at large scales is limited by the appropriateness of modeling interacting entities as disjoint. Corporations, for example, typically have interlocking boards of directors.

FCP supports a more flexible and general communication model which scales well. An FCP process can share logic variables used as communication channels with many different processes. The same logic variable can have multiple readers and writers. The communication channels of FCP can be actor-like (streams), multi-casting (broadcasting streams), one-shot, or branching (channels).

On the negative side, FCP is based upon atomic unification of terms. The notion of an atomic transaction for unification is very powerful, but it does not scale to very large activities. It is unreasonable to lock all the participants in a transaction which very extended in time and space. Atomic unification is not a part of the computational model underlying the concurrent logic programming languages GHC [23] and Parlog [24]. This makes it easier to offer any service written in GHC or Parlog for external use. The protocols of FCP services must be restricted to facilitate external use.

## 6.2   Suitability for Programming in the Small

In this paper we have concentrated on the properties of an abstract computational model suitable for supporting a diverse distributed open system. Such a model need not necessarily be suitable for programming in the small. We believe that it can be, bringing the benefits of greater uniformity. Additionally, if the machine model is unsuitable for programming in the small, we have grounds for suspicion of its generality and power.

The size and complexity of actor languages and concurrent logic programming languages are roughly comparable. They are both much simpler than most commonly used languages. The implementations of both are also comparable and small relative to the size of many existing non-distributed languages. One reason for this is that both languages are "kernel" languages which are sufficient for building higher level languages and abstractions but do not include such extensions as part of the language *per se*. The smallness and simplicity makes the languages well-suited for distributed implementations. The layering of extensions facilitates the evolution of these higher layers.

FCP as a kernel language is more expressive than primitive actor languages. Large applications have been written directly in FCP. The basic actor computation is normally customer based so that each communication contains a customer to be sent the response. This style of programming is very awkward and verbose. It is never done in practice. Instead, higher level languages are used which compile to customer style programs. The kernel language is the level which is distributed and standardized. It is clearly desirable for FCP and the actor kernel languages to be very expressive, even if the same higher layers of language can be built upon both. For example, both kernels can define very expressive object-oriented programming languages.

Much of the simplicity, conciseness, and expressiveness of FCP is due to the underlying unification mechanism and its support for logic variables. Unification in logic programming languages plays the same roles in other languages as argument passing, value return, pattern matching, term construction and access, and introduction of local variables.

There are other reasons to believe that FCP is well-suited for programming in the small. There is very promising research in logic programming on transforming, debugging, and verifying programs that depends critically upon the fact that the programs are collections of axioms in first-order logic [25]. Another aspect of FCP is that it has a short and simple meta-interpreter, variations of which have been found useful for many purposes [21]. This meta-programming technique, especially in combination with partial evaluation [22], promises a way to program in a much more modular and layered fashion while retaining efficiency. Actor researcher are also exploring the uses of meta-interpreters.

## 6.3 The Expression of Highly Concurrent Programs

The most effective way to exploit multiple processors is to express programs with maximal concurrency, thereby giving the implementation flexibility in allocating computations to processors. Frequently there is more concurrency in a problem than there are processors. It should not cost anything, however, for a program to allow more parallelism than is available.[5] It is also very important when communication latency is high, that while some part of a computation waits for a response from another processor that there be plenty of useful computation that can proceed in the meantime. As more concurrency is expressed, communication latency becomes less of a bottleneck relative to communication bandwidth.

Actor languages and concurrent logic programming languages facilitate the expression of large amounts of concurrency. In these languages concurrency is implicit, *i.e.*, it is the default and must be explicitly turned off. The mail system of actors, however, impose a total ordering upon incoming messages. In FCP, the programming technique using streams also imposes a total ordering. Streams are not, however, primitive notions of the language and other programming techniques such as channels [17] permit the communications to realize a partial order of messages. Servers are capable of detecting a branch in the ordering and spawning parallel processes to service each branch. This allows servers to mirror the parallelism among their clients.

Many sequential languages are poorly suited for concurrency expression. Common Lisp, for example, defines the order of argument evaluation to be left to right. Common Lisp as a notation does not distinguish between programs for which argument

---

[5]This argument for the expression of maximal concurrency breaks down when algorithm selection is concerned. A maximally concurrent algorithm may not run well sequentially.

evaluation is incidental from those for which it is essential.

A different sort of example of a language construct which is poorly suited for distributed execution is *cons* in Lisp. *Cons* creates pairs which are mutable. This means
that conses cannot be copied when communicated but must always be passed by remote reference. This restriction can lead to a great deal of costly communication even
in the very frequent cases where the conses will never be modified. The introduction of
read-only conses increases the complexity of the language significantly. It is unclear,
for example, which kind of conses Lisp functions such as *append* should construct.

# 7   Hewitt's Objections to Logic Programming

Hewitt has argued that logic programming is poorly suited for open systems [1,26].
Is this inconsistent with our claim that concurrent logic programming languages are
very good candidates for open systems programming? Our position is that Hewitt's
criticisms of logic programming in general are accurate, but believe they do not apply
to logic programming with committed-choice, concurrency, and dataflow synchronization. The essence of his argument is that logic requires a static globally consistent
model. We think that Hewitt has argued well against logic as a tool for modeling
the dynamics, inconsistencies, and lack of global notions of state and time which are
characteristic of open systems. Kowalski [27] essentially agrees with this argument
and proposes various changes to logic and semantics to alleviate these problems. His
solutions essentially retain logic as the basis for modeling individuals but not the
modeling of large collections of agents.

Logic programming attempts to provide a way of programming with logical axioms
and computing by controlled deduction. Prolog is one such attempt that gives the
programmer control over a depth-first search for solutions. We agree with Hewitt that
Prolog lacks notions of concurrency and communication essential for open systems.
But Prolog does not assume consistency any more or less than any language with
global environments. It does assume a global database, but since Prolog databases
cannot have negative facts, this is no different than any global naming environment.

FCP is a completely different realization of logic programming based upon committed choice non-determinism and dataflow synchronization of concurrent processes.
Like Prolog, FCP programs are collections of logical axioms (restricted to Horn clauses).
Like Prolog, the execution of FCP programs is performed by an incomplete, but sound,
theorem prover which is controllable to some extent by the programmer. The control
annotations, however, for FCP are very well-suited for open systems programming.
The control annotations of Prolog are useful for some kinds of search-oriented programming but not for open systems or even concurrency control.

# 8   Summary

We have presented arguments for why a distributed language can provide more flexibility and uniformity than a distributed operating system. For open systems pro-

gramming, a distributed language must support the definition of robust servers and dynamic ways of creating, removing, synchronizing and linking them together. Ideally, the language should enable the expression of maximal concurrency and should be based upon scalable principles.

We have attempted to show by examples that existing programming languages cannot be extended to become a distributed language suitable for open systems programming. Existing languages contain too many design choices which are inconsistent with building dynamic collections of interlinked secure robust servers. The negative examples have been primarily Lisp, Prolog, Smalltalk, CSP, dataflow, and functional programming. We believe that C, Pascal, Ada, Scheme, Fortran and Cobol could serve as negative examples as well. Actor languages and concurrent logic programming languages are, as we have argued, are notable positive examples. Argus [2], NIL [28], and quasi-functional languages [16] are possibly positive examples as well.

In this paper we have concentrated on kernel languages for distributed computing. We believe that higher level programming abstractions are needed to provide good support for building open systems. The abstractions needed range from thematically unified collections such as object-oriented programming, functional programming, constraint-based programming and so on to specialized abstractions for dealing with security, communication, resource allocation and the like. These abstractions need to fit together tightly and need to be supported by integrated programming tools. The choice of the appropriate kernel language upon which to build all this is very important.

Let us define, in the context of programming languages, the terms *omniscience* and *omnipotence*. Omniscience is the the ability to access all of some category of information defined without reference to where the information originates or is stored. Omnipotence is the similar ability to modify such categories of information. Most programming languages attempt to implement both – an attempt which must fail in a distributed open system. Perhaps the major culprit is the global scoping (naming) environment of most languages. From anywhere in a program in these languages one can set or access the value of any global variable. The presence of any globally accessible entity with atomically changeable state is an example of both omniscience and omnipotence. The closed-world assumption of Prolog and relational database systems – that one can know by inspection that an assertion is absent – is an example of an omniscience assumption. We suspect that the reason most languages assume omniscience and omnipotence (for some purposes) is that this carries no implementation penalty on a von-Neumann machine, and so is tempting.

To date, most interesting computation has occurred inside a single machine or a local cluster of machines. Programming languages have generally evolved to provide conceptual leverage for understanding and organizing computation in such systems. As more and more important aspects of computation take place across large open systems, similar conceptual leverage will be needed and become embodied in languages. A large part of language design is the characterization of an abstract computation model. Both the actor model and the concurrent logic programming model seem well-suited for building the robust servers which are the building blocks of open systems.

# 9 Acknowledgements

We wish to thank Curtis Abbott, Danny Bobrow, Mike Dixon, Carl Hewitt, Jacob Levy, Henry Lieberman, Jim Rauen and Eric Tribble for their comments on earlier versions of this paper.

# References

[1] C. Hewitt, "Concurrency in Intelligent Systems", *AI Expert*, premier issue, 1986, pp. 45-50.

[2] B. Liskov and R. Scheifler, "Guardians and Actions: Linguistic Support for Robust, Distributed Programs", this volume.

[3] B. Nelson, "Remote Procedure Call", Xerox PARC CSL-81-9, May 1981.

[4] R. F. Rashid, "From Rig to Accent to Mach: The Evolution of a Network Operating System", this volume.

[5] G. Agha, *Actors: A Model fo Concurrent Computation in Distributed Systems*, MIT Press, Cambridge, MA., 1987.

[6] W. Clinger, *Foundations of Actor Semantics*, MIT AI-TR-633, May 1981.

[7] H. Abelson and G. Sussman, *Structure and Interpretation of Computer Programs*, MIT Press, Cambridge, Mass., 1985.

[8] E. Shapiro, "Concurrent Prolog: A Progress Report", *Computer*, IEEE, August 1986, pp. 44-58.

[9] E. Shapiro and A. Takeuchi, "Object-Oriented Programming in Concurrent Prolog", *New Generation Computing*, Vol. 1, no. 1, July 1983.

[10] M. Ohki, A Takeuchi, and K. Furukawa, "An Object-Oriented Programming Language Based on the Parallel Logic Language KL1", *Logic Programming: Proceedings of the Fourth International Conference*, MIT Press, pp. 894-909.

[11] K. Kahn, E. Tribble, M. Miller, and D. Bobrow, "Vulcan: Logical Concurrent Objects", in Shriver, B. and Wegner, P. (eds.), *Research Directions in Object-Oriented Programming* and in Shapiro, E. (ed.) *Concurrent Prolog*, MIT Press, Cambridge, Mass., 1987.

[12] A. Davison, "POOL: A PARLOG Object-Oriented Language", Dept. of Computing, Imperial College, 1987.

[13] A. Goldberg and D. Robson, *Smalltalk-80 - The Language and its Implementation*, Addison-Wesley, 1983.

[14] A. Birrell, R. Levin, R. Needham, M. Schroeder, "Grapevine: An Exercise in Distributed Computing", *Communications of the ACM*, Vol. 25, No. 4, April 1982.

[15] J. Rees and N. Adams IV, "T: A Dialect of Lisp or, Lambda: The Ultimate Software Tool", *Proceedings of the 1982 ACM Symposium on Lisp and Functional Programming*, ACM, August 1982.

[16] G. Lindstrom, "Functional Programming and the Logical Variable", *12th ACM Symposium on Principles of Programming Languages*, New Orleans, 1985.

[17] E. Tribble, M. Miller, K. Kahn, D. Bobrow, C. Abbott, and E. Shapiro, "Channels: A Generalization of Streams", *Logic Programming: Proceedings of the Fourth International Conference*, MIT Press, pp. 839-857.

[18] D. Pountain, *A Tutorial Introduction to Occam Programming*, INMOS, 1986.

[19] C.A.R. Hoare, *Communicating Sequential Processes*, Prentice-Hall, New Jersey, 1985.

[20] B. Liskov, M. Herlihy, and L. Gilbert, "Limitations of synchronous communication with static process structure in languages for distributed computing", *Proceedings Thirteenth Symposium on Principles of Programming Languages*, St. Petersburg Beach, Florida, January 1986, pp. 150-159.

[21] M. Hirsch, W. Silverman, and E. Shapiro, "Layers of Protection and Control in the Logix System", Weizmann Institute Technical Report CS86-19, 1986.

[22] S. Safra and E. Shapiro, "Meta-interpreters for Real", *Proceedings of IFIP-86*, 1986.

[23] K. Ueda, *Guarded Horn Clauses*, The MIT Press, Cambridge, Mass., 1987.

[24] S. Gregory, *Parallel Logic Programming in PARLOG - The Language and its Implementation*, Addison Wesley, 1987.

[25] E. Shapiro, *Algorithmic Program Debugging*, The MIT Press, Cambridge, Mass., 1982.

[26] C. Hewitt, "The Challenge of Open Systems", *Byte*, April 1985, pp. 223-233

[27] R. Kowalski, "Logic-based Open Systems", Dept. of Computing, Imperial College, September 1985.

[28] R. Strom and S. Yemini, "NIL: An Integrated Language and System for Distributed Computing", *Proceedings of SIGPLAN '83 Symposium on Programming Language Issues in Software System*, June 1983.

The Ecology of Computation
B.A. Huberman (editor)
Elsevier Science Publishers B.V. (North-Holland), 1988

# The Next Knowledge Medium

Mark J. Stefik

*Xerox Corporation, Palo Alto Research Center*
*Intelligent Systems Laboratory*
*3333 Coyote Hill Road, Palo Alto, California 94304*

We are victims of one common superstition—
the superstition that we understand the
changes that are daily taking place in the
world because we read about them and know
what they are.

> —Mark Twain
> (from *About All Kinds of Ships*, 1892)

Warning: Flame follows.

> —Gregor Kiczales,
> (from an electronic network message,
> August 1985)

---

## Abstract

The most widely understood goal of artificial intelligence is to understand and build autonomous, intelligent, thinking machines. A perhaps larger opportunity and complementary goal is to understand and build an interactive knowledge medium.

---

Public opinion about artificial intelligence is schizophrenic. "It will never work" versus "It might cost me my job!" This dichotomy of attitudes reflects a collective confusion about AI. What is AI anyway? How can we think concretely about what it is, what it could be, or what it should be?

Reprinted from *AIP Magazine*, Vol. 7, Spring 1986.

Most technologists are consumed with the activity of designing, building, and fixing things that need to work this year, if not next week. There is not much time for planning very far ahead. Nonetheless, futurists believe that AI will fundamentally change our way of life. Predicting the future is always a difficult and notoriously unreliable process, at least in specifics, but it is important to try to understand trends and possibilities.

This article examines how AI technology could change civilization dramatically. The article is in three parts: stories, models, and predictions. The stories describe processes of cultural change that have been studied by historians and anthropologists. They provide a historical context for considering present and future cultural changes. To illuminate these stories and their lessons about technology, several models of systems drawn from the sciences are considered. The models provide analogies and metaphors for making predictions.

Predictions are then made, drawing on some projects and ideas that might point the way to building a new knowledge medium – an information network with semi-automated services for the generation, distribution, and consumption of knowledge. Such a knowledge medium could quite directly change our lives and, incidentally, change the shape of the field of AI as a scientific and engineering enterprise.

## Stories

Mankind's cultures are constantly evolving. In the following three stories, the growth of knowledge and cultural change are considered. The stories are representative; literature contains many similar ones. They form a natural progression.

## The Spread of Hunting Culture

At the end of the Pleistocene glaciations, a spear-throwing hunting culture swept from what is now the northwestern United States, throughout the length and breadth of North and South America. Paleo-Indian culture was characterized by the use of a spear with a distinctive fluted point and by the hunting of very large animals, such as bison and mammoths.

According to the archeological evidence, these artifacts, and presumably the culture, spread at a rate greater than one thousand miles per century. There is a debate as to whether the spread occurred through migration or through cultural diffusion by the observation, imitation, and integration of the spear technology and hunting methods by tribes at the edge of a spreading cultural wavefront (isochron). The weight of the sparse evidence, however, favors migration of hunting bands following as-yet-unhunted herds. In either case, it illustrates the very rapid spreading of a prehistoric culture over long distances.

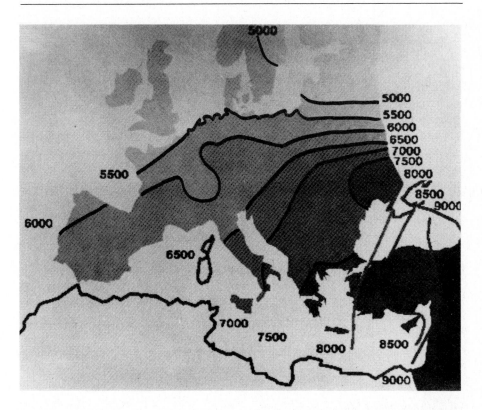

The spread of early farming from the near East to Europe. The lines (called isochrons) indicate equal times of arrival of farming artifacts in the regions, as determined using radiocarbon dating. The artifacts reach Great Britain about 4000 years after they leave Egypt, indicating a cultural diffusion rate of substantially less than 100 miles for each century. (Figure reprinted with permission from A. J. Ammerman and L. L. Cavalli-Sforza, The Neolithic Transition and the Genetics of Populations in Europe. Princeton University Press. 1984. p. 59.)

**Farming Culture.**

**Figure 1**

## The Spread of Farming Culture

The second story involves the diffusion of early farming culture across Europe from Eurasia. The spread of farming culture has been mapped using radiocarbon dating on the oldest discovered farming artifacts in the regions. Figure 1 shows a map of the land area of Europe, Asia, and Africa, stretching from Germany and England southeast to the north shore of the Mediterranean and then south to Egypt. The first artifacts appeared in Egypt approximately 9000 years ago. Wavefronts tracing the progress of cultural diffusion are spaced at 500-year intervals across Turkey, Italy, Spain, Germany, and France. Farming artifacts reach Great Britain about 4000 years after they first appeared in Egypt. This diffusion rate is substantially less than 100 miles for each century (Ammerman and Cavalli-Sforza, 1984).

It is easy to understand why the diffusion rate is so much slower for the farming culture than for the hunting culture. The farming culture is a much more complex form, containing several systems of knowledge. This culture brought about some dramatic shifts from food gathering and purposeful food collecting to the more organized behaviors of planting and harvesting. The collective investment in organization led to a great increase in population densities.

## Peasants into Frenchmen

In contrast with the previous stories, this one illustrates that a technology can accelerate cultural change. This story is about the introduction of roads and railroads into France between the years 1870 and 1914 and the subsequent sweeping changes and modernization that took place. Similar stories of rapid change just prior to the twentieth century can be told for countries around the world, including the United States. The story of the modernization of France is well documented and easily available for those with an interest in history and technology (Weber, 1976).

Until the 1860s the highway system of France was a mere skeleton. Highways led to and from Paris, the seat of the central government. They were for troops to march on and allowed tax revenues to reach the treasury. The railway lines, which were begun in the 1840s, had the same characterization. They did not connect with the farms and villages and did not serve the needs of ordinary people. Most of the real traffic was on the trails, paths, tracks, and lanes that covered the countryside. Along these trails traveled the people, goods, and ideas of the time.

A peasant's world was restricted to narrow corridors — the space of a village and familiar trails. Travel beyond the limits of a good hike was a difficult and costly undertaking. According to custom, the few who went to Paris, even if only once in a lifetime, were known as Parisians.

During the winter, the roads were so bad that they were classified according to how deep a person or a horse would sink in the mud — to the knees, to the shoulders, or to the head. Carts were unusable.

The exchange of goods was limited to neighboring regions. If a peasant wanted to sell wares at a distant location, that peasant faced the prospect of carrying them for hours and then arriving at a town with no means of storage. Once arriving, the peasant merchant was at the mercy of the buyers, who knew that the merchant was in no position to haggle. Consequently, farmers and regions tended to be self-sufficient.

The change came after 1881 when, in the public interest, a law was passed to promote the building of rural roads. Together, the railroads and the interconnecting secondary roads brought a new life to the villages, connecting isolated patches of countryside to the larger markets. The roads connected the villages together, and the railroads connected the nation together.

As the horizons of the peasant were expanded, new opportunities were perceived, and traditional orientations were abandoned. The peasant's apparent disinterest in trading evaporated. The necessary skills for shipping and receiving goods — reading, writing, and counting — were learned. The skills developed as part of a general education took on significance as occasions arose in which to use them.

Productivity expanded enormously. A rule of thumb of the time was that economic activity grew tenfold in any area serviced by the railroad. In the Correze region of south-central France, for example, transportation made fertilizer available. Its consumption increased 13 times over, and crop production increased 65 times between 1866 and 1906. Industries were transformed as France began to function as a unified marketplace. The oldest of the cottage industries — spinning and weaving — was replaced by the new textile mills. Coke, transported by trains, replaced charcoal. The local nailmakers came into competition with nail-making machines. Transportation expanded the marketplace and made possible what we now routinely call the economies of scale. (See Figure 2.)

The railroads and roads of France, like those of other nations, triggered a process of rapid transformation. In a scant 40 years, they brought the French people a common market, a common language, a unified nation, and a new prosperity. In the words of many French politicians, roads were the cement of national unity. In Weber's words, the roads transformed "peasants into Frenchmen."

Technology can accelerate processes of cultural change. Until the 1860s the highway system of France was a mere skeleton. Travel was difficult and a costly undertaking, and trade was limited mostly to neighboring villages. In 1881 a law was passed to promote the building of rural roads, connecting small villages to each other and to the railroads. This triggered a process of invigorated economic activity, in which cottage industries were displaced by large-scale production in an expanded market. The roads also transformed France into a marketplace for ideas. The ideas crisscrossed France along the roads and railroads, bringing about new ways of thinking and a more uniform language. (Reproduced from the cover of *Peasants into Frenchmen* by Eugen Weber. Stanford University Press, 1976.)

**Woodcut Print of the French Countryside.**

**Figure 2.**

# Models

The preceding stories illustrate processes of cultural change and the spread of knowledge. These processes can be accelerated by technology, as in the French roads example. Many other examples of technology accelerating change have been studied, such as the printing press, the post office, and the telephone.

In the following sections, four models of systems and change are examined: population genetics, ecology, economics, and processes in scientific communities. All of these models are well-known. They are reviewed here to establish some terminology and metaphors that will be useful for making predictions about a knowledge medium.

# Population Genetics

Beginning biology courses discuss the genetics of individuals, starting from the early plant experiments of Mendel to the more recent research that has revealed the chromosomal mechanisms of inheritance. Population genetics goes beyond the genes of individuals to consider the variations and percentages of genes in a population. The set of genes in a given population is called its *gene pool*.

In this model, living organisms are *gene carriers*, and a *species* is a single type of organism capable of interbreeding. Mutation occurs in the genes of individuals, and, over time, selection determines the percentages of different genes in a population.

As an environment changes, the selection processes also change; this is reflected by changes in the gene pool. *Genetic drift* refers to a change in the relative distribution of genes in a population. A fundamental hypothesis of population genetics is that when two groups become isolated from each other, there is always genetic drift between the two gene pools. Population geneticists have studied the mathematics of genetic drift and have related it to various factors such as the size of the gene pools. In general, larger populations have more stable distributions in their gene pools than smaller populations.

Sometimes, new species appear and displace related species much more rapidly than would be predicted by the apparent change of environment or expected rate of genetic drift. This phenomenon of speciation and displacement is called a *punctuated equilibrium* because of the characterization of a population that is stable for a long period of time and then experiences sudden changes. For example, the fossil record might show a sudden change in the shapes of teeth in a predator population.

The leading model for explaining this process takes place in three stages: isolation, drift, and displacement. First, a group becomes geographically isolated from the main population. In isolation, it undergoes selection and genetic drift across multiple genes more rapidly than does the larger body. Finally, the geographic isolation is removed, and the slightly fitter group competes against and displaces the original population.

The mathematics and concepts of genetic drift and gene pools can be adapted to other systems, even nonbiological systems. The systems must have replicating elements and analogous mechanisms for transmitting and recombining these elements.

## Ecological Models

*Ecology* is the study of systems of organisms in an environment. The first observation from ecology is that systems have levels. This concept is perhaps best exemplified by the so-called *food chains*, in which big animals eat little animals and so on, down to the most rudimentary plants and microorganisms.

Levels are the most simple order of relations: in complex ecological systems, the relations between species form an intricate web. To describe these relations, ecologists have developed a rich vocabulary of terms: predators, symbiotes, parasites, and pollinators.

From ecology comes a familiar metaphor: the *ecological niche*. An ecology has many nooks and crannies for all of the functions that must be performed, and everything has its niche.

When several species evolve together in ways that increase their mutual adaptation, they are said to *coevolve*. From this mutual adaptation can come increased efficiency, and this leads to an important ecological principle: life enables more life.

In an uninteresting sense, everything depends on everything. This degree of interdependency does not mean that ecologies are fragile. Ecologies are not constant, nor are they formed all at once. They develop under processes of coevolution. Multiple species compete for and create niches. As an ecosystem increases in complexity, it also becomes more redundant and thereby more robust.

Systems with populations of replicating elements can be described by metaphors based on either population genetics or ecology. Population genetics provides metaphors for drift, mutation, and selection. Ecology provides metaphors for describing relations between groups of elements and coevolution.

## Economic Models

Economic systems are similar in many ways to ecological systems. Businesses form economic subsystems and depend on each other according to intricate relations. There are suppliers, distributors, and consumers. Subcontractors supply parts and services to multiple manufacturers. Corporations and goods are said to occupy *economic niches*. New products can drastically change the shape of a market by displacing older products from existing niches or by creating different niches.

Economics brings us several concepts not found in ecology, including price, supply, and demand. These concepts provide a quantitative basis for explaining action in the marketplace. A market is said to "seek its own level," according to the laws of supply and demand.

When there are many suppliers in a market, some are more efficient than others, and consumers benefit from lower prices. Effects like this can ripple through an economy, as when a part that is used in many different products is made more cheaply. When there are many consumers, producers often can achieve economies of scale by switching to large-scale manufacturing processes and mass production.

Thus, business enables more business. This can also be seen in the spread of business. The first businesses in a rural area are basic and relatively inefficient. As a locality develops a rich mixture of businesses, its economy becomes robust.

Some economic systems require more sophisticated models than the essentially laissez-faire ideas just described. For example, an economy can interact with a legal system, it can be regulated, or more subtle phenomena might need explanation. Nonetheless, the above concepts form a reasonable first-order model for many situations and are enough for our purposes.

Stereoscopic view showing several forms of transportation in France. The Eiffel Tower was built in 1889. This view, from about 1895, shows barges, a horse-drawn cart, and a hot-air balloon. By this time, railroads and secondary roads had invigorated the French economy and had triggered a rapid process of change that made France into a unified nation. (Photograph by B. L. Singley. The Keystone View Company, Meadville, Pennsylvania.)

## French Transportation.

## Figure 3.

## Social Processes in the Scientific Community

Anyone with even a casual familiarity with science has heard about the *scientific method*. It is a principled approach for creating and validating new knowledge. Studies of the actual conduct of science, however, reveal a social richness in the conduct of science that goes beyond the scientific method.

Scientists are knowledge workers having important relationships with each other. Such relationships are the peer review and the "invisible colleges" of colleagues who share and collaborate on results prior to their publication. Some scientists are known to their colleagues as innovators. Some are best known for integrating the results of others or for reliably pursuing details. Some are best at theory, and others excel at overcoming difficult challenges in experiments. Some scientists are good at explaining things and contribute most with their teaching.

Thus, scientists have many different roles as knowledge workers. Science enables more science, or, perhaps, knowledge enables more knowledge. Yesterday's discoveries and unanswered questions drive today's experiments and provide the backdrop against which they are carried out. This additive effect is particularly evident in practical knowledge about the techniques of experimentation.

For example, a series of experiments about genes and nutrients might yield a well-characterized culture of microorganisms. This culture might then be used for fine-grained studies of genetic exchange, and these results, in turn, enable experiments about the mechanisms that regulate gene expression.

## Predictions

In the last chapter of his book, *The Selfish Gene*, Richard Dawkins suggests provocatively that ideas (he called them *memes*) are like genes and that societies have meme pools in just the same way as they have gene pools.

The central theme of Dawkins's work in biology was a shift to a "gene's eye view" for explaining the processes of evolution and selection. When mammals reproduce, they do not clone themselves, and their offspring are not identical to them. Genes are the (mostly) *invariant* units of inheritance. Taking this point of view goes a long way toward explaining many of the persisting conundrums of traits and behaviors that are linked genetically.

Almost an afterthought in his book, Dawkins's memes have been taken up by many writers since they were first introduced. Memes are carried by people. They are the knowledge units that are transmitted in conversations and that are contained in minds. Memes can be reinterpreted in new environments and expressed in new combinations, just like genes. Memes, like genes, often come in clusters that work together. Memes compete for their share in meme pools, just as genes compete in gene pools. If populations of memes become isolated, they undergo *memetic drift*, analogous to genetic drift.

## Toward a Meme's Eye View

Stories of cultural change can be reinterpreted from a meme's eye view. Cultural change occurs along a wavefront, with the memes competing and spreading to new carriers. Basic human capabilities for communication and imitation modulate the rate at which the memes spread. Differences in the rate of propagation, such as hunting culture versus the slower farm culture, can be explained by assuming that many more memes need to be communicated for farming than for hunting. Apprenticeship programs in science can be seen as a social mechanism for communicating memes about the techniques and practices of science that are not reported in publications.

The progression in our stories from hunting culture to farming culture to the modernization of France is of increasing cultural complexity. It is not, however, a sequence of decreasing speeds of propagation. Considering only the complexity of the cultural shift, it might be expected that the modernization of France took many centuries, if not millennia, but, in spite of the dramatic cultural changes that took place, the rate of propagation sped up enormously. To understand this, the effects of the roads in France must be reconsidered.

The roads did more than change France into a marketplace for goods. They also transformed it into a marketplace for memes. The isochron waves, which so faithfully described the orderly flow of memes for the hunting and farming cultures, are completely inadequate for tracing the flow along the roads and railroads of France. Technology changed the process. Imagine the memes crisscrossing France, along the roads and railroads, creating an intricate pattern of superimposed cultural wavefronts. Ideas from faraway places were continuously reinterpreted and reapplied.

By bringing previously separate memes into competition, the roads triggered a shift in equilibrium. The relaxation of constraints on travel led to meme "displacement." Cottage industries were replaced by mass production, and the way of life changed. Multiple equilibria were punctuated at once. The very richness of this process accelerated the generation of new *recombinant memes* with their own wavefronts. Whole systems of memes (*e.g.,* how to run railroad stations, what the value of education is, and even how to speak French) were created and transmitted. As Weber noted, peasants became Frenchmen in a mere 40 years.

Since 1914 several new communication media have been introduced, including improvements in the post office, telephones, and television. These communication media have quantifiable properties that govern the transmission of memes:   transaction times, fan out, community sizes, bandwidth, and storage. Better post offices mean that people can spend less time traveling and that they have more time for other activities. Shopping can be done by mail. The rise of the mail-order catalog stores at the turn of the century is a manifestation of this change. Today in the United States, the large catalog stores connect consumers and suppliers into a large national marketplace that has tended to reduce regional differences.

# AI Technology: Not Yet a Knowledge Medium

Precisely defining a knowledge medium is much like defining life, and, like life, it is better characterized in terms of processes rather than properties. Life usually is described in terms of processes such as reproduction, adaptation, growth, and the consumption of food. A knowledge medium is characterized in terms of knowledge processes such as the generation, distribution, and application of knowledge and, secondarily, in terms of specialized services such as consultation and knowledge integration.

For life there are many borderline cases that defy simple definition. Fires spread, change their burning patterns, increase in size, and consume fuel, but they are not considered living. Viruses and plasmids are classified as living because they take over the machinery of their hosts, lacking the machinery for reproduction. It can be said that mammals are "more alive" than viruses because the quality of their processes is so much richer. Knowledge media also have borderline cases: communication media without knowledge services and databases with limited distribution and services. Just as life is thought to have come from things that were "nearly alive," so too might knowledge media emerge from nearby media.

AI research includes topics relevant to knowledge media: the representation of knowledge in symbolic structures, the creation of knowledge bases for storing and retrieving knowledge, the development of problem-solving methods that can use and be advised by knowledge, and the creation of knowledge systems (or expert systems) that apply knowledge to solve problems.

However, AI technology, as it now exists, does not function in an important way as a knowledge medium in our society. Its influence has been far less important to the creation and propagation of knowledge than the secondary roads in France.

This is more than a matter of the youth of the field. The main goal of AI seems to lead off in a different, possibly contrary, direction. The term "artificial intelligence" expresses the most commonly understood goal of the field: to build intelligent, autonomous, thinking machines. Building autonomous thinking machines emphasizes ideas quite different from building a knowledge medium. It suggests the creation of machines that are intelligent and independent. In contrast, the goal of building a knowledge medium draws attention to the main source and store of knowledge in the world today: people.

## Books Versus Expert Systems

In the meme model, a *carrier* is an agent that can remember a meme and communicate it to another agent. People are meme carriers and so are books. However, there is an important difference: People can apply knowledge, whereas books only store it. Librarians, authors, publishers, and readers are the active elements in the printed knowledge medium. Computers can apply knowledge as well, and this makes them important for creating an active knowledge medium. When a medium includes computer systems, some of the knowledge services can be automated.

The most promising automated knowledge processors today are expert systems. They are the darlings of many high technology watchers; they are the business of several exciting start-up companies. In several well-publicized cases expert systems have proven to be of substantial economic value, far exceeding the cost of their development.

The tools for building expert systems continue to improve and the research tools of several years ago have become the programming and knowledge engineering power tools of today. We have our new AI Lisp machines or Prolog machines, and we have our knowledge base tools. Practicing knowledge engineers will correctly claim that these tools make a big difference. There are many anecdotal accounts of noncomputer specialists ("domain experts") successfully using these tools to build expert systems.

However, building an expert system is quite different from writing a book. In writing a book, an author needs to get the ideas together and to write them down clearly. Sometimes ideas will be missing or out of order or slightly wrong. But authors depend on the intelligence and knowledge of their readers to understand and integrate what they read. Not so with today's computers and expert systems. Today's computers are less sophisticated than humans. Knowledge must be acquired, represented, and integrated when programming an expert system. Moreover, the underlying tools, while providing assistance in the construction of the expert system (just as text editors provide assistance to an author) provide no memes of their own to help with the organization of new knowledge or to fill in its gaps. Each expert system requires careful handcrafting of its knowledge base, and for this reason, expert systems are expensive.

An operational economy enables the process of manufacturing complex artifacts such as automobiles and airplanes. To succeed at making modern airplanes, a manufacturer exploits a marketplace for materials and subassemblies. A manufacturer does not need to also make tires and batteries, to mine metals, and to produce glass and plastics. A manufacturer does not want to master all the details of the necessary technologies; but it does want to exploit the economies of scale of the marketplace. Specialized companies can produce batteries, glass, and tires less expensively than can an automobile manufacturer. The marketplace makes it possible to build complex goods that would otherwise be infeasible if everything had to be done from scratch. This recalls the abundance rules from our models: life enables more life, business enables more business, knowledge enables more knowledge.

For complex systems such as airplanes and automobiles, the feasibility of manufacturing turns critically on the availability of high-quality low-cost goods in the marketplace. The "goods" of a knowledge market are elements of knowledge, or memes if you will. In today's expert systems, knowledge bases are built from scratch.

To return to our comparison of books and expert systems, both are highly creative enterprises, both require research to collect the facts, and in both cases there is no (or very little) economy of scale in writing $N$ books or building $N$ expert systems. Compared with the number of people who are literate in the printed medium, knowledge engineers are few in number. They are the computer-literate monks of the twentieth century, illuminating their manuscripts in splendid isolation, awaiting perhaps the invention of the next printing press.

## Standardization and Shells

To reduce the cost of building expert systems, we need to be able to build them using knowledge acquired from a marketplace. This requires setting some processes in place and making some technical advances.

The technical issues are not just the usual problems of electronic connection; there are already networks for computers. Computer networks are used for many important tasks, such as booking airline reservations and clearing bank transactions. The networks carry mostly data, not knowledge; low-level facts, not high-level memes. This distinction eludes precise definition, but the general sense is that very little of what the computers are transmitting is akin to what people talk about in serious conversation.

Imagine drawing on a collection of knowledge bases for building expert systems. These knowledge bases would be developed for different purposes but would have some important terms in common. For example, consider the term "water." A chemistry knowledge base would specify when water freezes and boils and what dissolves in it. A cooking knowledge base would include information about its measurement or its use with different kinds of utensils. A desert-survival knowledge base would relate water to sweat and night travel. Farming and boating knowledge bases would relay other unique information.

Anyone who has tried to give a computer program common sense has found that there is a staggering amount of it which is acquired on the way to becoming adults, and none of it is readily accessible to computers. Some AI researchers have started to build generic knowledge bases of potentially wide value. For example, there are projects in common sense reasoning and qualitative and naive physics. Lenat's CYC project at Microelectronics and Computer Technology Corporation (Lenat, 1986) is encoding the knowledge of an encyclopedia in an explicit knowledge base. The success of this project will depend on whether the entry of additional knowledge becomes simpler as the knowledge base increases in size.

AI has very little experience with combining knowledge from different sources. There is plenty of experience in using protocols for getting low-level information (bits) from place to place, and there is an established practice for encapsulating higher-level information above the low-level protocols. Experience with protocols does not go high enough, however.

A partial approach to combining knowledge from different sources is *standardization*. The goal of standardization is to make interchange possible. Initially, railroads were designed with different-sized gauges for different sets of tracks. By now, though, the diversity of railroad gauges has mostly disappeared, and, for the most part, railway cars can be routed along any set of tracks.

The idea is to create standard vocabularies (for example, using words like water) and ways of defining things in terms of primitives. This is the conventional approach used to build knowledge bases, where the transmission language is a simple transformation of the representation language.

Work on standardization can be coupled naturally to work on expert system shells. A *shell* is an environment designed to support applications of a similar nature. Shells are an intermediate point between specific applications and general-purpose knowledge engineering environments. Shells could be built for broad applications, such as planning, scheduling, and a variety of specialized office tasks. Shells have four things that knowledge engineering tools do not: (1) pre-packaged representations for important concepts, (2) inference and representation tools tuned for efficient and perspicuous use in the application, (3) specialized user interfaces, and (4) generic knowledge for the application. For example, a shell for a planning application would have representations that integrate multiple alternatives and beliefs with time. It would have interfaces for dealing with plans and alternatives. It would have generic categories for items such as time, tasks, and serially reusable resources. It would include some generic domain knowledge, such as the fact that an agent can be at only one place at a time. Shells provide the potential for sharing and standardizing knowledge in communities larger than single expert system projects.

## From Standardization to Interoperability

Shells and experiments with standardization are the right next steps, but they are only a beginning. Indeed, if standardization is the only approach taken for knowledge combination it ultimately would defeat the whole enterprise. The fundamental problem is that memes are additive only when sufficient intelligence is applied for their integration. The fact that intelligence is needed to make knowledge "additive" is a lesson which has been painfully rediscovered several times. Early visions of the relevance of theorem proving to AI reflected this misconception. Much of the great appeal of building an artificial intelligence based on theorem proving was the notion that given a fast enough mechanical theorem prover, one could always add a few more facts and derive the consequences.

One lesson often cited from experience with theorem provers is that it is necessary for efficiency to be able to control search processes. There is an even more important lesson, however: A theorem prover is a fundamentally ignorant system. A child is often unable to make use of what it is told. Even an adult is often unable to work with ideas that are too far removed from familiar experience. Today's theorem provers know profoundly less than a young child; it is not realistic then to expect such systems to be able to integrate facts.

Nonetheless, this flawed notion has arisen in many visions of building intelligent systems. For example, a story similar to that about theorem proving could be told about the appeal and ultimate disappointment in schemes for encoding knowledge in terms of production rules. Additivity of knowledge requires more than a simple interpreter; it requires an intelligent agent.

When people read books, they actively integrate what they read with what they know. The process of learning from a book does not bear much resemblance to copying text (the "transmission language") to the end of a file.

A naive approach to developing standards for knowledge transmission is to repeat this mistake again, that is, to develop standard terms with simple fixed interpreters and to expect that, somehow, knowledge expressed in the transmission language will be additive. When people from different backgrounds share what they know, they must spend time mutually constructing a common background. Although standardization plays a role in shortening this process (because there is a substantial corpus of shared knowledge), people have also developed intricate means for discovering differences and developing communication.

Humans as knowledge carriers have developed techniques for "interoperability." The field of AI does not have much experience in understanding how to do this, and this is an open area for research. Building shells and combining large knowledge bases might trigger such research by providing a setting and examples for exploring limits. The use of intelligent agents to compile and integrate knowledge into usable knowledge bases will highlight the difference between languages for knowledge transmission and knowledge representation. Transmission languages need to be rich in the descriptions that enable integrators to connect memes together; representation languages need to provide the necessary hooks for efficient access, introspection, and application of knowledge.

## Roles in a Knowledge Market

Suppose there was a knowledge market. What would be the different roles in this market? From the economics model, we would expect to find knowledge producers, knowledge distributors (publishers), and knowledge consumers. Drawing on our practical knowledge of working markets, we might predict many other roles. Perhaps, there would be knowledge advertisers and knowledge advertising agencies. If the market were regulated, there might be knowledge certifiers. Experts who have participated in the creation of expert systems commonly report that the process of articulating their knowledge for explicit representation in computers has, itself, yielded a better body of knowledge and a more complete understanding of what they know. Reflecting on this experience, Michie has proposed the creation of *knowledge refineries*, where such processes could be used routinely to "purify" crude knowledge.

The model of the scientific community yields a different cut on the differentiation of roles. Integrators would combine knowledge from different places. Translators would move information between subfields, converting the jargon as needed. Summarizers and teachers would also be needed.

Workstations designed for professional knowledge integrators would need things unusual in today's AI workstations. An integrator needs to have ready access to the important knowledge media used in human affairs, so the workstation should provide technical bridges. It should include a scanner, so that books and journals can be read from their paper medium. The automated character recognition of text would not need to be perfect, because the integrator could help interactively with the rough spots. The process for converting a page of a book to a text file, however, should be convenient and mostly automatic. Similarly, it should be easy to scan in audio recordings or items from a remote database. The workstation should provide software tools for reorganizing the information, to aid the integrator in the profession of combining memes.

This vision of a knowledge medium might seem very distant in the future. There are a lot of objects and processes to create. How can such a process be bootstrapped?

## Bootstrapping a Knowledge Medium

The goal of building a new knowledge medium is not to replace work on expert systems with something else or to replace existing communication media. The goal is to tie these two elements together into a greater whole. A knowledge medium based on AI technology is part of a continuum. Books and other passive media can simply store knowledge. At the other end of the spectrum are expert systems which can store and also apply knowledge. In between are a number of hybrid systems in which the knowledge processing is done mostly by people. There are many opportunities for establishing human-machine partnerships and for automating tasks incrementally.

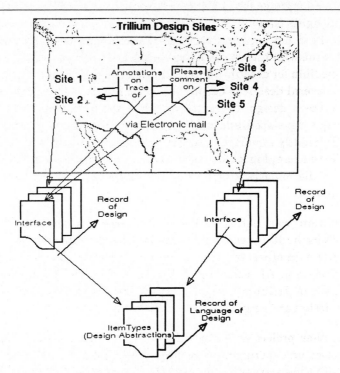

Trillium is a computer-aided design tool in which the controls for copiers can be designed. Trillium was not conceived as an expert systems project. Rather, it was built to augment existing media. It provides a language for expressing design concepts in terms of buttons, lights, actions, and constraints. Trillium quickly evolved into the best medium for describing user interfaces that Xerox copier designers ever had. Its use spread to several design teams within Xerox. It became a major (if not the major) medium for exchanging knowledge about user interfaces. Trillium has now been used for most of the major entries in the next generation of copiers made by the corporation.

**Trillium Map.**

**Figure 4.**

---

The best example of a knowledge medium using AI technology is the Trillium project at Xerox involving Austin Henderson and others. (See Figure 4.) Trillium created a knowledge economy of the memes of interface design for copiers. Modern copiers are being built with many more powerful functions than the early machines, and the design of user interfaces for them has become much more challenging. From one perspective, Trillium is a sort of computer-aided design tool in which the controls for a copier can be designed.

It provides a language for expressing the actions of a copier interface in terms of buttons, lights, actions, and constraints. Initially, Trillium was intended to facilitate the rapid prototyping of interface designs, so that designers could quickly try them and study the cognitive factors. Trillium quickly evolved into the best medium for describing interfaces that these designers ever had. Its use spread to several design teams inside Xerox, and soon these teams wanted to exchange their design concepts. Software to help them combine design concepts was developed and aided the teams in managing versions as they evolved differently at various sites. Trillium became a major (if not the major) medium for exchanging knowledge about user interfaces. It has now been used for most of the major entries in the next generation of copiers made by the corporation.

Trillium was not conceived as an expert systems project. Rather, Trillium was built to augment existing media. The computer integrates successfully with other existing media-in this case, phones and memos. What do computers and AI technology bring to bear in the Trillium project? The main benefit of Trillium is expressing the memes. In Trillium the memes of interface design are tangible artifacts in a knowledge medium.

Another project at Xerox that focuses on human collaboration is the Colab project, an experiment in inventing the team computer. This project was started with the observation that people spend much of their time in meetings, leaving their computers behind in their offices. The Colab is a computer-augmented meeting room in which computers are used as an essential medium in the process of meetings. Meeting software is developed for collaboration in organizing ideas for a paper and for arguing the merits, assumptions, and evaluation criteria for competing proposals. Tools support meetings through different phases,such as brainstorming, linking, and evaluating. The Colab also includes special hardware for group use, such as a large, touch-sensitive electronic blackboard. (See Figure 5.)

Colab is an experiment in inventing the team computer, in which a group of collaborators can jointly construct and organize ideas. This project was based on the observation that people spend much of their time in meetings, leaving their computers behind in their offices. The Colab is a computer-augmented meeting room, in which computers are used as an essential medium in the process of meetings. The Colab also includes special hardware for group use, such as a large, touch-sensitive electronic blackboard. Meeting software is developed for collaboration in organizing ideas for a paper and for arguing the merits, assumptions, and evaluation criteria for competing proposals. Tools support meetings through different phases, such as brainstorming, linking, and evaluating. If the Trillium project and the Colab project are harbingers of things to come, then new projects for knowledge media will be conceived in terms of the means that they create for collaboration. (Photograph by Brian Tramontana.)

**Colab.**

**Figure 5.**

In both the Trillium and Colab examples, computers bring special capabilities not available in competing, passive media. In both cases, the computer provides active knowledge services, ranging from simple storage and retrieval of information to processes that interact with and augment human social processes. The languages provided by the tools encourage an important degree of precision and explicitness for manipulating and experimenting with the knowledge in that form. Trillium provides a substantially better language and communication capability than designers had previously. The Colab offers computational support for organizing information, file storage for saving the information between meetings, and coordination that allows more than one person to write at the same time into a shared memory.

## Revising the Goals of AI

Building a knowledge medium has a set of overall goals quite distinct from those conventionally embraced by AI. The vision of AI, suggested by its name, is the understanding and building of an autonomous, artificial intelligence. While building an artificial intelligence is compatible with creating a knowledge medium, AI breakthroughs are not a prerequisite for building or experimenting with them. Intelligence can be added incrementally to a knowledge medium. The enterprise of building a knowledge medium shares much of the technology that has become important to AI.

Goldstein and Papert (1977) announced a shift of paradigm in AI from a power-oriented theory of intelligence to a knowledge-oriented theory of intelligence: The fundamental problem of understanding intelligence is not the identification of a few powerful techniques but rather the question of how to represent large amounts of knowledge in a fashion that permits their effective use and interaction. The bottleneck processes in building expert systems are recognized to be getting knowledge into expert systems (knowledge acquisition) and subsequently modifying it and updating it over time. Recognizing this puts the field of AI in a position to shift even closer to the foundations of knowledge: from a focus on mechanisms of intelligence to the role of knowledge in intelligent systems to the augmentation of knowledge processes in a medium.

Agencies that fund AI could play an important role in promoting or accelerating this shift. For example, over the past few years, there have been many workstation projects that aim to support specialized knowledge workers. There have been projects for building workstations for physicists, engineers, geneticists, doctors, and others. These projects could be conceived as isolated applications of AI. In this case, with few exceptions, the projects will be quite narrow and won't become particularly large or important for the proposed client community.

Alternatively, these projects could be conceived in terms of building experimental knowledge economies and knowledge media. Much of the same work needs to be done in either case. The difference is a change of emphasis. An expert system project is usually (and conventionally) conceptualized in terms of an isolated and independent widget that carries out certain tasks. The conventional goal of AI leads to projects for which the creators can say, "Look ma, no hands!"

The knowledge medium requires a change of goal focus from product to process and introduces new criteria for evaluating projects. Important questions need to be asked: As a project evolves, where will the knowledge come from? How will it be distributed? How is knowledge distributed now? What kinds of knowledge will be distributed, and what form will this knowledge take? Will it be of a grain size that encourages recombination and synergy? How will multiple experts interact?

A funding program intended to build a new knowledge medium would include many kinds of projects. It would include experiments with small expert systems, conceived around shared community knowledge bases. It would include projects dealing with expert system shells and knowledge-transmission languages. It would include the development of low-cost multimedia workstations for knowledge integrators and research on the processes of knowledge integration. It would include traditional work on AI, for incrementally automating knowledge-processing tasks. It would include experiments in creating viable knowledge markets, with mechanisms for distributing and renting knowledge.

The original proposal for the Japanese Fifth Generation Project described a number of roles for knowledge-processing systems: increasing their intelligence so they can better assist mankind, putting stored knowledge to practical use, learning, and associating data. In his keynote speech for the second ICOT conference, Hiroo Kinoshita of the Ministry of International Trade and Industry hailed the creation of an advanced information society:

> ...in it, different information systems will be linked into networks, and a variety of services will be offered. In addition, rather than individuals playing the passive role of merely receiving information, they will be able to obtain that information which they require, use it, and transmit it among themselves, in what is expected to be a society more closely reflecting human nature (Kinoshita, 1985).

Such a network would be a knowledge medium in the sense that this term has been used here. As a policymaker, Kinoshita cited several difficulties in bringing this network and society into existence, including the long time to write software, mechanisms for computer (and knowledge) security, interoperability, and better man-machine interfaces. His concerns are valid and focus on technological limitations which would affect the processes that need to operate in a knowledge medium.

However, the Fifth Generation Project does not have any projects for building experimental knowledge ecologies or knowledge markets. If the Trillium project and the Colab project are harbingers of things to come, then new projects need to be conceived in terms of the means that they create for collaboration.

Building a knowledge medium is a long-term goal, complementary to the goal of building artificially intelligent agents. Importantly, the vision of a knowledge medium might be the more useful guide to progress. Like the agent goal, it is for the long term. It stands on other work in the larger field of computer science, such as work on databases and network technology. It rests on the same core work of AI on language understanding, knowledge representation, and problem solving.

Creating a knowledge medium relates directly to the human condition and raises fundamental research issues for ultimately creating elements of widespread value, such as community knowledge bases and semiautomated knowledge markets. If it makes knowledge accessible, it might continuously trigger minor punctuations of knowledge equilibria, as memes cross the relatively impermeable boundaries of human specialization.

## Concluding Remarks

The AI systems of today are akin to the isolated villages of France before roads were built. Goods were made using time-consuming hand labor. The villages stood by themselves; in their poverty, they were relatively self-sufficient. Dialects were divergent, and experience was accumulated locally. There was little interest in the neighbors. The roads and larger markets were yet to be conceived and invented.

In the late 1890s, Robert Louis Stevenson persuaded the tribal chiefs of Samoa to cut a road through the wilderness. When it was opened, Stevenson said:

Our road is not built to last a thousand years, yet in a sense it is. When a road is once built, it is a strange thing how it collects traffic, how every year as it goes on, more and more people are found to walk thereon, and others are raised up to repair and perpetuate it, and keep it alive (Stevenson, 1896).

Stevenson's observation strikes me as profound; it illustrates a method for starting ideas or objects that will persist. It clarifies the idea that a successful knowledge medium cannot be just an autonomous widget, but instead it should be a medium for seeding knowledge processes.

The anthropological stories and the concept of memes were brought to my attention several years ago by Lynn Conway. Much of the vision and some of the material was drawn from a paper that we worked on together but never published. The important distinction between process and product was made crisp for me by John Seely Brown, who also has encouraged and made possible projects like Trillium, which I watched with interest, and Colab, in which I participated. Joshua Lederherg kindled my interest in biological issues and a respect which has not faded for knowledge processes and their partial automation. Dan Bobrow listened to my ramblings on several runs, agonized over my confusions, helped to get the kinks out of the arguments, and suggested the title for the article. Sanjay Mittal and I have spent many hours speculating together on the issues in building community knowledge bases and knowledge servers and in understanding the principles of knowledge competitions. Austin Henderson helped me to understand the Trillium story and to report it accurately. Austin and Sanjay hounded me to say, more precisely, what a knowledge medium is. Agustin Araya and Mark Miller participated in a Colab session in which we tried to jointly lay out these ideas, and together asked me to make the prescriptions clearer. Ed Feigenbaum persuaded me to be more precise in the discussion of the limits of today's expert systems technology.

Thanks to Agustin Araya, Dan Bobrow, John Seely Brown, Lynn Conway, Bob Engelmore, Ed Feigenbaum, Felix Frayman, Gregg Foster, Austin Henderson, Ken Kahn, Mark Miller, Sanjay Mittal, Julian Orr, Allen Sears, Lucy Suchman, and Paul Wallich for reading early drafts of this paper and for helping to clarify the ideas and improve the article's readability. Stephen Cross triggered the writing of this article when he invited me to give the keynote address at the Aerospace Applications of Artificial Intelligence Conference in Dayton, Ohio, in September 1985.

# References

Aceves, J. J. G. L., & Poggio, A. A. (1985) Computer-based multimedia communications (special issue). *Computer* 18(10):10-11.

Ammerman, A. J. & Cavalli-Sforza, L. L. (1984) *The neolithic transition and the genetics of populations in Europe.* Princeton, New Jersey: Princeton University Press.

Bobrow, D. G. (1985) Daniel Bobrow on artificial intelligence and electronic publishing. *Computer Compacts*, 6(3):55-57.

Boyd, R., & Richerson, P. J. (1985) *Culture and the evolutionary process.* Chicago: University of Chicago Press.

Brown, J. S. (1983) Process versus product: a perspective on tools for communal and informal electronic learning. In S. Newman & E. Poor (Eds.), *Report from the learning lab: Education in the electronic age.* New York: WNET Educational Broadcasting Corporation.

Crane, D. (1972) *Invisible colleges: Diffusion of knowledge in scientific communities.* Chicago: University of Chicago Press.

Dawkins, R. (1976) *The selfish gene.* New York: Oxford University Press.

Dobzhansky, T., Ayala, F. J. Stebbins, G. L., & Valentine, J. W. (1977) *Evolution.* San Francisco: W. H. Freeman.

Feigenbaum, E. A. & McCorduck, P. (1983) *The fifth generation: Artificial intelligence and Japan's computer challenge to the world.* Reading, Mass.: Addison-Wesley.

Fleck, L. (1979) *Genesis and development of a scientific fact.* Chicago: University of Chicago Press.

Freidland, P. (1985) Special section on architectures for knowledge-based systems. *Communications of the ACM* 28(9):902-903.

Goldstein, I., & Papert, S. (1977) Artificial intelligence, language, and the study of knowledge. *Cognitive Science* 1(1):84-123.

Hookway, C. (1984) *Minds, machines, and evolution: Philosophical studies.* Cambridge, England: Cambridge University Press.

Kinoshita, H. (1985) Towards an advanced information society. *ICOT Journal*, 6:9-19.

Lewin, R. (1986) Punctuated equilibrium is now old hat. *Science* 231:672-673.

Lederberg, J. (1978) Digital communications and the conduct of science: The new literacy. *Proceedings of the IEEE*, 66(11)1313-1319.

Lenat, D., Prakash, M., & Shepherd, M. (1986) CYC: Using common sense knowledge to overcome brittleness and knowledge acquisition bottlenecks. *AI Magazine,* 6(4):65-85.

Michie, D. (1983) A prototype knowledge refinery. In J. E. Hayes & D. Michie (Eds.), *Intelligent systems: The unprecedented opportunity.* Chichester: Ellis Horwood.

Moto-oka, T. (1981) Fifth generation computer systems: Proceedings of the international conference on fifth generation computer systems. Amsterdam: North-Holland.

Price, D. D. (1983) Sealing wax and string: A philosophy of the experimenter's craft and its role in the genesis of the high technology. Washington, D.C.: American Association of the Advancement of Science.

Stefik, M., Foster, G., Bobrow, D. G., Kahn, K., Lanning, S., & Suchman, L. (1987) Beyond the chalkboard: Computer support for collaboration and problem solving in meetings. *Communications of the ACM* 30(1):32-47.

Wallich, P. (1985) Computers and the humanities. *The Yale Review*: 472-480.

Weber, E. (1976) *Peasants into Frenchmen: The modernization of rural France, 1870-1914.* Stanford: Stanford University Press.

Wilson, E. O. (1980) *Sociobiology: The abridged edition.* Cambridge, Mass.: The Belknap Press.